Teach Yourself®
Microsoft® Windows®
2000 Professional

Teach Yourself®
Microsoft® Windows®
2000 Professional

Brian Underdahl

IDG Books Worldwide, Inc.
An International Data Group Company

Foster City, CA • Chicago, IL • Indianapolis, IN • New York, NY

Teach Yourself® Microsoft® Windows® 2000 Professional

Published by
IDG Books Worldwide, Inc.
An International Data Group Company
919 E. Hillsdale Blvd., Suite 400
Foster City, CA 94404
www.idgbooks.com (IDG Books Worldwide Web site)

ISBN: 0-7645-4602-3

Printed in the United States of America

10 9 8 7 6 5 4 3 2 1

1P/RQ/RR/ZZ/IN

Distributed in the United States by IDG Books Worldwide, Inc.

Distributed by CDG Books Canada Inc. for Canada; by Transworld Publishers Limited in the United Kingdom; by IDG Norge Books for Norway; by IDG Sweden Books for Sweden; by IDG Books Australia Publishing Corporation Pty. Ltd. for Australia and New Zealand; by TransQuest Publishers Pte Ltd. for Singapore, Malaysia, Thailand, Indonesia, and Hong Kong; by Gotop Information Inc. for Taiwan; by ICG Muse, Inc. for Japan; by Intersoft for South Africa; by Eyrolles for France; by International Thomson Publishing for Germany, Austria, and Switzerland; by Distribuidora Cuspide for Argentina; by LR International for Brazil; by Galileo Libros for Chile; by Ediciones ZETA S.C.R. Ltda. for Peru; by WS Computer Publishing Corporation, Inc., for the Philippines; by Contemporanea de Ediciones for Venezuela; by Express Computer Distributors for the Caribbean and West Indies; by Micronesia Media Distributor, Inc. for Micronesia; by Chips Computadoras S.A. de C.V. for Mexico; by Editorial Norma de Panama S.A. for Panama; by American Bookshops for Finland.

For general information on IDG Books Worldwide's books in the U.S., please call our Consumer Customer Service department at 800-762-2974. For reseller information, including discounts and premium sales, please call our Reseller Customer Service department at 800-434-3422.

For information on where to purchase IDG Books Worldwide's books outside the U.S., please contact our International Sales department at 317-596-5530 or fax 317-596-5692.

For consumer information on foreign language translations, please contact our Customer Service department at 800-434-3422, fax 317-596-5692, or e-mail rights@idgbooks.com.

For information on licensing foreign or domestic rights, please phone +1-650-655-3109.

For sales inquiries and special prices for bulk quantities, please contact our Sales department at 650-655-3200 or write to the address above.

For information on using IDG Books Worldwide's books in the classroom or for ordering examination copies, please contact our Educational Sales department at 800-434-2086 or fax 317-596-5499.

For press review copies, author interviews, or other publicity information, please contact our Public Relations department at 650-655-3000 or fax 650-655-3299.

For authorization to photocopy items for corporate, personal, or educational use, please contact Copyright Clearance Center, 222 Rosewood Drive, Danvers, MA 01923, or fax 978-750-4470.

Library of Congress Cataloging-in-Publication Data

Underdahl, Brian.
    Teach yourself Micrososft Windows 2000 professional / Brian Underdahl.
        p. cm.
    ISBN 0-7645-4602-3 (alk. paper)
    1. Micrososft Windows (Computer file) 2. Operating systems (Computers) I. Title.
QA76.76.O63 U93 1999
005.4'4769--dc21   99–049234
                                                                         CIP

ABOUT IDG BOOKS WORLDWIDE

Welcome to the world of IDG Books Worldwide.

IDG Books Worldwide, Inc., is a subsidiary of International Data Group, the world's largest publisher of computer-related information and the leading global provider of information services on information technology. IDG was founded more than 30 years ago by Patrick J. McGovern and now employs more than 9,000 people worldwide. IDG publishes more than 290 computer publications in over 75 countries. More than 90 million people read one or more IDG publications each month.

Launched in 1990, IDG Books Worldwide is today the #1 publisher of best-selling computer books in the United States. We are proud to have received eight awards from the Computer Press Association in recognition of editorial excellence and three from Computer Currents' First Annual Readers' Choice Awards. Our best-selling ...*For Dummies*® series has more than 50 million copies in print with translations in 31 languages. IDG Books Worldwide, through a joint venture with IDG's Hi-Tech Beijing, became the first U.S. publisher to publish a computer book in the People's Republic of China. In record time, IDG Books Worldwide has become the first choice for millions of readers around the world who want to learn how to better manage their businesses.

Our mission is simple: Every one of our books is designed to bring extra value and skill-building instructions to the reader. Our books are written by experts who understand and care about our readers. The knowledge base of our editorial staff comes from years of experience in publishing, education, and journalism — experience we use to produce books to carry us into the new millennium. In short, we care about books, so we attract the best people. We devote special attention to details such as audience, interior design, use of icons, and illustrations. And because we use an efficient process of authoring, editing, and desktop publishing our books electronically, we can spend more time ensuring superior content and less time on the technicalities of making books.

You can count on our commitment to deliver high-quality books at competitive prices on topics you want to read about. At IDG Books Worldwide, we continue in the IDG tradition of delivering quality for more than 30 years. You'll find no better book on a subject than one from IDG Books Worldwide.

John Kilcullen
Chairman and CEO
IDG Books Worldwide, Inc.

Steven Berkowitz
President and Publisher
IDG Books Worldwide, Inc.

VIII WINNER

Eighth Annual
Computer Press
Awards ≥1992

IX WINNER

Ninth Annual
Computer Press
Awards ≥1993

X WINNER

Tenth Annual
Computer Press
Awards ≥1994

XI WINNER

Eleventh Annual
Computer Press
Awards ≥1995

IDG is the world's leading IT media, research and exposition company. Founded in 1964, IDG had 1997 revenues of $2.05 billion and has more than 9,000 employees worldwide. IDG offers the widest range of media options that reach IT buyers in 75 countries representing 95% of worldwide IT spending. IDG's diverse product and services portfolio spans six key areas including print publishing, online publishing, expositions and conferences, market research, education and training, and global marketing services. More than 90 million people read one or more of IDG's 290 magazines and newspapers, including IDG's leading global brands — Computerworld, PC World, Network World, Macworld and the Channel World family of publications. IDG Books Worldwide is one of the fastest-growing computer book publishers in the world, with more than 700 titles in 36 languages. The "...For Dummies®" series alone has more than 50 million copies in print. IDG offers online users the largest network of technology-specific Web sites around the world through IDG.net (http://www.idg.net), which comprises more than 225 targeted Web sites in 55 countries worldwide. International Data Corporation (IDC) is the world's largest provider of information technology data, analysis and consulting, with research centers in over 41 countries and more than 400 research analysts worldwide. IDG World Expo is a leading producer of more than 168 globally branded conferences and expositions in 35 countries including E3 (Electronic Entertainment Expo), Macworld Expo, ComNet, Windows World Expo, ICE (Internet Commerce Expo), Agenda, DEMO, and Spotlight. IDG's training subsidiary, ExecuTrain, is the world's largest computer training company, with more than 230 locations worldwide and 785 training courses. IDG Marketing Services helps industry-leading IT companies build international brand recognition by developing global integrated marketing programs via IDG's print, online and exposition products worldwide. Further information about the company can be found at www.idg.com. 1/24/99

Credits

Acquisitions Editor
David Mayhew

Development Editor
Laura E. Brown

Technical Editor
John Preisach

Copy Editor
Marti Paul

Book Designers
Daniel Ziegler Design, Cátálin Dulfu,
Kurt Krames

Proofreading and Indexing
York Production Services

About the Author

Brian Underdahl has written more than 40 computer-related titles on a broad range of topics, including Windows 95, Windows 98, Microsoft Office, and the Internet. His recent efforts include *Teach Yourself Windows 98, Teach Yourself Microsoft Office 2000, Windows 98 One Step at a Time, Internet Bible,* and *Small Business Computing for Dummies.*

I dedicate this book to the people who have taught me so much in life. My family, my friends, and most of all, my wife, have shown me that the world can be a wonderful place.

Welcome to Teach Yourself

Welcome to *Teach Yourself*, a series read and trusted by millions for nearly a decade. Although you may have seen the *Teach Yourself* name on other books, ours is the original. In addition, no *Teach Yourself* series has ever delivered more on the promise of its name than this series. That's because IDG Books Worldwide recently transformed *Teach Yourself* into a new cutting-edge format that gives you all the information you need to learn quickly and easily.

Readers told us that they want to learn by doing and that they want to learn as much as they can in as short a time as possible. We listened to you and believe that our new task-by-task format and suite of learning tools deliver the book you need to successfully teach yourself any technology topic. Features such as our Personal Workbook, which lets you practice and reinforce the skills you've just learned, help ensure that you get full value out of the time you invest in your learning. Handy cross-references to related topics and online sites broaden your knowledge and give you control over the kind of information you want, when you want it.

More Answers . . .

In designing the latest incarnation of this series, we started with the premise that people like you, who are beginning to intermediate computer users, want to take control of their own learning. To do this, you need the proper tools to find answers to questions so you can solve problems now.

In designing a series of books that provide such tools, we created a unique and concise visual format. The added bonus: *Teach Yourself* books actually pack more information into their pages than other books written on the same subjects. Skill for skill, you typically get much more information in a *Teach Yourself* book. In fact, *Teach Yourself* books, on average, cover twice the skills covered by other computer books — as many as 125 skills per book — so they're more likely to address your specific needs.

Welcome to Teach Yourself

...In Less Time

We know you don't want to spend twice the time to get all this great information, so we provide lots of time-saving features:

▶ A modular task-by-task organization of information: any task you want to perform is easy to find and includes simple-to-follow steps.

▶ A larger size than standard makes the book easy to read and convenient to use at a computer workstation. The large format also enables us to include many more illustrations — 500 screen illustrations show you how to get everything done!

▶ A Personal Workbook at the end of each chapter reinforces learning with extra practice, real-world applications for your learning, and questions and answers to test your knowledge.

▶ Cross-references appearing at the bottom of each task page refer you to related information, providing a path through the book for learning particular aspects of the software thoroughly.

▶ A Find It Online feature offers valuable ideas on where to go on the Internet to get more information or to download useful files.

▶ Take Note sidebars provide added-value information from our expert authors for more in-depth learning.

▶ An attractive, consistent organization of information helps you quickly find and learn the skills you need.

These *Teach Yourself* features are designed to help you learn the essential skills about a technology in the least amount of time, with the most benefit. We've placed these features consistently throughout the book, so you quickly learn where to go to find just the information you need — whether you work through the book from cover to cover or use it later to solve a new problem.

You will find a *Teach Yourself* book on almost any technology subject — from the Internet to Windows to Microsoft Office. Take control of your learning today, with IDG Books Worldwide's *Teach Yourself* series.

Teach Yourself
More Answers in Less Time

Search through the task headings to find the topic you want right away. To learn a new skill, search the contents, chapter opener, or the extensive index to find what you need. Then find — at a glance — the clear task heading that matches it.

Learn the concepts behind the task at hand and, more important, learn how the task is relevant in the real world. Timesaving suggestions and advice show you how to make the most of each skill.

After you learn the task at hand, you may have more questions, or you may want to read about other tasks related to the topic. Use the cross-references to find different tasks to make your learning more efficient.

Viewing Thumbnails

Windows Explorer helps you to identify different types of files by using different icons that represent which application was used to create the file. This makes it easy to tell which document files are Word documents and which ones are Excel spreadsheets, for example. But simply identifying the file type isn't very useful when you are trying to locate specific files based on their content.

To help you identify files based on their content, Windows Explorer attempts to display a preview of files as they are selected. This preview, which appears between the Folders Explorer Bar and the file listing, can give you a pretty good idea of each file's content. Unfortunately, locating a specific file by previewing every file in a folder can be pretty time-consuming — especially if the folder contains a large number of files. Before you can see what is in each file you must first select the file and wait while Windows Explorer generates the preview. You may find yourself going back and forth as you need to compare the different files.

In Windows 2000, Windows Explorer offers a far easier method of locating specific files based on their content. If you choose the thumbnail view, Windows Explorer will automatically show a preview of every file in the folder so you don't have to select individual files to preview one at a time.

If a folder contains several different types of files you may find that it is useful to sort the file listing as discussed in the next task, "Sorting the File Listing." For example, sorting the files by type will sort the files based

① Select the folder containing the document files you wish to view in thumbnails.

② Click the down arrow at the right of the Views button.

③ Select Thumbnails from the drop-down list.

CROSS-REFERENCE

See Chapter 6 for more information about file types.

34

Ultimately, people learn by doing. Follow the clear, illustrated steps on the right-hand page of every task to complete a procedure. The detailed callouts for each step show you exactly where to go and what to do to complete the task.

Welcome to Teach Yourself

Go to this area if you want special tips, cautions, and notes that provide added insight into the current task.

The current chapter name and number always appear in the top right-hand corner of every task spread, so you always know exactly where you are in the book.

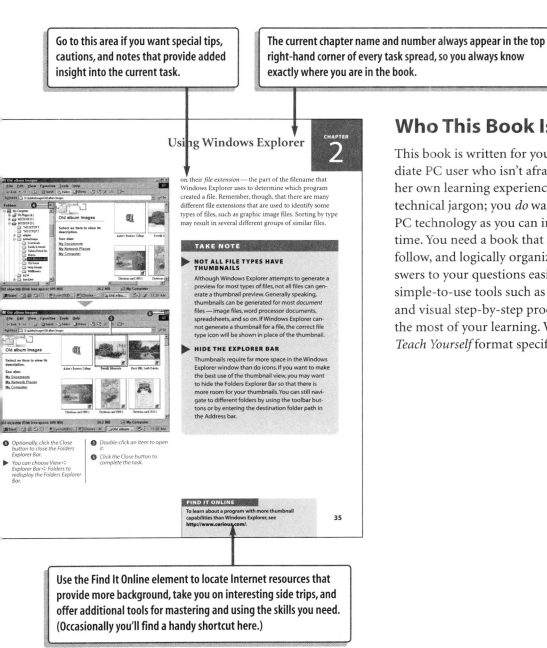

Who This Book Is For

This book is written for you, a beginning to intermediate PC user who isn't afraid to take charge of his or her own learning experience. You don't want a lot of technical jargon; you *do* want to learn as much about PC technology as you can in a limited amount of time. You need a book that is straightforward, easy to follow, and logically organized, so you can find answers to your questions easily. And, you appreciate simple-to-use tools such as handy cross-references and visual step-by-step procedures that help you make the most of your learning. We have created the unique *Teach Yourself* format specifically to meet your needs.

Use the Find It Online element to locate Internet resources that provide more background, take you on interesting side trips, and offer additional tools for mastering and using the skills you need. (Occasionally you'll find a handy shortcut here.)

Personal Workbook

It's a well-known fact that much of what we learn is lost soon after we learn it if we don't reinforce our newly acquired skills with practice and repetition. That's why each *Teach Yourself* chapter ends with your own Personal Workbook. Here's where you can get extra practice, test your knowledge, and discover ideas for using what you've learned in the real world. There's even a Visual Quiz to help you remember your way around the topic's software environment.

Feedback

Please let us know what you think about this book, and whether you have any suggestions for improvements. You can send questions and comments to the *Teach Yourself* editors on the IDG Books Worldwide Web site at **http://www.idgbooks.com**.

Personal Workbook

Q&A

❶ How can you display your personal Start menu items when you open Windows Explorer?

_____

_____

_____

❷ How can you run a program that doesn't appear on your Start menu?

_____

_____

_____

❸ What will happen if you click the History button?

_____

_____

_____

❹ How can you preview the contents of graphics files without opening them?

_____

_____

_____

❺ How can you make Windows Explorer display file previews in place of file type icons?

_____

_____

_____

❻ How can you locate all of the folders you opened last week?

_____

_____

_____

❼ Which Windows Explorer toolbar can you use to listen to music over the Internet?

_____

_____

_____

❽ Which Windows Explorer toolbar can you use to visit the "Best of the Internet" Web site?

_____

_____

_____

ANSWERS: PAGE 388

48

After working through the tasks in each chapter, you can test your progress and reinforce your learning by answering the questions in the Q&A section. Then check your answers in the Personal Workbook Answers appendix at the back of the book.

Welcome to Teach Yourself

Another practical way to reinforce your skills is to do additional exercises on the same skills you just learned without the benefit of the chapter's visual steps. If you struggle with any of these exercises, it's a good idea to refer to the chapter's tasks to be sure you've mastered them.

Using Windows Explorer

CHAPTER 2

Read the list of Real-World Applications to get ideas on how you can use the skills you've just learned in your everyday life. Understanding a process can be simple; knowing how to use that process to make you more productive is the key to successful learning.

EXTRA PRACTICE

1. Open Windows Explorer and explore your personal Desktop folder.

2. Compare the differences between the Move To and Copy To buttons.

3. Use the drag-and-drop method to copy a file.

4. Sort the view of the My Documents folder so that you can find your oldest files.

5. Customize one of your folders by adding a background image.

6. Use the history list to find the local folders that you opened yesterday.

REAL-WORLD APPLICATIONS

✔ You install a program but then don't find it listed anywhere on your Start menu. You use Windows Explorer to locate and run the program.

✔ You're working on a project on your office PC and realize you need to take the file with you on a business trip. Using Windows Explorer, you make a copy of your data file on a diskette.

✔ You have a new digital camera and you've downloaded a large number of images to your PC. You use thumbnail view to preview the images to decide which ones to keep and which ones to discard.

✔ You suddenly realize that a Web site you visited last week had information you need. You use the History bar to find the site again.

Visual Quiz

How does this view differ from the standard Windows Explorer view, and how can you make Windows Explorer display image previews like this?

_____

_____

_____

_____

_____

49

Take the Visual Quiz to see how well you're learning your way around the technology. Learning about computers is often as much about how to find a button or menu as it is about memorizing definitions. Our Visual Quiz helps you find your way.

Acknowledgments

I have many people to thank for making this book a reality:

At IDG Books Worldwide —

David Mayhew, acquisitions editor, for all of his support and understanding.

Laura Brown, development editor, for helping me get this project done on time.

John Preisach, technical editor, for making certain you don't have to deal with technical errors.

The copy editor, production coordinator, and the countless other wonderful people who work behind the scenes to make certain you get to read the best book possible.

At 3Com —

Dave DeVries, for making it possible to finally connect to the Internet with something better than a tin can and a string.

Ken Moreen, for providing excellent support and for understanding that you can't always write about products that are already on the market.

At Inner Media —

Glen R. Horton, Sr., for quickly providing an essential software patch that I couldn't have done without.

At Microsoft —

Jeff DeVos, Sam White, Stephen Mueller, and Rob Trace for all the excellent help in tracking down beta-related problems. Without these guys we wouldn't have Windows 2000 and I wouldn't have been able to write this book.

Contents

Contents

Contents

Contents

Contents

Contents

Contents

Teach Yourself®
Microsoft® Windows®
2000 Professional

Contents of 'Desktop'

Name

My Computer

Network Neigh

Internet Explore

Microsoft Outlook

Recycle Bin

My Briefcase

3252-9

3259-6

3261-8

3262-6

3281-2

3286-3

DE Phone List

Device Manager

In

Iomega Tools

PART

I

Learning Windows 2000 Basics

If you're new to PCs or even just getting your start with Windows 2000, you'll find all of the basics in this first part of the book. You'll learn about the important objects that you see on the Windows 2000 screen and how to use them. You'll learn how to find your way around so that Windows 2000 will be much more comfortable and easy to use.

Windows 2000 is designed to be easy enough for anyone to use. You don't have to be an expert nor do you have to spend hours learning new ways to do things. As you'll see in this part, it's even easy to find additional help when you need it.

CHAPTER 1

MASTER THESE SKILLS

▶ **Using the Start Menu**

▶ **Using Your Desktop**

▶ **Using My Computer**

▶ **Using My Network Places**

▶ **Using My Documents**

▶ **Using the Quick Launch Toolbar**

▶ **Using the System Tray Icons**

▶ **Switching between Programs**

Using Windows 2000

Every computer needs an *operating system* — a program that enables the computer to run programs, to work with devices such as printers, and that enables the user to interact with the computer. Windows 2000 is one such operating system and is a part of the Microsoft Windows family that includes Windows 98. Windows 2000 looks very much like Windows 98, but it includes significant improvements compared to Windows 98.

Windows 2000 is available in several different versions. From a user's standpoint, the basic tasks of Windows 2000 are the same no matter which version you use. All versions of Windows 2000 provide you with access to all the parts of your computing environment — documents, files, applications, e-mail, and the Internet.

As you can gather from the name, the Windows 2000 environment is heavily focused on *windows* — rectangular areas on the screen that present information. You open windows when you need them and close them when you don't need them. Individual windows can be resized and moved around the screen.

Windows 2000 uses small graphical *icons* — pictures — on the desktop to represent objects such as documents, applications, folders, devices, Web pages, and other computers. Icons often also have text labels to help make their purpose a bit clearer. If you move the mouse over an object on the desktop or in a window and click the right mouse button, Windows 2000 displays a menu with the object's common commands. Many Windows applications use this same convention, called a *context menu* or *right-click* menu.

You can *select* objects in several ways. For most types of objects, you *click* them: move the mouse cursor onto the object and then press the left mouse button once. A selected object is highlighted; its label is darkened and has a dotted line indicating that the selected object is ready to be chosen. You *choose* an object to activate its associated command. You choose the object by *double-clicking* its icon: move the mouse cursor onto the icon and then press the left mouse button rapidly twice. If the object is a menu selection or command button, however, you choose it with a single click.

You can also move or copy objects using *drag and drop.* To drag-and-drop an object, move the mouse cursor onto the icon of the object to be dragged. Press and hold the left mouse button while you move the mouse cursor to the destination object's icon. Then release the mouse button.

You'll learn more about all these terms as you follow along and try out the tasks for yourself.

Using the Start Menu

The Windows 2000 Start menu is a list of options that pops up when you click the Start button at the lower left corner of your desktop. This menu provides you with access to most of your programs, to your most recent documents, to options that enable you to search for items, to the Windows 2000 help system, and to the settings options that control how your system operates.

The Start menu includes three different kinds of items. You will find commands, cascading menus, and items that display dialog boxes.

Command selections run applications programs immediately. The Windows Update and Help commands in the figures on the facing page are command selections. When you click the command, the application starts.

A small arrow next to a label indicates cascading menus. These items display additional menus when you select them. Programs, Documents, Settings, and Search are cascading menu selections. If you move the mouse cursor to one of them, a second submenu pops out. Cascading menus can contain the same three selection types that the Start menu contains. In the first figure on the facing page, the Programs menu is open, as is the Accessories menu contained in the Programs menu. WordPad, an application program, is selected. If you click it once, WordPad will run.

Three dots (...) next to a label indicate menu selections that open dialog boxes. The Run and Shut Down menu selections are dialog box selections. Dialog boxes are special boxes that appear on your screen to display messages or to accept input from you.

The figures demonstrate several techniques rather than showing one complete task.

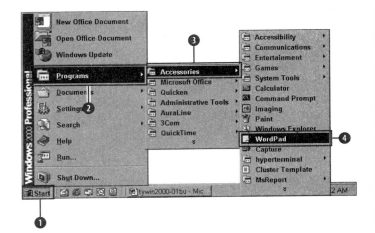

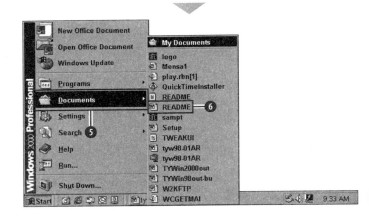

❶ Click the Start button to open the Start menu.

❷ Select Programs to open the Programs menu.

❸ Select Accessories to open the Accessories menu.

❹ Click an application such as WordPad to start the application.

❺ Select Documents to open your list of recently used documents.

❻ Click an item to open it.

CROSS-REFERENCE

See "Opening Items" in Chapter 2 for more information about opening programs that aren't on the Start menu.

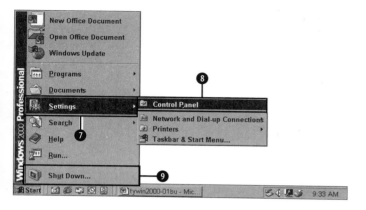

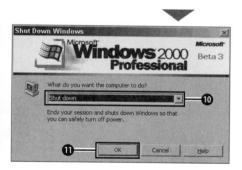

WINDOWS 2000 HAS NO FAVORITES

If you've used Windows 98 in the past, you'll notice one big difference with Windows 2000 as soon as you open the Start menu — there is no Favorites list on the Windows 2000 Start menu. You can still use Favorites in Internet Explorer in Windows 2000 — they just don't appear on the Start menu. In Chapter 12 you learn how to add Favorites back to your Start menu if you want.

STOP BY STARTING

It's important that Windows 2000 be shut down properly. Although it may seem that you need only turn off the switch when you're finished working, you'll damage your files and may lose some of your work if you don't close Windows 2000 correctly. Before you turn off your PC, always click the Start button and choose Shut Down.

SOME ITEMS REQUIRE ADMINISTRATOR PRIVILEGES

Because Windows 2000 includes several security features that are not found in operating systems such as Windows 98, you will need to be logged on as the System Administrator to perform certain functions. For example, certain types of programs can only be installed if you have System Administrator privileges. You will also need these privileges to adjust certain settings such as who will be able to access files over your network.

⑦ Select Settings to open the list of settings options.

⑧ Click an item to open it.

⑨ When you're ready to shut down your computer, click Shut Down.

⑩ Select the shut-down option you want to use.

⑪ Click OK to shut down your computer.

FIND IT ONLINE

See **http://www.microsoft.com/windows/default.asp** for the latest information on all versions of Windows.

Using Your Desktop

Your Windows 2000 desktop displays a number of icons that allow you to access your applications, files, documents, and other computers. These icons may be aligned in neat columns along the left side of your desktop or they may be spread randomly across the entire desktop.

There are five icons that appear on virtually all Windows 2000 desktops. My Documents provides access to the document files you create and save. My Computer provides access to the files, folders, disk drives, and so on that are on your PC. My Network Places provides access to the shared files and printers of other computers on your local network. Recycle Bin is where you place discarded items from the desktop and file folders. Internet Explorer provides access to the World Wide Web.

Because the icons on your desktop include both pictures and labels, you should be able to determine their purpose quite easily. Most of the desktop icons are program icons that will run the associated programs when you click the icon. This is true even if the icon represents a document, since Windows 2000 generally knows which program to use to open most document files.

Many of the desktop icons have a small arrow at the lower-left corner of the icon to indicate that the icon is a *shortcut* to the application or document. Shortcuts provide you with quick access to an item, but since shortcuts are only pointers to the real program or document, they save space and reduce the chance that you might accidentally delete an important item.

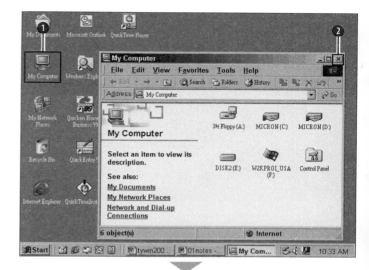

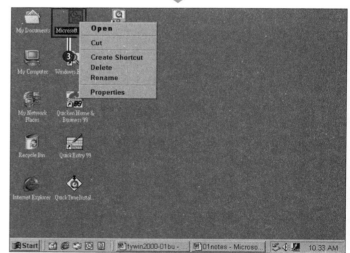

❶ Double-click an icon to open the item.

❷ Click the Close button to close an item you opened.

❸ Right-click an item to view its shortcut menu.

CROSS-REFERENCE

See "Configuring the Desktop" in Chapter 12 for more information on controlling how your desktop looks.

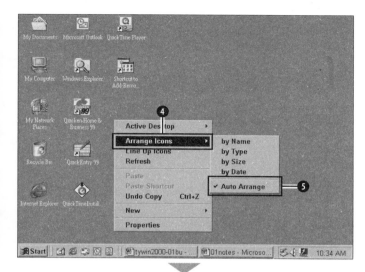

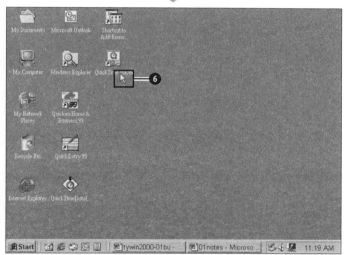

STRAIGHTENING UP YOUR DESKTOP

If your Windows 2000 desktop is a bit of a mess with icons scattered all over the place, you can tell Windows 2000 to automatically bring some order to the chaos. If you right-click a blank spot on the desktop and select Arrange Icons ➪ Auto Arrange, the icons will snap into orderly rows and columns. Any new icons that are added to your desktop will also move into place automatically.

USING YOUR MOUSE

If you find that it is confusing to remember when you need to click your mouse button once and when you need to double-click, you can change the way your mouse works. In Chapter 13 you'll learn more about using this option to allow you to open icons with a single click — much the same way you select menu items and Web page links. But as you'll also learn, setting up your desktop to use single clicks can make it a bit harder to copy and move items.

④ To view the desktop shortcut menu, right-click a blank space on the desktop.

⑤ Select Arrange Icons ➪ Auto Arrange to align the icons in neat rows and columns.

⑥ To rearrange the desktop, point to an icon, hold down the left mouse button, and drag the icon to a new location.

SHORTCUT

See **http://www.nthelp.com/** for more help in using Windows 2000.

Using My Computer

In Windows 2000, the My Computer icon opens a window that primarily shows you the disk drives that are connected to your PC. Typically this will include such things as a diskette drive, a hard disk, and a CD-ROM drive. Depending on your system configuration, you may see additional drives. In the figures on the facing page, the PC has a total of three different hard disks. My Computer also includes an icon to open the Control Panel.

The icons in the My Computer window represent your disk drives, folders, documents, data files, applications, shortcuts to devices and other PCs on the network, and so on. You can view the contents of a drive by double-clicking the drive's icon. You can also view the contents of a folder by double-clicking the folder's icon. Folders are subdirectories in the file system. To close a folder, click the Close button — the button with an X in the upper right corner of the open folder's window.

You can open documents by double-clicking the document's icon. When you do, Windows 2000 first opens the application that created the document and then the document opens within that application. If you double-click an application, the application opens directly. If you attempt to open an object that Windows 2000 does not recognize, Windows 2000 will ask you to choose the application to use for opening the item. In most cases it is safest to only open those documents that Windows 2000 automatically recognizes.

The Control Panel in My Computer contains many icons that enable you to manage the configuration of Windows 2000 and your PC. For example, one of the icons in the Control Panel opens the Add/Remove Programs dialog box so that you can install new programs or remove old programs that you no longer need.

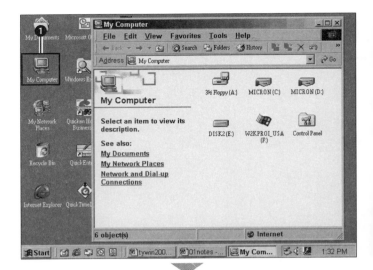

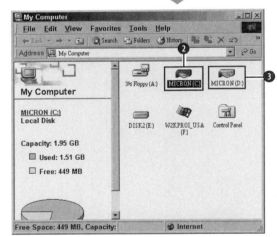

❶ Double-click the My Computer icon to open the My Computer window.

❷ Click an item to view its description on the left side of the window.

❸ Double-click an item to open it.

CROSS-REFERENCE

See "Controlling the View Detail Level" in Chapter 2 for more information about folder views.

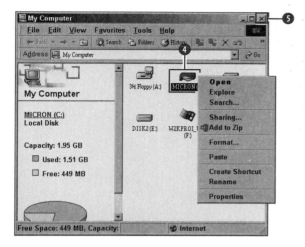

My Computer also contains links to your My Documents folder, to your My Network Places folder, and to the Network and Dial-up Connections folder. You will learn about each of these folders later.

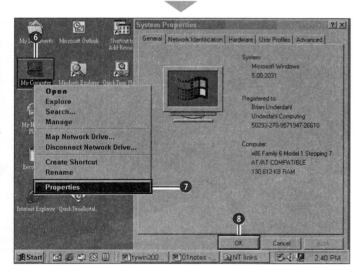

TAKE NOTE

▶ VIEW OBJECT DETAILS

Select View ➪ Details from the menu to see more information about each of the items in the My Computer window. Windows 2000 automatically provides a description of each item as it is selected, but changing to the Detail view provides additional information about all items even when they are not selected.

▶ EXPLORE MY COMPUTER

To view the objects in My Computer using the standard Windows Explorer view, right-click My Computer and choose Explore. Double-clicking the My Computer icon opens My Computer using the Open view rather than the Explore view. You may find that it is easier to navigate My Computer in Explore view since you can use the folder tree to locate items.

④ *Right-click an item to view its shortcut menu.*

⑤ *Click the Close button to close My Computer.*

⑥ *Right-click the My Computer icon to view its shortcut menu.*

⑦ *Select Properties to display the System Properties dialog box.*

⑧ *Click OK to close the dialog box.*

FIND IT ONLINE

See **http://www.mindspring.com/~ggking3/pages/ windmill.htm** for more Windows 2000 news.

Using My Network Places

The My Network Places icon opens a window that displays the computers and shared printers in your network. My Network Places displays an icon that represents the entire network, an icon that represents your *workgroup* or *domain*, and icons for some computers on the network. My Network Places initially shows you only the Computers Near Me and the Entire Network icons. The Computers Near Me icon includes those computers that are in your own workgroup or domain. The Entire Network folder contains icons for all the workgroups and domains in the network.

When you're browsing My Network Places, you may not be able to treat network resources in quite the same way you would if they were on your PC. For example, someone may share a folder but may not allow you to do anything except read the files in the folder. Your System Administrator may also set up rules that specify who has access to specific network resources. You might need to change your user name and password in order to save files on the network or to use shared printers. In addition, you won't be able to see quite as much information about network folders as you can for local folders unless you are logged on as the System Administrator (or have been granted the same rights as the System Administrator).

Networks are generally somewhat less responsive than what you may be used to. If you haven't browsed the network before, you may be surprised by the delays you can encounter when you're browsing My Network Places. This is especially true if you view folders where someone else is making changes to the files. When you select a new folder, the view will reflect the current status of the folder, but you may find it necessary to select View ➪ Refresh to see the changes.

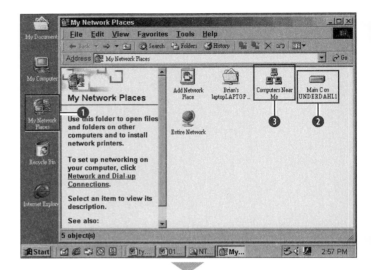

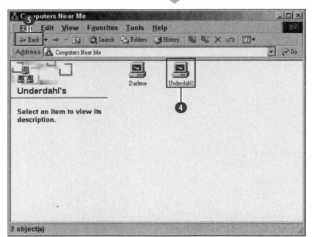

① Double-click the My Network Places icon to open the My Network Places window.

② Double-click a computer icon to view the shared resources on that computer.

③ Alternatively, double-click the Computers Near Me icon to view all the available computers in your workgroup or domain.

④ Double-click a computer icon to view its shared resources.

⑤ Alternatively, click the Back button to return to the previous window.

CROSS-REFERENCE

See "Sharing Your Files" in Chapter 7.

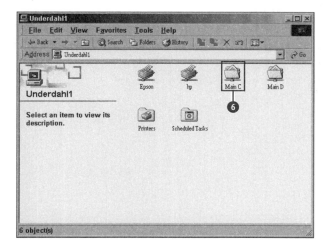

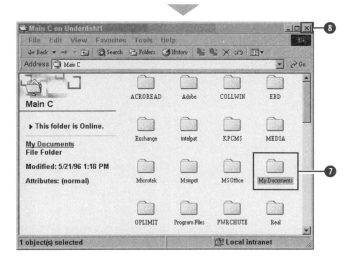

▶ UNDERSTANDING THE COMPUTERS NEAR ME ICON

Your My Network Places window will always include an icon named Computers Near Me. This icon provides quick access to the shared resources in your workgroup or your domain — depending on how your network is configured. Usually, opening the Entire Network is the same as opening My Network Places, especially if you have a small network. The Entire Network icon is useful only if your computer is part of more than one workgroup or domain and you need to view a workgroup or domain other than the one you logged on to when you started Windows 2000.

▶ VIEWING NETWORK RESOURCES

If you can't see any of the disk drives or printers on any of the computers on your network, it may be that none of the folders or printers has been set up for sharing on the network.

⑥ Double-click a folder to open the folder.

⑦ Click a shared resource to view its description.

⑧ Click the Close button to close the window.

FIND IT ONLINE

See **http://www.intel.com/anypoint/guide/index.html** for more networking basics.

Using My Documents

The My Documents folder is the default location that most Windows 2000 applications use when storing document files. By storing all of your documents in a central location, you not only have the convenience of being able to easily locate those files, but you also have a single main folder to back up when you want to make a copy of all of your document files. Windows 2000 does not force you to use the My Documents folder, but it's a very good idea to do so.

Even if you use the My Documents folder to store your work, you may want to add a little extra organization by creating additional folders that are contained within the My Documents folder. You can then use these additional folders to store the files for individual projects. You'll still be able to locate your files quickly and easily simply by opening the My Documents folder and then opening the project folder. The figures at the lower left and lower right on the facing page show you how to add new folders to the My Documents folder.

Although the My Documents folder is created automatically, in most ways it is a standard Windows 2000 folder. You could rename or move the My Documents folder, but be sure to see the "Take Note" section for special information on the best method for doing so. Since Windows 2000 supplies the name and location of the My Documents folder to applications, you'll want to make certain that the correct information is passed along.

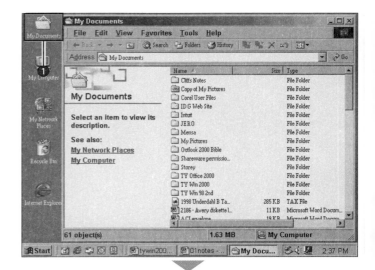

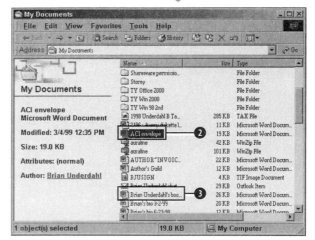

❶ Double-click the My Documents icon to open the My Documents folder.

❷ Click an item to view its description.

❸ Double-click an item to open it in the application in which it was created.

CROSS-REFERENCE

See "Sending Objects to the Recycle Bin" in Chapter 6 for more information about deleting unneeded files.

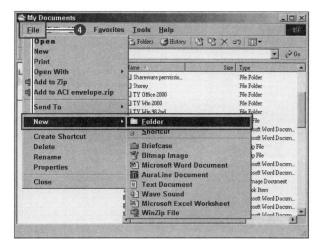

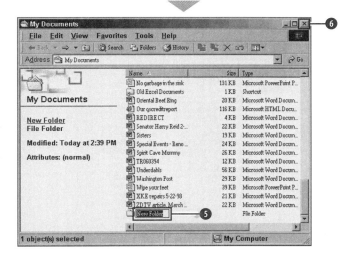

TAKE NOTE

MOVING THE MY DOCUMENTS FOLDER

By default, Windows 2000 creates a folder on your C drive named My Documents. If you'd rather save your documents in a different location — such as on your network — you can change the location of the My Documents folder. Right-click the My Documents icon, select Properties from the shortcut menu that pops up, and specify a new location in the Target folder location text box. If you can't remember the exact name of the new location, click the Browse button to find the folder you wish to use.

SAVING DOCUMENTS ON DISKETTES

If you save all of your document files in the My Documents folder, you may also wish to make backup copies of those files. But since most application programs remember the last file save location, saving your document files once in the My Documents folder and once on a diskette may not be very convenient. A better way to do this is to save your documents in the My Documents folder and then later open the folder. Right-click any files that you wish to save on diskettes and choose Send To ⇨ 3¹/₂ Floppy (A) from the context menu.

④ To create a new folder within the My Documents folder, select File ⇨ New ⇨ Folder.

⑤ Type a name for the new folder and press Enter.

⑥ Click the Close button to close the My Documents folder.

FIND IT ONLINE

To learn more about programs that use My Documents, see **http://officeupdate.microsoft.com/welcome/word.htm**.

Using the Quick Launch Toolbar

You have already learned that you can open applications by selecting them from the Start menu or by clicking their icons on your Windows 2000 desktop. In this section you will learn about another way to quickly access those programs that you use most often. You have probably noticed the icons that sit in the Windows 2000 taskbar just to the right of the Start button. These icons are a part of the Quick Launch toolbar.

The Quick Launch toolbar normally has three buttons. The Show Desktop tool button minimizes all open windows to buttons on the taskbar so that you can view the desktop. The Launch Internet Explorer Browser tool button launches Internet Explorer exactly as the Internet Explorer icon on the desktop does. The Launch Outlook Express tool button launches Outlook Express — a program that provides e-mail and newsgroup services. If you "hover" the mouse cursor over a button for a few seconds, the button's description will appear.

You have already seen that you can easily start your programs by clicking their desktop icons or by choosing them from the Start menu. Why, then, would you need the Quick Launch toolbar? One good reason is that the Quick Launch toolbar is visible whenever the Windows 2000 taskbar is visible. An open window might cover your desktop icons, and opening the Start menu so that you can wade through several layers of menus may not be the most convenient way to start your favorite programs.

What really makes the Quick Launch toolbar useful, however, is that you can add your own programs to the toolbar and gain the ability to launch them quickly. You can also remove some of the existing icons from the toolbar. In these ways you can customize the Quick Launch toolbar to make it more useful. The figures on the facing page show you how to make these changes.

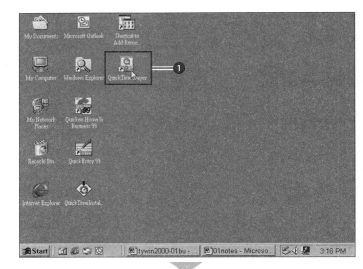

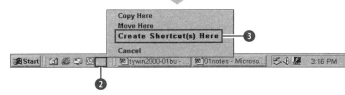

❶ To add an icon to the Quick Launch toolbar, select the icon.

▶ You can select items on your desktop or from Windows Explorer.

❷ Hold down the right mouse button and drag the icon onto the Quick Launch toolbar.

❸ Release the button and select Create Shortcut(s) Here.

CROSS-REFERENCE

See "Moving and Hiding the Taskbar" in Chapter 12.

MAKE ROOM FOR NEW ICONS

If you add too many of your own icons to the Quick Launch toolbar, you'll soon discover that you've run out of space. To adjust the size of the toolbar, drag the edge of the toolbar right or left. If you still don't have enough room, drag the top of the toolbar up to create a second row.

CORRECTING MISSING ICONS

If you drag items from the Quick Launch toolbar and later decide you'd like them back, you may discover that the icons are missing. In that case, you may need to manually copy the program items into the Quick Launch toolbar folder: C:\Documents and Settings*username*\Application Data\ Microsoft\Internet Explorer\Quick Launch. You should find any items you dragged from the toolbar in the E:\Documents and Settings\ *username* \Desktop folder. They will have a file extension of SCF. If you cannot find this folder, use the Tools ⇨ Folder Options command and make certain that you choose to view hidden files and folders on the View tab.

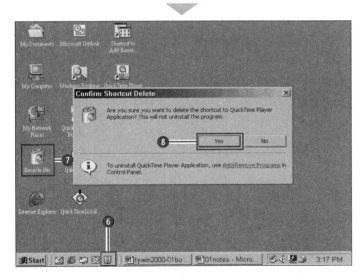

④ *If necessary, drag the edge of the Quick Launch toolbar so that you can see all the icons.*

⑤ *Click the icon to open the application.*

⑥ *To remove the icon from the Quick Launch toolbar, point to the icon and hold down the left mouse button.*

⑦ *Drag the icon onto the Recycle Bin and release the mouse button.*

⑧ *Select Yes to delete the icon.*

FIND IT ONLINE

If Show Desktop disappears, see
http://support.microsoft.com/support/

Using the System Tray Icons

At the bottom right-hand side of the Windows 2000 screen is a small area that is known as the *system tray*. The system tray usually contains several icons that vary depending on the software and hardware you have installed on your PC. You'll probably have at least three items in your system tray: the Unplug or eject hardware icon, the Volume icon, and the Time display.

The Unplug or eject hardware icon enables you to stop hardware so that it can be safely removed from your system. The Volume icon launches the Windows 2000 Volume Control applet. The Time display enables a continuous view of the time of day. You can view the date by moving the mouse cursor to the Time display and waiting a few seconds.

System tray icons represent programs or services that are currently running on your computer. For example, if you use a laptop computer, your system tray may include an icon for PC Card status whenever a PC Card is inserted into one of the slots. Clicking this icon will give you the option of stopping the card so that you can safely remove it from your system without shutting down your computer. When you are connected to the Internet through a modem, the Modem icon flashes to show you when data is being sent or received.

If you're not sure of the purpose of a system tray icon, hold your mouse pointer over the icon for a few seconds. Windows 2000 will pop up a ToolTip that tells you about the icon. If you still aren't clear about the icon's purpose, try right-clicking the icon. This usually pops up a shortcut menu. You should be able to obtain additional clues about the icon's purpose from the shortcut menu items.

❶ *Hold the mouse pointer over a system tray icon to view the ToolTip for the icon.*

❷ *Click the Volume control icon to display the master volume control.*

▶ *Alternatively, double-click the Volume control icon to display the more detailed Volume Control window.*

CROSS-REFERENCE

See "Installing and Uninstalling Programs" in Chapter 4.

DOUBLE-CLICK TO OPEN

Double-clicking most system tray icons will open the associated applet. The Volume icon is a bit unusual since a single click opens a smaller version of the Volume Control that is opened with a double-click.

DISABLE VIRUS CHECKERS

If you have an antivirus program installed, you will probably have an icon for the program in the system tray. Right-click this icon and choose Disable before you install new programs to prevent installation errors.

WATCH THE MODEM STATUS ICON

If you use a modem, you'll probably see a modem status icon on the system tray whenever the computer is connected. This icon has two spots that become bright blue when data is flowing to or from your PC. If both spots stay dark for a long time, your connection may be stalled, and you may wish to try reloading the current page or going to a different site. If neither works, you may need to restart your Internet connection.

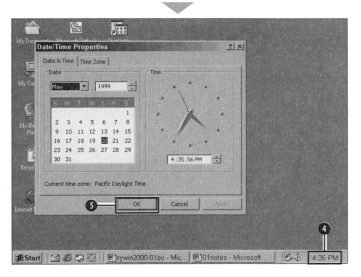

③ *Right-click a system tray icon to display the icon's shortcut menu.*

▶ *In this case the shortcut menu for the Time icon is displayed.*

④ *Double-click the Time icon to display the Date/Time Properties dialog box.*

▶ *You can use this dialog box to adjust the system date, time, and time zone settings.*

⑤ *Click OK to close the dialog box.*

FIND IT ONLINE

For tips on customizing the system tray, see
http://www.playernet.net/setup/win/tray.html.

Switching Between Programs

Windows 2000 is a *multitasking* operating system. This means that you can have several different programs running at the same time — each in its own window. To keep your computer from total chaos, only one window at a time interacts with you. That window is said to be *active* or to have the *focus*. Usually the most recent window you open is active. You can change the focus to another window whenever you choose. An active window displays on top of the others, receives the keystrokes that you type, and usually has a dark blue border — although the color may vary according to the color scheme that you are using.

Switching between open windows is easy. If you can see the window that you want to make active, simply click anywhere in it. If the window that you want to make active is not visible, you can use one of the methods that are shown on the facing page.

If you prefer to use your keyboard, you will probably like the task list method best. Because you only need to press two keys — Alt and Tab — to use the task list, you can keep your hands right on the keyboard and never touch your mouse. But even if you don't mind using your mouse, you may find that the task list is a bit more convenient. If you have a large number of windows open at the same time, the taskbar buttons can get too small to read unless you expand the taskbar.

If you feel that using your mouse is a very natural way to interact with your PC, you will probably prefer to click taskbar buttons. Because Windows 2000 shows a button for each open window, a quick click on the appropriate button is a fast method to switch between those windows. As you'll learn in Chapter 5, the taskbar buttons are also very convenient when you want to copy information that is in one window into a different one.

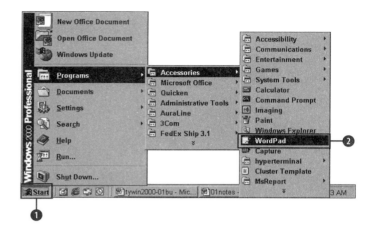

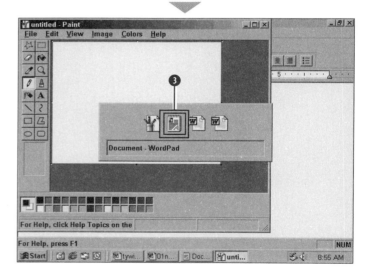

❶ Click the Start button.

❷ Open several programs, and then press Alt+Tab to display the task list.

❸ Press Tab until you have highlighted the window you wish to make active. Then release the Alt key.

CROSS-REFERENCE

See "Closing Programs" in Chapter 4.

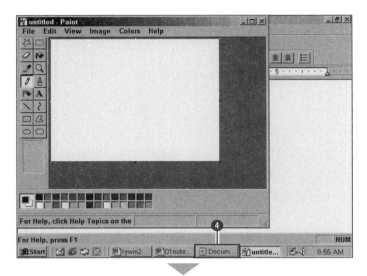

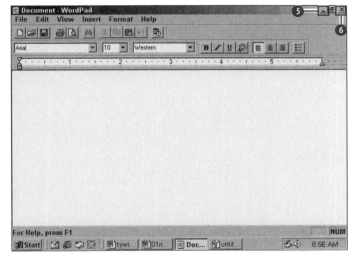

④ *Alternatively, click a button on the taskbar to switch to the associated window.*

⑤ *Click the Minimize button to hide the current window.*

⑥ *Click the Close button to close the current window.*

TAKE NOTE

▶ JUMP BETWEEN TWO PROGRAMS

If you quickly press and release Alt+Tab, you'll return to the last open window. If you have several programs open, you can quickly switch back and forth between two of them by using this technique without waiting for the task list to display.

▶ FORCING STALLED WINDOWS TO CLOSE

If you find that one of your applications stops responding, press Ctrl+Alt+Del, select the Task Manager button, and look for an item that says "Not Responding." Select the item and click the End Task button to close the item that has stopped working. In Windows 2000 you can close a stalled program and continue working without restarting your system.

FIND IT ONLINE

If Task Manager is unable to end a task, see
http://www.jsiinc.com/TIP0600/rh0656.htm.

Personal Workbook

Q&A

1 What are the three types of things that you will find on the Start menu?

_____

_____

_____

2 What do three periods following a menu item mean?

_____

_____

_____

3 What happens when you click an item on the Start menu that has a small arrow next to the item?

_____

_____

_____

4 What does a small diagonal arrow on a desktop icon mean?

_____

_____

_____

5 How can you make the icons on your desktop align automatically?

_____

_____

_____

6 What is the purpose of the Computers Near Me icon?

_____

_____

_____

7 How can you quickly view your desktop?

_____

_____

_____

8 How can you quickly switch between two programs without using your mouse?

_____

_____

_____

ANSWERS: PAGE 388

EXTRA PRACTICE

1. Open the Control Panel using the Start menu.

2. Open a program's Properties dialog box using one of the desktop icons.

3. Use My Computer to determine the free space on drive C.

4. Use My Network Places to determine the name of your workgroup or domain.

6. Use the Show Desktop button to view your desktop.

REAL-WORLD APPLICATIONS

✔ You have been assigned the task of writing a report about a group project. To enable yourself to complete the report at home, you use the My Documents folder to copy the report to a diskette.

✔ You have two computers in your home. To make it easy for everyone to share a color printer, you use My Network Places and share the printer.

✔ You like to include spreadsheets in your reports to explain the financial aspects, so you keep your spreadsheet program and your word processor open at the same time. When you're working on a report, it's easy to switch quickly between the two programs using Alt+Tab.

Visual Quiz

How can you display this folder? What must you do to make the folder display the message shown here?

_____

_____

_____

_____

_____

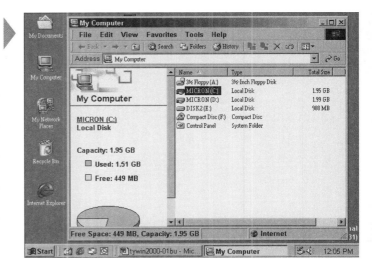

CHAPTER 2

Using Windows Explorer

I n addition to a basic operating system, every computer needs a method for users to interact with the computer. That method may be something as simple as a command prompt, or it may be as complex as a *graphical user interface* — GUI. In Windows 2000 the most recognizable part of the GUI is Windows Explorer.

Windows Explorer is the Windows 2000 component that shows you the contents of the folders that are available on your system. Whether these folders are on your local hard drive, on a removable drive, or even located somewhere on your network, Windows Explorer enables you to explore that folder structure. Folders are the directories and subdirectories that you use to store files on your disks. Folders are arranged in a hierarchical structure such that the set of folder and file names uniquely identify each file on a disk. Folders are arranged in a tree-like structure. Each folder can contain additional subfolders that branch off of it. These branches can extend several levels deep, but too many levels can make exploring your disk drives harder than necessary.

Windows Explorer displays information in *windows* — rectangular areas on the screen that present information. Individual windows can be resized and moved about the screen, and you can open and close them as necessary. You can even open several copies of Windows Explorer at the same time so that you can view the contents of different folders — perhaps to make it easier to copy or move files between those folders.

Windows Explorer can have several different appearances. You have a number of options that you can choose to control how Windows Explorer displays information. You can see a simple group of icons, a more detailed view that shows file size and date information, or even *thumbnail* views that enable you to preview the file contents before you open files. You can even use Windows Explorer to customize the appearance of your folders so that they take on the appearance of Web pages — complete with background images and links that you can click to jump to other pages.

In this chapter, you learn how to navigate in Windows Explorer, how to set Windows Explorer to display different types of information, and how to use it to copy and move files. You learn how to use the Windows Explorer toolbars so that you can more easily control Windows Explorer with a few mouse clicks. The chapter also explains how to sort file lists and how to use the Address Bar and History list to work with specific files.

Opening Windows Explorer

Y ou can use a number of different methods to open Windows Explorer. Each method offers a slightly different way to view your files and folders. In this section you'll learn about a few of the more common ones.

One problem with having many different ways to start Windows Explorer is that it's easy to become confused and choose a method that does not exactly suit your needs. An example is what happens when you right-click the Start button and choose Explore. Windows Explorer opens and displays the contents of the C:\Documents and Settings*username*\Start Menu folder — where *username* is the name that you used to log on to your PC. If, on the other hand, you right-click the Start button and choose Explore All Users, Windows Explorer opens and displays the contents of the C:\Documents and Settings\All Users\Start Menu folder. This behavior is very different from what you might expect if you are used to Windows 98, since Windows 2000 maintains separate settings for each authorized user. If you choose the wrong command, you may wonder why all of your program shortcuts have disappeared. They haven't really disappeared, but you just aren't looking in the correct location.

If you open Windows Explorer from the Start menu, the Windows 2000 Explorer will open in the My Documents folder. If you wish to view a different folder you must make a selection from the Folders Explorer Bar that appears in the left pane of the Windows Explorer window. To view the folders on your C drive you must first open My Computer and then select the C drive from the list of drives. You can then choose the folders that you wish to view.

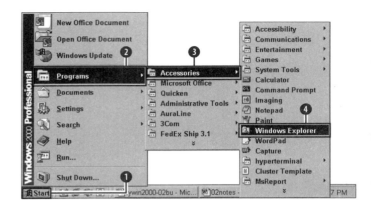

❶ Click the Start button to open the Start menu.

❷ Select Programs to open the Programs menu.

❸ Select Accessories to open the Accessories menu.

❹ Select Windows Explorer to open the program.

❺ Alternatively, right-click the Start button.

❻ Select Explore to explore your personal Start Menu folder.

CROSS-REFERENCE

See Chapter 1 for more information about using the Quick Launch toolbar.

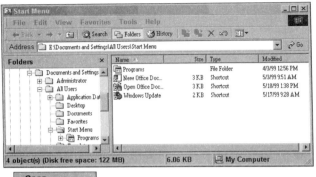

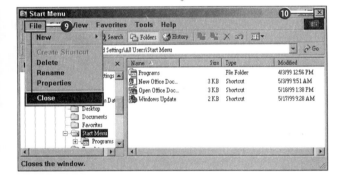

TAKE NOTE

CREATE A SHORTCUT TO FOLDERS

If you often explore a particular folder on your PC, you may want to use a Windows Explorer trick to make this task easier. While Windows Explorer is open, use the right mouse button to drag the folder onto your desktop. Choose Create shortcut here. Windows Explorer will place an icon for the folder on your desktop. Double-clicking the new icon will open the folder.

CREATE A SHORTCUT TO WINDOWS EXPLORER

You may also wish to create a shortcut to Windows Explorer on your Quick Launch toolbar. This will enable you to quickly open Windows Explorer whenever the Windows 2000 Taskbar is visible. To add Windows Explorer to your Quick Launch toolbar, open the Windows folder in Windows Explorer and use the right mouse button to drag the Explorer application to the Quick Launch toolbar. Choose Create Shortcut(s) Here from the context menu. If necessary, drag the border of the Quick Launch toolbar so that all of the icons are visible.

⑦ *Alternatively, right-click the Start button.*

⑧ *Select Explore All Users to explore the All Users Start Menu folder.*

⑨ *With Windows Explorer open Select File ⇨ Close to close the window.*

⑩ *Alternatively, click the Close button to close the Windows Explorer window.*

FIND IT ONLINE

For tricks on configuring Windows Explorer, see http://cpcug.org/user/clemenzi/technical/WinExplorer/index.htm.

Opening Items

In addition to simply using Windows Explorer to view the items on your disk drives, you can also open programs, folders, and documents from within Windows Explorer. In fact, in Windows 2000 this capability is visually emphasized — that's because Windows Explorer automatically opens the My Documents folder unless you have specifically selected a different folder to open.

The default Windows Explorer view includes two panes. The Folders Explorer Bar generally occupies the left-hand pane. The Folders Explorer Bar displays the hierarchical tree structure that is used for the folders on your disk drives. The Contents pane occupies the right-hand side of the Windows Explorer window. The Contents pane shows the files and folders that are contained within the currently selected folder. As you choose different folders in the Folders Explorer Bar, the Contents pane changes to show the items that are in the new folder.

Both the Folders Explorer Bar and the Contents pane use icons to represent the items that are being displayed. The same icons that appear on your desktop also appear in the Windows Explorer window — although not necessarily in the same sizes. You should be able to easily identify the items that are on your desktop in the Windows Explorer window.

The Folders Explorer Bar uses some special indicators to help you understand the status of the folders that are shown in the listing. An open folder icon shows the folder that is currently open. All of the other folders have icons that look like closed folders. Each folder's relationship to the other folders is shown by the vertical and horizontal dotted lines. If you follow the horizontal

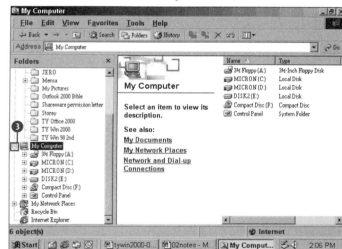

▶ If necessary, open Windows Explorer.

❶ Click a plus sign (+) to expand a folder.

❷ To collapse a folder, click a minus sign (-).

❸ Click the plus icon next to My Computer to expand the display so you can see the drive icons.

▶ The plus sign changes to a minus sign when you expand the display.

CROSS-REFERENCE

See Chapter 5 for more information about working with documents.

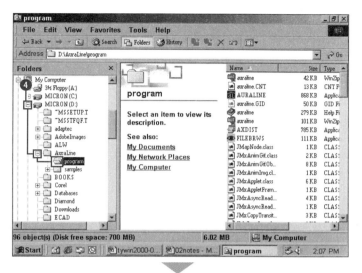

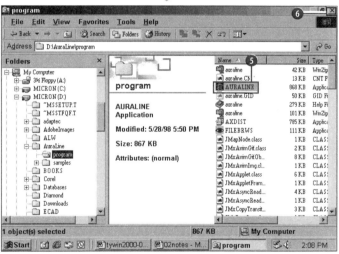

line to the left of a folder and then follow the vertical line up, you can see the *parent* folder — the folder that contains the folder where you started. Some folders have small boxes at the intersection of their horizontal and vertical lines. These boxes indicate that the folder contains additional folders. If the box contains a plus (+) sign, you can click the box to see the additional folders. If the box contains a minus (-) sign, all of the subfolders are already visible.

TAKE NOTE

▶ VIEW NETWORK FILES

If you click the My Network Places icon in the Folders Explorer Bar you can browse the shared resources that are available on your network. You may find that this is a good way to discover which of your folders are shared for network access. Only those items that have been shared will be visible, so if someone is having trouble accessing your files across the network, this is a good place to start your troubleshooting.

▶ REFRESH THE VIEW

If necessary you can cause Windows Explorer to re-examine the drives and refresh the view by pressing the F5 key.

④ *Click the icons to open the folder you wish to view.*

⑤ *Double-click an application's icon to run the program.*

▶ *Alternatively, select an item to view its description.*

⑥ *Click the Close button to close Windows Explorer.*

FIND IT ONLINE

For an online course on Windows Explorer, see
**http://thetangledweb.net/computing/
windows_explorer.htm.**

Copying and Moving Files

Y ou may have many different reasons to copy or move files. Whatever your reason, Windows Explorer makes both easy to do. In fact, there are even a couple of different methods that you can use depending upon which best suits your needs at the moment.

In Windows 2000 the Windows Explorer toolbar includes two buttons that you can use to copy or move files. The Move To button relocates the selected files to a different folder. The Copy To button adds a copy of the selected files to the new folder. If you are used to Windows 98, you may be surprised by the lack of a Paste button. In Windows 2000 this button is unnecessary because both the Move To and Copy To buttons handle the entire process — including specifying the destination for the selected files.

You can also use the drag-and-drop method to move or copy files. Using this method to move items, first select the items that you wish to move, then hold down the left mouse button, drag the selected items to the destination folder, and release the mouse button to move the selected items. To copy rather than move the selected items, hold down the Ctrl key as you drag.

If you want to completely skip using your keyboard, use the right mouse button to drag-and-drop the selection. When you use the right-button drag-and-drop method, Windows Explorer displays a context menu so that you can choose whether to copy or to move the items.

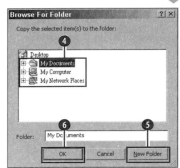

❶ Select the items that you wish to move or copy.

❷ Click the Move To button to move the items.

❸ Alternatively, select Copy To button to make a copy of the items.

❹ Select the destination folder.

❺ Optionally, click the New Folder button to create a new destination folder.

❻ Click OK to place the item in the new folder.

CROSS-REFERENCE

See Chapter 5 for more information about dragging-and-dropping data within documents.

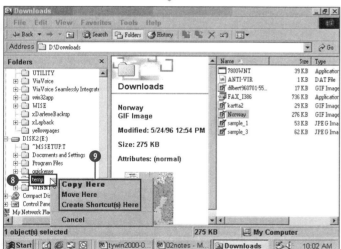

⑦ Select an item to drag-and-drop.

⑧ Hold down the right mouse button and drag the item to the new folder.

⑨ Choose the option that you prefer from the context menu.

TAKE NOTE

NAMES MUST BE UNIQUE

No two files or folders can have exactly the same name. This is less of a problem than it might seem since the entire *pathname* — the name of the disk drive and the folders leading to the file's location — is a part of each file's name. You could, for example, have a file named Norway.GIF in a folder named C:\Photos1 and another file named Norway.GIF in a different folder named C:\Photos2. But you could not have two different files named Norway.GIF in the same folder. Windows Explorer deals with this problem by asking if you wish to replace the existing file if you are moving a file, or by adding "Copy of" to the beginning of the file name if you are copying a file.

DRAGGING-AND-DROPPING BETWEEN DRIVES

Drag and drop works differently depending on destination and method. If you drag a file or folder to a different disk drive, the file or folder is copied when you use the mouse alone, and moved when you hold down the Shift key while you drag-and-drop. You may find that using the right mouse button is less confusing since that works the same regardless of the destination folder's location.

FIND IT ONLINE

To download an Internet file transfer utility that works like Windows Explorer, see **http://www.ftpvoyager.com/**.

Controlling the View Detail Level

Some years ago there was a sketch on the old Monty Python show about a restaurant that only served one product — Spam. Everything on the menu was Spam and if you didn't happen to want Spam, you were out of luck. In many ways a lot of computer programs were like that restaurant. If you wanted any variation from the way the programmer decided was best, you were out of luck.

Windows Explorer doesn't work like that restaurant. When it comes to viewing your files in Windows Explorer, you have a number of different options to get the view that you want. If you can't set up Windows Explorer to show the view that you want, you probably aren't trying hard enough!

In Windows 2000, Windows Explorer has five basic types of views you can select. The large icon view displays folder contents using the same large icons you normally see on your desktop. In this view the icons are displayed in rows beginning in the upper-left corner of the screen. All the folders are shown first, followed by any files. The small icon view is similar to the large icon view except for the size of the icons. You can see many more files on-screen in the small icon view than in the large icon view. The list view uses the same small icons as the small icon view but sorts the icons in columns rather than in rows. In details view you can see the icon, the file or folder name, the file size, the object type, the date the file was last modified, and, optionally, the file's attributes. The final view, thumbnails, is covered in detail on the next two pages.

Windows Explorer has a number of optional settings that you can set on the View tab of the Folder Options dialog box.

① Click the down arrow at the right of the Views button.

② Select the type of view from the drop-down list.

▶ The currently selected view is indicated by a dot.

③ Select Tools ➪ Folder Options to display the Folder Options dialog box.

CROSS-REFERENCE

See Chapter 6 for more information on how to find files.

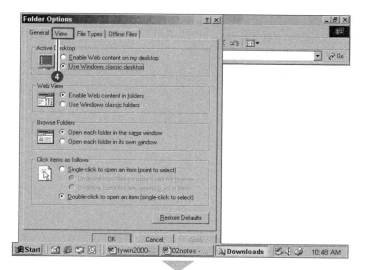

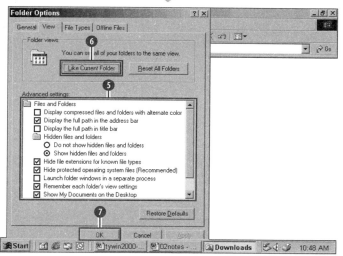

TAKE NOTE

LEAVE SOME FILES HIDDEN

It is a good idea to make certain that the *Hide protected operating system files* check box on the View tab of the Folder Options dialog box is selected. Because these files are vital to making certain that your PC runs properly, keeping them hidden offers some protection against accidentally moving or deleting these important files.

SHOW THE FULL PATH

Selecting either the *Display the full path in the address bar* or the *Display the full path in title bar* check box causes Windows Explorer to fully identify selected files. This can help you avoid mistakes in copying or moving files by reducing the possibility that you will accidentally select files in the wrong folder. Only one of these options needs to be selected since they serve essentially the same purpose.

④ *Click the View tab.*

⑤ *Select the view options that you prefer.*

⑥ *Optionally, click the Like Current Folder button to apply the selected settings to all folders.*

⑦ *Click OK to complete the task.*

FIND IT ONLINE

See **http://www.winzip.com** for a utility that will enable you to work with and view compressed files.

Viewing Thumbnails

Windows Explorer helps you to identify different types of files by using different icons that represent which application was used to create the file. This makes it easy to tell which document files are Word documents and which ones are Excel spreadsheets, for example. But simply identifying the file type isn't very useful when you are trying to locate specific files based on their content.

To help you identify files based on their content, Windows Explorer attempts to display a preview of files as they are selected. This preview, which appears between the Folders Explorer Bar and the file listing, can give you a pretty good idea of each file's content. Unfortunately, locating a specific file by previewing every file in a folder can be pretty time-consuming — especially if the folder contains a large number of files. Before you can see what is in each file you must first select the file and wait while Windows Explorer generates the preview. You may find yourself going back and forth as you need to compare the different files.

In Windows 2000, Windows Explorer offers a far easier method of locating specific files based on their content. If you choose the thumbnail view, Windows Explorer will automatically show a preview of every file in the folder so you don't have to select individual files to preview one at a time.

If a folder contains several different types of files you may find that it is useful to sort the file listing as discussed in the next task, "Sorting the File Listing." For example, sorting the files by type will sort the files based

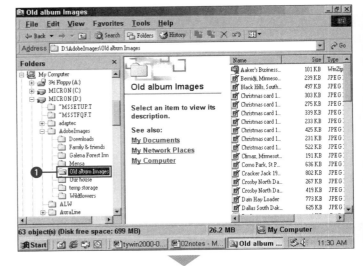

① Select the folder containing the document files you wish to view in thumbnails.

② Click the down arrow at the right of the Views button.

③ Select Thumbnails from the drop-down list.

CROSS-REFERENCE

See Chapter 6 for more information about file types.

on their *file extension*—the part of the filename that Windows Explorer uses to determine which program created a file. Remember, though, that there are many different file extensions that are used to identify some types of files, such as graphic image files. Sorting by type may result in several different groups of similar files.

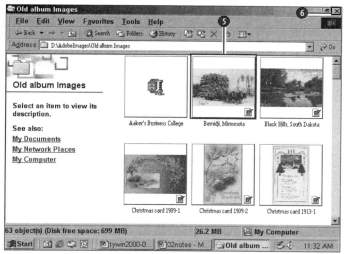

TAKE NOTE

▶ NOT ALL FILE TYPES HAVE THUMBNAILS

Although Windows Explorer attempts to generate a preview for most types of files, not all files can generate a thumbnail preview. Generally speaking, thumbnails can be generated for most *document* files — image files, word processor documents, spreadsheets, and so on. If Windows Explorer cannot generate a thumbnail for a file, the correct file type icon will be shown in place of the thumbnail.

▶ HIDE THE EXPLORER BAR

Thumbnails require far more space in the Windows Explorer window than do icons. If you want to make the best use of the thumbnail view, you may want to hide the Folders Explorer Bar so that there is more room for your thumbnails. You can still navigate to different folders by using the toolbar buttons or by entering the destination folder path in the Address bar.

④ *Optionally, click the Close button to close the Folders Explorer Bar.*

▶ *You can choose View ⤳ Explorer Bar ⤳ Folders to redisplay the Folders Explorer Bar.*

⑤ *Double-click an item to open it.*

⑥ *Click the Close button to complete the task.*

FIND IT ONLINE

To learn about a program with more thumbnail capabilities than Windows Explorer, see http://www.cerious.com/.

Sorting the File Listing

No matter what you are looking for, some organization can be very helpful. That's why the books in a library or in a bookstore are arranged in a specific order — otherwise you would have to be very lucky to find books according to their topic or ones written by a specific author. Arranging items in a specific order is also known as *sorting* the items.

Your computer probably contains thousands of files on its hard disks. Trying to find a specific file among all those files would be no easier than finding that gem in a bookstore full of unorganized piles of books. Of course there are several tools at your disposal to make the task somewhat easier. You already know that Windows 2000 creates a My Documents folder so that your document files aren't mixed in with hundreds of other types of files. Simply using the My Documents folder is a very good step towards making your documents easier to locate. But the My Documents folder is not a complete answer, because you may need to find other types of files than just document files, and there's no law forcing you to use the My Documents folder anyway.

Windows Explorer has the ability to sort file listings several different ways. You can choose the method that will be most effective in helping you locate specific files. You might want to use a date sort to help you find those files that were created during a specific time period — such as the week that you were on vacation. You might choose to sort by file type to help you locate any text

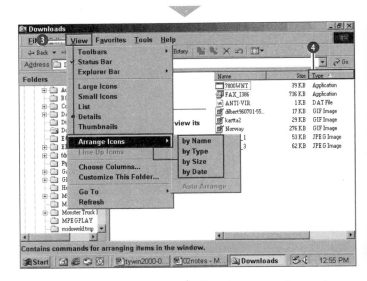

❶ Click the down arrow at the right of the Views button.

❷ Select Details as the type of view from the drop-down list.

❸ Select View ⇨ Arrange Icons and choose the sort order.

❹ Alternatively, click a column heading to sort the file listing in order of the values in the column.

▶ Click the column again to sort the listing in reverse order.

CROSS-REFERENCE

See Chapter 6 for more information about how to search for files.

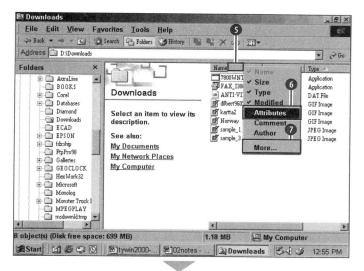

files that provide special configuration information to make certain that your programs are properly set up.

It is best to select the details view before sorting the file listing. Although you can use the View menu options to sort the other types of views, you will probably find that sorting by name is the only useful option in any view except for the details view.

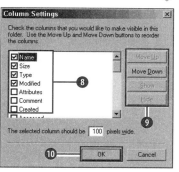

TAKE NOTE

SORT BY FILE ATTRIBUTES

As the figures on the facing page show, you can add additional columns to those that are displayed in the default details view.

If you include the attributes column, you can click the Attributes column header and sort the listing by file attributes. You might find this alternative useful, especially if you want to locate all the files with the "A" attribute, which shows the files that have not been backed up.

FOLDERS APPEAR FIRST

No matter which sort order you choose, Windows Explorer always separates the files and folders into two groups. The folders may appear first or last — depending on the sort order you selected — but they are never mixed in with the files.

---

⑤ Right-click the column headings to display the context menu.

⑥ Choose columns to show in the view.

⑦ Alternatively, choose More to select additional columns.

⑧ Select additional columns here.

⑨ Choose the display order options for the selected columns.

⑩ Click OK to complete the task.

FIND IT ONLINE

See **http://computingcentral.msn.com/topics/
windowsnt/refresh.asp** for a trick on how to make
Windows Explorer automatically refresh file listings.

Viewing Folders as Web Pages

You may have noticed that when you open certain folders on your Windows 2000 PC — such as the folder where Windows 2000 itself resides — those folders have a nonstandard appearance. The reason is that Windows Explorer can display your folders as if they were Web pages. This feature enables different folders to have unique appearances and to display customized messages.

By far the easiest appearance change you can make to your folders is to display a background image. When you add a background image to a folder, Windows Explorer places the image behind the file icons. If you want to add a digital photograph of your dog to a folder, that image will act as wallpaper for the folder.

You aren't limited to simply adding a background image. You can also add any of the items you might see on a Web page — such as colored text or links that you can click to jump to another location. If you want to get fancy, you can use sound or video files, too; but those types of elements will require some heavy-duty programming that is well beyond what can be covered in this book. That doesn't mean your folders can't be pretty impressive, though. As the figures on the facing page show, the Customize This Folder Wizard includes several templates you can use without doing any programming.

Web pages are HTML documents (*Hypertext Markup Language*). To give a folder a nonstandard appearance, you must customize it to add the background images, colored text, hypertext links, or other elements that you want to appear when the folder is opened.

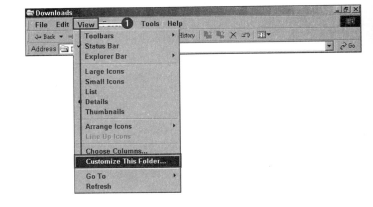

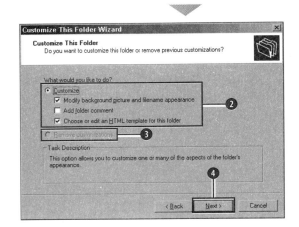

❶ Select View ⇨ Customize This Folder to open the Customize This Folder Wizard.

▶ Click Next at the first Customize This Folder Wizard page to continue.

❷ Choose the ways you wish to customize the folder.

❸ Alternatively, choose Remove customizations to return the folder to the default appearance.

❹ Click Next to continue.

CROSS-REFERENCE

See Chapter 12 for more information about changing the appearance of folders.

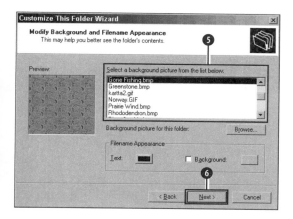

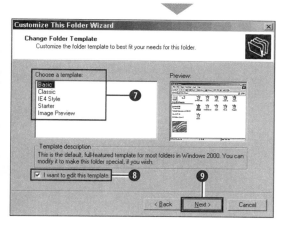

TAKE NOTE

▶ **USE THE TEMPLATES**

The Customize This Folder Wizard includes several templates you can choose to modify the appearance of your folders. You may be surprised when you see how sophisticated some of those templates are. For example, the image preview template includes tools that enable you to zoom in or out so that you can view graphic image files more easily.

▶ **MODIFYING THE TEMPLATES**

If you choose to add a template to a folder, you can modify the HTML code in the template if necessary. To do so you must first attach a template to the folder using the Customize This Folder Wizard. Once a template has been attached to a folder the *I want to edit this template* option becomes available and you can then edit the HTML code. You will find that the sample templates include a number of comments that may enable you to make simple changes without the necessity of learning a lot about HTML programming. If you make a mistake, you can always re-run the Customize This Folder Wizard and remove the folder customizations.

⑤ *If desired, choose a background image.*

⑥ *Click Next to continue.*

⑦ *Optionally, choose a template.*

⑧ *To edit the template's HTML code, select the I want to edit this template check box.*

⑨ *Click Next to continue.*

▶ *Complete your modifications and click the Finish button to complete the task.*

FIND IT ONLINE

See **http://www.camalott.com/html/htmltutor/** to learn a bit more about HTML.

Controlling the Toolbars

Toolbars were a great invention. Programs that include good toolbars are far easier to use because a single click of your mouse can accomplish so much. Instead of wading through the menus trying to find what you need, you simply point, click, and you're done.

Windows Explorer has several different toolbars that can help you use the program. In this section you'll learn about those toolbars.

The Standard toolbar includes navigation tools that will be very familiar to anyone who has spent any time browsing the Internet. You'll find a Back and a Forward button as well as an Up button to move you around through your folders. This toolbar also includes three buttons that quickly switch between the Search, Folders, and History Explorer Bars. Further to the right you'll find File and View management buttons.

The Address toolbar serves two primary purposes. The first is informational — the toolbar shows the currently active folder. The second purpose is navigational. You can either enter a folder address or click the down arrow and choose a destination folder from the list box.

The Links toolbar contains a number of interesting if not totally useful Web page links. Fortunately, you can click the Customize Links button and change to your own, more-relevant-to-Windows-Explorer set of links.

The Radio toolbar is the newest of the toolbars. If you have a fast Internet connection, you can use the Radio toolbar to listen to radio stations all around the world while you work. You can get the latest news, many different styles of music, and — if you want to waste a lot of the Internet's bandwidth — even talk radio.

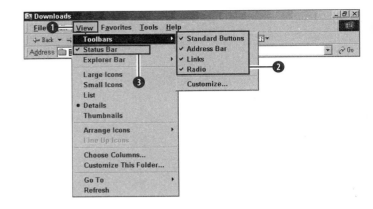

❶ Select View ➪ Toolbars to display the toolbar selections.

❷ Click any of the toolbar options to change the display.

❸ Optionally, deselect Status Bar to hide the status bar.

❹ Optionally, drag a toolbar to a new location.

CROSS-REFERENCE

See Chapter 12 for more information about adding toolbars to the Windows 2000 Taskbar.

The Windows Explorer toolbars may be quite useful, but they can also eat up quite a bit of space. Fortunately you can easily control the toolbar layout and even choose which toolbars are displayed on your screen.

Although the status bar — which appears at the bottom of the Windows Explorer window — is not really one of the toolbars, it is another Windows Explorer element that you can choose to display or hide. If you need the absolute maximum of usable space in the Windows Explorer window, you may want to consider hiding the status bar. You won't see quite as much information with the status bar hidden, but you can always put it back if you feel it is useful.

TAKE NOTE

▶ MOVE YOUR TOOLBARS

The toolbars can eat up a lot of space. You can regain some of that space by stacking the toolbars. You can drag the toolbars onto the same row as another toolbar.

▶ SHRINK THE TOOLBARS

Before you decide to remove toolbars that could be useful, consider removing the text labels as discussed in "Customizing the Toolbars" next in this chapter.

⑤ Drag the border of a toolbar to resize the toolbar.

⑥ Right-click one of the toolbars.

⑦ Select the toolbars you want to appear.

FIND IT ONLINE

See **http://www.microsoft.com/windows98/using windows/internet/tips/advanced/CustomizeLinks Bar.asp** to customize the links toolbar.

Customizing the Toolbars

A s an alternative to filling up a large portion of the Windows Explorer window with several different toolbars, you may want to consider doing some customization. Although you can't really duplicate the full set of Windows Explorer toolbars by customizing the Standard toolbar, you can make a number of changes you may find useful.

If you also use Windows 98, you may find it a bit confusing to have Cut, Copy, and Paste buttons on the Windows 98 Windows Explorer toolbar, and to have Move To and Copy To on the Windows 2000 Windows Explorer toolbar. You may want to customize the Windows 2000 Windows Explorer toolbar to look more like the one in Windows 98. You cannot customize the Windows 98 toolbar to add the Move To and Copy To buttons.

As you customize the toolbar, keep in mind the only modifications you can make to the first two sections on the left side of the toolbar are to choose the size of the icons and how any text labels are displayed. Even with small icons and no text labels these portions of the toolbar take about as much room as eight buttons. You'll want to make certain you add only those extra buttons that are truly useful — especially if you intend to make the Address toolbar share the same row. Also remember that you can use the Move Up and Move Down buttons in the Customize Toolbar dialog box to rearrange the button order.

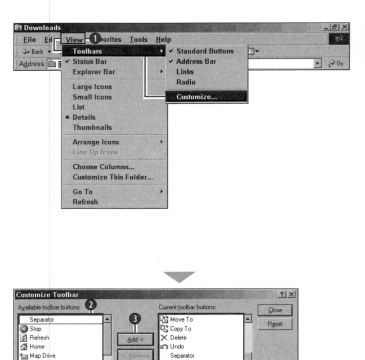

❶ Select View ➪ Toolbars ➪ Customize to display the Customize Toolbar dialog box.

❷ Choose the buttons you wish to add.

❸ Click the Add button to add the selected buttons to the toolbar.

❹ Optionally, choose buttons that you don't need.

❺ Click the Remove button to remove the selected buttons.

CROSS-REFERENCE

See Chapter 7 for more information about network drives.

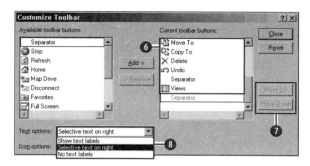

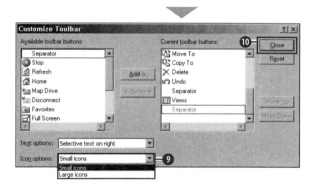

TAKE NOTE

SHRINK YOUR STANDARD TOOLBAR

The text labels on the Standard toolbar increase the amount of screen space that is needed for the toolbar. Once you have learned the purpose of the various toolbar buttons you can choose to remove the text labels so that the toolbar requires a bit less space. Because Windows 2000 will pop up a description of a button if you hold the mouse pointer over a button for a short while, you will still get the reminders you need if you aren't certain which button to select. After you remove the text labels, you may even find that the Address toolbar can share the same row as the Standard toolbar.

USING THE NETWORK DRIVE BUTTONS

If you add the Map Drive button to the toolbar, you can connect to a shared folder on the network using a drive letter. Most modern programs are perfectly happy using a folder anywhere on the network, but you may find that it is just a bit easier to refer to a deeply buried folder by using a single drive letter rather than a long pathname. You may also want to add the Disconnect button to remove the drive letter substitution when you no longer need the connection to the network folder.

⑥ Optionally, choose buttons you wish to move.

⑦ Use these buttons to move the toolbar buttons.

⑧ Choose the label text option you prefer.

⑨ Choose the icon size option you prefer.

⑩ Click the Close button to apply your changes and complete the task.

FIND IT ONLINE

To try out an alternative to Windows Explorer, see
http://www.cmaufroy.com/.

Using the Address Bar

If you have done any Web browsing you are probably quite familiar with the purpose of the address bar that appears in Internet Explorer. If so, you will quickly understand the address bar in Windows Explorer because it serves essentially the same purpose as the one you see in Internet Explorer.

You can type a folder address into the address bar or choose a folder from the drop-down list box that appears when you click the down arrow at the right side of the address bar. If you type in an address you must then press Enter or click the Go button to make the new folder the active folder. If you choose a folder by clicking in the Folders Explorer Bar, the address bar will change to show the new folder's address.

As the final figure on the facing page shows, you can choose to show the entire path or only the current folder name in the address bar. Showing the entire path offers one rather subtle but very useful advantage — you can right-click the address and choose Copy from the context menu to make an accurate copy of an address without the possibility of making a typing error. You can then paste this address into a document or into a dialog box as needed. You might, for example, keep a text file with the addresses of important files so it will be easier to access each of them as necessary in the future. You could later copy the addresses from the text file into the address bar to quickly locate the important files. You'll find this especially useful for files that are buried very deep under many layers of nested folders.

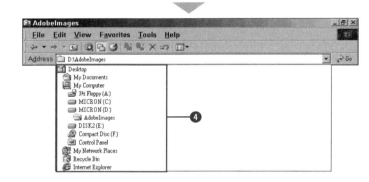

① Type an address in the address bar.

② Click the Go button or press Enter.

③ Alternatively, click the down arrow to display the drop-down address list box.

④ Click the address of the new folder that you wish to display.

CROSS-REFERENCE

See Chapter 9 for more information about Internet addresses.

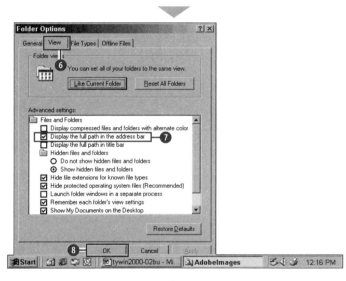

⑤ Select Tools ➪ Folder Options to display the Folder Options dialog box.

⑥ Click the View tab.

⑦ Select the Display the full path in the address bar check box.

⑧ Click the OK button to apply your changes and complete the task.

TAKE NOTE

▶ NETWORK ADDRESSES

If you want to access computers on your network using the address bar, it is important to understand the correct format for network addresses. Each computer in a workgroup or a domain has a unique name. In the address bar, the computer name is preceded by two backslashes as in \\Darlene. Following the computer name is the name assigned to a shared resource, such as \Darlene's C. This is followed by the pathname, such as \My Documents. Thus the complete address for the folder would be \\Darlene\DARLENE'S C\My Documents.

▶ INTERNET ADDRESSES

You can also access folders on the Internet by entering the correct address in the address bar. Internet addresses look quite similar to network computer addresses although there are some important differences between the two. Because the Internet is based on rules that were developed for Unix-based computers, the address separator is a forward slash (/) rather than a backslash (\) as used on Windows-based PCs. Also, Internet addresses cannot contain spaces, so an underscore is often used in place of a space.

FIND IT ONLINE

See **http://128.105.7.11/csl/faq/net/net-addr-faq.html** for more information on addresses.

Using the History List

The history list is a list of the folders and Web pages you have visited recently. By clicking a link in this list you can quickly reopen the same folder or Web page without searching for the correct address.

Because both your local folders and the Web pages you have visited are shown in the same list, finding a specific folder in the history list takes a bit of understanding. If you want to revisit a local folder, for example, you must first locate the My Computer icon in the history list. That icon will lead you to links for the local folders contained in the history list.

The history list is displayed using the History Explorer Bar. Unless you choose one of the optional views, folders and Web sites are listed by date. This can make it difficult to locate a specific folder or Web site if you don't remember the exact date you last used the folder or visited the Web site. You may want to choose one of the optional views to make it easier to find things in the history list.

The History Explorer Bar shows the history list using a series of folders. Each folder represents the main or *root* folder of the Web site. In the case of local folders, that folder is My Computer. When you click on a folder to open it, you will see links for each of the folders or Web sites you visited. Clicking one of those links returns you to that same location — if the Web page or folder is still accessible. Remember, though, that Web pages may quickly disappear and that local folders can be deleted, renamed, or have their sharing status changed. Any of these things can prevent you from reopening the folder or Web page.

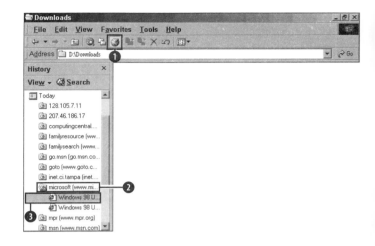

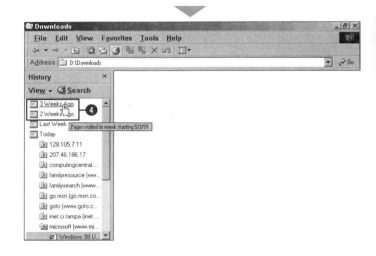

① Click the History button to display the History Explorer Bar.

② Click a folder icon to open the folder.

③ Click a link to open the Web page or local folder.

④ Hold the mouse pointer over a link to view a description of the link.

CROSS-REFERENCE

See Chapter 7 for more information about sharing files on a network.

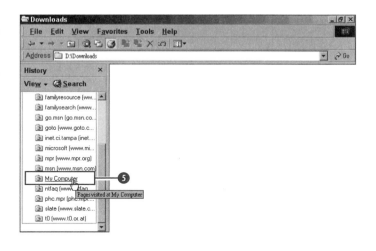

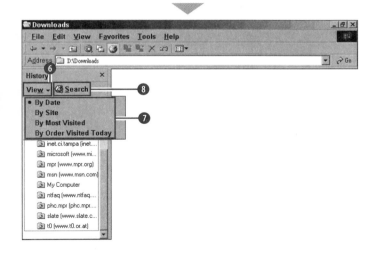

CONTROL THE HISTORY LENGTH

By default, the history list maintains links to folders and Web pages for the preceding three weeks. If you would prefer to specify a different time length, you must make the change from within Internet Explorer, not Windows Explorer. You can either open the Internet Options icon in Control Panel or choose Tools ⇨ Internet Options when Internet Explorer is open to access the Internet Properties dialog box. On the General tab use the *Days to keep pages in history* spin control to set the number of days of historical links to maintain.

CLEARING THE HISTORY

If you want to hide the fact you've been using certain folders, you can clear the history list by clicking the Clear History button on the General tab of the Internet Properties dialog box. This will not, however, clear the Documents list nor the recently used file lists that are maintained in many application programs.

⑤ *Open the My Computer folder to view the local folder history list.*

⑥ *Click the View button to choose a different sort order.*

⑦ *Choose a sort order from the drop-down list.*

⑧ *Alternatively, click the Search button to search for a folder or Web site.*

FIND IT ONLINE

See **http://www.t0.or.at/~txtserve/download/ie5beta5.htm** for more information the Explorer Bars.

Personal Workbook

Q&A

1 How can you display your personal Start menu items when you open Windows Explorer?

_____

_____

_____

2 How can you run a program that doesn't appear on your Start menu?

_____

_____

_____

3 What will happen if you click the History button?

_____

_____

_____

4 How can you preview the contents of graphics files without opening them?

_____

_____

_____

5 How can you make Windows Explorer display file previews in place of file type icons?

_____

_____

_____

6 How can you locate all of the folders you opened last week?

_____

_____

_____

7 Which Windows Explorer toolbar can you use to listen to music over the Internet?

_____

_____

_____

8 Which Windows Explorer toolbar can you use to visit the "Best of the Internet" Web site?

_____

_____

_____

ANSWERS: PAGE 388

EXTRA PRACTICE

1. Open Windows Explorer and explore your personal Desktop folder.

2. Compare the differences between the Move To and Copy To buttons.

3. Use the drag-and-drop method to copy a file.

4. Sort the view of the My Documents folder so that you can find your oldest files.

5. Customize one of your folders by adding a background image.

6. Use the history list to find the local folders that you opened yesterday.

REAL-WORLD APPLICATIONS

✔ You install a program but then don't find it listed anywhere on your Start menu. You use Windows Explorer to locate and run the program.

✔ You're working on a project on your office PC and realize you need to take the file with you on a business trip. Using Windows Explorer, you make a copy of your data file on a diskette.

✔ You have a new digital camera and you've downloaded a large number of images to your PC. You use thumbnail view to preview the images to decide which ones to keep and which ones to discard.

✔ You suddenly realize that a Web site you visited last week had information you need. You use the History bar to find the site again.

Visual Quiz

How does this view differ from the standard Windows Explorer view, and how can you make Windows Explorer display image previews like this?

_____

_____

_____

_____

_____

CHAPTER 3

MASTER
THESE
SKILLS

- Opening Windows 2000 Help
- Searching for Topics
- Copying and Printing Topics
- Using the Troubleshooters
- Getting More Help on the Web

Using Windows 2000 Help

Windows 2000 is a complex operating system. No one book — no matter how comprehensive — can possibly answer every question someone may want to ask about Windows 2000. Eventually there will be something you need to do in Windows 2000 where you will need a bit of extra help. Knowing how and where to look for that extra help can save you hours of frustration and probably a bit of money, too.

The Windows 2000 help system is intended to provide the additional information that may solve a problem. Since the Windows 2000 help system is right there on your computer, it should be one of the first places that you turn when you need more help.

In addition to providing answers to many of the questions that Windows 2000 users commonly ask, the Windows 2000 help system includes a series of powerful troubleshooters. When you encounter problems that keep you from making full use of your system, these troubleshooters can lead you through a series of steps that may well lead to solving the problem in just a few minutes. In this way, minor problems don't grow into major ones, and your PC runs the way that it should.

In this chapter, you learn how to find the answers that you need in the Windows 2000 help system. You'll see how you can search for specific topics, and then copy or print the information so that it is convenient to use. You will see that it often helps to get a little creative in trying to understand where the information that you need might be hidden within the hundreds of available help topics. You may need to play a little guessing game at times, but if you are persistent enough, you'll be rewarded with most of the answers that you need.

You will also learn how to obtain the absolute latest available information by accessing Windows 2000 help resources on the Web. Often these resources will include answers to questions that didn't even exist when the original Windows 2000 help system files were created.

Once you know how to make the best use of the Windows 2000 help system, you will find that using Windows 2000 will be far less frustrating. Rather than wondering how to accomplish the tasks that you need to do, you will know where to find the answers to help you become a bit more successful.

Opening Windows 2000 Help

When you need help, the last thing that you want is trouble finding that help. That's why the Windows 2000 help system is so easy to open and navigate. You wouldn't want to have to use a help system that compounds your problems.

If you have used Windows 98 or Windows NT 4, you have probably found that some of the familiar things you knew in those operating systems seem to have disappeared. In some cases this is true, but in reality, most of the missing items are still there someplace. Some things have been renamed, while others have been combined into new, more powerful tools. To help you find out where you can find the items that seem to be missing, the Windows 2000 help system includes a Where is it now? index that explains the changes. The figures on the facing page show how you can access this extremely useful tool.

Some help topics are simple enough that you can understand the subject after reading it through the first time. Many other help topics, however, are much more complex. You may need to refer to these topics several times in order to obtain their full value. But with literally hundreds of help topics, you can spend quite a bit of time trying to get back to an important topic. That is where you will find the new Favorites feature, as shown in the final figure on the facing page, so useful. When you find a useful topic that you may wish to refer to in the future, you simply click the Favorites tab and click the Add button to add it to your list. Once you have added topics to the Favorites list, returning to them is a simple matter of choosing the topic from the list. Of course you can also remove topics once you no longer need them.

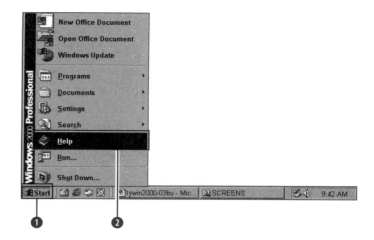

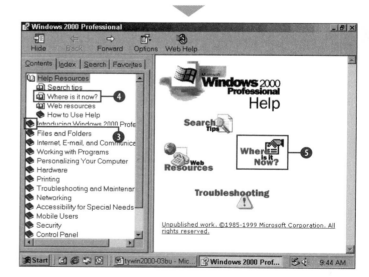

❶ Click the Start button to open the Start menu.

❷ Select Help to open the online help system.

▶ Alternatively, press F1 if no program windows are maximized.

❸ Click a closed book icon to open the book and display the topics.

❹ Click a topic to show the topic.

❺ Alternatively, click a link in the contents pane.

CROSS-REFERENCE

See Chapter 1 for more information about using the Start menu.

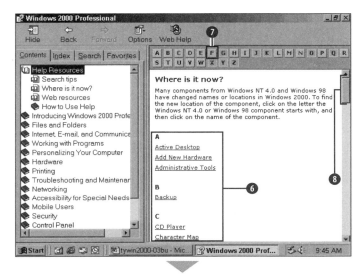

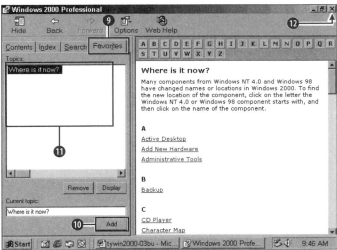

TAKE NOTE

USE FAVORITES AS A LEARNING TOOL

If you discover an interesting topic while you are browsing the Windows 2000 help system, add the topic to your Favorites list. That will enable you to return to the topic when you have more time to study and digest the subject. This is an excellent way to learn more about Windows 2000 at your own pace.

HIDE THE LEFT PANE

You can click the Hide button to remove the left-hand pane from the Windows 2000 help window. Once you have located a topic, this step can be helpful so that you have more room to work on resolving a problem. When the left-hand pane is hidden, the Hide button changes to a Show button that you can use to again display the left-hand pane so that you can locate additional help topics.

⑥ Choose a topic.

⑦ Click a letter to jump to a different section in the list.

⑧ Alternatively, use the scroll bars to view additional topics.

⑨ Optionally, click the Favorites tab.

⑩ Click the Add button to add the current topic to your list of favorites.

⑪ Select a topic to display the topic.

⑫ Click the Close button to close the help window.

FIND IT ONLINE

For referrals to companies that can provide additional assistance, see **http://www.microsoft.com/isapi/referral/default.asp**.

53

Searching for Topics

Have you ever tried to find a relatively obscure type of product by looking in the yellow pages of your local telephone directory? If you have, you know that different people may use different names for the same thing. For example, suppose your sister asked you to take care of her horse while she went on a trip around the world. Two days after she left, the horse started limping and you discovered it had lost one of its horseshoes. Would you know to look under farriers to find someone who could fix the problem?

This same difficulty can occur in any online help system. Sure, the help system includes a whole list of help topics in the contents list, but will you always know where to begin looking? Would you think of looking under the *Personalizing Your Computer* category to learn how to adjust your PC's time setting? No matter how careful the manufacturer is in setting up the help system categories and list of topics, there will still be occasions when you know that the topic is there someplace, but you just can't figure out where.

The Windows 2000 help system includes both an Index tab and a Search tab that you can use to locate topics. At first glance it may seem as though the two tabs perform similar functions, but this is really not the case at all. The Index tab displays topics that have been *indexed*—linked to specific subjects by someone who felt they were relevant to the subject. The Search tab displays any topic that contains the *keyword* that you specify. Both tabs are useful in finding topics. You may want to

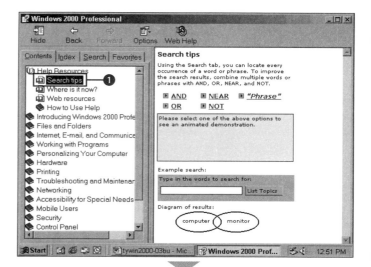

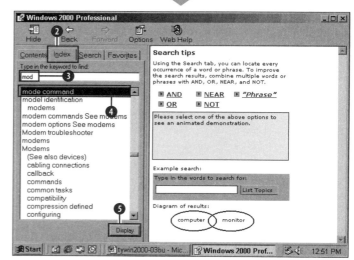

❶ Click the Search Tips topic to learn more about creating an effective search.

❷ Click the Index tab.

❸ Type a keyword to display the topics.

❹ Double-click a topic to show the topic.

❺ Alternatively, select a topic and click Display to show the topic.

CROSS-REFERENCE

See "Copying and Printing Topics" later in this chapter for information about printing topics.

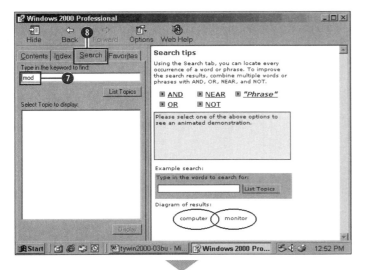

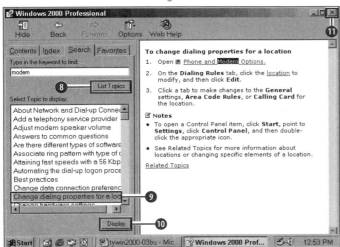

see the "Take Note" section to learn more about the circumstances under which each might be most effective.

Even when you are searching for help topics, it pays to have an open mind. If your search doesn't produce the results that you are seeking, try the creative approach. See if you can think of a different name for the topic, and also look for the *Related Topics* link at the bottom of many help topics.

TAKE NOTE

▶ USE THE INDEX TAB

If you know the correct name of the item that you seek, use the Index tab to locate topics. The Index tab will generally produce fewer results than the Search tab, but the results are usually more focused.

▶ USE THE SEARCH TAB

If you know the general topic but not necessarily the correct name for the item that you seek, use the Search tab to locate topics. You may have to wade through a number of items that seem quite far off the subject, but if the term that you enter is mentioned anywhere in a topic, you can locate it using the Search tab.

---

⑥ *Click the Search tab.*

⑦ *Type a keyword.*

⑧ *Click List Topics to view the topics list.*

⑨ *Double-click a topic to show the topic.*

⑩ *Alternatively, select a topic and click Display to show the topic.*

⑪ *Click the Close button to close the help window.*

FIND IT ONLINE

For some tips on searching for help, see
http://search.microsoft.com/us/quicktips.htm.

Copying and Printing Topics

O n-screen help is great, but there are times when nothing beats a printed copy. For example, you probably wouldn't remember all of the steps to setting up and configuring a new network connection, so if you were using the Windows 2000 help system on-screen, you would probably find yourself switching back and forth a whole bunch of times trying to get it all correct. Rather than doing that, why not simply print out a copy of the instructions so that you can go right through the process without stopping?

If you are creating a document that contains user instructions for performing various Windows 2000 tasks, there's no reason to type everything by hand. You can copy help topics into your document as discussed in the "Take Note" section. Remember, though, that the material in the Windows 2000 help system is copyrighted, and you must be careful to respect that copyright if you wish to avoid legal problems. You aren't likely to have problems if you copy something for your own personal use, but you will need permission to use the copied material commercially.

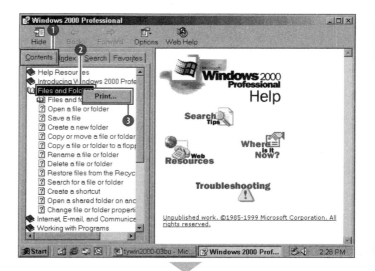

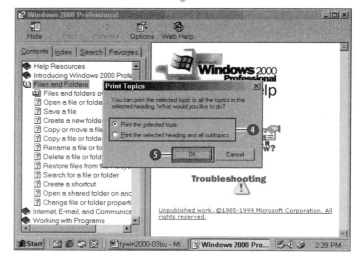

❶ Click the Contents tab to display the help topics.

❷ Select the topic to print.

❸ Right-click the topic and click Print.

❹ Choose the printing option you prefer.

❺ Click OK.

▶ You may also need to confirm your printer selection.

CROSS-REFERENCE

See Chapter 5 for more information about printing documents.

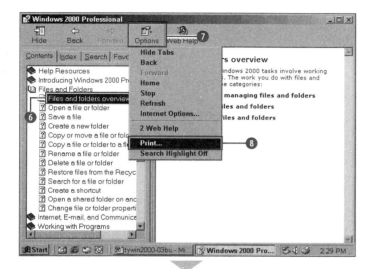

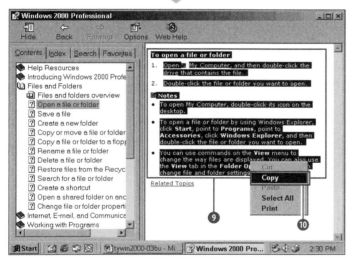

⑥ *On any tab, choose the topic you wish to print.*

⑦ *Click the Options button.*

⑧ *Click Print and then confirm your print options to print the selected topic.*

⑨ *Drag your mouse across a topic.*

▶ *Alternatively, select a topic and press Ctrl+A to select the entire topic.*

⑩ *Right-click the selection and choose Copy.*

▶ *Paste the material into a document before copying anything else to the Clipboard.*

TAKE NOTE

▶ USE THE CONTEXT MENU

The Windows 2000 help system doesn't exactly make it easy for you to copy information for your own use. You won't find an Edit ⇨ Copy command or even a Copy button in the help window. The key to copying help topics is to use the right-click context menu and choose the Copy command from that menu to copy any selected material to the Windows 2000 Clipboard. You can use your mouse to first select part of a topic or you can press Ctrl+A to select the entire topic before you select the Copy command. Once you have copied a help topic to the Clipboard you can paste the material into a document using the Edit ⇨ Paste command or the Paste button in the application that you use to create the document.

▶ PRINTING COMPLETE TOPICS

Many help topics lead to a series of related topics. Although you can print each of the topics individually, it is generally far more efficient to print an entire topic along with all subtopics. The trick to doing so is to right-click the main topic in the contents window and choose the Print option. If the selected topic has subtopics, you can then choose to print only the selected topic or the selected topic and any subtopics. If you choose to print all of the subtopics in addition to the selected topic, you will use far less paper than you would printing them individually, because the entire subject prints as a single document. This will also make it far easier to follow the topic flow because everything will be printed in order.

FIND IT ONLINE

For information on solving printing problems, see
http://support.microsoft.com/support/kb/articles/
q93/5/03.asp.

Using the Troubleshooters

There aren't too many things as frustrating as a computer that doesn't work correctly.

Unfortunately, problems can occur on almost any system. That's one reason why companies often employ large computer staffs — so there will be someone to troubleshoot and correct problems.

The Windows 2000 help system also has a number of troubleshooters that are designed to help you discover the cause of certain types of problems and to resolve those problems. While these troubleshooters cannot solve every problem you might encounter, they are quite capable at fixing the most common problems.

One of the design goals for Windows 2000 was to greatly reduce the number of situations that would require you to restart your computer. Still, there are problems that cannot be resolved without restarting your system. To avoid unnecessary delays or even the potential for data loss, be sure to close all open applications before you begin working with the troubleshooters.

There are some types of problems that the troubleshooters simply cannot resolve. For example, if you attempt to run application programs that were not designed to run on Windows 2000-based PCs, those programs may not be able to run correctly no matter what you do. This is especially true for older programs such as those designed for 16-bit versions of Windows. Because Windows 2000 is a far more secure operating system than even Windows 98, certain types of programs cannot be used on a Windows 2000 system. Many games and other programs that attempt to directly access the hardware fall into this category.

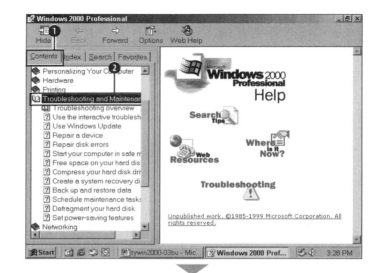

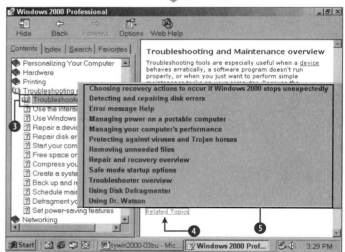

❶ Click the Contents tab to display the help topics.

❷ Click the Troubleshooting and Maintenance category to display the topics.

❸ Click the Troubleshooting and Maintenance topic to view the topic.

❹ Click the Related Topics link to view the list of troubleshooting tools.

❺ Choose the tool you need from the list.

▶ Follow the steps for the topic you choose.

CROSS-REFERENCE

See Chapter 15 for information about maintaining your PC.

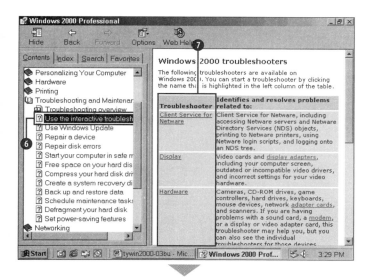

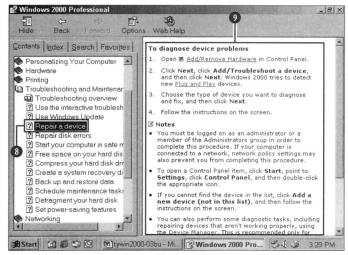

6 *To use the interactive troubleshooters, open the Use the interactive troubleshooters topic.*

7 *Click the link for the troubleshooter you need and follow the displayed steps.*

8 *Alternatively, choose a specific topic.*

9 *Follow the steps to work through the problem.*

▶ *You may wish to print the topic.*

INTERACTIVE VERSUS PASSIVE TROUBLESHOOTERS

Some of the Windows 2000 troubleshooters are interactive — they lead you though the process step-by-step. These troubleshooters are generally easiest to use if your screen is set to a high enough resolution so that you can see the troubleshooter at the same time as any dialog boxes or other windows that might be displayed during the troubleshooting process. The passive troubleshooters generally consist of a set of specific steps that you will need to follow to resolve a problem on your own. You will probably find that printing out the steps will make it easier to follow along with the passive troubleshooters.

FIND ALL THE TROUBLESHOOTERS

As the figures on the facing page show, you may have to look in several different places to find all of the Windows 2000 troubleshooters. If you are having a problem and don't immediately see a troubleshooter that relates to the problem, be sure to look in the other topics of the *Troubleshooting and Maintenance* category. You may find that the help you need is buried within one of the related topics.

Getting More Help on the Web

The Internet has changed modern life in many important ways. For the Windows 2000 PC user, one of the changes comes in the form of up-to-date help that is available 24 hours a day, every day of the year. If you happen to be a person who works at odd hours, you no longer have to wait until "normal business hours" to get assistance with your computer-related problems.

There are many different types of help resources on the Internet. Some of the ones you may find useful include *FAQs,* the *knowledgebase,* and *forums.* FAQs are lists of frequently asked questions. The knowledgebase is a vast resource that covers thousands of different problems with suggested solutions or workarounds. Forums are places where people can ask questions online. Other users answer some forum questions, while an official tech support person may answer others.

When you access the Windows 2000 Support Web site, you may see an almost overwhelming series of options. In most cases the option that will be of the greatest benefit is the search option. When you choose this option you will be able to enter a phrase that defines the problem and then look for related topics. When you enter multiple-word search phrases, remember to enclose the phrase in quotation marks so that the search engine looks for the complete phrase rather than just the individual words.

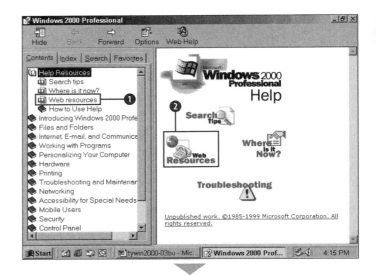

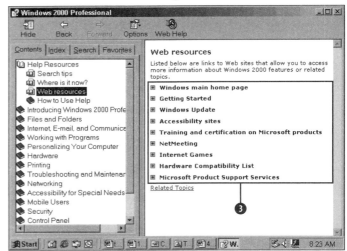

❶ Click the Web resources topic.

❷ Alternatively, click the Web Resources link.

❸ Choose a link to visit the associated Web site.

CROSS-REFERENCE

See Chapter 9 for information about finding things on the Internet.

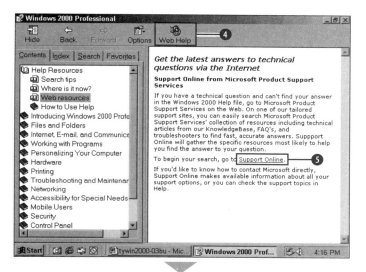

④ *Alternatively, click the Web Help button.*

⑤ *Click the Support Online link to connect to the Microsoft Product Support Services Web site.*

⑥ *Use the Search link to find a specific help topic.*

⑦ *Alternatively, choose a different online support option.*

⑧ *Click the Close button to close Internet Explorer — you may need to confirm that you wish to disconnect.*

TAKE NOTE

▶ THE WEB CONSTANTLY CHANGES

You will likely notice quite a few differences in the appearance of the Windows 2000 support pages whenever you visit those pages. In fact, you will probably notice changes in those pages almost daily if you visit the Web site often. Don't let those changes throw you — they are a big part of what makes Web-based help so useful. Since Web pages can be updated so quickly and frequently, they are an ideal place to provide all of the latest information in a location that anyone can access easily.

▶ YOU NEED INTERNET ACCESS

Although it may seem obvious, you can only use the Web-based Windows 2000 help resources if you already have Internet access. As a result, you won't find this option very useful for resolving problems with your Internet connection. For these types of problems you will probably have to open the *Internet, E-mail and Communications* category on the Windows 2000 help system Contents tab.

▶ VISIT IDGBOOKS

One of the best sources of Windows 2000 help on the Web isn't provided by Microsoft. At the IDG Books Worldwide site at **http://www.idgbooks.com** you'll find all sorts of resources that can make Windows 2000 easier to use. You can even subscribe to free newsletters and find daily tips in addition to looking for the latest titles by your favorite IDG authors.

FIND IT ONLINE

Register at **http://technet.microsoft.com/reg/ support/default.htm** for help resources you won't find elsewhere.

Personal Workbook

Q&A

1 How can you print an entire topic and all of its subtopics as one document?

_____

_____

_____

2 How can you copy a help topic?

_____

_____

_____

3 What is the Favorites tab used for?

_____

_____

_____

4 How can you find a topic the quickest when you know the correct keyword?

_____

_____

_____

5 How can you find a topic if your keyword is not indexed?

_____

_____

_____

6 How can you toggle the display of the left pane of the help window?

_____

_____

_____

7 Which help system component is intended to step you through solutions to problems?

_____

_____

_____

8 How can you get more help if you can't find the answer in the Windows 2000 Help system?

_____

_____

_____

ANSWERS: PAGE 389

EXTRA PRACTICE

1. Open Help and find out where the Active Desktop settings are in Windows 2000.

2. Locate the help topic on setting the system clock.

3. Find the fourth topic under Sound in the Index tab.

4. Copy the Sounds and Multimedia section from that topic to a document.

5. Print the *Sound notification for incoming faxes* topic.

6. Add a help topic to your Favorites tab.

REAL-WORLD APPLICATIONS

✔ You install a modem but then can't use it. You use the troubleshooters to diagnose the problem.

✔ You're working on a document and realize that you need to add a recorded message to it. Using Windows Help, you learn how to use Sound Recorder.

✔ You want to add a new component to your system but the system requirements say that your BIOS must be dated after a certain date. You look in the help system Glossary to find out what the term BIOS means.

✔ You want to buy a new scanner but aren't sure if it will work with Windows 2000. You use the hardware compatibility list help topic to see if the scanner is supported.

Visual Quiz

How would you display the list shown in the figure? How would you print the entire MS-DOS command list in one document?

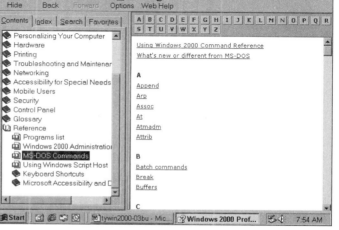

_____

_____

_____

_____

_____

PART

II

Using Windows 2000

This part really gets to the meat of using Windows 2000. You'll learn how to use your favorite programs, how to work with your documents, how to open and save files, how to use your network, and how some special options may provide you with a bit of extra help when it is needed.

You can do a lot with a Windows 2000 PC. Since most programs that are designed for Windows 2000 work in similar ways, the skills that you learn in this part will help you get more done with far less work and frustration in almost any program that you use. You'll see that there are many ways that Windows 2000 can help you become more efficient and productive.

CHAPTER 4

**MASTER
THESE
SKILLS**

▶ **Installing Programs**

▶ **Uninstalling Programs**

▶ **Installing Windows 2000 Components**

▶ **Installing Program Shortcuts**

▶ **Starting Programs Automatically**

▶ **Adding an Entry to the Start Menu**

▶ **Using Menu Bars**

▶ **Using Scroll Bars**

▶ **Using Dialog Boxes**

▶ **Closing Programs**

▶ **Troubleshooting Programs**

Using Programs

Programs are what make your computer useful. They are the applications such as word processors, spreadsheets, and games you use to accomplish different tasks with your PC. Windows 2000 enables you to use most of the popular software that is available today. Not only that, but in most cases you will find that your programs run somewhat more efficiently in Windows 2000.

Because Windows 2000 is a *multitasking operating system* you can generally have many applications running at the same time — if your system has enough memory. This enables you to accomplish a lot more with your PC because you don't have to exit from one program before you start a different one. You simply load the programs you need and switch between them as necessary.

This chapter covers some program basics. It starts by showing you how to install new programs and how to uninstall them if necessary. It then explains how to make your programs easier to use. You can, for example, easily set up programs so they automatically load whenever you start Windows 2000.

You'll also learn how to use common elements such as the menus, dialog boxes, and scroll bars you'll find in most programs. Of course, this chapter doesn't show you how to use specific programs, but it explains what you need to know to at least open and navigate within programs.

Windows 2000 can run most Windows 98-compatible and Windows NT 4-compatible programs. There are exceptions, of course. Because Windows 2000 is a secure operating system, certain things that could do damage to your PC or to your data are not allowed. Programs cannot, for example, bypass Windows 2000 and directly address the hardware on a Windows 2000-based computer. This is most likely to affect older game programs — especially those that require MS-DOS rather than running under Windows.

Because programmers are only human, you may occasionally encounter programs that don't run quite as well as you might like. Fortunately, Windows 2000 is far better equipped to deal with troublesome programs than is Windows 98. In the final task of this chapter you'll learn how you can make use of some of the Windows 2000 troubleshooting techniques if problems do occur.

Installing Programs

Installing most programs on your Windows 2000 PC is generally a pretty easy task. In most cases, you'll probably find that once you've answered a few questions about where you want the program installed and which optional features you want, you'll just sit back and wait for the installation to complete. Windows 2000 registers the programs that you install so that you can later go back and change the installation or uninstall the program.

Programs you install from a CD-ROM often use *AutoPlay* to automatically launch their installation program. If you install a program that uses AutoPlay, you won't need to start the Add/Remove Programs window yourself. You can still use the Add/Remove Programs window to change the installation options after the program has been installed or to run the installation program if you canceled out of the installation the first time.

Although most programs are now distributed on CD-ROM, not all programs come that way. Applications distributed on a diskette cannot use the AutoPlay feature, and you must launch the application's setup program manually. Applications you download from the Internet typically arrive as a single executable file that expands into a setup configuration and then runs its own setup program. You can download and execute the installation file in one step, or you can download it, save it to disk, and manually execute it later.

The figures on the facing page show you the first steps in installing a new program. This task continues on the following two pages.

Continued

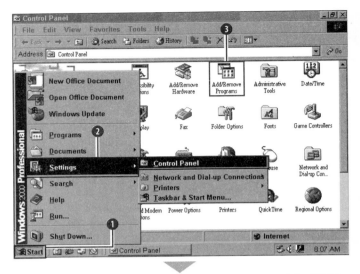

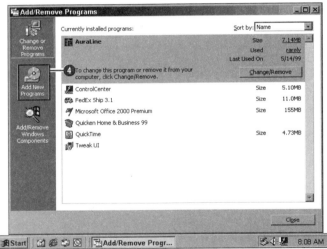

➊ Click the Start button to open the Start menu.

➋ Select Settings ➪ Control Panel to open the Control Panel.

➌ Double-click the Add/Remove Programs icon.

➍ Click the Add New Programs item.

CROSS-REFERENCE

See Chapter 3 for more information about troubleshooting program installation problems.

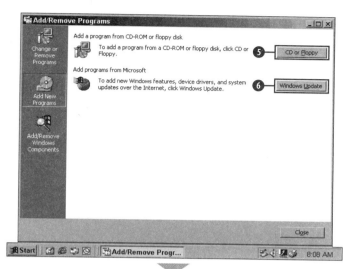

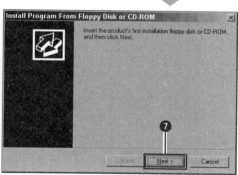

TAKE NOTE

PROGRAMS MUST BE INSTALLED

Although it might seem like the logical thing to do, you generally cannot install programs simply by copying them from another computer. Windows 2000 programs often share components so that they will use less disk space and consume less memory while they are running. In addition, most Windows 2000 programs add special settings to the *Registry* when they are installed. The Registry is a special Windows 2000 database that stores system and program settings. If you simply copy programs from another PC, the Registry will not be modified with the correct settings and certain necessary shared files may be missed. These omissions will often cause errors that appear once you attempt to run the program, and can usually be corrected only by doing a proper installation.

SOME PROGRAMS ARE NOT WINDOWS 2000-COMPATIBLE

Although most Windows 98-compatible programs will work just fine in Windows 2000, some will not. One example of this — programs that use *virtual device drivers,* VxDs, — will not run in Windows 2000. Windows NT 4 had the same restriction on VxDs, so if a program is listed as Windows NT 4-compatible, it does not use VxDs and should be Windows 2000-compatible.

⑤ Click the CD or Floppy button to install a new program.

⑥ Alternatively, click the Windows Update button to install system updates.

⑦ Insert the installation disk in the drive and click Next to continue.

FIND IT ONLINE

See **http://www.winmag.com/windowsnt/links.htm** for information on Windows 2000 compatibility issues.

Installing Programs

Continued

You will find that most program installations go smoothly. Still, you'll probably have to answer several questions to get just the installation that you really want.

By default, most programs will offer to install themselves in a folder under the \Program Files folder located on the same disk drive as your Windows 2000 installation. This new folder will generally be named such that it indicates the name of the program that is installed in the folder. Some installation programs won't even offer you any options and will automatically choose the program folder. Fortunately, most programs will give you the choice of selecting a different destination.

You may choose to specify a different folder for your programs for any number of reasons. You might, for example, have more than one hard disk, and you may want to place programs on the disk that has the most space available. Or perhaps you simply want to organize your folders in some other order that makes it easier for you to use your system.

Often you will be given the option to choose which program features are to be installed. If you choose a custom or advanced option, you will have to make additional selections, but you can make certain that just the feature set that you need is installed.

Although Windows 2000 generally does not need to be restarted very often, it's usually a good idea to restart your PC after installing a new program. This is true even when the installation program does not prompt you to restart. Otherwise, some configuration changes may not be completed properly.

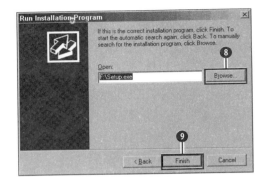

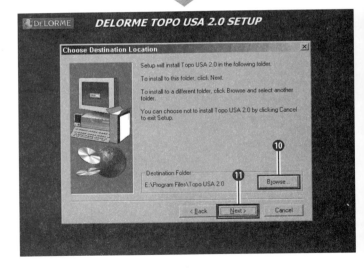

8 If the correct installation program is not shown in the Open text box, click Browse and locate the correct program.

9 When you've finished the installation, click Finish.

▶ Each installation program varies — follow the onscreen instructions to continue.

10 Optionally, click the Browse button and choose a destination folder.

11 Click Next to continue.

CROSS-REFERENCE

See Chapter 1 for more information about different methods for starting programs.

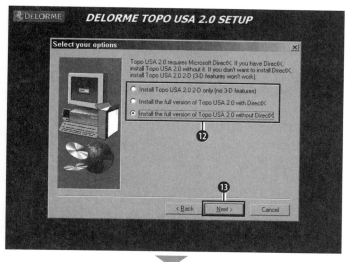

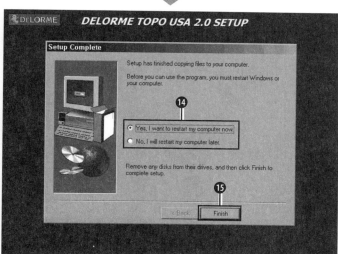

TAKE NOTE

TAKE NOTE

▶ **DUAL-BOOT CONSIDERATIONS**

If your PC is set up to run more than one operating system, you'll need to exercise a bit more than normal care when you install programs. It is generally considered safest to install different operating systems on different disk drives, or at least on different *partitions* of the same physical drive. If you use the same program in more than one of those operating systems you may be tempted to use the same program folder for each operating system. While this may work, it is usually not a good idea. The program may need different versions of certain shared files for different operating systems, and this could mean the program will only work correctly on the last operating system for which it was installed.

▶ **WATCH FOR OLD FILES**

If you see messages during a program's installation that tell you a newer file is about to be overwritten by an older version, be careful not to allow the newer file to be overwritten. This is especially true if the program you are installing is several months old. In almost every case, you should choose to use the newest versions of files. Otherwise, some of your other programs or even Windows 2000 itself may not function properly.

---

⑫ *If you are given the option, choose the type of installation you want.*

⑬ *Click Next to continue.*

⑭ *If you are given the option, choose when you want to restart your system.*

⑮ *Click Finish to complete the installation.*

FIND IT ONLINE

See **http://www.execsoft.com/diskeeper/why-diskeeper.htm** for information on Windows 2000 performance issues.

Uninstalling Programs

You will no doubt encounter some programs that really serve no useful purpose and are simply taking up space on your hard disk. This could be a result of finding a newer program that does a better job, or it could simply mean the old program just doesn't suit your needs. Whatever the reason, you will probably want to uninstall programs from time to time.

Even if you have plenty of spare disk space, there are still good reasons to uninstall old programs you no longer need. Windows 2000 programs often share certain types of files. These shared files are usually installed in one of the Windows 2000 *system* folders rather than in the individual program folders. In many cases there are Registry entries that load these files into memory even when they are not being used, and this can cause your system to lose performance. By uninstalling those old programs you may free up some memory and make your PC run a bit faster.

The task of removing unwanted programs often runs into a few small snags. In some cases, folders cannot be removed. This is usually due to data files that you have stored in those folders. You may want to make a copy of any such files before you manually delete the folders. A system restart is often necessary in order to complete the uninstall process.

One problem that can occur during either installing or uninstalling programs is that you lack the proper level of permission for the task. Generally you will need administrator-level permissions in order to successfully complete these tasks.

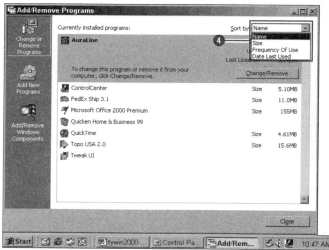

① Click the Start button to open the Start menu.

② Select Settings ➪ Control Panel to open the Control Panel.

③ Double-click the Add/Remove Programs icon.

④ Optionally, choose a sort order to help you choose the program to remove.

CROSS-REFERENCE

See Chapter 14 for more information about backing up files.

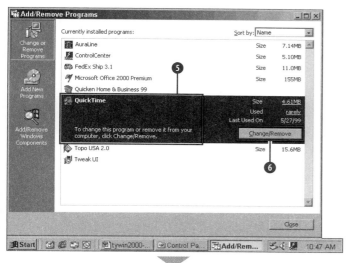

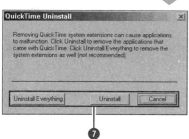

TAKE NOTE

SHOULD YOU REMOVE IT?

When you uninstall programs you no longer need, you may see messages telling you that it appears a certain shared file is no longer in use. You are then given the option to delete the shared file or to leave it in place. While the dialog box may also tell you there is no harm in leaving the file on your hard disk, there is also very little risk in deleting it. The worst thing that can happen is that the shared file really is still needed by another program — in which case you'll receive an error message when you try to load the other program. If this happens you can always reinstall the program that displays the error message. Reinstalling the program will also reinstall any necessary shared files.

ADD THE ADD/REMOVE PROGRAMS ICON TO YOUR DESKTOP

You can make the Add/Remove Programs window a little easier to use by placing a shortcut to it on your desktop. When the Control Panel is open, use the right mouse button to drag the Add/Remove Programs icon to your desktop and choose Create Shortcut(s) Here.

⑤ Choose the program to remove.

⑥ Click the Change/Remove button to continue.

⑦ Choose the Uninstall option you prefer.

▶ Different programs will vary in the steps necessary to remove the program. Follow the onscreen prompts.

FIND IT ONLINE

See **http://www.symantec.com/sabu/qdeck/ cleansweepdlx/fs_cs45_dlx.html** for information on an alternative way to uninstall programs.

Installing Windows 2000 Components

Although most of the components of Windows 2000 that most users will ever need are installed automatically along with Windows 2000, there are some additional optional components that you may have need for. These optional pieces provide additional services for many different tasks, including such things as running a Web server, network management tools, and special networking protocols.

You will need administrator-level access to your system to add most of the optional components. You will also need your Windows 2000 CD-ROM, because these components are installed from the CD-ROM.

As you will learn in Chapter 15, Windows 2000 uses another method to add new system components. This method, known as Windows Update, is not used to add optional components. Rather, it is used to make certain that the latest bug fixes and other system updates have been applied to your system.

Of the optional Windows 2000 components, the Internet Information Services category is the most significant. This category of services is used to support a Web site. You do not need these components to create Web sites that you will place on someone else's Web server, nor do you need them for browsing the Web. You only need to add these components if your computer is always connected to the Internet, and you will be using it to host your Web site.

If you have used Windows 98 (or Windows 95) in the past, you may be surprised to find that the Windows Component Wizard does not include the types of categories that you are used to seeing. You will not, for example, find things such as an Accessory category, a

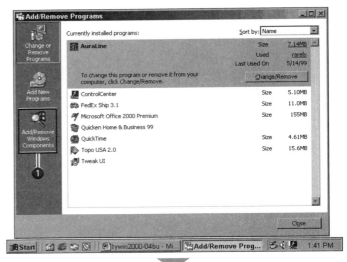

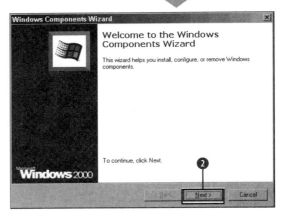

❶ Click the Add/Remove Windows Components button.

❷ Click Next to continue.

CROSS-REFERENCE

See "Installing Programs" earlier in this chapter.

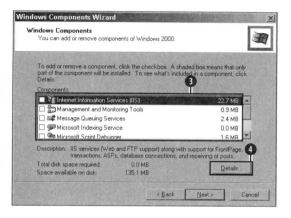

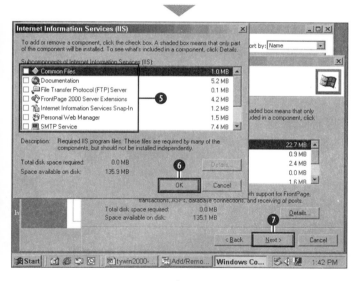

Multimedia category, or Web TV. In Windows 2000, all of the items that would be in these categories are either installed automatically, or are not available. Web TV is an example of a Windows 98 component that is not offered in Windows 2000.

③ Chose the components to install.

④ To learn more about the individual pieces of a component, click the Details button.

⑤ Choose the individual items you wish to install.

⑥ Click OK.

⑦ Click Next to continue.

▶ Depending on the components you selected, you may need to make some additional selections to complete the task.

FIND IT ONLINE

See **http://www.mediavis.com/tech/tips/Mar98/ index8.htm** for many drivers for Windows.

75

Installing Program Shortcuts

You have most certainly noticed that your Windows 2000 desktop has icons that you can use for starting many of your programs. Often using a desktop icon is much more convenient than wading through several levels of the Start menu. Clicking a desktop icon is certainly a lot faster than looking for an application in the Windows Explorer windows! Of course you can use whichever of these methods you prefer, but this task will show you how to add your own Windows 2000 desktop shortcuts.

You can create desktop shortcuts to any type of file, but application programs, document files, and folders are the most likely candidates for creating useful shortcuts. Each of these will do something that is actually useful when you click their shortcut icon. In most cases, Windows 2000 will know what to do when these types of shortcuts are opened. The same may not be true if you create shortcuts to most other types of files.

In addition to the procedures shown in the figures on the facing page, you can create desktop shortcuts very quickly by right-clicking an item and choosing Send To ⇨ Desktop (create shortcut) from the context menu. No matter which method you choose for creating desktop shortcuts, you may want to look at the program documentation to learn if there are any optional *startup parameters* you can add to the command line. These can often provide additional functionality that would otherwise be missing.

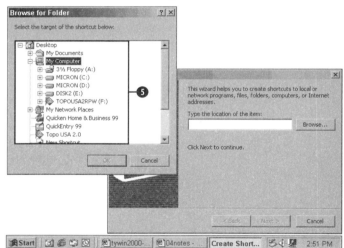

❶ Right-click a blank spot on the desktop.

❷ Select New ⇨ Shortcut.

❸ Enter the command to start the program.

❹ Alternatively, click the Browse button.

❺ Locate the folder containing the item you wish to add to the desktop.

CROSS-REFERENCE

See Chapter 6 for more information about finding files.

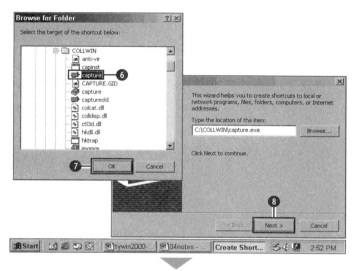

TAKE NOTE

▶ **USING DESKTOP ICONS**

Even if you prefer to keep your desktop quite clean and to start your programs using the Start menu, there is one handy trick that may make you reconsider. Although Windows 2000 knows which application programs to use to open many different types of document files, you may sometimes want to open a document using a different program. You might, for example, want to use a particular graphics program to create some special effects in an image file, even though the file's graphic format is associated with a different program. One of the easiest ways to open a document using a different application is to drag-and-drop the document onto the icon for the program that you wish to use. You can do this in Windows Explorer or by using desktop icons.

▶ **TAKE THE EASY WAY**

When you install new programs on your system, you may be given the option of having an icon placed on your desktop. It's easier to go ahead and allow this desktop icon to be created than to create your own later. If you don't want to allow all your program icons to remain on your desktop, consider creating a new folder on your desktop and dragging the unwanted icons into the new folder.

⑥ Select the file you wish to add.

⑦ Click the OK button.

⑧ Choose the Next button to continue.

⑨ Edit the name for the shortcut if you wish. This name will appear in the label of the icon.

⑩ Click Finish to complete the task.

FIND IT ONLINE

To learn more about shortcuts, see **http://www. microsoft.com/windows/downloads/contents/ wutoys/ntshrtcttarget/default.asp?site=ntw.**

Starting Programs Automatically

You probably have a number of things that you do quite regularly with your PC. Some of these are tasks your computer can handle automatically — such as downloading your e-mail messages at regular intervals or perhaps alerting you to important changes in your stock market investments. To ensure these important tasks are running whenever your PC is running, you may want to make them run automatically when you start Windows 2000. In this section you will learn an easy way to accomplish that goal.

The Windows 2000 Start menu includes an item called Startup that is located on the Programs submenu. Anything appearing in the Startup menu will automatically load whenever you start Windows 2000.

The Startup menu is actually a shortcut to the \Documents and Settings*username*\Start Menu\Programs\Startup folder. You can add items to the Startup menu by copying them to the folder, or you can add them directly to the menu. The figures on the facing page show you how to add them to the Startup menu. You can also use the methods that you learned in Chapter 2 to copy the files into the Startup folder.

It is easy to add shortcuts to the Windows 2000 Startup folder, but it is also easy to get carried away and add programs you only use occasionally. Even though Windows 2000 is a multitasking operating system, if you load every program you might ever use, you will likely discover your PC starts to run very slowly. Unless your computer has enough memory for all of the loaded programs, some will have to be swapped out to *virtual memory* space on your hard disk. When this happens, switching between programs can be quite slow. It is far better to load only the most important programs at startup, and then load other programs when you need them.

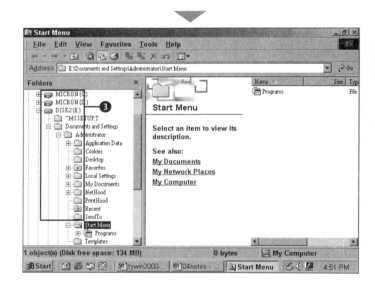

❶ Right-click the Start button.

❷ Click Explore on the context menu to open Windows Explorer.

❸ Locate the folder containing the program you want to add to the Startup folder.

CROSS-REFERENCE

See "Installing Programs" earlier in this chapter for more information about adding new programs to your system.

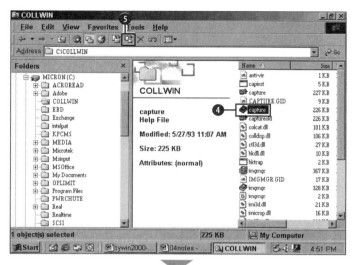

TAKE NOTE

SOME THINGS DON'T USE THE STARTUP FOLDER

Although you use the Startup folder to automate the loading of applications, that's not the only method of automatically starting programs. It is also possible to start programs by making changes to the Windows 2000 Registry. This method is often used for programs that must be run automatically with no possibility of the user deleting them from the Startup folder.

PREVENT AUTOMATIC STARTUP

It is possible to prevent the items in the Startup folder from loading automatically. To do so you must hold down the Shift key after Windows 2000 completes the logon process but before the Startup programs begin to load. It may take some experimentation to discover the exact moment when to hold down the Shift key. It is generally easier to simply remove the shortcuts from the Startup folder than to try and prevent them from running using the Shift key.

④ Click the program to select it.

⑤ Click the Copy To button.

⑥ Select the Startup folder as the destination.

⑦ Click the OK button.

FIND IT ONLINE

For a utility to control startup options, see
**http://www.microsoft.com/windows/downloads/
contents/wutoys/nttweakui/default.asp?site=ntw.**

Adding an Entry to the Start Menu

The Windows 2000 Start menu is probably the most convenient way to start most programs. No matter what you are doing, you can always display the Start menu by clicking the Start button, pressing the Windows key, or by pressing Ctrl+Esc. At least one of these methods is always available.

When you install new programs you will usually find that the installation program automatically places an entry for the program on the Start menu. Even so, you may find that there are program items that do not appear on your Start menu, but which you would like easy access to. In this section you will learn how to add these items to the Start menu yourself.

The figures on the facing page show one of the methods you can use to add items to the Start menu. In Windows 2000 you can also use the drag-and-drop method to add items to the Start menu. In the drag-and-drop method, you drag a shortcut onto the Start button and wait for the Start menu to appear while you continue to hold down the mouse button. Then you drag the shortcut to the desired location and drop it. Placing a shortcut just where you would like it is a bit trickier than it sounds, and you may find yourself trying several times before you get the hang of it.

As you browse your PC looking for programs to add to your Start menu, keep in mind that some applications are not intended to be run manually. Some items that are listed as applications in Windows Explorer are actually a part of another program. Although you usually

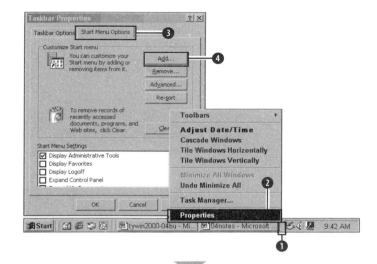

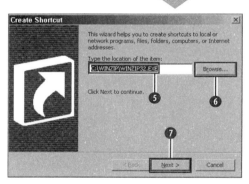

1. Right-click a blank space on the Taskbar.
2. Select Properties.
3. Click the Start Menu Options tab.
4. Click the Add button.
5. Enter the command to start the program.
6. Alternatively, click the Browse button to locate the program you want to add to the Start menu.
7. Click the Next button.

CROSS-REFERENCE

See "Starting Programs Automatically" earlier in this chapter.

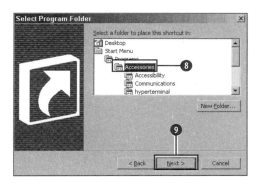

won't do any harm by attempting to run these applications, there's no guarantee that it's safe to try to run an application you don't recognize. You should be able to recognize most of your programs by their file names, but, when in doubt, try right-clicking the application and selecting Properties. This should provide some additional clues about the program.

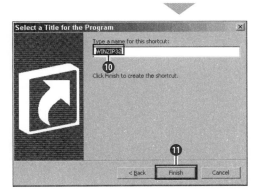

TAKE NOTE

► CORRECTING THE START MENU ORDER

If you make any changes to the Start menu, Windows 2000 will no longer automatically sort the menu items. The menu will instead remain in the same order in which you left it. You can drag-and-drop the menu items into whatever order you prefer. If you would like Windows 2000 to re-sort the Start menu, see "Controlling the Start Menu" in Chapter 12.

► USE SUBMENUS

Rather than just dumping everything into the Programs menu, organize your Start menu by creating several related submenus under the Programs menu. You will find it is far easier to deal with these smaller and simpler menus than to have one huge menu containing so many items that you end up scrolling through the menu to find your programs.

⑧ Select the Start menu folder where you want to place the new program item.

⑨ Click Next to continue.

⑩ Enter a name for the item.

⑪ Click Finish to complete the task.

FIND IT ONLINE

To learn more about the Windows 2000 Start menu, see
http://www.microsoft.com/Windows/professional/
overview/whatsnew/Easiest/interface.asp.

Using Menu Bars

You will use menus quite often as you use Windows 2000 programs. Fortunately most of the programs you encounter follow certain rules that result in similar menus in most cases. For example, most programs display a menu bar just below the title bar at the top of the window. This menu bar generally includes a number of drop-down menus that organize commands into logical groupings. Different programs have different menus that fit the needs of the individual programs, of course, but most applications have File, Edit, and Help menus.

The File menu typically contains commands to open and close documents; print documents, open recently used documents, and exit the application. The Edit menu often contains cut, copy, and paste commands. Edit menus may also include commands for searching documents and for search-and-replace operations. If there is a View menu, it typically has commands to control the appearance of the program and documents. Most applications have a Help menu to provide access to online help information.

Menus all work the same way. You can use either your mouse or keyboard commands to open menus and to select commands. The end result is the same whether you point and click or use your keyboard to select.

Menu items often have an underline under one of the characters. For example, the F in the File menu is usually underlined. If you press the Alt key to activate the menu bar, you then press the underlined character to activate the associated menu or menu selection. Some menu items also work with a shortcut, or *hotkey* combination. Many of these hotkeys are common to a wide range of Windows 2000 programs. Ctrl+C is a common hotkey that copies a current selection to the Clipboard. Ctrl+Z usually selects Edit ➪ Undo.

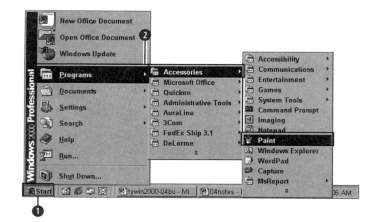

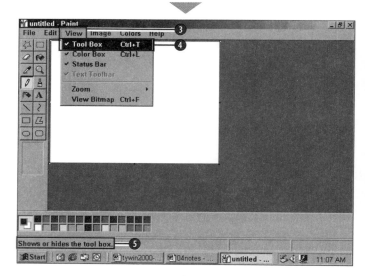

1 Click the Start button.

2 Select Programs ➪ Accessories ➪ Paint.

3 Click View to drop down the View menu.

4 Press the down arrow to highlight the first choice.

5 Read the menu selection description in the status bar.

CROSS-REFERENCE

See Chapter 13 for more information on changing how your mouse works.

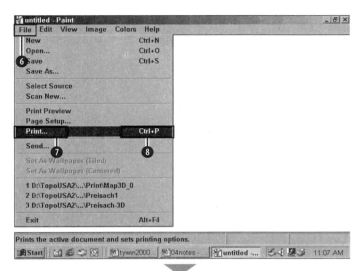

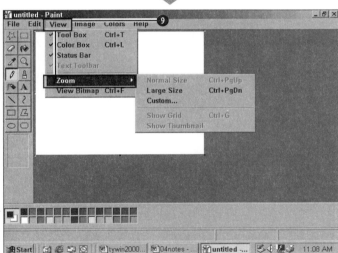

USE YOUR ARROW KEYS

If you're not certain which menu selection you need, click the menu name in the menu bar and then use your arrow keys to scroll down through the choices. Programs often provide menu item descriptions in either the title bar or the status bar, but only if the menu item is highlighted rather than clicked. You can highlight items using your mouse, but this requires holding down the left mouse button while you scroll through the menu. If you release the mouse button the currently highlighted item will be selected. If you scroll using the arrow keys, items are only selected when you press Enter.

MENUS USE SINGLE CLICKS

A single click of a mouse button always activates a menu selection. Cascading menus automatically open when you highlight them. You can then scroll over to the new window, highlight an item, and release the mouse button to select the item.

⑥ Press Alt+F to open the File menu.

⑦ Click Print.

⑧ Alternatively, press Ctrl+P to print the document without opening the menu.

⑨ Select View ➪ Zoom to display a cascading menu.

FIND IT ONLINE

To learn more about menu bars, view
http://computingcentral.msn.com/guide/beginner/
default.asp.

Using Scroll Bars

When you open a large document file it's often impossible to view the entire document onscreen without the display being too small to be usable. As a result, it may be possible to only show part of the file at once. To view the rest of your file — whether it is a multiple page word processing document or a large graphic image — you may need to *scroll* the window vertically or horizontally. The easiest way to scroll most documents is to use the scroll bars. This section explains how to use the scroll bars in typical Windows 2000 programs.

You may not see any scroll bars when you first open a program. That's because the scroll bars often are hidden until they are needed. If the current view can display the entire document without scrolling, the scroll bars are unnecessary. If you zoom in so that the document is too large to view entirely or add more text so the document is too long to show, the scroll bars will appear.

Although using your mouse and the scroll bars is usually the easiest way to scroll through large documents, you can often scroll using the keyboard, as well. To scroll small distances with the keyboard, press the arrow keys to move in any of the four directions. When the cursor reaches the edge of the workspace, the window will move. To move one page at a time using the keyboard, press the PgUp and PgDn keys to page through the workspace vertically. In many applications, you can also press Ctrl+PgUp and Ctrl+PgDn to page horizontally.

❶ If necessary, select a zoom percentage that activates the scroll bars.

❷ Click a blank space in the scroll bar to scroll one screen in that direction.

❸ Drag the scroll box in the direction you want to scroll.

CROSS-REFERENCE

See "Configuring Mouse Speed" in Chapter 13 for more information on controlling your mouse.

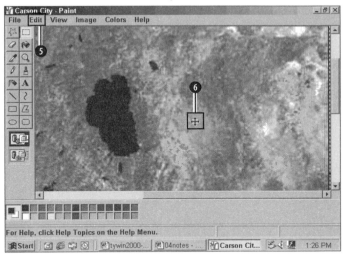

As the figures on the facing page show, there are several techniques that you can use for scrolling with the scroll bars and your mouse. Clicking the arrows at the ends of the scroll bars generally scrolls by a smaller amount than clicking in the open space of the scroll bar. Dragging the scroll box is usually the fastest way to move large distances within the document.

TAKE NOTE

SCROLL BOXES ARE OFTEN PROPORTIONAL

In many programs the scroll bars contain scroll boxes whose size indicates the percentage of the total document that is visible. While this is not true in all programs, it is a fairly common convention.

SCROLLING WITH A WHEEL MOUSE

Some mice, such as Microsoft's Intellimouse, have a wheel between the two buttons. The wheel is used for scrolling. You can turn the wheel to scroll, and often you can hold down the wheel to power scroll in the direction you move the mouse. In some programs you can also zoom in or out if you hold down the Ctrl key while you turn the wheel. Not all programs work with the mouse scroll wheel.

④ *To scroll one line at a time, click the arrow at either end of a scroll bar.*

⑤ *Select Edit ⇨ Select All to select the entire image.*

⑥ *Point to the image, hold down the left mouse button, and drag the image to scroll.*

FIND IT ONLINE

For more information on computing basics, view **news://msnnews.msn.com/msn.computingcentral. newcomputerusers.general**.

Using Dialog Boxes

nother of the elements that you will encounter in most Windows 2000 programs are dialog boxes. Dialog boxes are windows that are often used to set program options or to gather user input. Within dialog boxes you will find items such as command buttons, radio buttons, list boxes, text boxes, spin controls, and so on. These items are often referred to as *controls*.

Command buttons are controls that execute commands immediately. The OK button and the Cancel button are typical command buttons.

Check boxes are small square boxes that are either empty or contain a check mark. When the check box contains a check, the associated option is selected — otherwise it is deselected.

Radio buttons — which are sometimes called option buttons — are always located in groups of two or more. The selections in a group of radio buttons are mutually exclusive. When you choose one of the options in a group, the other options are deselected.

Text boxes are rectangular boxes where you can enter text. User name and password boxes are typical text boxes.

List boxes are also rectangular boxes, but they include a small down arrow at the right side of the box. When you click the down arrow you can choose an option from the drop-down list.

Spin controls are boxes with small arrows pointing both up and down at the right edge of the box. You can enter an integer number in a spin control by typing a number or by using the up or down arrows.

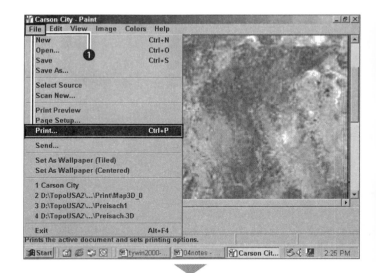

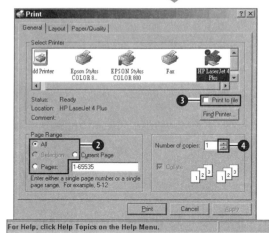

① Select a command, such as File ➪ Print, that displays a dialog box.

② Click one radio button to select one of the options and deselect the others.

③ Click a check box to select or deselect its option.

④ Click an up or down arrow to change the value of a spin box.

CROSS-REFERENCE

See Chapter 3 for more information on using the Windows 2000 help system.

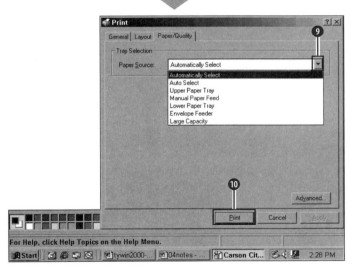

Only one of the controls in a dialog box is active at any one time. A dotted line box that surrounds the control usually indicates the active control. You can make another control active by clicking the new control or by using your keyboard. You can press the Tab key to move forward or Shift+Tab to move backward through the controls. The up and down arrow keys change the selection in a list box or in a set of radio buttons.

TAKE NOTE

CANCEL DIALOG BOXES

If you discover that you don't want to make any of the changes in a dialog box, click the Cancel button. You can also cancel the dialog box by clicking the Close button (the X in the upper right corner). In addition, you can usually press Esc to back out of dialog boxes without entering any changes.

GET SOME HELP

Dialog boxes often have a help button — a button with a question mark — near the right side of the title bar. If you're not certain what a dialog box control does, click the help button to change the mouse pointer into a question mark, and then click the question mark on the control. You'll see a quick help tip about the control.

⑤ *Click a tab to view the options on that tab.*

⑥ *Click a button that displays a dialog box.*

⑦ *Make your selections in the dialog box and click OK to confirm your choices.*

⑧ *Alternatively, click Cancel.*

⑨ *Click the down arrow at the right side of a drop-down list box to display the list box contents.*

⑩ *Click Print to print the document and close the dialog box.*

FIND IT ONLINE

For more information on common Windows 2000 elements see **http://computingcentral.msn.com/ guide/mastercomputing/**.

Closing Programs

Closing programs properly is an important part of using your PC. If you don't use proper procedures you can end up losing your work. In extreme cases you could even prevent a program from working correctly in the future, although that outcome isn't very likely.

Windows 2000 programs will generally warn you if you have unsaved changes in an open document when you attempt to close the program. If you ignore the warning, any changes made since the last time the document was saved will be lost.

If you have used Windows 98 (or Windows 95), you have probably encountered program crashes that caused either a single program or your entire computer to stop responding. This is far less likely to happen on a computer that is running Windows 2000. On a Windows 2000-based PC, programs generally cannot affect each other because their use of system memory is tightly controlled by the operating system. This greatly reduces the chances that one program can cause another program to lock up, and almost completely eliminates the possibility that Windows 2000 itself can be adversely affected.

Most programs have a File menu, and most File menus have an Exit command. To close a program from the File menu, select File ➪ Exit. In addition, most programs have a Close button at the right end of the title bar at the top of their main window. You can click the Close button to terminate the application. You can also press Alt+F4 to close a program or Ctrl+F4 to close a document window in a program that has multiple documents open. Of course, it is always a good idea to save your work first.

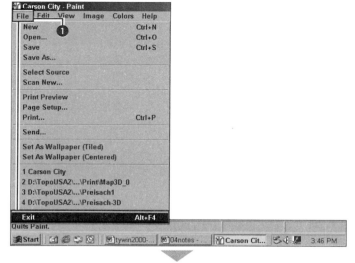

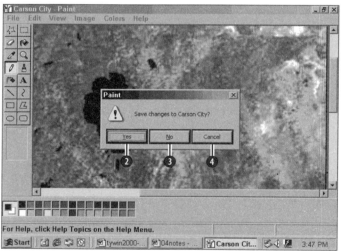

❶ Select File ➪ Exit to begin an orderly shutdown.

❷ Click Yes to save any changes you've made.

❸ Alternatively, click No to abandon any changes and close the program.

❹ Alternatively, click Cancel to return to the program.

CROSS-REFERENCE

See "Switching Between Programs" in Chapter 1.

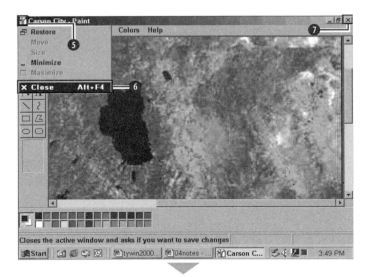

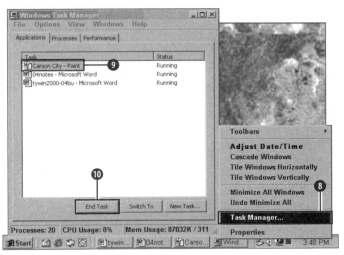

⑤ Click the system menu icon.

⑥ Select Close to close the application.

⑦ Alternatively, click the Close button.

⑧ If an application has stopped responding, right-click the Taskbar and choose Task Manager.

⑨ Select the application that has frozen.

⑩ Click End Task to close the program.

FIND IT ONLINE

For more information on safe computing practices see **news://msnnews.msn.com/msn.computingcentral. safecomputing.general**.

Troubleshooting Programs

Even though Windows 2000 is far more stable than operating systems such as Windows 98, not all programs can run properly on a Windows 2000 PC. Some programs simply won't start, while others may load and then fail to function properly. In this section, you'll learn about some techniques that you can use to troubleshoot those types of problems.

Some types of programs simply cannot be used with Windows 2000. If a program tries to directly access the hardware, Windows 2000 will block the attempt and shut down the program. Disk utility programs are one example of this type of program. Programs that were designed for Windows 3.x often bypassed Windows and tried to directly access hardware in order to improve their performance, and these, too, will not function in Windows 2000. Game programs commonly did this, too. If you are having trouble running any of these types of programs on Windows 2000, your only choices are to upgrade to a compatible program, or dual boot your PC with a less secure operating system than Windows 2000.

Although you troubleshoot problems you might encounter, the figures on the facing page give you some clues where to go for help. The error log example provided enough information for me to determine that certain Registry entries had not been added properly. By sharing the information shown in the log with the program manufacturer's tech support department, I quickly determined that manually running a batch file would solve the problem. Rather than spending hours being frustrated, I resolved the problem quickly. Of course, you may have to play detective in order to make your favorite program run correctly, but Windows 2000 will provide as much help as possible.

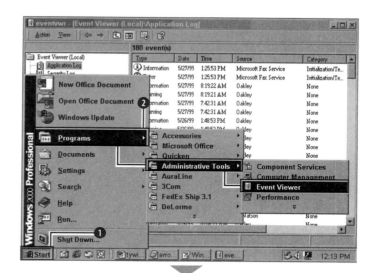

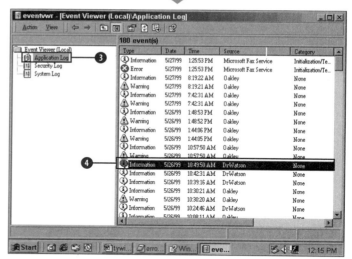

❶ Click the Start button.

❷ Select Programs ➪ Administrative Tools ➪ Event Viewer.

❸ Click the Application Log.

❹ Double-click an event generated by Dr Watson.

▶ Dr Watson is a Windows 2000 tool that tracks program errors.

CROSS-REFERENCE

See "Using the Troubleshooters" in Chapter 3.

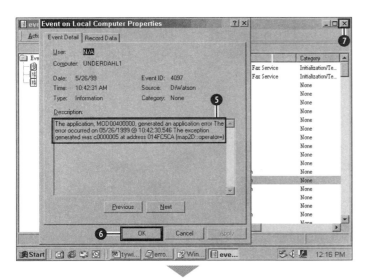

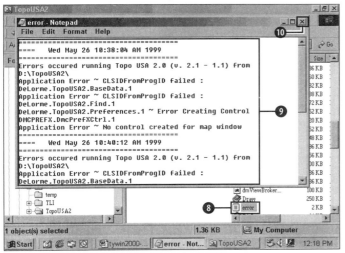

SEND ERROR LOGS TO TECH SUPPORT

When a program fails and Windows 2000 creates an error log file, that file can be a key factor in helping the program manufacturer's technical support department find a solution. The error log is created in a file named ERROR.LOG in the folder where the application program is located. Although the notations in the error log may not make much sense to you, they do provide vital information about exactly what failed in the program. If you need to contact the manufacturer for assistance, be sure to advise them that you have the error log file and can e-mail it to them. Doing so will likely reduce the amount of time you spend looking for a solution.

TRY THE WINDOWS 2000 TOOLS

Rather than trying to use old utility programs that may not be Windows 2000-compatible, try the tools that are built into Windows 2000. You can be sure that they are safe to use on your system.

⑤ View the description — you may need help from tech support.

⑥ Click OK to close the event.

⑦ Click the Close button.

⑧ Locate and double-click the error log file that Windows 2000 generated.

⑨ View the information to determine the problem.

⑩ Click the Close button.

FIND IT ONLINE

For more information on finding answers online, view
**http://support.microsoft.com/support/howto/
services.asp.**

► Personal Workbook

Q&A

1 If you have items you want to run automatically whenever you start Windows 2000, where should you place them?

_____

_____

_____

2 How many options can you select at the same time from a group of radio buttons?

_____

_____

_____

3 Which Control Panel icon do you use when you want to install a new program?

_____

_____

_____

4 What does the size of the scroll box often indicate?

_____

_____

_____

5 What type of action prevents some older programs from running on Windows 2000?

_____

_____

_____

6 What are _desktop shortcuts_?

_____

_____

_____

7 What window would you use to add the services you would need to use your PC as a Web server?

_____

_____

_____

8 What will happen if you select No when Windows 2000 tells you that you are closing an application and haven't saved your work?

_____

_____

_____

ANSWERS: PAGE 390

EXTRA PRACTICE

1. Install a new program using the Add/Remove Programs dialog box.

2. Add a shortcut to Paint to your desktop.

3. Set up Notepad to start automatically when you start Windows 2000.

4. Experiment with the hotkeys on the WordPad menus.

5. Open the Print dialog box and try out the various controls.

6. Try the different methods of closing programs.

REAL-WORLD APPLICATIONS

✔ You get a CD-ROM that contains several programs, each in its own folder. To install each individual program, you use the Add/Remove Programs dialog box and browse for the correct installation programs.

✔ You depend on e-mail messages to keep in touch with your office. To make certain you get your e-mail frequently, you add your e-mail program to the Startup folder so that it starts whenever you run Windows 2000.

✔ You've just purchased a new program but you get errors whenever you try to print from it. You send the error log to the tech support department to help resolve the problem.

Visual Quiz

How can you display this window? What can you tell from the status column?

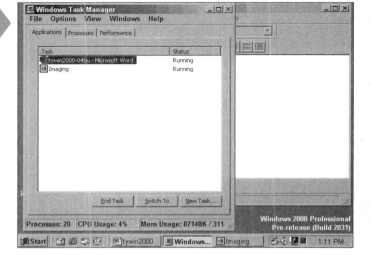

_____

_____

_____

_____

_____

CHAPTER **5**

MASTER
THESE
SKILLS

▶ **Opening Documents**
▶ **Opening Recently Used Documents**
▶ **Saving Documents**
▶ **Organizing Your Documents**
▶ **Changing the My Documents Location**
▶ **Selecting Text**
▶ **Cutting, Copying, and Pasting to the Clipboard**
▶ **Dragging-and-Dropping Data**
▶ **Setting Printer Properties**
▶ **Putting a Printer on the Desktop**
▶ **Printing Documents**

Working with Documents

I f someone were to ask you what was the most valuable thing on your PC, would you have a good answer? Actually, the answer is an easy one. Your *documents* represent the time and effort that you have expended working on your computer. Everything else — your monitor, your disk drives, your programs, and so on — are items that could be replaced or repaired quite easily. Your documents are unique and are therefore more important than any of these other items.

Windows 2000 makes it very easy to work with your documents. You can place them where you want, you can copy or move them easily, and you can open them without first figuring out which program you should use. This means that you can think about what you want to do rather than which tools you need. And since the same general techniques apply in most Windows 2000 applications, you can concentrate on results rather than procedures.

If you have used a Windows 98 or Windows 95 PC, many of the techniques that you will use for working with your documents in Windows 2000 will seem quite familiar. You won't have to learn a whole new way of working to become productive in Windows 2000. What you will find, though, is that Windows 2000 often provides better or easier ways of doing things.

When you have documents rather than programs as your focus, it is far easier to manage your projects productively. For example, imagine how difficult it would be to plan a family picnic if you spent all of your time trying to figure out which mode of transportation each family member was going to use rather than what food everyone should bring. Since the ultimate goal is to put together the feast, why would you care if some family members came by bicycle, some by car, and others by bus?

The same principal applies to your documents. When you are working on a project, you will find that it is far easier to keep all of the project documents together regardless of whether you used a word processor, a spreadsheet program, or a graphics editor to create those documents. Then you can think about the results, not the tools.

Opening Documents

When you want to work with one of your document files in Windows 2000, you don't need to first figure out which program was used to create the document. That's because Windows 2000 *associates* document types with the application programs that create those types of documents. When you double-click a document file, Windows 2000 uses that association to open the document in the correct program. You don't have to first open the program and then open the document, because opening the document opens the correct program.

When you right-click a file in Windows Explorer, you open a context menu that displays a number of actions that you can perform. The item at the top of the context menu is the default action that Windows 2000 will perform if you double-click the file. In most cases the default action is to open the file. If the file is a document file, Windows 2000 uses the associated program to open the document.

You can also open documents by first opening the program that you wish to use. Once the program is open, you generally open documents using the File ⇨ Open command or by using the Open button on the program's toolbar. If you are already working on a document, it is usually far easier to use one of these methods to open additional documents rather than by returning to Windows Explorer.

Windows 2000 associates document types with specific programs by using the *file extension*. The file extension is the three characters that follow the filename. Common document file extensions include .doc for word processing documents, .xls for Excel spreadsheets, and .jpg for certain graphic image files.

You may not even realize that your Windows 2000 programs are using file extensions to designate their

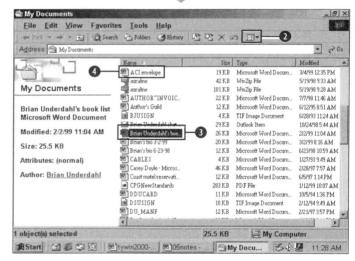

❶ Double-click the My Documents icon on your desktop to open the folder.

❷ If you want to change the way document files are displayed, click the Views button.

❸ Select a file to view its description.

❹ You can double-click a document to open it.

CROSS-REFERENCE

See "Opening Recently Used Documents" later in this chapter.

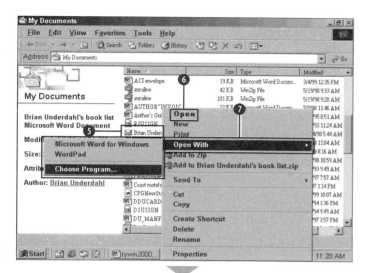

document files. Windows 2000 normally does not show the file extensions, and most programs automatically add the extensions after you indicate the filename that you wish to use.

TAKE NOTE

▶ VIEW THE FILE EXTENSIONS

If you want to see the file extensions for your files, you will need to change one of the default settings for Windows Explorer. To do so, first open Windows Explorer. Then select Tools ⇨ Folder Options and click the View tab. Remove the check from the *Hide file extensions for known file types* check box. Click OK to close the dialog box. Be careful not to change any file extensions that are displayed.

▶ OPEN DOCUMENTS AS YOU LIKE

If you wish to open a document using a program other than the one that Windows 2000 associates with the document, right-click the document and choose Open With to display a cascading menu. You can then choose one of the programs that are listed, or you can choose the Choose Program option.

⑤ *Right-click a file to view the context menu.*

⑥ *Click Open to open the file using the default application.*

⑦ *Alternatively, select Open With and choose an alternate application to open the document.*

⑧ *Choose the application.*

⑨ *Click OK to open the document.*

FIND IT ONLINE

See **http://home.zdnet.com/pcmag/pctech/content** for information on file associations.

Opening Recently Used Documents

Whenever you work on a document, Windows 2000 adds that document to a list that it maintains of the documents that you have opened recently. The list of your most recently used documents appears on the Start menu, and you can reopen one of the listed documents by selecting it from the list. This makes it easy to open those documents because you don't have to open the My Documents folder and search for them.

The Start menu Documents list shows the 15 most recently accessed documents. This list is made up of document shortcuts that are stored in the \Documents and Settings*username*\Recent folder. This folder may actually contain far more than 15 shortcuts, but only 15 will show on the Documents list.

If you work with a large number of documents in the course of a day, it's easy for important documents to get bumped off the Documents list. To keep this from happening, you may want to manually delete unimportant documents from the list, as shown in the figures on the facing page.

You can open any of the items on the Documents list by clicking the item. You can also open a shortcut menu for any of the items on the Documents list by right-clicking the item. This shortcut menu includes the same context-sensitive choices you'd see if you opened the item's shortcut menu in Windows Explorer. The items on the shortcut menu vary according to the type of object you've selected. You'll always see an Open choice, a Delete choice, and a Properties choice, along with several others. Open is always the first choice at the top of the shortcut menu, and selecting Open is the same as clicking the item. Use Delete to remove the shortcut without affecting the actual document file.

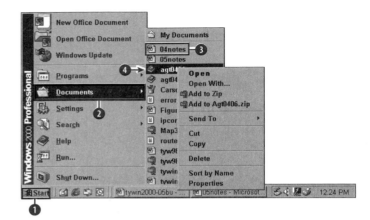

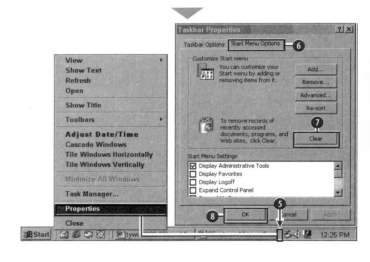

① Click the Start button.

② Select Documents to open the list of recently used documents.

③ Click a document to open the document file.

④ Right-click a document to open the context menu.

⑤ Right-click the Taskbar and select Properties.

⑥ Click the Start Menu Options tab.

⑦ Click Clear to delete the shortcuts to recently accessed documents.

⑧ Click OK to close the Taskbar Properties dialog box.

CROSS-REFERENCE

See "Sending Objects to the Recycle Bin" in Chapter 6.

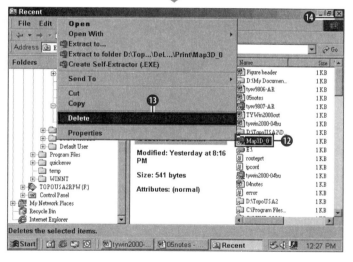

THE DOCUMENTS LIST CAN BE WRONG

Just because an item is on the Start menu's Documents list doesn't mean that you'll be able to open the document file by selecting it from the list. If you delete a document file, the shortcut may remain in the list for some time. If you move a document file without opening the file, the shortcut won't be corrected to point to the new file location.

PROTECTING YOUR PRIVACY

Anyone who examines your Documents list can easily see which document files you've been using. Clearing the Documents list is an important first step in protecting your privacy, but it does not provide a complete solution. Most application programs also maintain a list of the documents you opened using the application, and if you use a program such as Microsoft Outlook, you may find that the Outlook Journal also records which documents you open. If you need to protect your privacy, you will probably want to prevent anyone from using your PC.

⑨ *Right-click the Start button.*

⑩ *Select Explore.*

⑪ *Click the Recent folder to view the contents of the folder.*

⑫ *Right-click an item to display its context menu.*

⑬ *If you want to remove the shortcut, select Delete.*

⑭ *Click the Close button to complete the task.*

Saving Documents

Unless you like wasting your time redoing the same work each time you work on a document, you will probably want to save your documents in files. Any program that you use to create documents will give you the option to save your work (although the Save function may be disabled on trial versions of some software packages).

Most Windows 2000 programs follow certain conventions so that users will have an easier time using the software. One of the standard conventions followed by Windows 2000 programs is to include a File ⇨ Save command so you can easily save your documents.

The first time that you save a new document you will have to supply a name for the file. After you have saved the file, the same name will be used when you save the file again to incorporate any changes that you have made.

You can also save your work using a new filename by selecting the File ⇨ Save As command. This command enables you to not only specify a different name, but also a different destination folder or even a different file format in most instances. One example of why you might use this option is if you need to convert a graphics file from one format to another — perhaps so that you can use the image on your Web site. Because only a few graphics file formats can be used on the Web, using File ⇨ Save As and choosing one of the Web-compatible formats would enable you to use an image file that might not work otherwise.

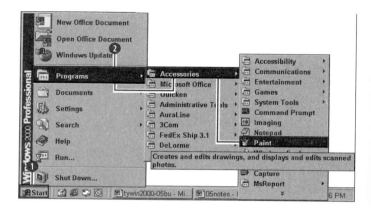

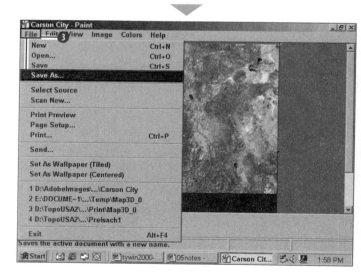

① Click the Start button.

② Select Programs ⇨ Accessories ⇨ Paint.

③ Select File ⇨ Save As to open the Save As dialog box.

CROSS-REFERENCE

See "Copying and Moving Files" in Chapter 2.

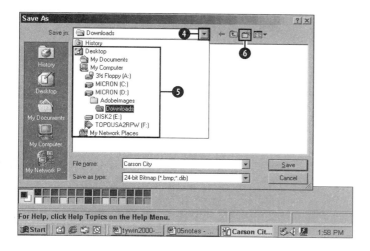

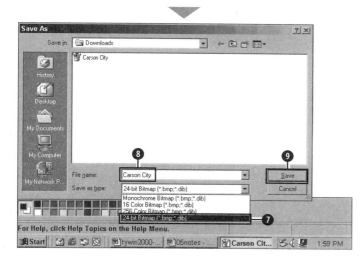

ADD THE CORRECT FILTERS

Programs often use add-in features that are called *filters* to convert files from one format to another. If you want to use File ➪ Save As to save a document file in a different format, you may need to install some extra filters that were not installed by default. In most cases, you will need to use the application's install program and choose a custom or advanced option to select the filters to be installed.

USE THE SEND TO OPTION

Many Windows 2000 programs remember the last location where you opened or saved files, and they offer the same location when you save a new file. Although this practice is usually convenient, it can cause problems. For example, if you use the File ➪ Save As command to save a copy of your document onto a diskette, you may see an error message if you later try to open a new file after the diskette is no longer in the drive. To avoid this situation, you may want to always save your documents on your hard disk, and then use the right-click context menu Send To command to save a copy on the diskette.

④ Optionally, click the down arrow at the right edge of the "Save in" list box to drop down the list box.

⑤ Select a location for saving the file.

⑥ Click here if you want to create a new folder to hold the file.

⑦ Optionally, select the file type from the "Save as type" list box.

⑧ Enter a name for the file here.

⑨ Click Save to save the file and close the dialog box.

FIND IT ONLINE

For document-saving tips, see **http://www. computertips.com/Windows/WindowsNT40/ Files%20and%20Folders/aheader.htm.**

Organizing Your Documents

Proper organization can be the key to getting more done in less time. If you find that you simply cannot get everything that you need to do finished, maybe you just need to be a little more organized.

You already know that most Windows 2000 application programs use the My Documents folder as the default location for saving document files. What you may not realize, though, is that this folder should be the starting point rather than the ending point as you organize your documents. If you use the My Documents folder as a base for creating new document folders, you can easily separate your documents by project so that each of your projects will be well organized.

Imagine that your boss has assigned you four different projects that you are to work on over the next several months. Each of those projects has some similar elements, but each also requires separate documentation. By creating four separate project folders under the My Documents folder you can keep each project's files together and you don't have to worry about using the same filename in two or more projects.

There's no reason why you can't take this concept a few steps farther. You can create new folders within other folders, so you might even want to add new folders to your project folders. Remember, though, that Windows Explorer sorts folder contents into two separate groups. Any folders that are contained within a folder are sorted together as one group, and all other files make up the second group. Shortcuts — even shortcuts to folders — are grouped with files rather than with folders.

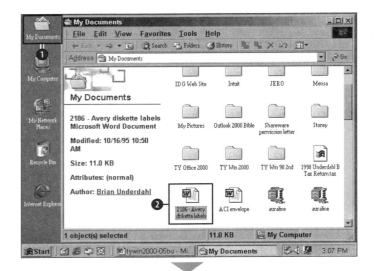

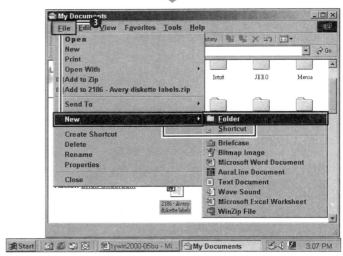

① Double-click the My Documents icon to open the folder.

② Select a document to view its properties.

③ Select File ➪ New ➪ Folder to create a new project folder.

▶ Give the new folder a descriptive name so that it is clear which project's files belong in the folder.

CROSS-REFERENCE

See "Finding a File" in Chapter 6.

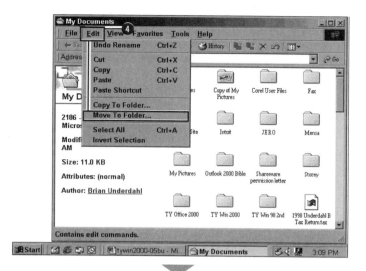

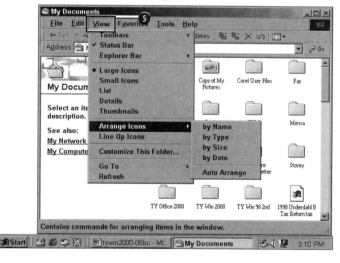

▶ *Select the project files that you wish to move to the new folder.*

❹ *Select Edit ⇨ Move To Folder and choose the new folder for the project files.*

❺ *Optionally, select the view options for the new project folder.*

▶ *You can select different options for organizing each project folder.*

TAKE NOTE

REUSE DOCUMENTS

If you are working on several projects that will require you to create a number of similar documents, you can save some time by reusing some of those documents. For example, if each project requires a budget analysis, it's likely that most of the basic details will be quite similar in each budget analysis document. You can create a master document and then use the File ⇨ Save As command to save the individual copies in their separate locations. Then you can plug in the proper numbers and have the separate documents completed in no time.

USE THE CONTEXT MENUS

The context menus that appear when you right-click an object in Windows Explorer are also available in the Save As and the Open dialog boxes. You can use these context menus for many different file management tasks including renaming files, deleting files, or copying files. Using the context menus in one of the dialog boxes can save you considerable time because you won't have to open Windows Explorer to handle these tasks. In most cases you can use the context menus to perform several actions without closing the dialog box.

FIND IT ONLINE

For tips on the My Documents folder, see **http://windowsupdate.microsoft.com/nt5help/Server/en/my_documents.htm**.

Changing the My Documents Location

In most ways the My Documents folder functions just like any other folder on your PC. You can add files and folders to it, you can clean out old items that you no longer need, and you can view the My Documents folder using Windows Explorer.

Even with these important similarities to the other folders on your hard drive, the My Documents folder is just a bit different from most other folders. Because My Documents is the default location where most Windows 2000 programs save document files, you have to be careful about renaming or moving the folder. The reason for this is simple — you want to make certain that your programs can locate the folder, both for saving new files and for opening your existing documents.

As the figures on the facing page show, you use the My Documents Properties dialog box to move, rename, or share the My Documents folder. By using this dialog box, you record the changes in the Registry so that your programs will also be informed of any changes. This will also enable new programs that you install later to locate the new folder.

If your PC has more than one hard disk, you may want to move the My Documents folder to the disk with the most free space. You may also want to consider using a network drive as your document storage location — especially if your network has a file server that is backed up automatically.

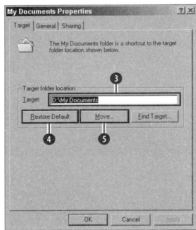

❶ Right-click the My Documents icon to open the context menu.

❷ Select Properties.

❸ To specify a new folder, type the folder name here.

❹ To revert to the original My Documents folder location, click the Restore Default button.

❺ Alternatively, click the Move button to browse for a new location.

CROSS-REFERENCE

See "Sharing Your Files" in Chapter 7.

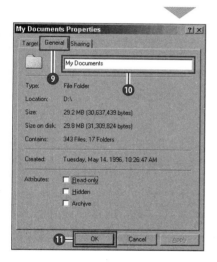

KEEP A SHORT PATH

If you decide to move the My Documents folder to a new location, don't bury the folder several levels deep in the file system. Although you can use over 250 characters in a filename, the complete path of folder names that lead to a file is a part of the filename. If you bury the My Documents folder as a subfolder within other folders, each of the folder names contributes to the number of characters in your document filenames. Although it is unlikely that you will approach 250 characters, even with a deeply buried My Documents folder, you may encounter other problems. For example, if you happen to use a CD-R or CD-RW drive to create backups of your document files, you will find that the ISO-9660 standard prevents you from using filenames longer than 64 characters and will not accept directory structures that are more than eight levels deep.

DON'T SHARE MY DOCUMENTS

The My Documents Properties dialog box has a Sharing tab that you can use to share the My Documents folder on your network. Rather than sharing the My Documents folder, consider sharing project folders that are contained within My Documents. Otherwise you will be providing access to all of the folders contained within My Documents.

⑥ Select the new folder.

⑦ Alternatively, click the New Folder button and specify a name and location to create a new folder.

⑧ Click OK to continue.

⑨ Optionally, click the General tab to rename the existing My Documents folder.

⑩ Enter a new name for the folder here.

⑪ Click OK to complete the task.

FIND IT ONLINE

You can download a trial version of software to view and compress documents at **http://www.pgcc.com/turbozip/downloads.html**.

Selecting Text

When you work with documents there's a very good chance that you'll need to select text so that you can move, copy, or delete words or phrases. Once you have selected text, you can store it on the Windows 2000 Clipboard so that it can be added to another location in the same or another document.

Selecting text is generally pretty easy, although it might take some practice to become comfortable with the techniques that you need to use. If you have still not made peace with your mouse, now is definitely the time to learn. While you can select text with the keyboard alone, using the mouse is far faster and simpler. Here is a comparison of the two techniques:

To select a block of text with the mouse, move the cursor to the first character of the block. Next, press and hold the left mouse button and drag the cursor to the last character of the block. As you move the mouse, the text is highlighted to indicate the range of the selected block. When you have selected the text block that you want, release the mouse button.

To select text using the keyboard, use the arrow keys to move the cursor to the first character of the block. Next, press and hold the Shift key and move the cursor with the arrow keys. The highlight indicates which text has been selected.

Most programs make it somewhat easier to select text with the mouse by using *automatic word selection*. When automatic word selection is enabled, you don't have to start at the beginning of a word. Instead, you can start dragging the pointer anywhere within the first word of your selection; the selection automatically expands to select complete words as soon as you drag the pointer onto a new word. Automatic word selection usually does not work when you are selecting text using the keyboard.

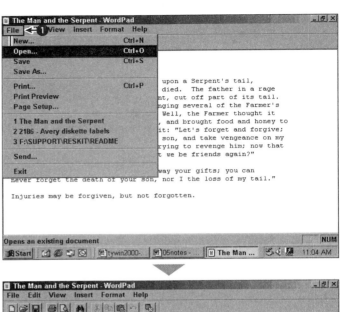

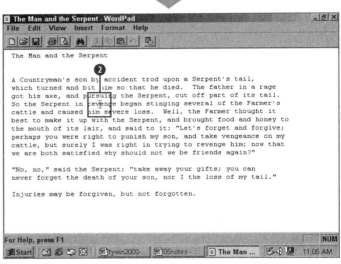

▶ Open WordPad or your word processor.

❶ Select File ➪ Open and open a document that you can use to practice selecting text.

❷ Move the mouse pointer over the middle of a word.

CROSS-REFERENCE

See "Cutting, Copying, and Pasting to the Clipboard" later in this chapter.

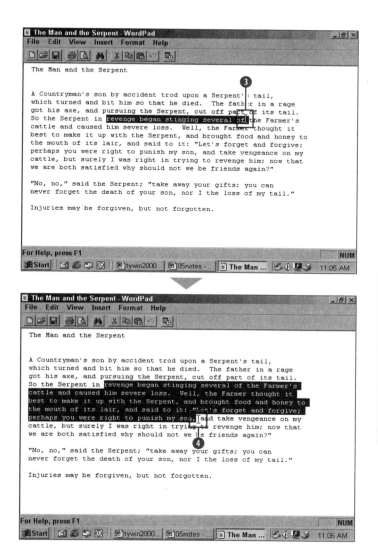

REDUCE TYPING ERRORS

To reduce the chance of making a typing error — especially in something that must be absolutely perfect, such as a Web page address — select the text and copy it to the Clipboard rather than retyping it.

SELECT ALL TEXT

You can usually select all the text in a document by clicking Edit ⇨ Select All. Most programs use Ctrl+A as a shortcut for this command. In Windows Explorer, you use this shortcut to select the entire contents of a folder.

SELECT WORDS AND PARAGRAPHS

To select a word, you can double-click within the word. To select an entire paragraph at once, you can generally triple-click within the paragraph. If you accidentally select more text than you intended, click outside the selection and try again. You can also extend a selection by holding down the Shift key and clicking the new end point.

③ Hold down the left mouse button as you drag the mouse pointer across several words.

▶ The selection automatically expands one word at a time as you continue dragging.

④ Continue holding down the left mouse button and drag the pointer down several rows.

▶ As you extend the selection downward, it includes all words from the first to the last selected word.

FIND IT ONLINE

See **http://www.sandybay.com/pc-web/index.html** to learn about computer terms.

Cutting, Copying, and Pasting to the Clipboard

After you have selected something, you can copy or cut the selection to the Clipboard. Copying leaves the original selection in place, while cutting removes the original selection. If you wish to make a duplicate without removing the original selection, use copy. If you wish to move the selection to another location, use cut.

With text on the Clipboard, you can paste the data to a new location in the same or in another document. As long as the original data remains on the Clipboard, you can paste as many copies of the data as you like.

Although the figures on the facing page use text, you can actually copy, cut, and paste many different types of data. Of course, you can only paste data that is compatible with the destination document type. You would not, for example, be able to paste a graphic image into a plain text document.

There are several ways to copy or cut data. Once you have selected the data, you can use the Edit ⇨ Copy or Edit ⇨ Cut commands on the program's menu, the Copy or Cut buttons on the toolbar, or the Copy or Cut commands on the right-click context menu. Regardless of the option that you choose, a copy of the selected data will be placed onto the Clipboard.

Before you paste Clipboard data into a document, make certain that the insertion point — generally the cursor — is at the point where the inserted data should begin. The easiest way to do this is usually to click the mouse pointer where you want to place the data.

You can also replace existing data with the data from the Clipboard. To replace existing data rather than simply inserting the new data, select the data that you want to replace before you paste.

Data on the Clipboard can exist in several different formats. When you paste the data into a document, it is

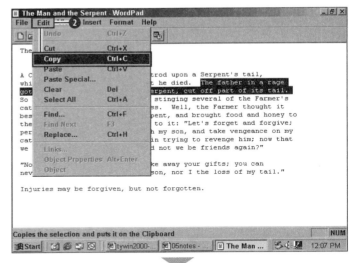

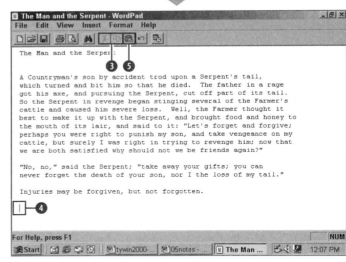

① Select the text you want to copy or cut.

② Select Edit ⇨ Copy, to copy the text to the Clipboard.

③ Alternatively, click the Copy or the Cut button to move the selection to the Clipboard.

④ Move the insertion point to the place where you'd like to insert the data.

⑤ Click the Paste button to paste data from the Clipboard.

CROSS-REFERENCE

See "Dragging and Dropping Data" later in this chapter.

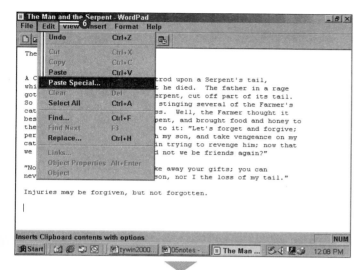

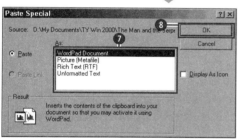

pasted using whichever format contains the most information about the data that is compatible with the document. If you'd like more control over how the data is pasted into the document, choose the Edit ➪ Paste Special command. You will then be able to choose the format and, depending on the type of data on the Clipboard, whether to link or embed the data.

TAKE NOTE

NEW REPLACES OLD

Any new data you copy to the Clipboard replaces any existing data that might already be on the Clipboard. If you cut earlier data from a document and haven't already pasted it into a new location, you'll lose the older data when the new data is sent to the Clipboard.

USE THE CONTEXT MENU

You will often find that the Edit menu and the toolbar buttons cannot be used when a dialog box is open. In most cases you can still right-click an item and use the context menu to copy, cut, or paste.

⑥ Alternatively, select Edit ➪ Paste Special.

⑦ Select the data format to paste into the document.

⑧ Click OK to paste the data and complete the task.

FIND IT ONLINE

See **http://www.sharewarejunkies.com/9zwd5/ apsezr.htm** for an interesting Clipboard utility.

Dragging-and-Dropping Data

lthough the commands that use the Clipboard — copy, cut, and paste — can be pretty handy, there is a more direct way to copy or move data. Drag and drop is a visual method of accomplishing the task using your mouse. Using drag and drop, you select data in a document and then drag-and-drop it into another location — even a location in another document or application.

You may find that using drag and drop can be a little confusing initially. You must first select the data and then release the mouse button. Then you point to the selected data and hold down the left mouse button while you drag the mouse pointer to the destination location. You must wait for the mouse pointer to return to the standard arrow pointer after first selecting the data — otherwise you won't be able to move the selected block because you'll end up changing the selection instead of dragging the data to the new location. Usually it's best to select the data, move the mouse slightly, and then point to the selection before you press and hold the left mouse button to initiate the drag.

While you are dragging data, it is important to remember that you must not release the mouse button until you are pointing to the intended destination. As soon as you release the mouse button the data will be dropped in the current location. If you make a mistake, select Edit ⇨ Undo or click the Undo button in the destination window. Do not use any other commands before selecting Edit ⇨ Undo or you will not be able to reverse the drag-and-drop action.

Dragging-and-dropping between two documents doesn't work quite the same way as it does within a single document. Within a single document, the data is moved unless you hold down the Ctrl key; if you hold the Ctrl key the data is copied rather than moved. If you

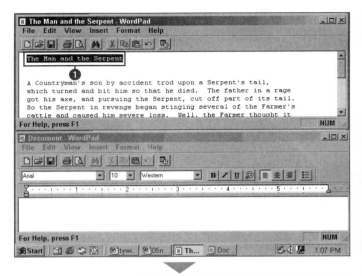

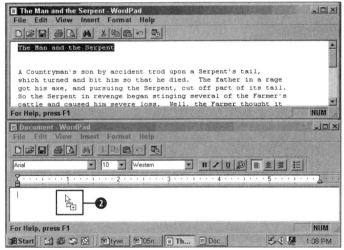

❶ Select the text you want to drag-and-drop.

❷ Point to the selected text, hold down the left mouse button, and drag the pointer to the desired location.

▶ Dragging-and-dropping between two applications copies the data unless you hold down Alt while you drag and drop.

CROSS-REFERENCE

See "Configuring Mouse Speed" in Chapter 13.

drag-and-drop between two documents, the data is always copied unless you hold down the Alt key; in that case the data is moved rather than copied.

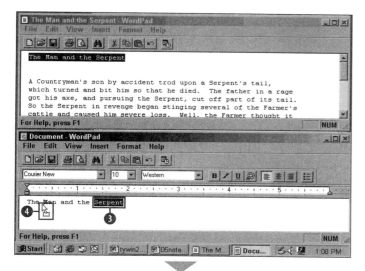

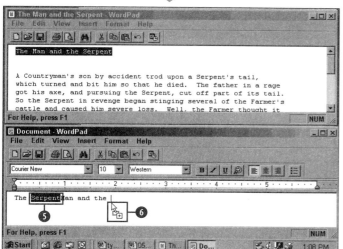

TAKE NOTE

DRAGGING-AND-DROPPING BETWEEN TWO WINDOWS

If you wish to drag and drop data into a document window that is not currently visible, you need to take a two-step approach. First drag the data onto the Taskbar icon for the destination window, but do not release the mouse button. Wait for the destination windows to open and then move the mouse pointer to the destination location before releasing the mouse button.

DRAGGING-AND-DROPPING FILES

Drag and drop works the same way in Windows Explorer as it does in documents, and it is often the easiest method of copying or moving files.

③ Select the text you want to move.

④ Point to the selected text, hold down the left mouse button, and drag the pointer to the destination location.

▶ Dragging-and-dropping between locations within one document moves the data unless you hold down Ctrl while dragging-and-dropping.

⑤ Select the text you want to copy.

⑥ Point to the selected text, hold down the left mouse button, hold down Ctrl, and drag the pointer to the destination location.

FIND IT ONLINE

See **http://www.canyonsw.com/index.htm** for a selection of drag-and-drop shareware programs.

Setting Printer Properties

In spite of the predictions that we will all soon be enjoying the paperless office, it's pretty clear that printing is a big part of working with documents in today's world. Printing documents is typically not a difficult task, but there are several things that you should know in order to obtain the best possible output.

The first step towards putting your documents onto paper is to make certain that your printer is set up properly. Printers have a number of properties, such as resolution and color settings, that you can adjust to get the desired type of output.

The settings that you choose may represent a compromise between the highest quality of printing and speed, or between the cost per page of output and the purpose of the document you're printing. You might, for example, choose to use a draft setting to quickly produce proof copies of a report and then switch to a high-quality setting to print the final report. The higher-quality setting might take several times as long to print and could also cost several times as much per page for toner or color ink. For day-to-day printing you might decide on a combination of settings that falls in the middle of these two extremes.

There are a number of ways to access the properties of your printer. You usually have access to more properties when you use the Printers folder as your starting point as shown on the facing page. If you prefer to set your printer options from the Print dialog box, look for a Properties button or an Advanced button.

Different types of printers will have different options that you can select. For example, color printers will generally include settings that adjust items such as color balance. Printers that can automatically print on both sides of the paper usually have settings that relate to duplex printing.

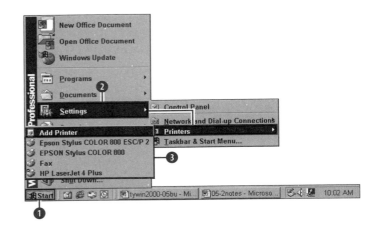

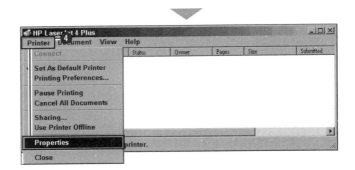

❶ Click the Start button.

❷ Select Settings ⇨ Printers to display the list of printers in the Printers folder.

❸ Select the printer whose properties you wish to set.

❹ Select Printer ⇨ Properties.

CROSS-REFERENCE

See "Sharing a Printer" in Chapter 7.

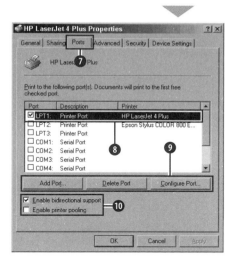

The figures on the facing page show how you can access some printer properties. This task continues on the next two pages, where you will learn about additional settings.

Continued

⑤ *Optionally, specify a name for the printer.*

⑥ *Click Print Test Page to make certain the printer is working correctly.*

⑦ *Click the Ports tab.*

⑧ *Select the correct printer connection.*

⑨ *Use these buttons to add, remove, or configure the connection.*

⑩ *Select the options that apply to your printer.*

FIND IT ONLINE

See **http://windowsupdate.microsoft.com** for printer driver updates.

Setting Printer Properties

Continued

Because Windows 2000 is far more network-oriented than Windows 98, there are more settings that you can use in Windows 2000 to control how your printer is used on the network. Both the Advanced and the Security tabs on the printer Properties dialog box — as shown on the facing page — are primarily intended to give you this extra level of control.

You may not be familiar with a few of the printer settings that are shown in the figures. For example, the availability settings on the Advanced tab can be used to prevent your printer from being used during certain times of the day. You might find this setting quite useful if your network has several shared printers, and you wish to prevent others from disturbing your noontime nap by printing long documents between noon and 1 p.m.

The Separator Page option enables you to specify a page that is printed at the beginning of each print job. Typically separator pages are used to identify the author of a document so that when a printer is shared the finished documents can be routed to the correct person.

The settings on the Security tab are used to specify who can use and manage printers. You might use these settings to make certain that those printers that are loaded with expensive glossy film are only available to the people who really need that capability. Then you won't find someone printing their personal letters on paper that costs a dollar or more per sheet.

Although there is not room to show this in the figures, you can also click the Printing Defaults button to obtain access to printer settings such as page orientation and print quality. Typically, though, these settings are ones that you might be more inclined to select for individual documents as the need arises.

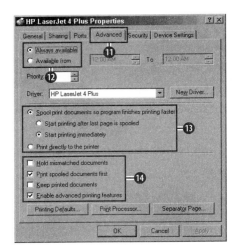

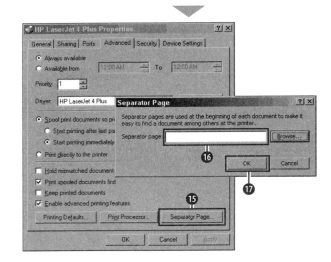

⓫ *Click the Advanced tab.*

⓬ *Choose when the printer will be available for use.*

⓭ *Select the print spooling options that you prefer.*

⓮ *Select the document printing options.*

⓯ *Optionally, click the Separator Page button.*

⓰ *Enter the name of the separator page or use the Browse button to locate one.*

⓱ *Click OK.*

CROSS-REFERENCE

See "Printing to Network Printers" in Chapter 7.

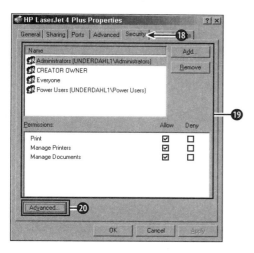

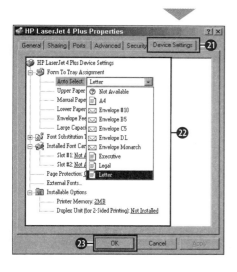

SPOOL YOUR PRINTING

Make certain that the *Spool print documents so pro-gram finishes printing faster* check box is selected. This setting enables you to continue to work even when your printer is printing a long document. If you select the alternative, *Print directly to the printer*, you will have to wait for the printer to finish before you will be able to do more work in the application that is printing. No matter which option you choose, however, you will be able to use other ap-plications while the first program is printing.

USING FONT SUBSTITUTION

The Font Substitution Table option on the Device Settings tab enables you to specify which fonts to use in printed documents. You might want to use this option to ensure consistency in your printed documents — especially those that arrived from an outside source. This setting allows you to choose the fonts to substitute in place of those that are specified in your documents.

⑱ *Click the Security tab.*

⑲ *Select the printer permissions for this printer.*

⑳ *Optionally, click Advanced to specify individual access control settings.*

㉑ *Click the Device Settings tab.*

㉒ *Choose the options that suit your needs — these will vary according to your printer.*

㉓ *Click OK to complete the task.*

FIND IT ONLINE

See **http://oak.oakland.edu/simtel.net/win95/print.html** for printer utilities.

Putting a Printer on the Desktop

Your Windows 2000 desktop is a handy place. You can place all sorts of shortcuts on your desktop so that you have quick access to your programs, documents, or folders. In this section you will learn that placing a shortcut on your desktop for your printer can be handy too.

Desktop shortcuts to your printers serve several purposes. Using the shortcut enables you to quickly check the status of the print queue or to pause printing when you receive an important phone call. You can also do something interesting with a desktop shortcut to a printer — you can print documents by dragging-and-dropping them onto the shortcut. These is no need to first open the document or the application that created the document, because Windows 2000 will automatically open and close these as necessary.

The printer dialog box that appears when you open a desktop shortcut to a printer provides quite a bit of information about your printer. You can see the names of any documents that are waiting to be printed, the current status of each print job, the name of the person who sent the document to the printer, the number of pages, the file size, the time that the print job was started, and which printer port was used. This information might be useful to help plan when to add more paper or change your printer's ink cartridge.

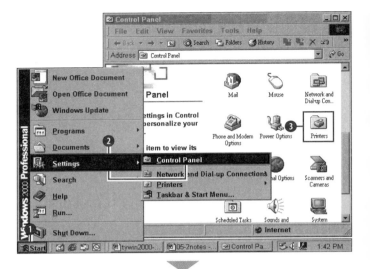

❶ Click the Start button.

❷ Select Settings ➪ Control Panel.

❸ Double-click the Printers icon.

❹ Point to the printer icon, hold down the right mouse button, and drag it onto your desktop.

❺ Select Create Shortcut(s) Here from the context menu.

CROSS-REFERENCE

See "Managing Shares" in Chapter 7.

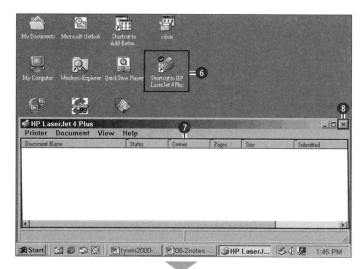

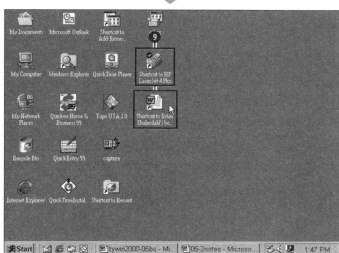

6 *Double-click the printer icon to open the printer status dialog box.*

7 *View the current print queue here.*

8 *Click the Close button to close the dialog box.*

9 *Drag-and-drop a document onto the printer icon to print the document.*

TAKE NOTE

USING THE PRINT QUEUE

The print queue is the list of documents that are waiting to be printed. If you have sufficient access rights, you can control the print queue. You might, for example, note that someone sent a huge print job to your printer and that it is ahead of your more important document in the print queue. If you select the documents that are ahead of the one you wish to print first, you can use the Document ⇨ Pause command to prevent those documents from printing. Once your document is completed, don't forget to use Document ⇨ Resume to allow the paused documents to print.

YOU MUST HAVE THE RIGHT PROGRAM

A desktop shortcut makes it easy to print documents because you can print simply by dragging the document icon and dropping it on the printer icon. But this technique works only if you have the correct application program installed on your PC. You must have the application that created the document, and that application must be one designed for Windows 2000. If you do not have the application that created the document installed on your system but you do have another program that is associated with that type of document, the program that you do have will probably be able to handle the printing task without a problem.

FIND IT ONLINE

See **http://tucows.tierranet.com/** for shareware programs that can help you manage your printers.

Printing Documents

Even though a desktop shortcut to your printer is handy for quickly printing a copy of an existing document, in most cases you will probably print documents while you have them open. When a document is open in an application you have the option to change the print settings — something that you have no chance to do when you drag-and-drop a document onto the desktop shortcut to the printer. Besides, when the document is already open you don't need to hunt for it.

Most programs include a Print command on the File menu. In many cases you will also find Print (or Page) Setup and Print Preview commands on the File menu. In some cases you may need to be a little creative in determining where to find the print preview and setup options. Often these can be found somewhere on the Print dialog box.

You may also see a Print button on the toolbar. Typically this button will print a single copy of the entire active document using the current default settings. If you want to make any changes to the defaults, be sure to select File ⇨ Print rather than using the Print button.

Although the default settings of individual programs vary, most programs allow you to specify certain page setup options. Typically, these options include the orientation of the printing — portrait or landscape — along with the paper size and the margin settings. When you adjust the page setup options, the onscreen view of the document will likely change to reflect the new settings. If you're trying to control the final document appearance, it's best to make the page setup changes before you begin formatting your document.

You can use the Print dialog box to select a different printer, change the printer properties, select the page range you wish to print, and choose the number of copies to print.

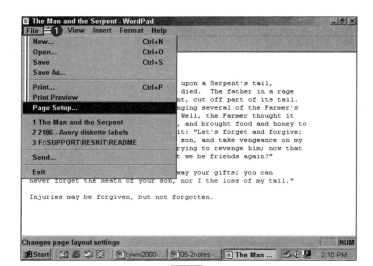

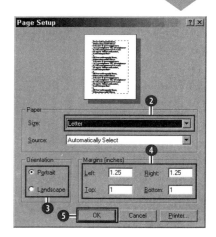

❶ Select File ⇨ Page Setup to display the Page Setup dialog box.

❷ Select the correct paper size.

❸ Select the proper page orientation.

❹ Adjust the margin settings as necessary.

❺ Click OK to close the dialog box.

CROSS-REFERENCE

See "Printing to a File" later in this chapter.

Correct page setup depends on the printer. Different printers have different features that affect the page layout, so if you have more than one printer installed, select the printer before trying to change the page settings. Otherwise, you may find that the page settings change when you select the correct printer.

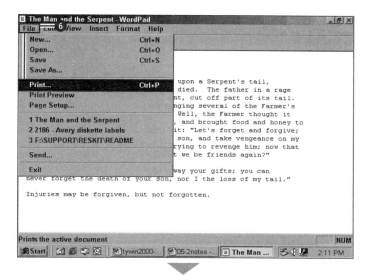

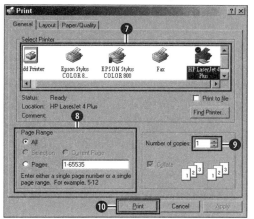

TAKE NOTE

▶ USE THE NUMBER OF COPIES OPTION

To print multiple copies of the same document, it's usually more efficient to select the number of copies in the Print dialog box than to issue several print commands.

▶ CHOOSE MARGIN SETTINGS CAREFULLY

Printers often have limits to how close they can print to the edge of a page. If you set the print margins too small, you may get a warning from the application program, or there may be no warning and your document may be printed minus the characters closest to the edges of the page.

⑥ Select File ⇨ Print to display the Print dialog box.

⑦ Select a printer.

⑧ Select the range that you want to print.

⑨ Select the number of copies you want to print.

⑩ Click Print to print the document.

FIND IT ONLINE

See **http://support.microsoft.com/support/Word/ServiceWare/Wrd97/76CQWCEB2.ASP** for help with printing issues.

Personal Workbook

Q&A

1 What happens when you drag and drop data between two different documents without holding down any keys?

_____

_____

_____

2 How can you save paper while still seeing how your printed output will appear?

_____

_____

_____

3 How can you control the format of data you paste from the Clipboard?

_____

_____

_____

4 What shortcut can you use to copy selected text to the Clipboard?

_____

_____

5 What happens to data that you've copied to the Clipboard when you copy additional data to the Clipboard?

_____

_____

_____

6 What is the best way to print multiple copies of the same document?

_____

_____

_____

7 How can you print using a printer that isn't connected to your PC or your network?

_____

_____

_____

8 If you are unable to open a document that appears on the Documents list, what might be the cause?

_____

_____

ANSWERS: PAGE 391

EXTRA PRACTICE

1. Remove a document from the Documents list.

2. Copy some text to the Clipboard and then paste it into a new location in your document. Examine the Documents list to see your most recently used documents.

3. Copy some new text to the Clipboard and paste it to confirm the original text is no longer available.

4. Print three copies of the same document using a single print command.

5. Change the paper orientation for your printer to landscape and print another copy of the same document.

REAL-WORLD APPLICATIONS

✔ You have a standard form that you print frequently, so you create a copy of the document on your desktop. Now you can easily print a copy simply by dragging and dropping the document onto your desktop printer icon.

✔ You're creating a report that includes a document file you created in Word and a photo you've retouched in Paint. After you complete work on the different pieces, you drag and drop them into one document to consolidate them.

✔ You are creating a new brochure to promote your company's new product line. To have the brochure printed professionally, you create a print file that works with the PostScript printers at your local print shop.

Visual Quiz

How can you display this dialog box? How can you change the number of copies that are printed?

_____

_____

_____

_____

_____

_____

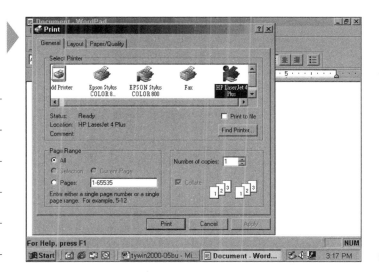

CHAPTER 6

Working with Files and Folders

Your computer probably has hundreds of folders and thousands of files. Keeping track of all of those elements can be a major project. This chapter shows you how to make managing your files and folders easier as well as how to avoid problems in dealing with so many different things.

Two of the most important file management tasks that you are likely to encounter are locating specific files and preventing your hard disk from becoming full of old junk. In many ways these two are related. It is far easier to lose track of important items if you have to search through tons of trash to find them. It's also a lot easier to make a mistake and throw out something that you really need if there is no order in the chaos.

Finding things on your PC can be pretty simple. Windows 2000 has a search tool that enables you to look for items based on simple or complex search criteria. You can look for files and folders based on their names, or you can look for files that exhibit specific sets of content or dates.

Keeping your files under control also means that you must delete old files that are no longer needed. No matter how large a hard disk your computer has, eventually that hard drive will become full if you don't remove the obsolete files.

Unfortunately, anyone can make a mistake. If that mistake involves deleting a file and then discovering that you really did need it, you will be happy to learn that the Windows 2000 Recycle Bin can give you a second chance. When you delete files, Windows 2000 stores those files in the Recycle Bin for a time so that you may be able to recover from a quick mouse click that could otherwise cost you hours of work.

Just like everything else on your PC, the Recycle Bin does have its limits. There is only so much space on a hard drive, so only the most recently deleted items can be saved for future recovery. But as you'll learn, there are some things that you can do to ensure that the Recycle Bin protects you from major disasters.

Finding a File

Losing track of where you have saved a file is easy to do and quite common, too. You might be sure that you have saved your work, but can't quite remember where you put it or what you named it. Everyone who uses computers has probably lost more than one file simply because he or she didn't pay close enough attention. To make matters worse, the lost file always seems to be an important one that would be hard to duplicate.

In the early days of personal computing it was pretty easy to misplace files. One reason for this was the limitations on filenames. You could use only 11 characters to name your files: eight characters for the filename and three characters for the file extension. With these limitations it was hard to come up with filenames that were adequately descriptive.

Windows 2000, of course, allows you to use long, descriptive names for your files. If you want to name a file "Western region budget for 2001" you can, and this should make it far easier to determine the file contents without even opening the file. Unfortunately, as the figures on the facing page show, long filenames can also complicate the search for lost files.

Long filenames are a problem for one simple reason. When Windows 2000 searches for files or folders, it uses the search criteria that you specify as alternate conditions that can be met and still satisfy your requirements. That is, if you search for *region budget for* in the hopes of finding the budget files for all regions no matter what year, Windows 2000 will look for any file that contains "region," "budget," or "for" in the filename. The figures on the facing page illustrate this problem.

As you can see in the figures, the search results in this case probably won't be what you want. One solution is shown on the following two pages.

Continued

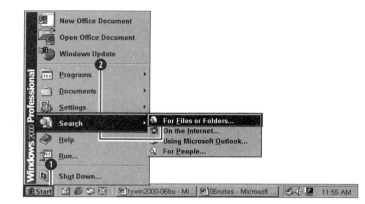

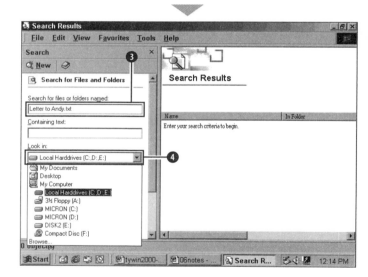

❶ Click the Start button.

❷ Select Search ➪ For Files or Folders.

❸ Enter the filename.

❹ Optionally, choose a drive to limit the search area.

CROSS-REFERENCE

See "Searching for Web Sites" in Chapter 9.

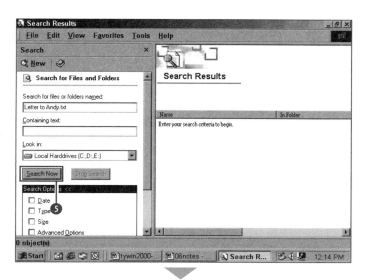

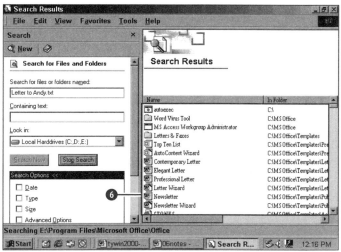

⑤ Click the Search Now button to begin the search.

⑥ Because the search is not producing the desired results, click Stop Search so you can refine the search.

Finding a File
Continued

It's clear that the search wasn't finding what you had intended. This is a common problem with file searches because it is easy for Windows 2000 to understand your search phrase differently than you expected. Rather than looking for the file using the complete filename that you specified, Windows 2000 looked for any file that had any of the words anywhere in its name.

There are several ways to solve this problem. The figures on the facing page show one of the methods that you can use. Since you know some of the text that is contained within the file you are seeking, you can add a condition that says that only those files meeting both the filename and contained text specifications can meet the criteria.

Notice too that limiting the search to drive D has further narrowed the search. Since the My Documents folder is on drive D on the PC used in the figures, limiting the search to that drive will shorten the search considerably. When you click the Search Now button, your search will conclude much faster because the search is far less ambiguous.

Of course, even solutions to problems can introduce new problems. Unless you are absolutely certain that the text really is in the file, specifying text to search for can bypass the file that you really want to find. For example, if the file that you are seeking uses the term "cash" instead of "money" you might not find the file that you want.

When you've found a file that was hiding in an unexpected location, you can use the File ⇨ Open Containing Folder command to see what else you may have saved there. Before using this command, you must first select the file in the list of found files.

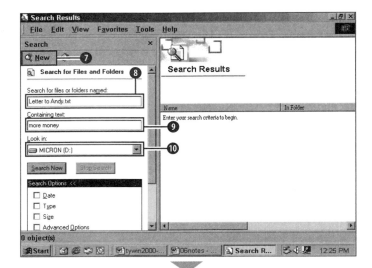

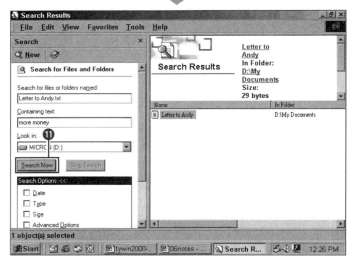

7 Click the New button to begin a new search.

8 Enter the filename.

9 Enter text that you know is contained in the file.

10 Optionally, choose a drive to limit the search area.

11 Click the Search Now button to begin the search.

CROSS-REFERENCE

See "Specifying a Date Search" later in this chapter.

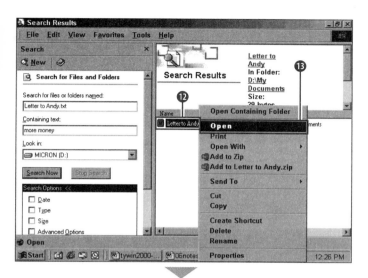

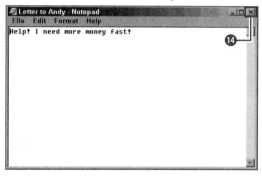

AVOID SPACES IN FILENAMES

Because Windows 2000 assumes that words separated by spaces in search phrases are separate search phrases, you can eliminate a lot of search problems by not including spaces in your filenames. You could, for example, use an underscore (_) between words rather than a space when you name files. You can also eliminate the problem by simply running the words in the filename together.

MOVE YOUR FOUND FILES

If you discover that a lost file was saved in an out-of-the-way folder, you may want to move the file to a better location — such as your My Documents folder if the file is a document folder. To move the file to My Documents, right-click the file and choose Send To ⇨ My Documents from the context menu. To move the file to a different folder, select Cut from the context menu and then open Windows Explorer. Right-click the destination folder and choose Paste from the context menu.

⑫ Right-click a found file to open the context menu.

⑬ Select Open to verify that you have found the correct file.

⑭ Click the Close button to complete the task.

FIND IT ONLINE

See **http://support.microsoft.com/support/NTWorkstation/ServiceWare/Ntw40/E9JVWMB34. ASP** for more on using path names in searches.

Specifying a Wildcard Search

It's pretty clear that searching for files that have several words in their filenames can be somewhat imprecise. Even when you add the condition of looking for text that is contained within the file, the results may not always be just what you are hoping for. There is a good chance that you either won't find the file that you want or that you will find dozens of unrelated files in addition to what you are seeking.

You may wish to try another search method that may produce better results. This method uses *wildcards* to refine the search criteria so that the results may be more acceptable. Wildcards are characters that Windows 2000 interprets in special ways.

Windows 2000 recognizes two wildcard characters. These wildcard characters are the asterisk (*) and the question mark (?). You use an asterisk to take the place of any number of characters in a text string. You use a question mark to take the place of a single character. For example, TY*.DOC would find any files that start with the letters TY and use the DOC extension. TY??.DOC would also find any files that start with TY and use the DOC extension, but would limit the search to filenames that were exactly 4 characters in length. Each question mark in a wildcard specifies that there must be a character in that position.

You can also use wildcards in the *Containing text* box. You might find this option useful if you were only certain about a part of the filename but knew that the file contained two words in a certain sequence. In most cases, though, you will probably have better results if you try to limit the search criteria to a single field in the Search Explorer bar. It can be easy to create a search that produces no useful results.

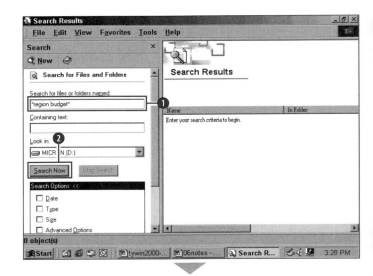

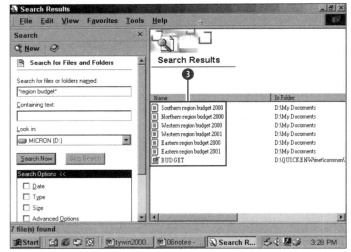

① Enter the filename using wildcards.

② Click the Search Now button to begin the search.

③ View the search results to determine if the wildcards are producing the expected results.

▶ In this case, the final file in the list was not expected, because it did not contain the word "region" in the filename.

CROSS-REFERENCE

See "Finding Specific File Types" later in this chapter.

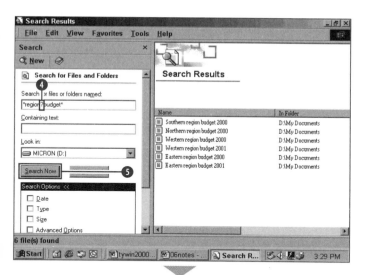

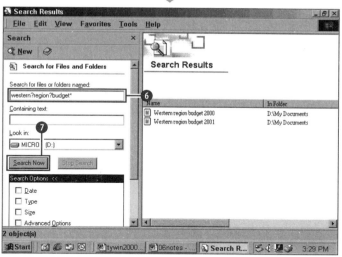

④ *Add another wildcard to refine the search.*

⑤ *Click the Search Now button to redo the search.*

▶ *In this case, the results were what was expected because the files all contain both "region" and "budget" in the filename.*

⑥ *Optionally, limit the results by adding additional words and wildcards.*

⑦ *Click the Search Now button to redo the search.*

FIND IT ONLINE

See **http://www.compendia.freeserve.co.uk/ winkeyboardgif.html** for information on keyboard shortcuts.

Specifying a Date Search

Even though you can use wildcards to enhance a search for files using the filename, there simply are times when searching by name won't produce the results that you seek. You might not even know anything about the filenames in some cases. Windows 2000 gives you many different ways to search for files. In this section you learn how to conduct a search based on the date the file was created, modified, or last accessed.

Searching for files based on these dates can help you find files that you might not otherwise be able to locate. You could, for example, discover which files were changed or added when you installed a new program so that you could troubleshoot a problem that developed later. You could also determine which files someone was snooping in while you were on vacation. Finally, you might want to find all of the files that were used during the time you worked on a big project. These are just a few examples of how searching for files using dates can be useful.

When you specify a date search, you can also specify whether you're searching for the time the file was created, modified, or last accessed. For document files, you'll likely want to look for files that were modified within a time period. In that way you can tell which files were changed and not only those that were originally created during the specified date range.

When you specify dates, be sure the period that you specify is large enough. It's always possible that you could be off a day or two, and this could affect your results.

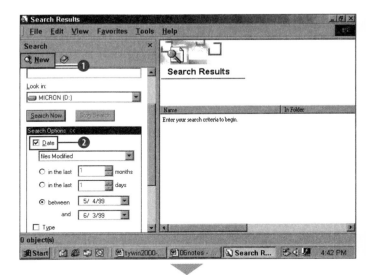

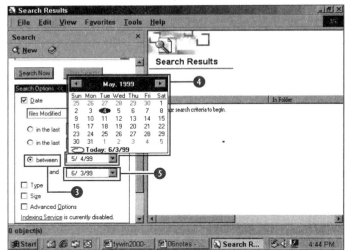

❶ Click the New button.
❷ Click the Date check box.
❸ Click the "between" button.
❹ Enter the start date.
❺ Enter the end date.

CROSS-REFERENCE

See "Saving Documents" in Chapter 5.

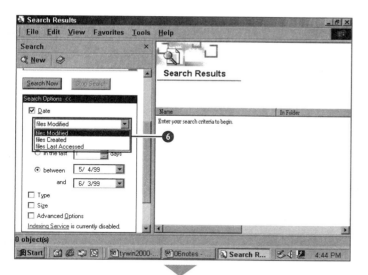

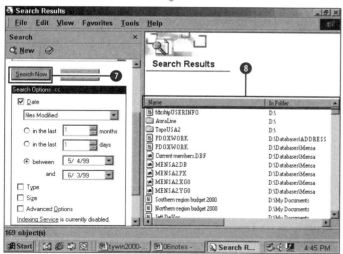

CREATE COMPLEX SEARCHES

You don't have to limit yourself to making simple searches that use a single search condition. You could, for example, specify that you wanted to find all documents created in the past two weeks that contain the word *budget* in their filename. A complex search that specifies more than one search condition narrows the results list considerably, but you must use care in setting up a complex search. Remember that each one of the search conditions must be satisfied. If a file contains *budget* in the filename but was created three weeks ago, the file won't appear in your result list. Similarly, a file you created last week that lacks the term *budget* in the filename won't make it into the list.

START A NEW SEARCH

Unless you're attempting to build a complex search based on multiple conditions, be sure to click the New button to clear the old search before you begin. Otherwise, Windows 2000 will allow any existing search conditions to remain as they were, and your search probably won't find the files you expect.

⑥ Select the type of date you're specifying.

⑦ Click the Search Now button to start the search.

⑧ If you want to sort the results, click the column header to sort by that column.

SHORTCUT

See **http://support.microsoft.com/support/ NTWorkstation/ServiceWare/Ntw40/ E9JVWMFQY.ASP** for finding information within a file.

Finding Specific File Types

In most cases, when you are searching for a file you probably know what type of file you are seeking. You might be looking for a specific type of document file or perhaps graphic images in a particular format. The hundreds of Windows 2000 system files that may appear in a typical file search aren't likely to be of much interest, even if their filenames somehow fit the filename or date modified criteria. In fact, having those files displayed in the search results just makes it harder for you to locate the specific files that you're trying to find.

One solution is to search for files by using the file type as either the sole criteria or, depending on your needs, in conjunction with some of the other search options. By basing your search on the type of file, you can focus on the specific files that you want and won't have to manually wade through a long list.

To search for files by file type, use the Type check box that appears in the list of search options. When this check box is selected, you can choose a file type from the list box that appears below the check box. This list box includes entries for every file type that is registered on your system. It does not, unfortunately, contain an entry for generic documents. If you wish to find document files, you must specify which type of document files you want to find. You can specify Microsoft Word document files, Lotus 1-2-3 spreadsheet files, or Paradox database files — but you cannot specify a search that finds all three at one time. If you specify a search by type, you can only choose one file type per search unless you choose the *All Files and Folders* option.

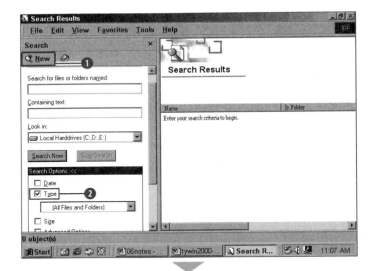

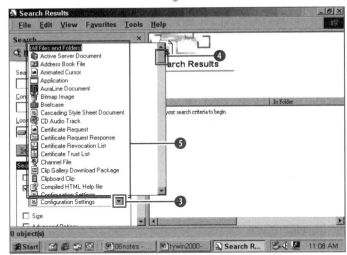

❶ Click the New button.

❷ Click the Type check box.

❸ Click the down arrow at the right edge of the type list box.

❹ Use the scroll bar to see the available file types.

❺ Choose the type of file you wish to find.

CROSS-REFERENCE

See "Saving a Search" later in this chapter.

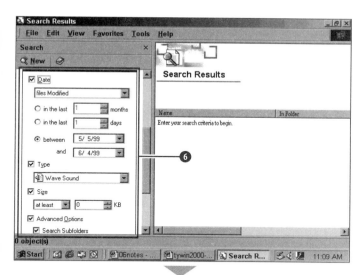

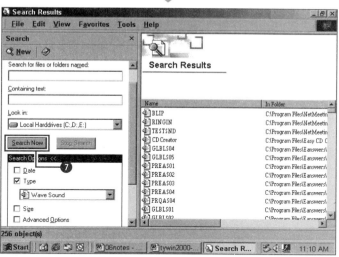

6 Optionally, select any additional search conditions that you wish to apply.

7 Click the Search Now button to start the search.

MOST DOCUMENTS CANNOT BE SEARCHED

In theory, you should be able to use the "Containing text" box to specify text that you'd like to find in a file — but don't count on it. The text in a document file is seldom stored as plain text, and this makes it difficult to locate the actual text within the files. It's unlikely that you'll find what you want by using this text box. You can try, but don't count on the results being complete.

NOT ALL TYPES WILL BE FOUND

The file type list box contains a listing of every type of file that is registered on your PC. But just because a file type is listed does not mean that any files of that type actually exist on your system. To be certain that a particular type of file is stored on your computer, make certain that you do not use any other criteria when executing the search.

FIND IT ONLINE

See **http://support.microsoft.com/support/ NTWorkstation/ServiceWare/Ntw40/E9JVWMF5P. ASP** for more search tips.

Saving a Search

If you spend time refining a search, it's likely that you will want to perform the same type of search at some future time. If so, it makes sense to save the search so that you don't have to go through all of the steps setting up the same set of criteria the next time.

Saving a set of search criteria makes a lot of sense because it allows you to quickly find the same types of files. You might use this saved criteria in several ways. For example, suppose you want to copy all of your modified files to a recordable CD once a week. You could set up a search for files that were modified during the past week, select all of the files that appear in the results list, and copy them to the CD. If you make this a part of your Friday afternoon routine, you can have your weekly backup done in just a few minutes with very little fuss. You might even decide that backing up your files is fun!

If you attempt to save a set of search criteria, you may encounter a subtle idiosyncrasy in the Windows 2000 search program. Until you actually execute a search, you cannot save the search. In fact, when you first open the search program you won't even find the Save Search command on the File menu. That command will appear once you have clicked the Search Now button or when you have opened a previously saved search. Also, you must click the Search Results pane before the command will be made available.

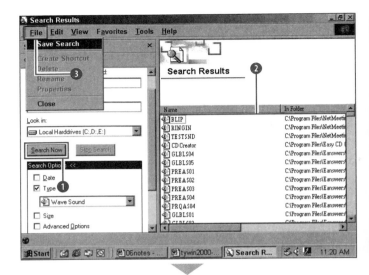

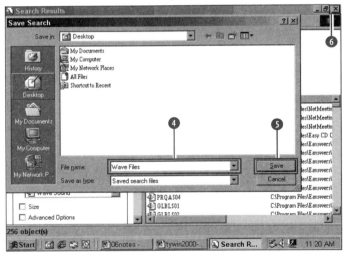

❶ Click the Search Now button to start the search.

❷ Click the Search Results pane.

❸ Select File ⟹ Save Search.

❹ Specify a name for the saved search.

❺ Click the Save button.

❻ Click the Close button to close your search.

CROSS-REFERENCE

See "Specifying a Date Search" earlier in this chapter.

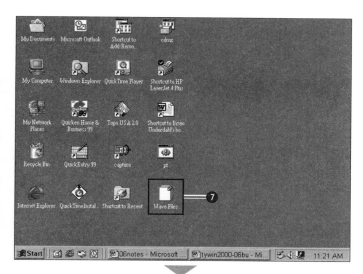

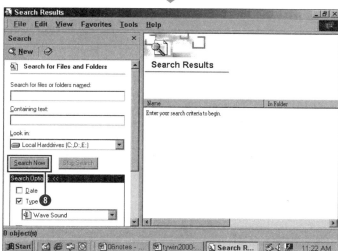

When you save a search, Windows 2000 creates an icon on your desktop so you can later perform the same search by double-clicking the icon. The desktop icon will have the name that you specify when you save the search. For example, saving the search shown in the figures on the facing page results in a desktop icon named "Wave Files." You can save as many different searches as you like on your desktop. Each one will have a different name, but if you save multiple copies of the same search, the names will differ by a number appended to the icon name.

TAKE NOTE

SAVED SEARCHES ARE EMPTY

When you save a search, Windows 2000 only saves the set of criteria that you specified — not the results of the search. This enables you to click the Search Now button to quickly execute the same search again.

CREATE A SEARCH FOLDER ON YOUR DESKTOP

If you save a large number of searches, you may want to create a new folder named "Search" on your desktop. You can then drag all the saved searches into the Search folder and reduce desktop clutter.

⑦ Double-click the saved search to reopen the same set of search criteria.

⑧ Click the Search Now button to start the search.

FIND IT ONLINE

See **http://www.chami.com/tips/windows/ 122596W.html** for information on Windows searches.

Using the Indexing Service

Windows 2000 offers another method of searching for the information that is contained within documents — the Indexing Service. This service makes it easy for you to search the contents of documents and also to search for certain document properties, such as the author. You can perform keyword searches to find documents that relate to specific topics.

The Indexing Service works by creating *catalogs* of information about your documents. A catalog contains both an *index* of the document contents and a listing of the document properties. When the Indexing Service is activated, the catalogs are created automatically.

You can control which folders are indexed using the Computer Management console. The "Take Note" section explains how to use the Computer Management console to control the index settings. By opening the Directories folder in Computer Management you can choose the folders that should be included or excluded. When you include or exclude a folder, all of its subfolders are also included or excluded.

You can use the Indexing Service regardless of the system access rights that you have been assigned. You may not be able to adjust the settings unless you are logged in as the system administrator or are allowed equivalent rights.

For more information on using the Indexing Service query language, click the Help button in the Indexing Service Settings dialog box, as shown in the first figure on the facing page.

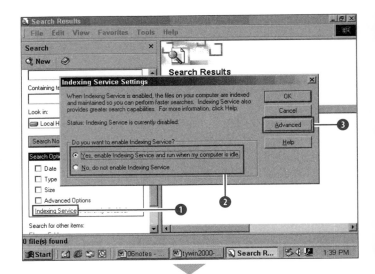

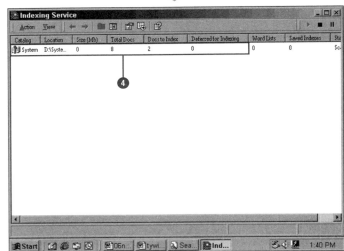

❶ Click the Indexing Service link to open the Indexing Service Settings dialog box.

❷ Choose whether to enable the Indexing Service.

❸ Optionally, click the Advanced button.

❹ View the catalog information here.

CROSS-REFERENCE

See Chapter 15 for more information on using Computer Management.

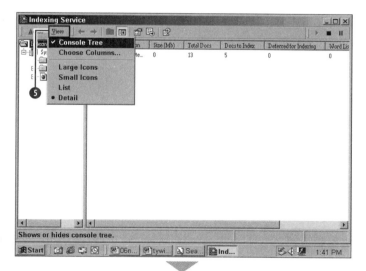

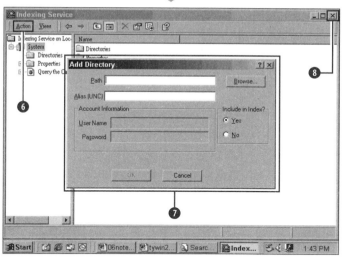

⑤ Select View ⇨ Console Tree to access the list of indexed folders.

⑥ Select Action ⇨ New ⇨ Directory to specify folders to include or exclude.

⑦ Fill in the information in the Add Directory dialog box.

⑧ Click the Close button to close the Indexing Service window.

TAKE NOTE

▶ EVERYTHING IS NOT INDEXED

As you can imagine, the Indexing Service filters the document content so that only useful information is contained within the index. Many words, such as "and" and "the," found in virtually every document, are filtered out. The Indexing Service uses an *exception list* to choose the words that should be ignored. Because of this filtering, the index will generally run about one-fifth the size of the document files that are indexed.

▶ CUSTOMIZE THE INDEXING SERVICE

To modify Indexing Service performance, click the Start button and choose Programs ⇨ Administrative Tools ⇨ Computer Management. Click the plus sign to expand Server Applications and Services. Choose Action ⇨ Stop. Then choose Action ⇨ All Tasks ⇨ Tune Performance. Choose the option that best fits the way Indexing Service is used on your computer. If you select Customize, you can click the Customize button to further adjust the settings. In the Desired Performance dialog box, move the Indexing slider to Lazy for less immediate indexing or to Instant for immediate indexing of new or changed documents. Move the Querying slider to Low load if you expect to process only a few queries at a time or to High load if you expect to process many queries at a time. Setting the sliders to the right uses more system resources. You must restart the Indexing Service for your changes to take effect.

FIND IT ONLINE

See **http://www8.zdnet.com/pcmag/pctech/content/17/06/tf1706.003.html** for related information.

Sending Objects to the Recycle Bin

Everyone makes mistakes, but most of the mistakes that you make are pretty minor. Few of them can be as costly as the hours of work that you could lose by accidentally deleting an important file on your computer. That's why the Recycle Bin is so important. The Recycle Bin protects you by temporarily storing most of the files that you delete so that you can get them back if it turns out that you made a mistake.

When you delete a file, Windows 2000 does not really remove the file from your hard drive. In most cases it simply moves the file to the Recycle Bin. Eventually the disk area that the file is using will be released so that the space can be reused, but until that happens, your deleted file is actually intact. This makes restoring an accidentally deleted file a simple task.

You don't have to do anything special to use the Recycle Bin. Files that you delete are automatically sent to the Recycle Bin unless you make a special effort to prevent that. When you consider that you probably wouldn't purposely delete files if you knew that you were going to need them in the future, it's easy to understand why the Recycle Bin is so easy and automatic to use. You wouldn't want to have to depend on guessing when it might be important to preserve a file that you were about to delete, would you?

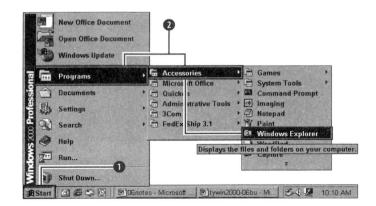

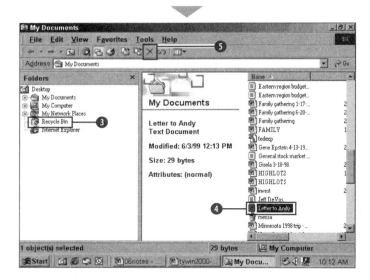

❶ Click the Start button

❷ Select Programs ➪ Accessories ➪ Windows Explorer.

❸ Drag-and-drop an object from wherever it is onto the Recycle Bin.

❹ Alternatively, first select the object.

❺ Then click the Delete button, or hit the Delete key on your keyboard.

CROSS-REFERENCE

See "Setting Recycle Bin Properties" later in this chapter for information about controlling how the Recycle Bin works.

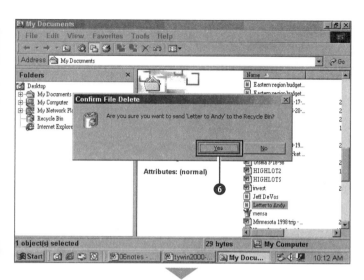

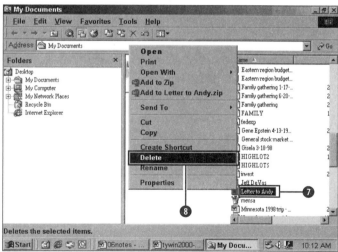

TAKE NOTE

FINDING THE RECYCLE BIN ICON

You have probably noticed the Recycle Bin icon on your desktop, but you may have missed the Recycle Bin icon that appears in the Windows Explorer window. Both icons enable you to access the same Recycle Bin folder. The one that you choose to use is simply a matter of convenience.

WATCH THE RECYCLE BIN MESSAGE

When you delete files, Windows 2000 will display a dialog box that asks you to confirm the deletion (unless you have configured the Recycle Bin so this message does not appear). Be sure to make note of the message that appears in this dialog box. In most cases the message will ask you to confirm that you want to send the files to the Recycle Bin. In some instances, however, the message will ask you to confirm that you want to delete the files. This difference is important because you can only recover files that were sent to the Recycle Bin — not those that were deleted. The delete confirmation message will appear when you delete files from diskettes, if you hold down the Shift key while you delete files, or if you configure your PC to bypass the Recycle Bin. In each of these cases, the Recycle Bin is not used, and deleted files are really gone.

⑥ Click Yes to send the file to the Recycle Bin.

⑦ Alternatively, right-click the object.

⑧ Select Delete from the context menu.

FIND IT ONLINE

See **http://support.microsoft.com/support/ windows/ServiceWare/Win2000/E9S70TCGV.ASP** for more on deleting without sending to the Recycle Bin.

Viewing and Restoring Recycle Bin Contents

One of the really great features of the Recycle Bin is also one of its faults. The Recycle Bin can store hundreds of different files, so the file that you just accidentally deleted is probably in the Recycle Bin. But along with that one important file you'll probably find a lot of pure junk, too. You certainly wouldn't want to have to restore the deleted files on an all-or-nothing basis! If you did, you might end up having to decide whether it was more trouble to recreate the one important file or to put up with having all those other deleted files return too.

Fortunately, once you've deleted files or folders, you can open the Recycle Bin to view its contents. You can choose specific files or folders to restore or to delete permanently. You can also choose to restore or remove all the files at once.

When the Recycle Bin contains deleted objects, its desktop icon changes. The empty Recycle Bin icon looks like an empty wastebasket. Once the Recycle Bin contains files or folders, its icon looks more like a wastebasket full of papers. The change is subtle, so it's easy to miss unless you're observant.

The Recycle Bin has an important difference from the other folders on your hard disk. The Recycle Bin is the only place where two files or more can appear to have the same name. In reality, though, there is more to this than you might notice at first glance. In the Recycle Bin, file descriptions include their name, their original location, and the time that they were deleted. It is this complete description that is unique — not just the filename on its own.

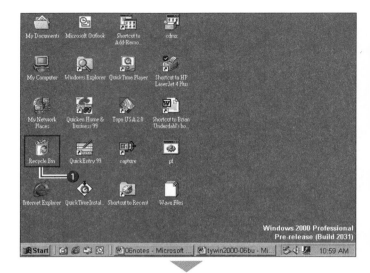

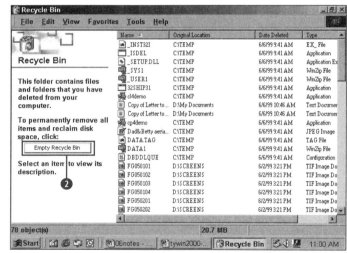

1 Double-click the Recycle Bin icon on the desktop to open the Recycle Bin.

2 Click Empty Recycle Bin to permanently delete everything from the Recycle Bin.

CROSS-REFERENCE

See "Emptying the Recycle Bin" later in this chapter for information about making the Recycle Bin more manageable.

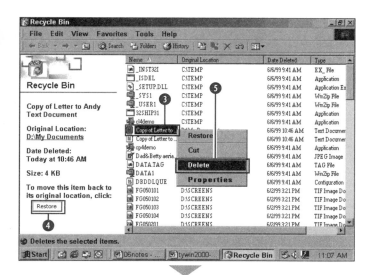

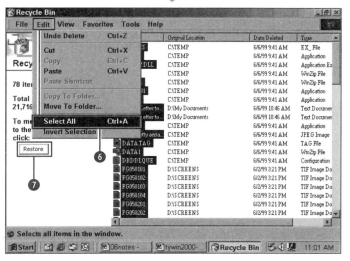

You may be surprised to discover that Windows 2000 doesn't have a Recycle Bin for files you delete from diskettes. That's because the Recycle Bin stores the deleted files on the disk, and there isn't enough room to allow deleted files to remain on the diskette. Windows 2000 does warn you of this when you delete files from diskettes, but the warning simply comes in the form of slightly different wording in the confirmation dialog box.

TAKE NOTE

THE RECYCLE BIN IS A SYSTEM FOLDER

The Recycle Bin is a *system* folder — a folder that is important to the operation of Windows 2000. This means that the Recycle Bin has some unique properties. For example, you won't find either a Delete or a Rename command on the Recycle Bin context menu, because these operations are generally not permitted for system folders.

THE RECYCLE BIN REMEMBERS FILE ORIGINS

Fortunately, the Recycle Bin remembers each file's origin, so you can more easily determine which copy of the file you wish to restore by looking in the Original Location column.

③ Click an object to view its description.

④ Click Restore to return the selected object to its original location.

⑤ Alternatively, right-click the item and select Delete to permanently delete the file.

⑥ Alternatively, select Edit ⇨ Select All to select all objects in the Recycle Bin.

⑦ Click Restore to return all objects to their original locations.

▶ Alternatively, right-click the selection and select Delete to permanently delete the files.

FIND IT ONLINE

See **http://www.execsoft.com/undelete/eudfree/ eudguest.htm** for a free downloadable version of Emergency Undelete.

Emptying the Recycle Bin

Windows 2000 uses the *first in, first out* method of automatically removing items from the Recycle Bin when it becomes too full. This means that the items that have been in the Recycle Bin the longest are deleted first to make room for new items. This arrangement prevents the Recycle Bin from completely filling up your hard disk, so you need not empty the Recycle Bin yourself unless you want to do so. But as you'll soon see, letting Windows 2000 handle the Recycle Bin contents automatically may not be the best idea.

By default, Windows 2000 sets the size of your Recycle Bin to 10 percent of the size of your hard disk. On a typical 2GB hard disk, this means that 200MB of disk space might be set aside to hold the Recycle Bin contents. Depending on the size of the typical files on your system, this amount of space could represent hundreds or even thousands of files. It could also be completely used up by a few large files (or possibly even one).

You can choose to remove all of the Recycle Bin contents in one step, or if you prefer you can select individual objects to delete (or restore). Remember, though, that there's no Recycle Bin for the Recycle Bin. Once you delete items from the Recycle Bin, they're gone forever and can't be restored. The Undo button does not restore a file that was deleted from the Recycle Bin. The Recycle Bin gives you a second chance, but there's no third chance. If you have any doubts, don't empty the Recycle Bin.

You may want to sort the Recycle Bin file listing to help determine which files to delete and which ones to restore. The easiest way to sort the file listing is to click one of the column heads to sort using the selected column. Click the column again to sort the items in reverse order.

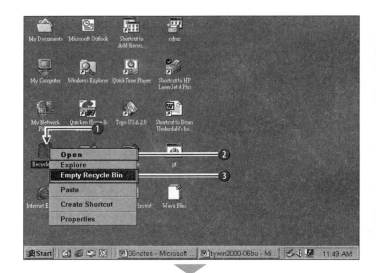

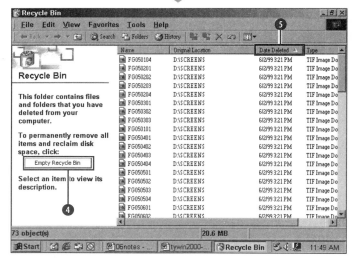

① Right-click the Recycle Bin icon on the desktop to open the context menu.

② Click Open to view the Recycle Bin contents.

③ Alternatively, click Empty Recycle Bin to permanently delete everything from the Recycle Bin.

④ Click Empty Recycle Bin to permanently delete everything from the Recycle Bin.

⑤ To sort the listing, click a column heading.

CROSS-REFERENCE

See "Setting Recycle Bin Properties" (next) for information about controlling the Recycle Bin.

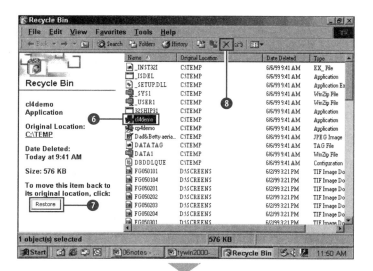

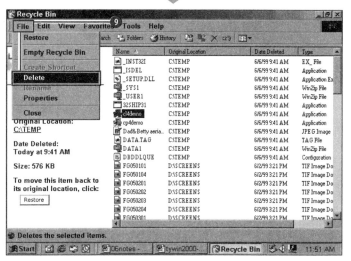

INVERT YOUR SELECTION

When you first open the Recycle Bin you have the option of completely emptying it by deleting all the objects. If you'd rather save some of the items in case you might need them in the future, the best course is to select the files and folders you want to keep. Choose Edit ⇨ Invert Selection, and then delete the selected files. Inverting the selection removes the objects you selected and adds all the others to the selection. This technique makes it easy to remove objects you won't ever need from the Recycle Bin.

CONTROL THE RECYCLE BIN TOOLBARS

If you don't see the Recycle Bin toolbar buttons when you open the Recycle Bin, select View ⇨ Toolbars ⇨ Standard Buttons to display them. This will enable you to use the buttons, such as Move To, Delete, and Undo.

⑥ Click an object to view its description.

⑦ Click Restore to return the selected object to its original location.

⑧ Alternatively, click the Delete button to permanently delete the selected file.

⑨ Another way to permanently delete the file is to select File ⇨ Delete.

See **http://support.microsoft.com/support/kb/articles/Q132/5/79.asp** for information if Shift+Delete does not bypass the Recycle Bin.

Setting Recycle Bin Properties

There is no reason for you to use any of the default Recycle Bin settings unless they suit your needs. You may find that some of the default settings are simply annoying and provide you with no useful service. Depending on the size of the files that you commonly use, you may also want to set aside more or less than the default 10 percent of your hard disk space for the Recycle Bin. It's even possible that you might want to use different settings for different drives, or perhaps you'd rather not use the Recycle Bin at all.

One of the most satisfying Recycle Bin setting changes you can make is to eliminate the dialog box that appears when you delete an object. Normally, Windows 2000 asks you to confirm that you want to move the object to the Recycle Bin. The first few hundred times you see the message you may find it helpful, but eventually you may tire of it. In that case, you can change a setting and thereafter skip the dialog box. Then when you delete an object, Windows 2000 will send it straight to the Recycle Bin without asking for your permission.

Windows 2000 normally uses the same Recycle Bin settings for all of your hard disks. In most cases there is little reason to change this, but you might have reason to if you've set aside one hard disk for a special purpose such as creating master layouts for CD-ROM discs. If you need to dedicate an entire hard disk to the CD-ROM layout, you might be concerned about running out of space if the Recycle Bin uses up disk space. You might also want to increase the Recycle Bin size on a separate hard disk that you have set aside for your document files to provide additional protection for those files.

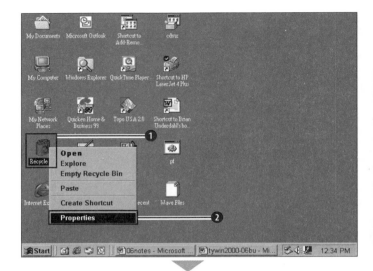

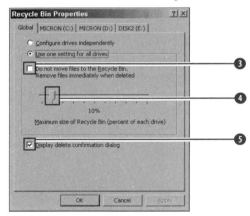

❶ Right-click the Recycle Bin icon on the desktop to open the context menu.

❷ Click Properties to view the Recycle Bin Properties dialog box.

❸ Check here to delete files without using the Recycle Bin.

❹ Drag the slider to adjust the size of the Recycle Bin.

❺ Remove this check to skip the confirmation dialog box that appears each time you delete a file.

CROSS-REFERENCE

See "Sending Objects to the Recycle Bin" earlier in this chapter for information about skipping the Recycle Bin.

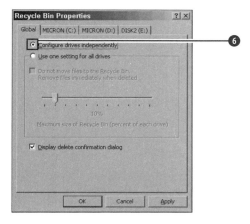

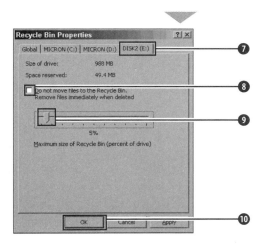

▶ DON'T SKIP THE RECYCLE BIN

You can choose to skip the Recycle Bin and delete files directly. It's hard to make a good case for using this option, because it eliminates any chance to recover from an accidental file deletion. Rather than choose to skip the Recycle Bin, it's better to eliminate the dialog box that confirms your deletions. If you like, you can combine this step with reducing the Recycle Bin size to the minimum effective size, which is 1 percent of your hard disk space.

▶ THE CONFIRMATION DIALOG BOX IS GLOBAL

Even if you choose to use different Recycle Bin settings for each of your hard drives, you can only choose one setting for the delete confirmation dialog box. The delete confirmation dialog box will either appear for all of your drives or for none of them. This uniform setting is intended to reduce confusion and the possibility of errors.

⑥ *Click here to configure each drive separately.*

⑦ *Click the tab for the drive you want to configure.*

⑧ *Click here to delete files from this drive without using the Recycle Bin.*

⑨ *Drag the slider to adjust the size of the Recycle Bin for this drive.*

⑩ *Click OK to complete the task.*

FIND IT ONLINE

See **http://support.microsoft.com/support/ NTWorkstation/ServiceWare/Ntw40/35HZNHH4.AS P** for information on how to tell if the Recycle Bin is deactivated.

Personal Workbook

Q&A

1. What will happen if you don't click the New button between searches?

   _____

   _____

   _____

2. How can you specify that you want to limit your search to files larger than a certain size?

   _____

   _____

   _____

3. How can you temporarily bypass the Recycle Bin and delete a file permanently?

   _____

   _____

   _____

4. Why is it more dangerous to delete files from diskettes than from hard disks?

   _____

   _____

   _____

5. How can you change the Recycle Bin sort order?

   _____

   _____

   _____

6. What steps must you take before saving a search for future use?

   _____

   _____

   _____

7. How can you reuse a search you've saved?

   _____

   _____

   _____

8. How can you find a file if all you know are two words that occur together somewhere in the filename?

   _____

   _____

   _____

ANSWERS: PAGE 391

EXTRA PRACTICE

1 Find all the files *created* in the past month.

2 Search for all the bitmap image files on your hard disk.

3 Select and restore one of the files in the Recycle Bin.

4 Prevent the delete confirmation dialog box from appearing when you delete files.

5 Create and save a search that finds all your word processor document files for the past two weeks.

6 Find all the files that are more than 750KB in size.

REAL-WORLD APPLICATIONS

✔ You do a lot of work on your PC. To make it easy to back up your files, before you stop work for the day you create and save a search that locates all the files you've created each day.

✔ You suspect that someone has been modifying your files while you were away from the office for a few days. You do a search for files created or modified during that time so that you can see if they changed any critical information.

✔ You've been assigned to prepare a confidential report that must not appear on your hard disk. After you make a backup on a diskette, you hold down the Shift key when you delete the file from your hard disk so that it is not saved in the Recycle Bin.

Visual Quiz

How do you display this dialog box? Which part of the dialog box do you use to control how much disk space the Recycle Bin uses? What would you do if you didn't want to confirm that deleted items should go to the Recycle Bin?

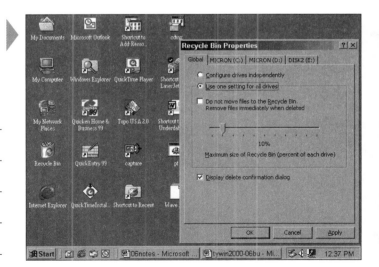

_____

_____

_____

_____

_____

CHAPTER 7

MASTER
THESE
SKILLS

▶ **Finding Computers on Your Network**
▶ **Adding Network Places**
▶ **Sharing Your Files**
▶ **Managing Shares**
▶ **Finding Files on Your Network**
▶ **Sharing a Printer**
▶ **Creating Network and Dial-up Connections**
▶ **Adding an Internet Connection**
▶ **Sharing an Internet Connection**
▶ **Allowing Outside Access**

Using Local Networks

If your PC is running Windows 2000, there is a good chance that it is also connected to a network. Windows 2000 inherently supports networking and can connect to computers running many different operating systems.

In most cases, the tasks that are covered in this chapter won't vary too much no matter what other types of computers are on your network. You may notice a few small differences in a few instances, but the procedures that are shown are quite typical of what you will encounter.

Even if you don't have several computers connected in a local network, you will likely make use of the biggest network of all — the Internet. This chapter shows you how to make a connection from your PC to the Internet, and how to share that connection with the other PCs that are on your network. You will also learn how to allow outside access to your system using a dial-up connection. Using this feature, you can connect to the PC in your office while you are on the road with your laptop, and access those files that you just can't live without.

Before starting on this chapter, you should make certain that your network is completely installed and that it is working correctly. If you are having problems making your network function properly, you may want to refer to Chapter 3 for more information on using the Windows 2000 troubleshooters before you continue.

Even if you don't yet have a network, you'll probably want to browse through this chapter. Seeing the examples may make it easier for you to determine whether a network would offer you enough benefits to make it worthwhile. Installing a network is generally not too difficult as long as you are careful to follow the directions.

If you haven't used a network before, you're in for a pleasant surprise. It is amazing how much easier it can be to get things done when you can share network resources without ever leaving your chair. If you need to use the fancy color printer that is in the next office, or open a report that a coworker has been creating, you can do so with a few clicks of your mouse. That's a lot more convenient than copying things to diskettes and running down the hall to borrow someone's PC!

Finding Computers on Your Network

One of the best ways to introduce yourself to using a network is to learn how to find out what other computers are on the network. Because you can only share those resources that you can see on the network, finding computers on the network is a good place to start. In this section you'll learn how to find out which computers are available on the network.

Your Windows 2000 desktop includes an icon — My Network Places — that enables you to locate and view the shared resources on the network. *Shared* resources are files, folders, drives, or printers that have been made available for your use on the network.

My Network Places only shows those items which have been shared and which you have permission to access. This can result in some confusion when you first set up a network, because resources must be shared explicitly before they'll appear on the network. Initially nothing is shared, so nothing will be available in My Network Places until some items are shared.

Your network will use *workgroups* or *domains* to organize groups of computers. Domains generally have higher levels of security than do workgroups, and are most often used on larger networks.

In most cases individual users are limited to accessing the resources within a single workgroup or domain, but your system administrator can grant you permission to access other workgroups or domains as necessary. The Computers Near Me icon in My Network Places shows the shared resources in your assigned workgroup or domain.

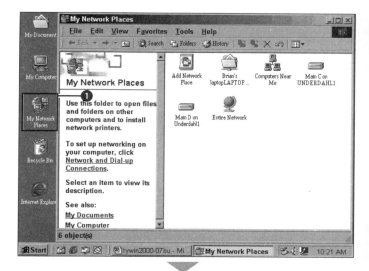

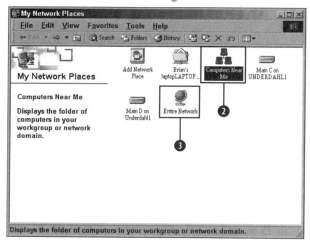

❶ Double-click the My Network Places icon to open the My Network Places folder.

❷ Double-click the Computers Near Me icon to view your workgroup or domain.

❸ Alternatively, double-click the Entire Network icon to view the workgroups or domains on the network.

CROSS-REFERENCE

See "Sharing Your Files" later in this chapter.

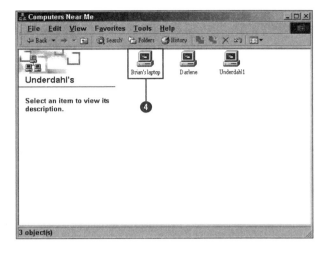

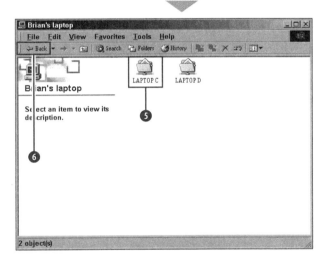

④ *Double-click a computer icon to view the shared resources on that computer.*

⑤ *Double-click an item to open it.*

⑥ *Alternatively, click the Back button to return to the previous folder.*

FIND IT ONLINE

To learn how to change the icon for My Network Places, see **http://support.microsoft.com/support/ NTWorkstation/ServiceWare/Ntw40/E9JVWHV6V.ASP.**

Adding Network Places

Although there may be many different shared resources that you can access on your network, it's likely that you'll use some of the same things quite often and others hardly at all. You can make the task of opening the items that you need to use often a bit easier by adding them as *network places*. A network place is simply a quick shortcut that takes you directly to a computer or a folder somewhere on your network. You can also use network places as shortcuts to folders on the Internet — such as Web folders or FTP sites.

Once you have added a folder as a network place, an icon for that folder will appear in the My Network Places window and in Windows Explorer. You can then use the icon to quickly open the shared folder without navigating through several different levels to reach your destination.

When you click the Browse button in the Add Network Place Wizard, you will see a list of *servers* as shown in the second figure on the facing page. In this context, a server is simply a computer on your network that has shared folders available.

If you create a network place icon that is a link to an FTP site — a *File Transfer Protocol* site where you can upload or download files, you will also have to specify how to log on to the site. In most cases FTP sites use an anonymous logon. If a site requires a specific logon, you should obtain the proper user name and password before you attempt to set up a network place icon for the site.

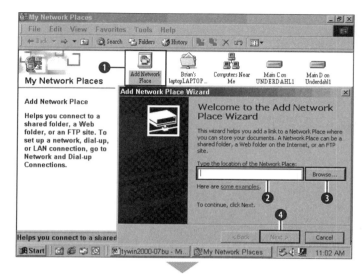

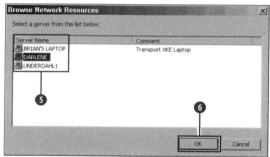

❶ Double-click the Add Network Place icon to open the Add Network Place Wizard.

❷ Type the network place address.

❸ Alternatively, click the Browse button to view the servers on the network.

❹ If you typed the address, click Next to continue.

❺ Select the computer that contains the shared folder you wish to use.

❻ Click OK to continue.

CROSS-REFERENCE

See "Finding Files on Your Network" later in this chapter.

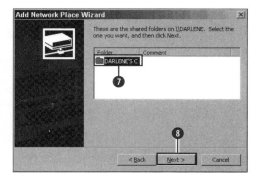

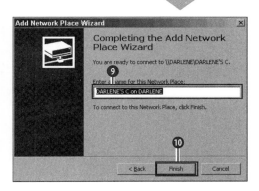

⑦ Select the shared folder you wish to use.

⑧ Click Next to continue.

⑨ Optionally, enter a new name for the new network place.

⑩ Click Finish to continue.

▶ After you have added a new network place, you can double-click the new icon to open the folder directly.

FIND IT ONLINE

For an FTP site that makes a great network place, see **ftp://ftp.microsoft.com/softlib/MSLFILES/**.

Sharing Your Files

Networks serve no purpose unless things on the network are shared. *Sharing* is the process of allowing other people access to files, folders, and printers. Initially, nothing on the network is shared — you must initiate sharing explicitly for each resource that you want to be available on the network. If you are connected to a large network, you may find that the network administrator has already set up a limited amount of sharing. But if you are responsible for your own network, you must set up sharing yourself.

Windows 2000 file sharing is generally done at the folder level. If you want to share a set of files, you do so by sharing the folder containing those files. If you wish to restrict the access to certain files you can either place those files in a different folder or change the permissions to specific groups of users. For example, you can allow certain users to read but not change files that are contained within a folder. You can allow other users more complete access, or even completely deny access to some users. Some application programs also allow you to specify passwords for access to specific documents.

There are several access settings you can use. You can allow *read* access so that visitors can open or copy a file but cannot delete, modify, or create a file. *Change* access allows someone to modify a file, but not to delete it. *Full* access allows a visitor to do anything that you can do.

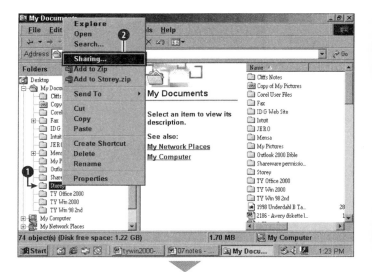

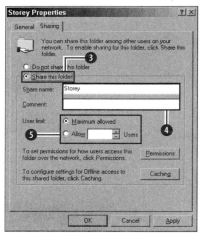

▶ Open Windows Explorer.

❶ Right-click the folder you wish to share.

❷ Select Sharing from the context menu.

❸ Click Share this folder to allow sharing.

❹ Optionally, enter a share name or a comment for the folder.

❺ If you wish to control the number of concurrent users, choose one of these options.

CROSS-REFERENCE

See "Allowing Outside Access" later in this chapter.

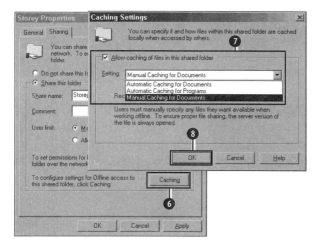

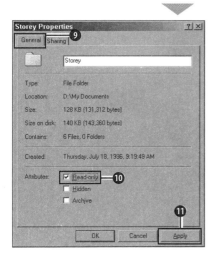

UNDERSTANDING NETWORK SECURITY

By default, when you share a folder Windows 2000 provides full control permission to anyone who can access the folder on your network. If you have a need for more security on your network, you must use the Permissions controls to restrict the access that is granted to specific users. This is very different from a Windows 98-based network where anyone who knows the password has the same level of access to shared folders. In Windows 2000, you can set different access levels for each user on your network if you wish.

CONTROLLING WHAT YOU SHARE

When you share a drive or a folder, everything contained in it is also shared. You can restrict access to a folder on a shared drive or to a folder contained within a shared folder, but you must do so explicitly. So, for example, if your \My Documents folder contains a folder named "Resume" and you share \My Documents, anyone on the network can access \My Documents\Resume unless you specifically restrict the access to the \My Documents\Resume folder. For this reason, it is generally better to explicitly share specific folders rather than to share your entire hard disk.

⑥ To control the use of shared files offline, click the Caching button.

⑦ Choose the caching options that suit your needs.

⑧ Click OK to continue.

⑨ Optionally, click the General tab.

⑩ Select Read-only to prevent anyone from making changes in the shared folder.

⑪ Click Apply to apply your changes.

FIND IT ONLINE

For more information on sharing Files on your network, see **http://it.stlawu.edu/~Infotech/ techbytes/930fileshare.htm.**

Managing Shares

Simply allowing unrestricted access to your shared folders may be all that is needed on a small network with a limited number of users. As your network grows and there are more people on the network, you may need to exercise more precise control over who can access your files. For example, if you keep the company payroll records in a shared folder, you probably want to allow certain members of the accounting staff to have access to those records, but you likely don't want other employees to have such access.

In Windows 2000 you can control each individual's access to any shared resources. Some people can be given full access to a folder so that they can create, delete, or modify files as necessary. You can set the folder permissions to allow other people more restricted access. You might use this control to allow everyone in the company to have read-only access to a folder that contains document templates, for instance, to ensure that no one could accidentally infect those templates with a macro virus. Only the person with higher-level access to the folder would be able to add anything to the folder — thus preventing viruses from being spread by your users.

As you are adding users to the permissions list, be certain that your list is complete enough so that you have covered all of the different user groups. It may be helpful to write out a list that shows which users should have Full Control, Change, Read, or no access to the folder. Then use your list to create the permissions, starting with the most restrictive set of permissions. Explicitly granting someone higher levels of access overrides the restrictions that you place on a more inclusive user group — such as the Everyone group.

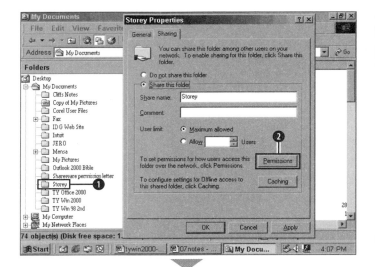

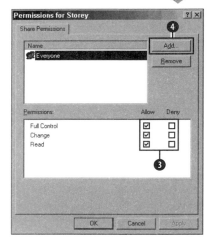

▶ If necessary, open Windows Explorer.

❶ Right-click the shared folder you wish to control and select Sharing from the context menu.

❷ Click the Permissions button.

❸ You may want to adjust the existing permissions.

❹ Click Add to select a new user.

CROSS-REFERENCE

See "Sharing Your Files" earlier in this chapter.

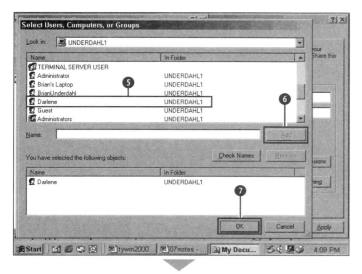

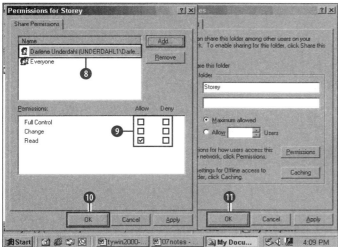

5 Choose the users from this list.

6 Click Add to add them to the selected users list.

7 Click OK to continue.

8 Select a user to modify.

9 Choose the permission levels for the selected user.

10 Click OK to continue.

11 Click OK to complete the task.

FIND IT ONLINE

For more information on sharing resources, see
http://www.huntley.claremont.edu/win98tcr/othernet/6.htm#1.

Finding Files on Your Network

In the last chapter you learned several techniques that you can use to find your files. Those techniques generally work pretty much the same when you are looking for files on your network, but there are some important differences that you need to consider. In this section you will learn how to quickly locate what you need on a network.

Using a network can produce some interesting surprises. A computer that contains files that you need may not always be available, and you probably won't have any advance warning when a computer disappears from the network. A user may have turned his or her system off, its physical connection may have been disrupted, or the owner may have decided to stop sharing files.

When you are looking for files on the network, you can only search one computer at a time. You cannot search the entire network at once, so if you aren't sure where a file is located, you may end up searching several times before you are successful.

Just as when you're searching your PC, you can narrow the search by specifying the starting folder rather than searching the entire drive. This is often a good idea because it reduces network traffic and speeds the search. Depending on the speed of your network, the network traffic level, and the number of files that are contained in the folders being searched, a network file search can take considerably longer to complete than a search on your own PC.

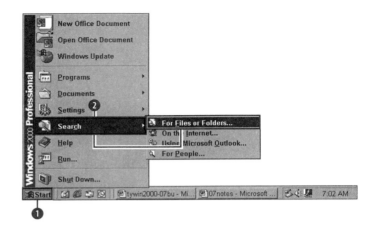

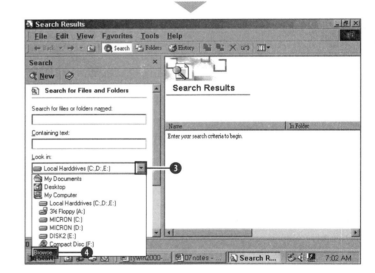

① Click the Start button.

② Select Search ➪ For Files or Folders.

③ Click the down arrow at the right side of the Look in list box.

④ Select Browse.

CROSS-REFERENCE

See "Finding Computers on Your Network" earlier in this chapter.

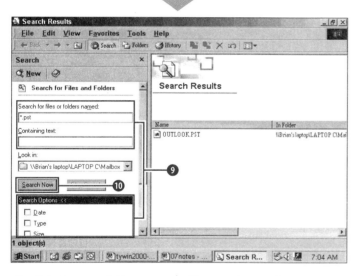

5 Click My Network Places.

6 Select the computer you wish to search.

7 Select the folder you wish to search.

8 Click OK to continue.

9 Enter the search criteria.

10 Click Search Now to complete the task.

TAKE NOTE

▶ **UNIVERSAL NAMING CONVENTIONS**

Windows 2000 needs a means to identify the computers on a network so that it can specify the exact location of network files. On your computer, Windows 2000 uses the drive letter, a colon, and a backslash to identify the drive where files can be found. This approach isn't practical on the network because there would be no way to discern whether C:\ referred to drive C on your local PC or to drive C on one of the other computers on the network. To remedy this problem, Windows 2000 uses *UNC* — Universal Naming Conventions — to designate computers that are on the network. For example, if a computer is named Brian, that computer would be referred to as \\Brian on the network.

▶ **NETWORK PLACES ICONS REMAIN**

If you have created Network Places icons for various network folders, those icons will remain, even if the folder they refer to is no longer available. As a result, you may see an error message telling you that the Network Place is no longer accessible if Windows 2000 cannot find the folder that is referred to by the shortcut. If you receive this type of error message, make certain that you can access the rest of the network — the error could be your network connection.

FIND IT ONLINE

For information about online file storage and sharing, see **http://www.fileshark.com/FileShark/Login.asp.**

Sharing a Printer

Networks are good for a lot of different things, and sharing printers is often one of the most important of them. Even if your network is so small that it consists of two computers and a printer, the efficiency of network printer sharing simply makes good sense. It's certainly far easier to justify the expense of a fancier printer when it is shared between several computer users — especially because few people spend a great percentage of their time printing anyway.

When you share a printer on your network, it's important to remember that the correct printer driver software must be installed on each PC that will use the printer. It isn't enough to simply install the printer on the computer where the printer is physically attached. The reason for this is simple. When you print a document, your application program works through the operating system to send out the correct series of commands to the printer. The operating system knows what commands to send by interacting with the printer driver. These printer commands are the same regardless of whether the printer is connected directly to your PC, whether it is located somewhere on the network, or whether you are printing to a file. The end result is that you must install the printer before you can use it — even if the printer is not connected to your PC.

The major difference between using a locally attached printer and one that is elsewhere on your network is the *port* that you choose for the connection. The port is simply the address where your PC sends the print commands. When you select a network printer, you are sending those commands across the network to the PC connected to the printer. That PC then forwards the commands to the printer.

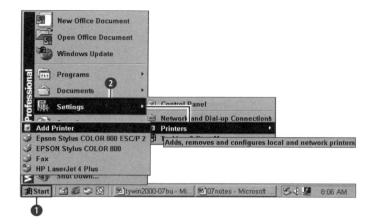

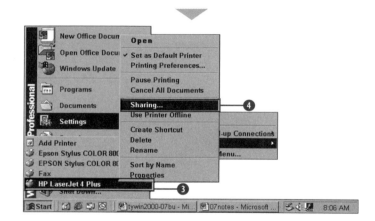

➊ Click the Start button.

➋ Select Settings ➪ Printers.

▶ These steps will display either the list of printers or the Printers folder.

➌ Right-click the printer you wish to share.

➍ Select Sharing from the context menu.

CROSS-REFERENCE

See "Adding New Hardware" in Chapter 13.

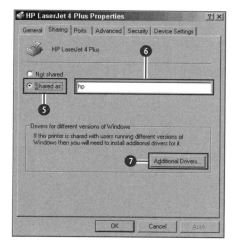

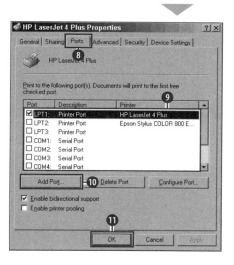

TAKE NOTE

▶ ELIMINATE HARDWARE HASSLES

Adding a second printer to a PC is certainly possible, but it is not always the easiest task to successfully accomplish. In most cases you will have to locate an open expansion slot in your PC, and you may encounter problems with system conflicts, too. But because virtually all PCs already include one printer port as standard equipment, you can avoid these problems by spreading extra printers around your network and sharing them. You eliminate the hassle and expense of adding extra hardware, and you spend far less time dealing with configuration issues, too.

▶ INSTALL ON THE PRINTER SERVER FIRST

Be sure to first install the printer on the *print server* — the computer connected to the printer — and then share the printer before you attempt to install it on the other computers. Otherwise, you may see error messages when the printer cannot be found on the network.

⑤ Select the Shared as button.

⑥ Optionally, enter a network name for the printer.

⑦ If the other network PCs are not running Windows 2000, you may need to click the Additional Drivers button and follow the directions.

⑧ To connect to a network printer, you may need to click the Ports tab.

⑨ Select the network printer port.

⑩ If the port is not shown, click Add Port and follow the onscreen directions.

⑪ Click OK to complete the task.

FIND IT ONLINE

For information about network printer sharing, see
http://www.circuitmasters.com/tech/network3.html.

Creating Network and Dial-up Connections

Windows 2000 treats all connections to other computers pretty much the same — essentially as network connections. This makes it far easier for you to create and manage your connections, because they all can be accessed from one central location.

There are several different types of connections that you can create. These include the following:

Dial-up to a private network enables you to connect to another computer using your modem. You might use this type of connection to connect to your company's office in a different location. Because you connect directly, you do not have to worry about someone intercepting your messages as you might using the Internet.

Dial-up to the Internet enables you to connect to the Internet through a modem or through your network if you have a shared connection.

Connect to a private network through the Internet enables you to make a secure connection to your network even though you are using the Internet to carry your messages. This option uses *Virtual Private Networking* — VPN — to encase your messages in a special "wrapper" that keeps them secure while they are traveling across the Internet.

Accept incoming connections enables you to set up your PC as an access point so that other computers can access your network through your computer. You could, for example, allow someone to dial in to your modem and download files to their computer.

Connect directly to another computer enables you to create a direct connection between two PCs. You could use this to transfer files between your desktop PC and a laptop PC that lacked a network adapter.

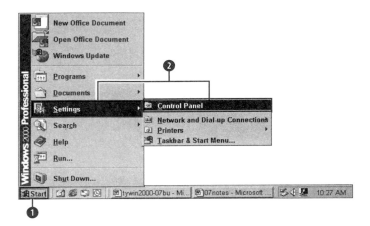

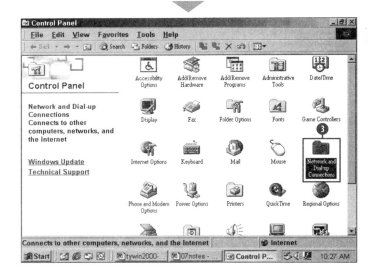

❶ Click the Start button.

❷ Select Settings ⇨ Control Panel.

❸ Double-click the Network and Dial-up Connections icon.

CROSS-REFERENCE

See "Adding New Hardware" in Chapter 13.

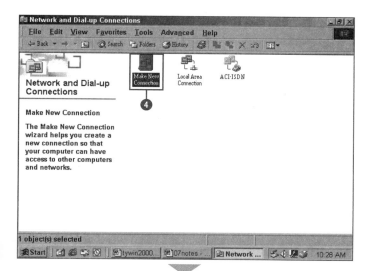

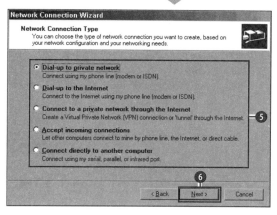

The figures on the facing page show how to access the Network Connection Wizard, but not how to create specific types of connections. Later in this chapter you will see two specific examples that step you through the process of creating a new connection.

TAKE NOTE

▶ COLLECT INFORMATION FIRST

Regardless of the type of connection that you want to create, the task will go much smoother and faster if you collect all of the information that you will need before you begin. Although the types of information that you will need will vary according to the kind of connection you are creating, typical bits and pieces include your login (or user) name, a password, the dial-up telephone number for telephone connections, the protocols that you must use, and any special addressing information. You may not need every piece of information that you gather, but having as much of it as possible makes it less likely that you will have to stop and hunt for the missing data.

▶ LOCAL CONNECTION IS AUTOMATIC

You don't need to use the wizard to create a connection to your local network. That connection is created automatically.

④ Double-click the Make New Connection icon.

▶ To continue, click Next in the information dialog box that appears.

⑤ Select the type of connection that you wish to create.

⑥ Click Next to continue.

▶ You will now need to follow the on-screen directions for the selected type of connection. See the next section for a specific example.

FIND IT ONLINE

For information on Virtual Private Networking, see
http://msdn.microsoft.com/workshop/server/
feature/vpnovw.asp?RLD=90.

Adding an Internet Connection

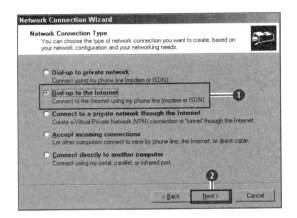

Of all the types of connections that you can create with the Network Connection Wizard, the one that is likely to be of most interest to you is a connection to the Internet. In this section you will learn how to create an Internet connection on your Windows 2000-based PC.

To connect to the Internet, you need a physical connection to an Internet server, either via a modem or through your network. You also need an account that grants you Internet access. For dial-up connections, an Internet Service Provider — an ISP — generally provides this account. You can choose any ISP that meets your needs, from a large ISP, such as Earthlink, to a local service provider that you will find listed in the Internet category of your telephone directory.

In choosing an ISP, make certain there is a local access number that you can use. Paying long distance charges on top of your monthly access fees could quickly result in huge bills. Also be sure to check the type of local access that is provided. You'll want fast access that is compatible with your modem. In some areas you can use 56K modems, ISDN or DSL connections, or even cable modems, but you'll need to check to see which service is available in your area. If your only option is to use a standard 56K modem, keep in mind that your connection speed will likely be quite a bit less than 56K. In reality, fewer than half of the phone lines in the country support 56K connections. Depending on your location, you may not have any other option.

In most cases, setting up a dial-up connection is very simple and straightforward. Although the example shown in the figures on the facing page and the next two pages show you how to set the advanced connection options, you probably won't have to make any changes to these settings for most connections.

Continued

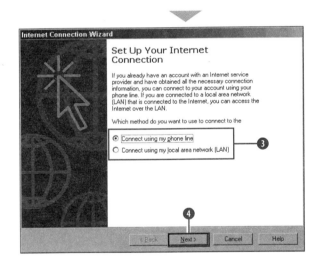

▶ *If necessary, open the Network Connection Wizard as described in the previous task.*

❶ *Select the Dial-up to the Internet option.*

❷ *Click Next to continue.*

❸ *Select your connection method.*

❹ *Click Next to continue.*

CROSS-REFERENCE

See "Starting Internet Explorer" in Chapter 9.

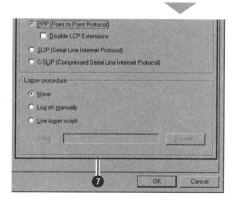

TAKE NOTE

▶ USE THE DIAL-UP OPTION

Although the Network Connection Wizard calls the type of connection that you will create a "dial-up" connection, you use this same option — Dial-up to the Internet — to create an Internet connection that uses your local network. See the next section for more information on sharing Internet connections on your network.

▶ WHY YOU NEED AN ISP

Although no one actually owns the Internet, to connect to the Internet you will probably need to use the services of an *Internet Service Provider*. An ISP provides the physical connection between the Internet and your PC. In most cases this connection is through your modem and phone line, but it may also be through an ISDN adapter, a DSL adapter, or through a cable modem. ISPs generally charge for the right to connect to the Internet through their equipment.

⑤ Enter the dial-up telephone number.

⑥ Optionally, click the Advanced button to configure the advanced settings.

⑦ If your ISP has instructed you to use nonstandard Connection type or Logon settings, select the correct settings.

FIND IT ONLINE

See **http://dir.yahoo.com/Business_and_Economy/ Companies/Internet_Services/Access_Providers/Free _Internet_Access/** for ways to get free Internet access.

Adding an Internet Connection

Continued

In addition to setting up the access number and any advanced settings that may be required for your account, you will need to enter your user name and password. In most cases this will not be the same user name and password that you use to log on to Windows 2000. Your ISP may refer to your user name as your account name or your logon name.

When you enter your password, the password will not appear in the Password text box. You will see an asterisk in place of each character that you type, and, because you cannot see what you are typing, it is easy to make a mistake. If you are unsure whether you typed in the correct password, re-enter it to make certain it is correct. Both user names and passwords may be case-sensitive. Entering either your user name or your password incorrectly can prevent you from logging on.

If you are concerned about security, you may not want to enter your password when you are setting up your Internet connection. If you do enter both your user name and password, anyone who uses your PC will be able to access your Internet account simply by opening Internet Explorer. Of course, if you do not enter your password, it will be necessary to enter it manually when you wish to connect to the Internet. This will prevent your system from automatically opening your Internet connection, and will effectively prevent other people from accessing the Internet through your PC unless you provide them with your password.

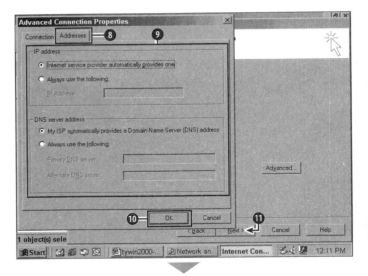

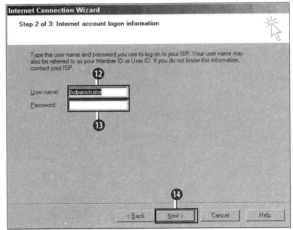

- ❽ *Click the Addresses tab.*
- ❾ *Make any necessary IP or DNS address changes.*
- ❿ *Click OK.*
- ⓫ *Click Next to continue.*
- ⓬ *Enter your Internet account name.*
- ⓭ *Optionally, enter your Internet password.*
- ⓮ *Click Next to continue.*

CROSS-REFERENCE

See "Visiting Web Sites" in Chapter 9.

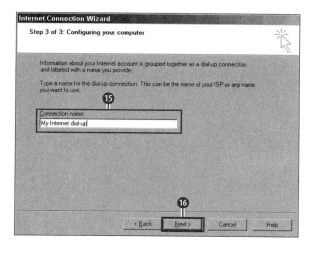

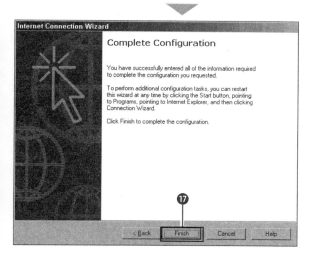

⑮ Enter a name for this connection.

⑯ Click Next to continue.

⑰ Click the Finish button to complete the task.

STATIC IP ADDRESSES

If you connect to the Internet through a dial-up connection, you will probably be assigned a different IP address each time you log on to the Internet. As the first figure on the facing page shows, you can also specify a specific IP address if one has been assigned by your ISP. The option to use a *static* IP address — one that is always the same — is generally needed only if your PC is acting as a Web server. If you have a Web page that is hosted on a server that is provided by your ISP, you do not need a static IP address.

DNS ADDRESSES

The second advanced address setting that you may need to configure is the DNS server address. *DNS servers* are the computers on the Internet that translate Web page addresses that you type into a series of numbers that are the true Web page addresses. Although DNS servers are normally accessed automatically, your ISP may specify specific addresses that you should use to access these servers. Using a specific DNS address may make accessing Web pages slightly faster and more reliable for some connections.

FIND IT ONLINE

See **http://free.msn.com/msncom/** for a free trial of MSN.

Sharing an Internet Connection

Even though it may sometimes seem as though no Internet connection is fast enough, the truth is that most of the time your connection is probably sitting idle. Even when you are actively browsing the Web, you're likely spending quite a bit of that time just viewing a Web page that you have downloaded. This usually means that even though you are connected, no data is flowing across your connection.

Since your Internet connection sits idle most of the time, it makes sense to share that bandwidth by providing your entire network with Internet access. Unless you have a specially restricted Internet access account or must pay for connect time, most Internet accounts allow unlimited access as long as someone is actually using the PC.

In order to share an Internet connection on your network, each of the computers that will use the shared connection must use the TCP/IP protocol on the network adapters that they use to access the network. When you enable connection sharing, each network adapter must be assigned a static IP address. This IP address is then used to send Web pages to the correct computer on your network. These IP addresses are used only on your local network, and are not visible to computers that are not connected to the network.

When you set up sharing on your Internet connection, the PC that is providing the Internet access to the network is automatically configured with the correct IP addresses. The remaining computers must be configured manually — a process that will depend on which operating system they are using. You can find out more about the necessary settings for the other computers on your network by looking for "Shared Access" in the Windows 2000 help system.

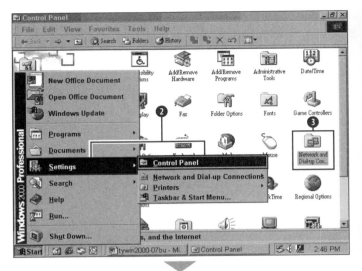

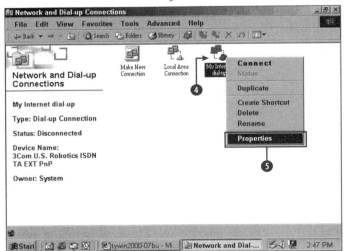

① Click the Start button.

② Select Settings ⇨ Control Panel.

③ Double-click the Network and Dial-up Connections icon.

④ Right-click your Internet connection.

⑤ Select Properties from the context menu.

CROSS-REFERENCE

See Chapter 3 for more information on using the Windows 2000 help system.

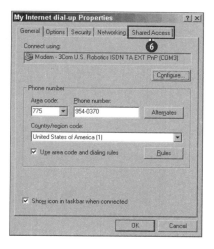

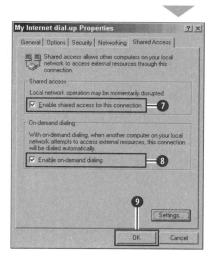

TAKE NOTE

► BE CAREFUL WITH YOUR ISP

Most ISPs only allow a single logon at one time for each account. In many cases they require that each user have his or her own Internet access account. If you share your Internet connection with all of the PCs on your network, you may be technically violating your account agreement with your ISP. But since you will only be using a single connection to access the Internet, your ISP will have no way to determine how many users are accessing the connection unless you tell them. It's probably best not to ask your ISP for assistance configuring Internet connection sharing!

► BANDWIDTH SIMPLIFIED

Bandwidth is a term that is often used to describe the capacity of an Internet connection. Higher bandwidth means faster connections and shorter delays while Web pages are downloaded. If you upgrade to a higher bandwidth connection — such as ISDN, DSL, or a cable modem — you should easily be able to allow several people to share a single Internet connection and still be satisfied with the results.

---

⑥ *Click the Shared Access tab.*

⑦ *Select the Enable shared access for this connection check box.*

⑧ *Select the Enable on-demand dialing check box.*

⑨ *Click OK to close the dialog box.*

► *You will have to manually configure PCs on your network that are not using Windows 2000.*

FIND IT ONLINE

For information about sharing a Cable Modem, ADSL, or ISDN Connection, see **http://www.rangelan2.com/ symphony/solution/cablemod.shtml.**

Allowing Outside Access

People who travel for business — even if it's just across town — often find that they would benefit greatly by being able to have access to the files on the office network. Somehow it always seems as though there is at least one important document that would be very useful, but which you don't have with you. Fortunately, Windows 2000 makes it quite easy for you to set up a connection that allows someone to access your network remotely so that these problems can be quickly solved.

Even if your Windows 2000 PC is a standalone PC that is not connected to a network, you can still create an incoming connection. In fact, there really is no difference between creating an incoming connection to your network or to a standalone PC.

When you are choosing the type of device that will provide the incoming connection, make certain that it is one that will be compatible with the type of access you want to provide. One of the options that the Network Connection Wizard may offer is a direct parallel connection that uses your PC's printer port. Although this option may seem strange in the context of a dial-up connection, it does offer the ability to connect a PC to your network without requiring that PC to have a network card. While this may seem similar to the *Connect directly to another computer* option, there is an important difference. The *Connect directly to another computer* option is really only intended for connecting two computers — not for providing access to your network.

Continued

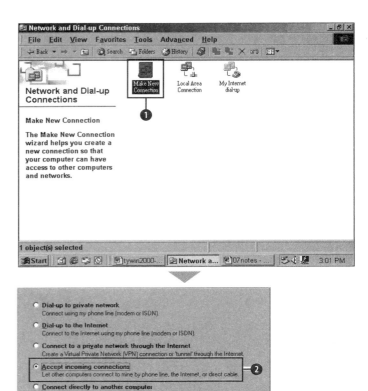

▶ If necessary, open the Network and Dial-up Connections folder.

❶ Double-click the Make New Connection icon.

▶ Click Next in the information dialog box to continue.

❷ Select the Accept incoming connections button.

❸ Click Next to continue.

CROSS-REFERENCE

See "Finding Files on Your Network" earlier in this chapter.

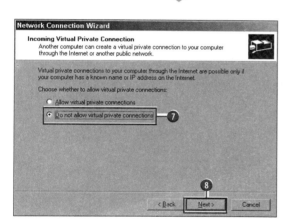

DON'T EXPECT HIGH SPEED

One of the biggest problems with a dial-up connection to the network is simply the speed limitation that is imposed by using standard telephone lines to transmit data. If you're used to quickly moving large files across your network, you're in for a reality check if you try to do the same thing over a dial-up network connection. Remember that the highest speed that two standard modems can achieve is 33.6KBps. You need a special (and expensive) modem on the network side of the connection to get higher transmission speeds, and that's only in one direction. If possible, limit your dial-up network access to transferring smaller files that won't take forever to send.

USE THE NETWORK CONNECTION WIZARD TO CONNECT

Just as you use the Network Connection Wizard to set up your system to accept incoming calls, you also use this wizard to set up an outgoing connection. To configure an outgoing connection, select the *Dial-up to private network* option shown (not selected) in the second figure on the facing page. You will need to know the phone number, your correct user name, and your password to set up the connection.

④ Select the device that you wish to use for incoming connections.

⑤ Optionally, click Properties to configure the device.

⑥ Click Next to continue.

⑦ Unless you are setting up a VPN connection that uses the Internet, select the Do not allow virtual private connections button.

⑧ Click Next to continue.

FIND IT ONLINE

See **http://filedudes.lvdi.net/win95/nfs/ridewayp.html** for another way to create a virtual private network for secure file sharing through a Web browser.

Allowing Outside Access

Continued

Incoming connections to a Windows 2000-based PC can be quite secure. As the figures on the facing page show, you are able to not only control which users are allowed to access the network through the dial-up connection, but you can also make certain that they use secure passwords.

Windows 2000 treats dial-up connections no differently than it does any other network connection. If you allow someone to access the network through a dial-up connection, that person will have exactly the same access rights as if they were logged on to a PC that was directly connected to the network. Any resource permissions that are granted to a user remain the same regardless of the type of connection.

In most cases, the default set of networking components that Windows 2000 uses for incoming connections can be left alone. If the computers on your network are able to successfully communicate using the installed protocols and services, a PC that is using the dial-up connection should be able to communicate using them, too. If you have trouble connecting, make certain that the PC that is dialing in has the same protocols and services installed as are shown for the incoming connection.

Be wary of allowing the default accounts such as administrator or guest accounts to have dial-up access to your network. Although you may feel that it is convenient to use these accounts, remember that they would be easy for someone to guess, and these accounts often do not have passwords set by default.

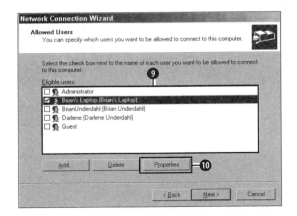

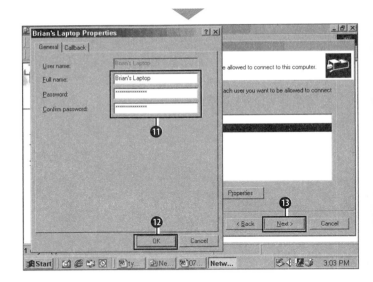

⑨ Select each of the users who will be allowed to use this connection.

⑩ Optionally, click Properties to set the properties for a selected user.

⑪ If necessary, set the user password.

⑫ Click OK to continue.

⑬ Click Next to continue.

CROSS-REFERENCE

See Chapter 11 for another way to connect PCs.

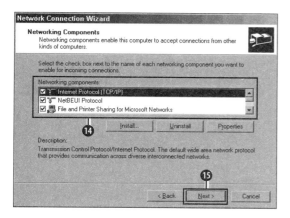

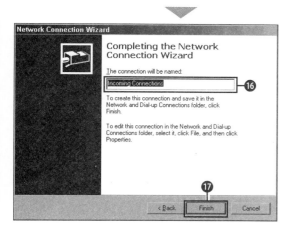

CONSIDER SEPARATE DIAL-UP ACCOUNTS

Because users have the same permission levels regardless of how they are connected to the network, it may be wise to provide mobile users with two separate accounts. When they are in the office and connected directly to the network they use one account that provides more complete access to network resources. When the user is connected through dial-up access, you could assign them an account with more limited privileges. As the first figure on the facing page shows, you can set up the dial-up access to allow only a logon using the more restricted account.

BE CAREFUL WITH PASSWORDS

When you enable outside access to your network, you are creating the potential for unauthorized people to enter your network. User names and passwords help reduce the threat, but only if you are careful in creating and protecting them. User names are often fairly easy to guess, so passwords should not be. If you allow your users to pick their own passwords, set a minimum length — such as eight characters — and insist on passwords that include both letters and numbers. Above all, make certain that passwords are not written on sticky notes, and that they are changed at regular intervals.

⑭ If necessary, select the networking components that you wish to use for incoming connections.

⑮ Click Next to continue.

⑯ Optionally, enter a name for the connection.

⑰ Click Finish to complete the task.

FIND IT ONLINE

See http://support.microsoft.com/support/ntserver/serviceware/nts40/e9mse6rhw.asp for information on using the callback feature.

Personal Workbook

Q&A

1 How can you tell that you're seeing the name of a computer that is on the network?

_____

_____

_____

2 When you're trying to find a file, how much of the network can you search at any one time?

_____

_____

_____

3 What happens to folders that are contained in a folder that you share on the network?

_____

_____

_____

4 What happens to your Network Places icons when the computers they refer to are no longer available?

_____

_____

_____

5 What network protocol is necessary if you want to share an Internet connection?

_____

_____

_____

6 Why does a network printer need drivers installed on PCs that aren't connected to the printer?

_____

_____

_____

7 How can you allow people access to master documents in a shared folder without allowing them to make changes?

_____

_____

_____

8 What do you use to control who has access to shared resources?

_____

_____

ANSWERS: PAGE 392

EXTRA PRACTICE

1 Find all the files with a DOC extension that are available in one of the shared folders on your network.

2 Figure out a method of allowing access to some of your document files without making all the files available on the network.

3 Open My Network Places and determine how many computers are on the network.

4 Look in your Printers folder to see which printers are shared on the network.

5 Create a new connection to the Internet.

6 Enable the other users on your network to share your Internet connection.

REAL-WORLD APPLICATIONS

✔ You're about to order a newer, faster computer to help you get more done. You network your new and old systems so that you have a backup system in the event of problems with the new computer.

✔ You install an ISDN line in your office and then allow everyone to share the same Internet connection. This ends up saving you money since you don't need separate accounts for everyone.

✔ You need to make your company's documents look more professional. You buy a color laser printer and share it on the network so that everyone can have high quality output.

Visual Quiz

How can you display a window like this one? Why does it show three computers but no Entire Network icon?

_____

_____

_____

_____

_____

CHAPTER 8

MASTER THESE SKILLS

▶ **Using the Accessibility Wizard**

▶ **Using the Magnifier**

▶ **Using the Narrator**

▶ **Using the On-Screen Keyboard**

▶ **Using the Utility Manager**

▶ **Changing the Accessibility Settings**

Using the Accessibility Options

Computers are supposed to be easy to use, but not everyone finds them to be quite as easy as they should be. People who have physical difficulties can feel left out in a world that seems to require excellent vision and great manual dexterity.

Windows 2000 includes several tools that are designed to help people overcome these problems so that they can make effective use of their PC in spite of physical limitations. These tools address the needs of people who have limited vision, hearing problems, or an inability to use a standard keyboard. This chapter shows you how to use these tools. You will learn how to start the tools as well as how to configure them so that they are of the most use when you need them.

People sometimes feel that the accessibility tools are only useful for people who have physical disabilities. The fact is, however, that these tools can be quite useful in many different circumstances. Almost everyone has encountered situations where a computer screen has been difficult to read due to poor lighting conditions or very small text. But quite aside from this obvious case, the accessibility tools offer solutions to other problems, too. Imagine how much easier it would be to teach a novice PC user to use a computer if the computer could actually read aloud information that is shown on the screen. Or consider how an amateur astronomer might benefit from having their PC speak while they were attempting to view heavenly bodies rather than having their night vision ruined by reading data from a brightly lit computer screen. With a little imagination you can probably think of a number of other innovative uses for these tools.

Even if you have no real need for the accessibility options yourself, you may know someone who could benefit from them. If so, it's important to remember that those who need these tools might have a difficult time setting them up without a bit of assistance. By learning how these tools work you can be ready to provide that assistance if the need arises.

The accessibility options consist of several different tools. You will likely find that some of them are much more useful than others. That's okay — these tools were designed to be used in many different combinations to best suit the needs of the individual user.

Using the Accessibility Wizard

The Accessibility Wizard is a tool that enables you to set up the various accessibility options for use on your computer. This wizard provides an easy method for choosing the correct options without giving the whole process a lot of advance thought or planning. You simply make a few easy choices and the Accessibility Wizard selects the options that seem appropriate, based on your selections.

The Accessibility Wizard has four main options. You can choose as many of the options as you need to configure your PC properly for your situation.

There are a number of features designed to assist people who have limited or no vision. Access these settings by choosing the *I am blind or have difficulty seeing things on screen* check box. This group of features includes relatively simple items such as higher contrast color schemes and larger text displays. Both of these tools are designed to help with less severe vision difficulties. A more sophisticated tool is the Magnifier, which greatly magnifies a portion of your screen as you move the mouse around your desktop. Finally, there is the Narrator — a tool that uses speech synthesis to read aloud text that appears on the screen. Both the Magnifier and the Narrator are covered in detail later in this chapter.

Several features are intended to aid people whose hearing is limited. You access these settings by choosing the *I am deaf or have difficulty hearing sounds from the computer* check box. Windows 2000 normally uses sounds to alert you when certain system events occur.

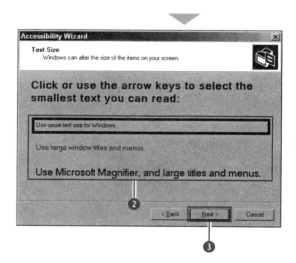

▶ Select Programs ⇨ Accessories ⇨ Accessibility ⇨ Accessibility Wizard from the Start menu.

❶ Click Next to continue.

❷ Choose the text size option that works the best for your needs.

❸ Click Next to continue.

CROSS-REFERENCE

See "Changing the Accessibility Settings" later in this chapter.

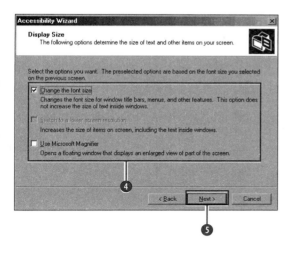

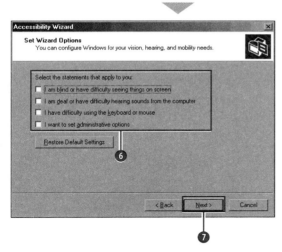

Using the options accessed through this section of the Accessibility Wizard, you can specify that Windows 2000 provide more visible onscreen alerts of these types of events. For example, Windows 2000 can flash a new warning message window several times to make certain that you notice the new message.

If you have difficulty with typing or using the mouse, select the *I have difficulty using the keyboard or mouse* check box. This option enables you to use the On-Screen Keyboard or one of the options such as Sticky Keys that can make these devices easier to use.

The administrative options enable you to fine-tune the accessibility tools. These settings can also be changed using the Accessibility icon in the Control Panel, as you'll see later in this chapter.

TAKE NOTE

OPENING THE ACCESSIBILITY TOOLS

You can open the accessibility tools by clicking the Start button and then choosing Programs ⇨ Accessories ⇨ Accessibility to display a menu of the accessibility tools. Select the tool you wish to use from the list. You can also use the Accessibility Wizard or the Accessibility icon in the Control Panel to configure the accessibility tools to run automatically whenever your computer is started.

④ Choose any of the display size options necessary to make your screen easier to see.

▶ The option to switch to a lower resolution will not be available if your screen is already set for 640 × 480 resolution.

⑤ Click Next to continue.

⑥ Choose the areas where you would like Windows 2000 to make accessibility adjustments.

⑦ Click Next to continue.

▶ Follow the on-screen directions for the different options that you have selected.

FIND IT ONLINE

To learn more about the Accessibility Wizard, see http://support.microsoft.com/support/windows/inproducthelp98/accessibility_options_installs.asp.

Using the Magnifier

The Magnifier is an accessibility tool that acts similar to a magnifying glass — it increases the size of anything that is displayed on your Windows 2000 screen. As you move the mouse around the screen, the area that is displayed in the Magnifier window moves along with the mouse pointer. This enables you to simply move your mouse over something to view it in a much larger size. The Magnifier window can also follow the keyboard cursor when you are typing or making selections using the keyboard.

The Magnifier can be set to several different magnification power levels. Depending on your needs, you can select power settings up to nine times normal size. Of course, higher power settings also reduce the amount of data that will be visible in the Magnifier window at any one time. If you choose a very high power level you may need to slow the mouse response speed so that everything doesn't zoom past too quickly when you move your mouse. You will learn how to adjust the mouse speed in Chapter 13.

In some ways, you'll find that balancing the screen resolution setting along with the size and magnification power of the Magnifier window is a delicate balancing act. If you adjust the screen resolution to a higher setting, everything on your screen will be smaller, but there will be more room for the Magnifier window. But this will also mean that the items within the Magnifier window will appear somewhat smaller, so you may need to use a higher magnification level to comfortably view them. Setting the screen resolution to a lower setting has the opposite effect, and it also means that there will be less room left over outside of the magnifier window. You may need to experiment to find an optimal setting.

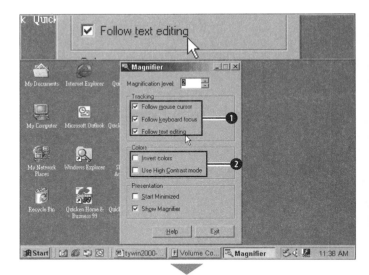

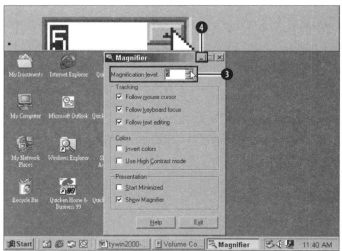

▶ Select Programs ⇨ Accessories ⇨ Accessibility ⇨ Magnifier from the Start menu.

❶ Choose the tracking options that you prefer.

❷ Choose the color and contrast options that work best for you.

❸ Use the Magnification level spin control to adjust the magnification power.

❹ Click the Minimize button to minimize the Magnifier controls.

CROSS-REFERENCE

See "Changing the Resolution" in Chapter 12.

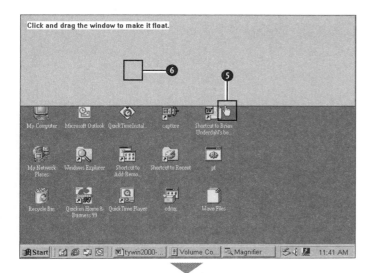

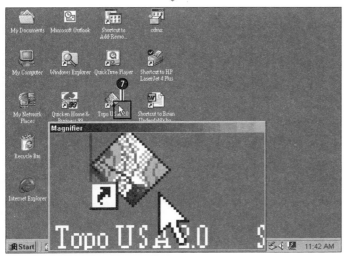

RESIZE THE MAGNIFIER AS NECESSARY

You'll probably quickly discover that the default size of the Magnifier window can be too small to be very useful. You can correct this problem by changing the size of the window so that you can see more information in the window. There are two ways to resize the Magnifier window. When the window is docked at the top of your screen, you can drag the lower edge of the window up or down to change its size. If you have undocked the window by dragging the whole window onto your desktop, drag one of the corners to resize the window.

LEAVE THE MAGNIFIER DOCKED

Although you can drag the Magnifier window onto your desktop, you may want to leave it docked at the top of the screen. When the window is docked, your Windows 2000 desktop begins below the Magnifier window, and this prevents the Magnifier window from covering up other windows.

5 *Drag the lower edge of the Magnifier window to resize the window while leaving it docked at the top of the screen.*

6 *Alternatively, drag the window to undock it and move it to a new location on the screen.*

7 *Move the mouse pointer over the screen area that you would like to magnify.*

▶ *Right-click the Magnifier window and choose Exit to close the Magnifier.*

Using the Narrator

The Windows 2000 Narrator is a text-to-speech tool that reads aloud text that appears on your screen. This tool is intended to help people who cannot see the screen or who have difficulty reading text that is displayed.

The Narrator reads the contents of message boxes, describes the command buttons that appear in dialog boxes, and announces the contents of menus. When you switch to a new window, the Narrator tells you which window is active and briefly describes the window contents.

When you open a document, Narrator will first announce the name of the document, and then it will describe the visible menus and toolbars. In applications that Narrator supports — such as Notepad and WordPad — Narrator then reads the first part of the document. Narrator does not read an entire document, so it would not be a good choice for someone who wanted their computer to read e-mail messages or long document files.

One of the Narrator options enables the program to announce each character as you are typing. This audible feedback might be quite useful in helping make certain that you were typing the characters that you intended.

You can choose from several different voice options. Although all of the voices that are used by the Narrator are synthesized, some are much easier to understand than others. You're likely to find that some of the voices seem to be more of a novelty than a real help.

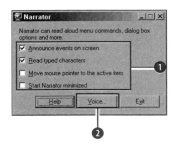

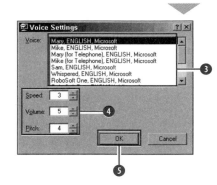

▶ Select Programs ➪ Accessories ➪ Accessibility ➪ Narrator from the Start menu.

❶ Choose the options that you prefer.

❷ Optionally, click Voice to adjust the speaking voice.

❸ Choose a voice from the list.

❹ Use the spin controls to adjust the Speed, Volume, and Pitch settings.

❺ Click OK to continue.

CROSS-REFERENCE

See Chapter 17 for information on using the Windows 2000 multimedia capabilities.

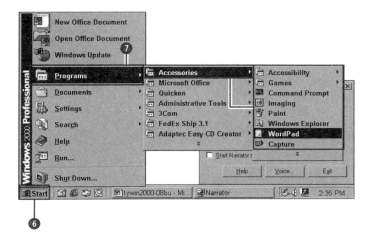

In addition to choosing a specific voice for the Narrator, you can adjust the speed, volume, and pitch of the voice. These types of adjustments can be critical in making certain that the spoken prompts are understood correctly. For example, if the speed is too fast, it can be easy to mistake one word for another. You may want to adjust these three settings several times until you have a combination that has the clarity that maximizes your understanding of the spoken prompts.

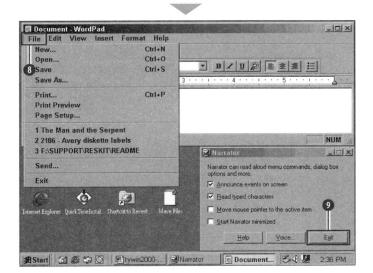

6 Click the Start button.

7 Move the highlight over the Start menu to have Narrator vocalize the current selection. Press Enter to choose the current item.

8 Open a menu in an application to hear a description of the choices.

▶ Move the highlight or use the shortcut described by Narrator to make a selection.

9 Click Exit to close Narrator.

▶ You will also have to select Yes to confirm your selection.

TAKE NOTE

THE NARRATOR IS LIMITED

The Narrator is not intended as a full-featured text-to-speech program. It is designed to work with Notepad, WordPad, Control Panel programs, Internet Explorer, the Windows 2000 desktop, and Windows 2000 setup. You will probably find that Narrator won't read words correctly in other programs. It is far better to use Narrator as it was intended — as a limited aid that provides audible clues to what is happening on your screen.

IMPROVE YOUR SOUND CAPABILITIES

While the Narrator will certainly work with most PC sound card and speaker systems, you can greatly improve the vocal qualities by making certain that you have a high-quality sound card and decent speakers or a good headset. Electronically synthesized voices can be rather difficult to understand — especially if your sound system is of poor quality.

FIND IT ONLINE

To learn more about these tools, see the Accessibility home page **http://www.microsoft.com/enable/.**

Using the On-Screen Keyboard

The On-Screen Keyboard is intended to help people who have limited mobility to type on their PC. You can use the On-Screen Keyboard with a mouse or with an alternative pointing device, and you don't need to manipulate the keys on an actual keyboard.

You can choose several different appearance settings for the On-Screen Keyboard. As the second figure on the facing page shows, you can choose an enhanced or a standard keyboard, a regular or block layout, and the number of keys. Of these settings, the layout settings are probably the most important. The regular layout looks most like a real keyboard, but that layout might be somewhat difficult to use with a pointing device, because there are variable gaps between the various keys, and there are keys of different sizes. Block layout uses uniform spacing and key sizes that can make using the On-Screen Keyboard far easier.

Because the On-Screen Keyboard is intended as a replacement for a physical keyboard, it works as much like a normal keyboard as possible. Typing on the On-Screen Keyboard only produces results if another Windows 2000 application is open and can accept keystrokes. You can use the On-Screen Keyboard to enter text into documents as well as into dialog boxes.

When you are typing on the On-Screen Keyboard, the Shift, Ctrl, and Alt keys act as toggles. That is, when any of these keys are selected, they remain selected until you select another key. This enables you to easily use capital letters because selecting the Shift key causes the

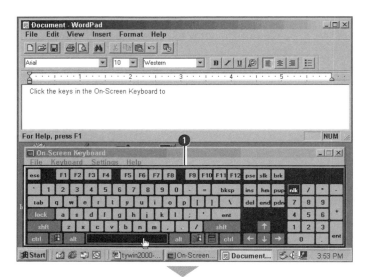

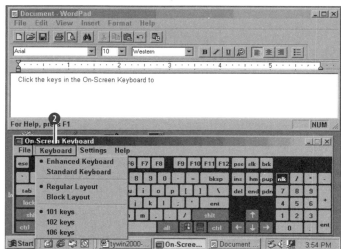

▶ Select Programs ➪ Accessories ➪ Accessibility ➪ On-Screen Keyboard from the Start menu.

▶ Open the application (such as WordPad) that you wish to use in conjunction with the On-Screen Keyboard.

❶ Select the keys on the On-Screen Keyboard to enter characters into the active application.

❷ Optionally, select Keyboard to choose the keyboard appearance and layout options as necessary.

CROSS-REFERENCE

See Chapter 13 for information on configuring the standard keyboard.

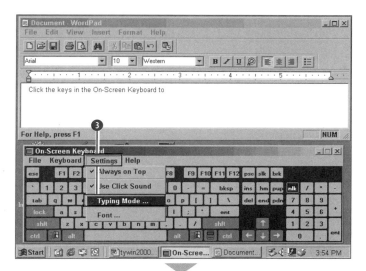

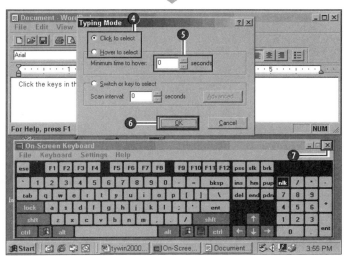

next character you select to be capitalized. The keys that appear on the On-Screen Keyboard always reflect the current Shift key state. That is, selecting Shift causes the keys to be displayed as uppercase characters. You can select the Shift key again if you selected it in error. After you enter a capitalized character, the On-Screen Keyboard returns to lowercase.

TAKE NOTE

CHOOSE THE CORRECT MODE

The On-Screen Keyboard has two typing modes. You can choose to select characters by clicking or by hovering. Click mode requires the user to move the pointer over a key on the On-Screen Keyboard and then to click the mouse button to select a character. Hover mode selects characters without clicking. When the pointer is held over a character for a specified period of time, that character will be selected. Choose the mode which best enables the user to make the proper selections with whatever pointing device they use.

FOCUS IS IMPORTANT

In order for the On-Screen Keyboard to enter characters into an application, that application must be active and its window must have the *focus* — it must be the window that is currently receiving keystrokes. You can make certain that a window has the focus by clicking anywhere within the window.

③ Optionally, select Settings ⇨ Typing Mode to adjust the typing method.

④ Select the typing mode as appropriate for your needs.

⑤ If you select hover mode, choose the hover time interval before characters are selected.

⑥ Click the OK button.

⑦ Click the Close to close On-Screen Keyboard.

FIND IT ONLINE

Visit the Web Access Project online at **http://www.wgbh.org/wgbh/pages/ncam/ webaccess/index.html** to learn about additional accessibility options.

Using the Utility Manager

The Utility Manager functions as a control center for the accessibility tools. With the Utility Manager you can easily control the status of any of these tools.

The accessibility tools wouldn't be of much help to anyone if they were cumbersome to start and use. The Utility Manager makes the process a bit easier by enabling you to automatically start any of the accessibility tools that you might need whenever Windows 2000 starts. For each tool you can also choose to load the tool but to have it remain inactive until you need it. In addition, the Utility Manager allows you to pause any of the tools without removing it from memory. This enables you to restart a paused tool with one click rather than by wading through several levels of the Start menu.

By default, the Utility Manager automatically loads the Magnifier and the Narrator. If you have system administrator access rights, you can also add the On-Screen Keyboard to the list.

Each item that is loaded by the Utility Manager has several options. To select the options for any item, you must open Utility Manager and select the item that you wish to control. Then you can choose to start or stop the selected tool while leaving it loaded in memory using the Start and Stop buttons. You can also choose to load a selected tool into memory when Windows 2000 starts or when the Utility Manager is started.

Because the Utility Manager has no menus, you can only add the On-Screen Keyboard to the Utility Manager using the File ➪ Add to Utility Manager com-

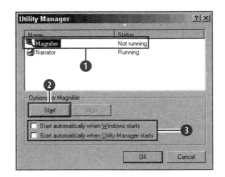

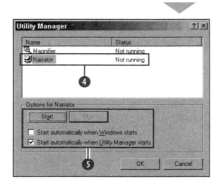

▶ Select Programs ➪ Accessories ➪ Accessibility ➪ Utility Manager from the Start menu.

❶ Select the accessibility tool you wish to modify.

❷ Click Start to run the tool.

❸ Optionally, select the start up options for the selected tool.

❹ Select a different tool to modify its status.

❺ Select the options you want for this tool.

CROSS-REFERENCE

See "Starting Programs Automatically" in Chapter 4.

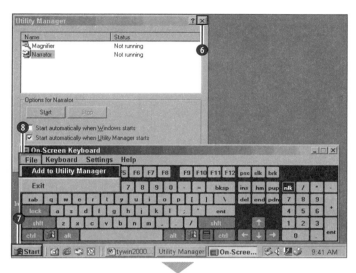

mand on the On-Screen Keyboard as shown in the third figure on the facing page. You must also use the On-Screen Keyboard File menu to remove the On-Screen Keyboard from the Utility Manager if it is no longer needed. You cannot add other programs to the Utility Manager — Magnifier, Narrator, and On-Screen Keyboard are the only three options that can be used with the Utility Manager.

TAKE NOTE

WINDOWS 2000 SERVICES

Windows 2000 loads many different tasks into memory as *services*. These are essentially processes that your PC can perform without necessarily having an application appear on your Taskbar. When the Utility Manager loads some of the accessibility tools at system startup but does not automatically run those tools, the loaded tools could be thought of as services that are loaded but not running. This status makes starting the tools quick and easy whenever they are needed.

USE THE SHORTCUT KEY

The fastest way to start the Utility Manager is to press the Windows key and the letter U at the same time. This key combination can be considerably faster than navigating through the Start menu.

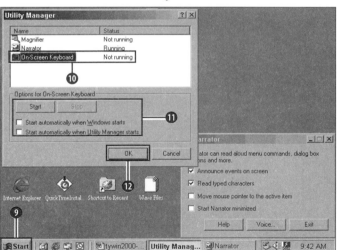

⑥ *Click the Close button to close Utility Manager.*

⑦ *Click the Start button and select Programs ➪ Accessories ➪ Accessibility ➪ On-Screen Keyboard.*

⑧ *Optionally, select File ➪ Add to Utility Manager.*

⑨ *Select Programs ➪ Accessories ➪ Accessibility ➪ Utility Manager from the Start menu.*

⑩ *Select On-Screen Keyboard.*

⑪ *Choose the desired options for On-Screen Keyboard.*

⑫ *Click OK to complete the task.*

FIND IT ONLINE

Visit **http://www.microsoft.com/enable/news/default.htm** for information on accessibility news and events.

Changing the Accessibility Settings

Although they aren't shown on the Programs ⇨ Accessories ⇨ Accessibility menu, Windows 2000 includes a number of additional capabilities that are designed to help people who need a bit of extra assistance using a PC. In this section, you will learn about these additional options and how to configure them so they provide the utility you need.

The additional accessibility options include a number of useful tools. The figures on the facing page show how to configure the keyboard-related accessibility options. The remaining options are covered in detail on the following two pages.

StickyKeys enables a user to simulate the use of the Shift, Ctrl, and Alt keys in combination with another key. These keys are also known as *modifier keys*. When StickyKeys is active, you can first press Shift, Ctrl, or Alt, release it, and then press the next key that you would normally have pressed at the same time. For example, rather than hold down Ctrl while you press A, you can press Ctrl, release it, and then press A to accomplish the same task. StickyKeys makes it possible to use the menu shortcuts found in many programs even if you are able to press only one key at a time.

FilterKeys causes Windows 2000 to ignore keys you press in error or keys you hold down so long that they are repeated in error. You can tell Windows 2000 to ignore key repeat. In this way, no matter how long a key is held down it won't repeat. You can also choose to have Windows 2000 ignore repeated pressing of the same key unless there is a delay between pressing the keys.

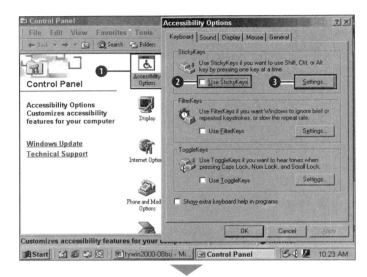

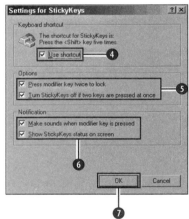

▶ Select Setting ⇨ Control Panel from the Start menu.

❶ Double-click the Accessibility Options icon.

❷ Click the Use StickyKeys check box to enable this option.

❸ Click here to configure StickyKeys.

❹ Click here to enable the shortcut.

❺ Select the desired StickyKeys options.

❻ Select the desired notification methods.

❼ Click OK to close the dialog box.

CROSS-REFERENCE

See "Using the On-Screen Keyboard" earlier in this chapter.

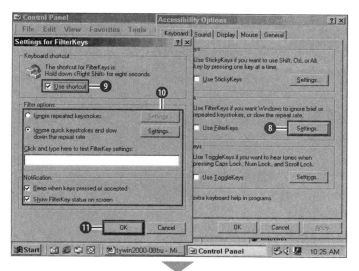

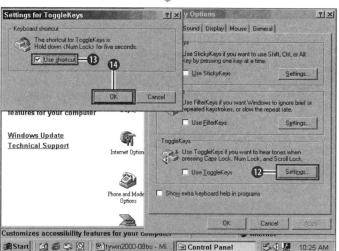

StickyKeys and FilterKeys can be a help to someone who has limited mobility or who types using a touch stick.

ToggleKeys plays sounds when the Caps Lock, Num Lock, or Scroll Lock keys are pressed. These keys can have an adverse effect on the way your PC operates, but if you have limited vision you might not realize that you had pressed them in error.

Continued

Continued

TAKE NOTE

▶ **USING THE SHORTCUTS**

The keyboard accessibility options use shortcuts to turn on the options. The figures on the facing page show the shortcuts, such as pressing Shift five times to turn on the StickyKeys option.

▶ **OFFER SOME ASSISTANCE**

If you assist someone who needs the accessibility options, be sure to take the time to fine-tune the settings to meet his or her needs. It may not occur to them to ask for assistance in adjusting these options for optimal performance, but a few extra minutes of setup time will pay many dividends. Be sure the user understands the full range of tools that Windows 2000 provides.

8 *Click here to configure FilterKeys.*

9 *Click here to enable the shortcut.*

10 *Select the FilterKeys options.*

11 *Click OK to close the dialog box.*

12 *Click here to configure ToggleKeys.*

13 *Click here to enable the shortcut.*

14 *Click OK to close the dialog box.*

FIND IT ONLINE

Visit the Accessibility Aids catalog at
**http://www.microsoft.com/enable/products/
aids.htm.**

Changing the Accessibility Settings

Continued

In addition to the keyboard options, these extra accessibility options include a number of other tools for making your PC easier to use. The figures on the facing page provide a quick look at the extent of these additional options.

The sound options are designed to assist Windows 2000 users who have a hearing impairment. These options supplement the sounds that Windows 2000 normally uses to advise you of system events. Rather than simply playing a sound, when you activate *SoundSentry*, Windows 2000 will flash the title bar or window border to alert you of the event. *ShowSounds* displays text captions in addition to audible messages from your programs.

The display options use high-contrast color schemes to make the screen easier to read. You can choose the color scheme that is the easiest to read; the default high-contrast color scheme displays white lettering on a black background.

Users who have difficulty using a mouse may find that the *MouseKeys* option makes life simpler. When you enable this option you can use the arrow keys on your numeric keypad to move the mouse pointer. To make the MouseKeys pointer work more like a real mouse pointer, you can press and hold Ctrl to speed up the movement or Shift to slow down the movement.

On the General options tab shown in the lower right figure on the facing page, you'll find the option to allow the accessibility features to expire if they aren't used for a period of time. Because the accessibility options can be confusing to users who aren't familiar with them or who don't expect them, this option makes it easier to share a PC in which the accessibility options have been activated. You can set the accessibility features to turn off after 5 to 30 minutes.

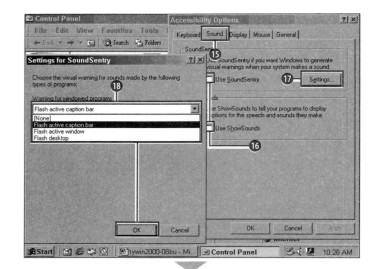

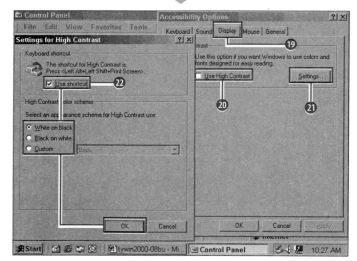

⑮ *Click the Sound tab.*

⑯ *Select the sound options you wish to enable.*

⑰ *Click here to configure SoundSentry.*

⑱ *Configure SoundSentry, and then click OK.*

⑲ *Click the Display tab.*

⑳ *Click here to enable the high-contrast display.*

㉑ *Click here to configure the high-contrast settings.*

㉒ *Select the options and click OK.*

CROSS-REFERENCE

See "Using the Accessibility Wizard" earlier in this chapter.

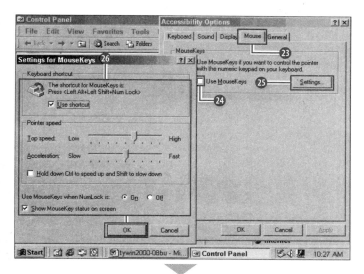

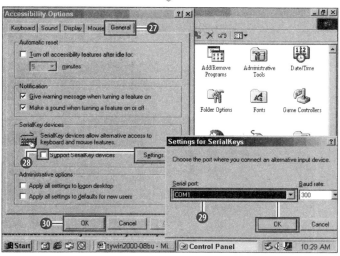

TAKE NOTE

USING VOICE ACTIVATION

Although we normally think of the keyboard as the way to input information into a computer, voice recognition is an alternative that may assist users who have difficulty using the keyboard. Windows 2000 does not offer any built-in voice recognition capabilities, but modern PCs are powerful enough to allow voice recognition software to do a creditable job. Dragon System's NaturallySpeaking (**http://www.dragonsys.com/**) is one example of this type of software that seems to work well, especially when used with the included high-quality headset.

KEYBOARD ALTERNATIVES

Users who cannot use a standard keyboard or mouse can still use a Windows 2000-based PC. *SerialKey* devices connect to the PC's serial port and allow the user to communicate with the system using specially adapted devices. For example, the Eyegaze device enables a user to interact with the computer completely through eye movements. Many other devices are available. See **http://www.lctinc.com/doc/egwin95.htm** for information on the Eyegaze system.

㉓ *Click the Mouse tab.*

㉔ *Click here to enable MouseKeys.*

㉕ *Click here to configure MouseKeys.*

㉖ *Select the options and click OK.*

㉗ *Click the General tab.*

㉘ *Select the check box to enable SerialKey devices, and click the Settings button to configure your device.*

㉙ *Select the options and click OK.*

㉚ *Click OK to complete the task.*

FIND IT ONLINE

For more documentation on configuring accessibility options, see **http://www.microsoft.com/enable/products/windocs.htm**.

Personal Workbook

Q&A

1 Where do you go to add the On-Screen Keyboard to the Utility Manager?

_____

_____

_____

2 What tool do you use to view screen contents at up to nine times normal size?

_____

_____

_____

3 What tool do you use to listen to dialog boxes?

_____

_____

_____

4 How can you make it possible to press the Shift, Ctrl, or Alt key first and then a second key without holding down the first key?

_____

_____

_____

5 How can you make Windows 2000 ignore keys that are held down too long?

_____

_____

_____

6 What option can you use to flash a window when Windows 2000 plays a sound?

_____

_____

_____

7 How can you make it possible to use the keyboard to move the mouse pointer?

_____

_____

_____

8 What tool can you use to control when the Magnifier, Narrator, and On-Screen Keyboard start?

_____

_____

_____

ANSWERS: PAGE 393

EXTRA PRACTICE

1 Open the Magnifier and set the power to 3.

2 Move the Magnifier into a floating window at the lower right edge of your screen.

3 Open Notepad and use the Narrator to vocalize the Edit menu.

4 Enable StickyKeys and practice pressing one key at a time.

5 Use SoundSentry to give you a visual warning when Windows 2000 plays sounds.

6 Set the accessibility options to turn off after 10 minutes.

REAL-WORLD APPLICATIONS

✔ You broke your arm skiing and find that it is quite difficult to type using one hand. You use the accessibility options to make the process a little easier.

✔ You need to help an elderly relative who has impaired vision create a record of your family tree. You use the Magnifier to help them read the details as you enter them.

✔ You need to use your PC to take notes during an important board meeting but don't want to disturb the board members. You disconnect your speakers and use ShowSounds and SoundSentry to provide visual clues.

Visual Quiz

How can you display a window like this one? Why does it show 4 in the spin box?

_____

_____

_____

_____

_____

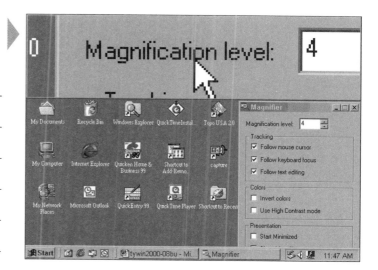

Contents of 'Desktop'

Name

My Computer

Network Neigh

Internet Explore

Microsoft Outlook

Recycle Bin

My Briefcase

3252-9

3259-6

3261-8

3262-6

3281-2

3286-3

DE Phone List

Device Manager

In

Iomega Tools

PART

III

Using the Internet

The Internet is by far the biggest change that has occurred in the computing world in the past ten years. Now it seems like everyone is using the Internet for research, e-mail, or just plain recreation. Windows 2000 has the capabilities to enable you to do what you want on the Internet. Windows 2000 is so Internet-integrated that you may discover that it is sometimes hard to know where your computer ends and the Internet begins!

In this part, you'll learn how to use Windows 2000 to browse the Internet and find Web sites that are important to you. You'll learn how to send and receive e-mail, and how you can access areas of the Internet that remain hidden to people who only use a Web browser.

CHAPTER 9

Connecting to the Internet and the World Wide Web

The Internet is a fascinating place. You could easily set out to research one subject on the Internet and end up spending hundreds of hours going off in different directions finding all sorts of interesting material. With millions of unique places to visit, the Internet almost cannot be described in mere words!

When most people today talk about the Internet, what they are really referring to is that part of the Internet that is known as the World Wide Web. The Web is the graphical portion of the Internet that is connected by millions upon millions of *links*—which are the addresses of other pages that you can visit by clicking the link.

To access the Internet you need a way to connect to it. An *Internet Service Provider*—ISP—provides this access for most people. If you do not already have Internet access, you'll want to refer to Chapter 7 before you begin this chapter. There you will find the information that you need to set up your Internet access account.

When you are browsing the Internet you are viewing *Web pages*. In most instances several Web pages are linked together to form a Web *site*. Web pages can contain text, graphics, sounds, and many other elements that provide visitors with a colorful and often quite entertaining view of the information that is being presented.

In Windows 2000 you don't need to look very far to find the software that you need to view all of these Web pages. Internet Explorer is a *Web browser* that is very tightly integrated into the Windows 2000 interface. In fact, you'll soon discover that when you're working in Windows 2000 you can browse the Web just about as easily as you can browse your own computer or your local network. In some cases browsing the Web may even be easier!

As you read through this chapter, keep in mind that the Internet is constantly changing and evolving. Web sites come and go. Links that worked perfectly well this morning may be history by this afternoon. If an interesting-looking site seems to have disappeared, there will probably be another site that's just as interesting if you spend a few minutes looking for it. Keep your sense of adventure and you'll be rewarded with all sorts of interesting treats.

Using Internet Explorer

Web pages are documents that are created using *HTML* — HyperText Markup Language. A Web browser such as Internet Explorer is a program that understands how to convert the HTML code into the graphical images that is represented by that code. Fortunately, you don't have to understand anything about HTML to use Internet Explorer. All you have to do is to start the program and point it in the right direction.

There are several methods that you can use to start Internet Explorer. The figures on the facing page show the most common ones, but you can also start Internet Explorer in other ways, too. For example, if you click a Web page address link that appears in an e-mail message, Internet Explorer will likely open automatically so that you can view the Web page.

While you are surfing the Web, you're likely to do most things by clicking links or Internet Explorer toolbar buttons. Still, as the figures on the facing page show, you can do a lot using the Internet Explorer menus. As an example, you can click the Print button to print the currently displayed Web page using the default printer settings. But if you wish to change any of the defaults, you'll want to use the File ➪ Print command.

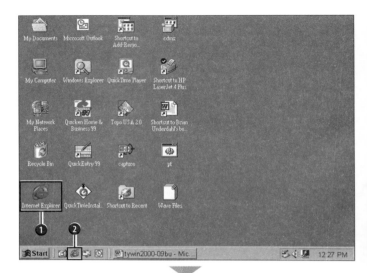

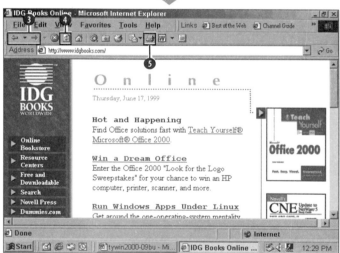

1 Double-click the Internet Explorer icon on your desktop.

2 Alternatively, click the Internet Explorer icon in the Quick Launch toolbar.

3 Click the Back and Forward buttons to return to pages that you have just visited.

4 If the page does not load correctly, try clicking the Refresh button to reload the page.

5 If you want to print the page using the default settings, click the Print button.

CROSS-REFERENCE

See "Saving Your Favorite Web Sites" later in this chapter.

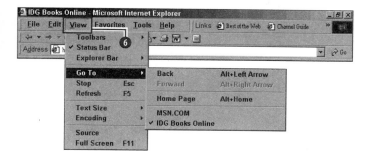

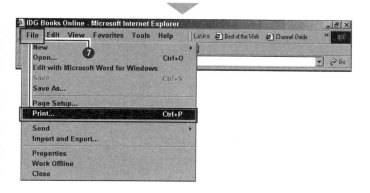

CLEAN UP YOUR SCREEN

A large portion of the Internet Explorer window can easily be used up by elements such as the menu, the toolbars, and the status bar. This can make it difficult to view very much of a Web page — especially if your display is set to a low-resolution setting such as 640 × 480. There are several things that you can do to increase the area that is used to display Web pages. You can drag the toolbars to new locations using the handle at the left edge of each toolbar. You can stack more than one toolbar on the same row. You can even use the View menu options to remove some of these elements from the screen.

USE THE ADDRESS TOOLBAR

When you click one of the Internet Explorer icons, Internet Explorer will attempt to open your default home page. From there you can click links or manually enter an address to go to the Web page that you really wanted to visit. A more direct route to a Web page is to right-click the Windows 2000 Taskbar and choose Toolbars ⇨ Address from the context menu. This will place an address box on the Taskbar. If you enter a Web page address into this box and press Enter, Internet Explorer will go directly to that page without first loading your home page. You can close the Address toolbar once the page begins loading.

⑥ *Open the View menu to select view options to suit your needs.*

⑦ *If you want to print the page and control the settings, select File ⇨ Print.*

FIND IT ONLINE

Learn Internet Explorer tips and tricks at
http://www.activewin.com/ie/ie5/tips/index.shtml.

Visiting Web Sites

Every Web page has an address that is used to locate the page. That address is called the *Uniform Resource Locator* or URL. When you click a link or enter an address manually in the Address toolbar, Internet Explorer uses that address to send out a request across the Internet for a copy of the associated document file.

A URL typically consists of a protocol identifier, the domain or server name where the page can be found, and sometimes directory and file names. For Web pages, the most common protocol identifiers are http:// for standard pages and https:// for pages on secure servers. A typical server name looks like this — www.idgbooks.com (although not all Web servers include the www portion of the address). If directory and file names are used, they are separated from each other and the server name with slashes, and they indicate specific documents that Internet Explorer should attempt to open. If no directory and file names are used, the server will send the default page (which is often index.html).

Certain Web pages may take a long time to load. This can be caused by overloaded servers or simply by a Web page that is very large and includes a lot of text and graphics. While Internet Explorer is waiting for a page to complete loading, it displays a progress bar in the status bar. To stop trying to load a slow page any further, click the Stop button. You may wish to try clicking the Refresh button after you click Stop. Sometimes a second request to load a page goes considerably faster — especially if loading the page seemed to be stalled the first time.

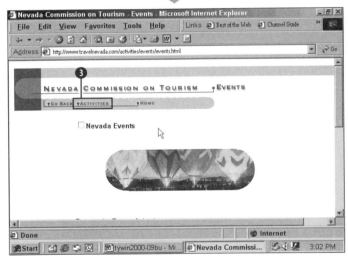

① Enter the address of a Web page that you wish to visit.

② Alternatively, click a link to visit a new page.

③ Click another link to view a different page.

CROSS-REFERENCE

See "Searching for Web Sites" later in this chapter.

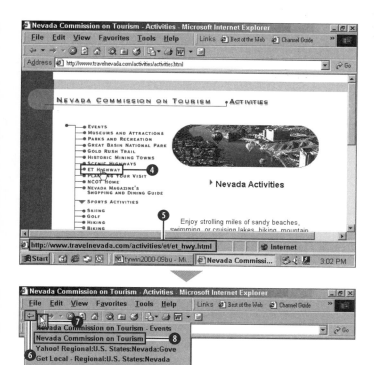

TAKE NOTE

UNDERSTANDING LINKS

A *link* is text or a graphic on a page that, when you click it, causes the browser to request the new page (represented by the link) from the server. Links can be underlined text, graphical representations of buttons or banners, or anything else the page designer chooses. When you move the mouse cursor across a link, the cursor changes to a pointing finger, and the URL is displayed. Most Web pages include links you can click to view related pages. Often, you'll find that those links will take you to interesting sites you probably would not have found on your own.

RETURN TO PREVIOUS PAGES

After you've visited several Web pages, you may find yourself wanting to return to a page that is several pages before the current one. Click the down arrow next to the Back button to display a list of recently visited pages. Choose the page you want from the list. If the page you want has scrolled off the list, click the History button to display the complete list of pages that you have visited.

④ *Move the mouse pointer over a link to view the link's address.*

⑤ *When the pointer changes to a hand, view the link address here.*

⑥ *Click the Back button to return to the preceding page.*

⑦ *Alternatively, click the down arrow to view the list of recently visited pages.*

⑧ *Click a page to return to that page.*

FIND IT ONLINE

See **http://computingcentral.msn.com/topics/ bandwidth/speedtest50.asp** to test your Internet connection speed.

Searching for Web Sites

The Web has millions of pages that cover almost any imaginable topic. Locating Web sites that contain the information you're looking for would be virtually impossible if there weren't an easy way to search for them. Fortunately, there are special services that you can use to search for Web sites. These services are called *search engines*, and they index Web pages so you can find what you need.

Most of the search engines are free, although you will see advertisements on almost all of them. Search engines often use *keywords* to find sites of interest. A few search engines examine the complete text on each Web page to find those sites that match your search goals.

To find Web sites you enter a *search string*— one or more words that should define the content of the Web sites you'd like to see. Most search engines treat each word in a search string as a separate phrase, so a search for *Nevada tours* would find sites that relate to Nevada and sites that relate to tours. One way around this is to enclose the search phrase in quotation marks, as in "Nevada tours" — most search engines will then find only sites where the two words appear together.

Placing your search string in quotation marks may not always produce the desired results. If you wanted to find Web sites that mentioned both Nevada and tours but didn't necessarily have the two words directly together, you would need to use a different technique. Most search engines allow some type of *Boolean* search techniques so that you can search for sites that include both words somewhere on the page. In this case you might specify your search string as *Nevada AND tours*— with the word *AND* in all capital letters. Read the "Take Note" section for more information about using advanced search techniques.

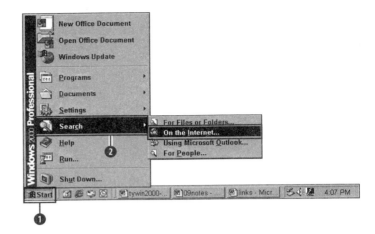

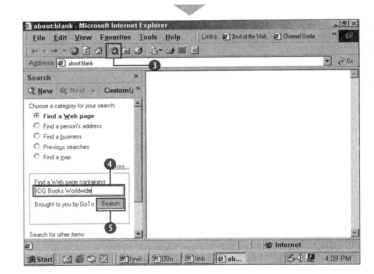

1. Click the Start button.
2. Select Search ⇨ On the Internet.
3. Alternatively, click the Search button if Internet Explorer is already open.
4. Type your search phrase in the text box.
5. Click the Search button to begin the search.

CROSS-REFERENCE

See Chapter 6 for more information on finding files on your computer.

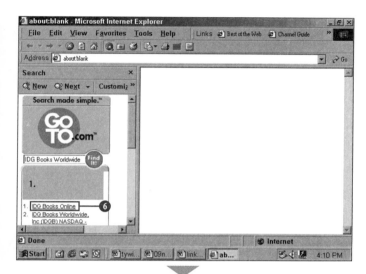

TAKE NOTE

▶ REFINE YOUR RESULTS

If your search doesn't produce the desired results, consider using some advanced search techniques. Most search engines offer advanced methods of searching for Web sites. These advanced methods enable you to refine your search by specifically including or excluding multiple words or phrases in the search string. To access the advanced search capabilities, look for a button labeled "Advanced Search" or something similar.

▶ TRY ANOTHER SEARCH ENGINE

If the first search engine that you try either produces no results or includes so many matches that you couldn't possibly visit all of them, try a different search engine. Different search engines often produce quite different results. Each search engine uses somewhat different methods of categorizing Web sites, so you'll likely find that only some of them produce the results you want. You may want to compare the results from several different search engines.

⑥ *Click a link that appears to meet your needs.*

⑦ *Click the Close button to close the Search bar and maximize the browser window.*

⑧ *Alternatively, click another link to see if the site has the information you were looking for.*

FIND IT ONLINE

To download a tool that allows you to use 32 search engines at once, see **http://computingcentral.msn. com/topics/ie4/dbdetails.asp?downloadID=44631**.

Saving Your Favorite Web Sites

After you've been browsing the Web for some time, you'll likely discover that certain Web sites have become favorites that you return to quite often. Internet Explorer makes it easy to keep track of those sites so that you can return to them with just a few clicks.

If you have spent any time on the Web, you have probably discovered that URLs can be a little complicated to type correctly. And because even the slightest typing error prevents Internet Explorer from finding the correct page, being able to eliminate the possibility of those errors can be a real boon.

Internet Explorer offers two different options for saving your favorite Web sites. You can choose to simply save the URL or to save the entire page. If you choose to save only the URL, Internet Explorer will attempt to load the page from the Internet whenever you click the saved link. If you choose to save the entire page for offline viewing, Internet Explorer will display the saved page without attempting to load it from the Internet. In most cases, it makes the most sense to simply save the URL so that you can always be sure of viewing any updated content. However, if a page contains valuable information that you don't want to risk losing, save the page for offline viewing.

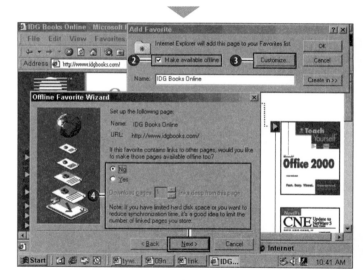

▶ If necessary, open a Web page that you wish to add to your list of favorite sites.

❶ Select Favorites ⇨ Add to Favorites.

❷ Optionally, click here to make the page available offline.

❸ If you wish to change the storage options, click Customize.

▶ If the introductory page appears, click Next to continue.

❹ Select the link level options you prefer and click Next to continue.

CROSS-REFERENCE

See "Sending E-mail and Files" in Chapter 10.

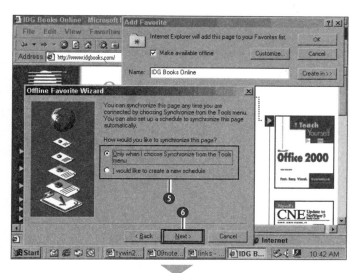

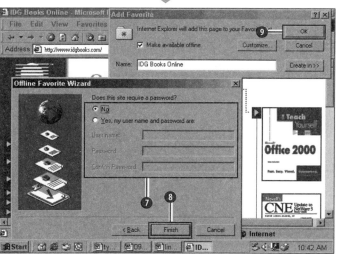

CHANGE IS CONSTANT

On the Internet, change is the one constant that you can depend on. Your favorite Web pages can disappear as quickly as they appeared in the first place. If you attempt to visit one of the Web sites you saved in your favorites list but you see only a message that the page cannot be found, it's likely that it has moved or no longer exists. Before you decide to delete the link, however, you may want to try the link later to see whether the problem was only temporary.

OFFLINE VIEWING

If you choose to make a Web page available for offline viewing, Internet Explorer stores the entire page on your hard disk. This procedure enables you to view the page again without first connecting to the Internet. This option also enables you to specify how many additional levels of linked pages to store. Saving the linked pages makes them available offline too, but can use considerable disk space — especially if you choose to store more than one level of links. For example, if the page that you are saving is linked to ten other pages and each of them links to ten more pages, you'll actually be downloading and storing over 100 pages if you choose to save two link levels. Rather than storing the linked pages, you can click the links on the stored page to open your Internet connection and view the linked pages online.

⑤ Choose the options for updating the page.

⑥ Click Next to continue.

⑦ If necessary, enter the correct password options.

⑧ Click Finish to continue.

⑨ Click OK to complete the task.

FIND IT ONLINE

See the Safe Computing Forum's newsgroups at **http://computingcentral.msn.com/topics/ safecomputing/newsgroups.asp**.

Organizing Your Favorites

If you save a lot of favorite Web sites, you'll soon discover a small problem. The Favorites list can easily become so full that finding the site that you want is almost more work than simply re-entering the URL in the Internet Explorer Address toolbar.

Organizing your list of favorite Web sites isn't a whole lot different from organizing your My Documents folder. Just as you can organize your documents by creating extra folders under the My Documents folder, you can also organize your favorite Web sites by creating new folders. In addition, you can move, rename, or delete favorite links.

In Windows 2000 you use the Organize Favorites dialog box to modify the favorites list. Although you can use Windows Explorer to modify the list, you'll find that the Organize Favorites dialog box makes the process somewhat easier because you don't have to search your hard disk for the correct location.

When you choose Favorites ⇨ Add to Favorites, one of the options in the Add Favorite dialog box is the Create In button. If you have created folders for organizing your favorite Web sites, you can add those links directly to the appropriate folder rather than moving them later.

Once you have organized your favorite Web sites into folders, the Favorites menu will show each folder as a cascading menu. To view one of the saved sites, choose it from the Favorites menu or one of the cascading menus. If you have a lot of favorite Web sites, you can also create folders within folders for even more organization.

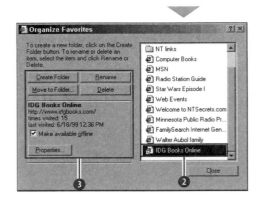

❶ Select Favorites ⇨ Organize Favorites.

❷ To modify an item, first select it.

❸ Select the appropriate options.

CROSS-REFERENCE

See "Organizing Your Documents" in Chapter 5.

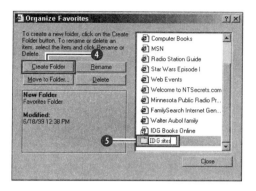

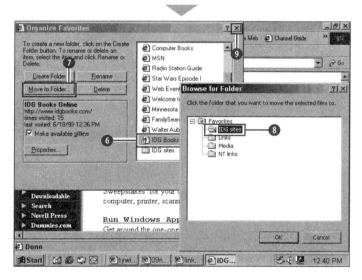

CONTROL OFFLINE PAGES

If you have saved Web pages and selected the *Make available offline* option, you can use the Organize Favorites dialog box to control how those pages are saved and updated. To do so, you click the Properties button when the page is selected in the Organize Favorites dialog box. You can then modify the number of link levels that are stored as well as placing an absolute limit on the disk space that can be used by the selected page and any linked pages that are saved along with it. You might use this option to reduce the number of saved link levels if you discover that updating the page using the Tools ⇨ Synchronize command takes too long to complete.

CREATE RELATED ITEM FOLDERS

When you are organizing your list of favorite Web sites, try to think of ways that the sites you have saved may be related. That way you'll be able to create folders for storing the related items, and using your Favorites list will be much easier. For example, if you frequently visit a number of pages at the IDG Books Worldwide Web site, you might keep all of those links organized in a folder called IDG sites.

④ To create a folder, click the Create Folder button.

⑤ Enter a name for the new folder.

⑥ To move an item, first select it.

⑦ Click the Move to Folder button.

⑧ Choose the destination folder and click OK.

⑨ Click the Close button to complete the task.

FIND IT ONLINE

See the **http://computingcentral.msn.com/topics/ie4/questions.asp** for answers to common questions about Internet Explorer.

Configuring Internet Explorer

You can change almost any aspect of how Internet Explorer functions using the extensive set of options that are available in the Internet Options dialog box. The figures on the facing page and the following two pages give you some idea of how many different items you can modify to make Internet Explorer work the way you like.

It is not possible to go into very much detail about the Internet Explorer options in the limited space that is available, so you should try to examine those options on your own. For example, you might want to use the Colors, Fonts, and Accessibility options to make your Web browsing a little easier if you have difficulty seeing Web page content.

The final figure on the facing page shows the Security tab of the Internet Options dialog box. You can use the options on this tab to make certain that your computer is not damaged by content that is sent by the Web sites that you visit. By default, sites on the Internet are assigned to the Internet zone, which really only offers minimal security. If you visit sites that you feel you cannot trust, add them to the Restricted Sites list. When you choose one of the zones other than the Internet zone, you can click the Sites button to specify sites that belong in the selected zone. One of the side benefits of placing sites in the Restricted Sites zone is that *cookies* are disabled when the security level is set to high, as it is for this zone.

Continued

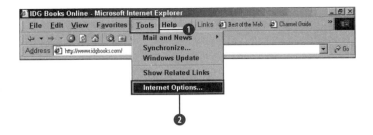

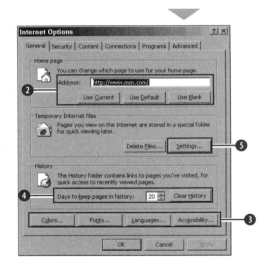

❶ Select Tools ⇨ Internet Options.

❷ Select the Internet Explorer start page options.

❸ Alternatively, use these buttons to control the appearance options.

❹ Use these options to control how long links remain in the History folder.

❺ Click Settings if you wish to adjust the temporary file options.

CROSS-REFERENCE

See "Visiting Web Sites" earlier in this chapter.

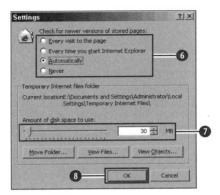

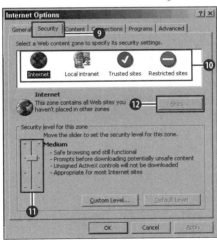

SET YOUR OWN START PAGE

You can choose any page that you prefer as the page that is loaded when you start Internet Explorer. If you choose a page that is located on your PC rather than a page on the Web, Internet Explorer will immediately load your selected page instead of first attempting to log on to the Internet. This choice might be useful if you create your own HTML page that includes links to both Web pages and local documents. You can also choose the Use Blank option to load a blank page when Internet Explorer starts — this will also prevent Internet Explorer from always starting your Internet connection when Internet Explorer loads.

CONTROL YOUR DISK SPACE

Whenever you visit a Web site, Internet Explorer stores information on your hard disk. This information consists of two elements: content from pages, so that those pages can be reloaded faster in the future, and the history list that logs all of the URLs that you have visited over a specified period of time. You can use the options on the General tab of the Internet Options dialog box to control how much disk space is used by these items.

⑥ If you wish to change the update options, choose the update frequency.

⑦ To control the amount of space used by temporary files, use these options.

⑧ Click OK to continue.

⑨ Click the Security tab.

⑩ Choose the zone to adjust.

⑪ Select the security level for the selected zone.

⑫ Click the Sites button to add sites to a security zone.

FIND IT ONLINE

See **http://www.wizsys.com/** to download TweakIE, a program designed to customize Internet Explorer.

Configuring Internet Explorer
Continued

The previous two pages showed the first of the Internet Explorer options that you could customize. There are many more options that you can change to suit your exact needs. The figures on the facing page show you how to access these additional items.

You can use the Content Advisor to control the types of Web sites that can be visited on your PC. This option enables you to restrict access to sites that you find offensive. See the "Take Note" items for information on the remaining Content tab options.

The Connections tab enables you to configure the way you connect to the Internet. One of the options on this tab — LAN Settings — can be used to enable other computers on your network to share your Internet connection.

You use the Programs tab to specify which application programs Internet Explorer should use for various tasks. Often you may find that there are several different programs installed on your system that can serve some of these functions. This tab enables you to select the programs you prefer.

The Advanced tab has many different options that you can use to fine-tune Internet Explorer. Although many of these options are pretty much self-explanatory, some of them will require a little extra explanation if you are to understand their true purpose. The best way to determine what each option does is to click the question mark icon near the upper-right corner of the Internet Options dialog box and then click the item that you want explained. When you do, Windows 2000 will display a pop-up message that describes the option's purpose. If you still aren't positive about the best choice after reading an option's pop-up help message, it's probably safest to leave the option set to the default value.

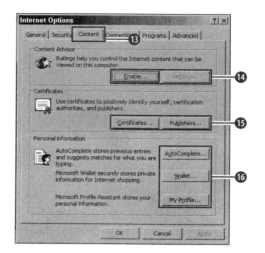

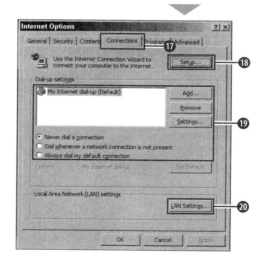

⑬ *Click the Content tab.*

⑭ *If you wish to restrict Web content that can be viewed, use the Content Advisor options.*

⑮ *To obtain a certificate or view existing certificates, use these options.*

⑯ *Use these options if you want to change your personal information settings.*

⑰ *Click the Connections tab.*

⑱ *To create a new Internet connection, click the Setup button.*

⑲ *Use these options to adjust your existing connection.*

⑳ *If you want to adjust your network settings, click LAN Settings.*

CROSS-REFERENCE

See Chapter 12 for information on changing the appearance of Windows 2000.

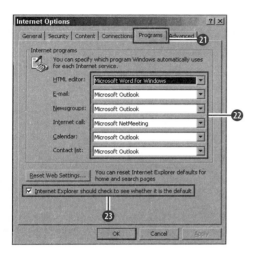

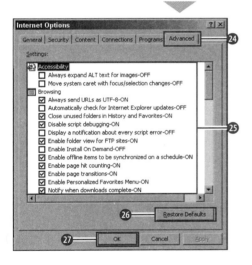

ABOUT CERTIFICATES

Certificates are electronic identity codes that provide positive identification of people and content on the Internet. You can obtain a free or low-cost personal certificate from one of the *certificate authorities* by clicking the Certificates button and following the instructions. Having a personal certificate means that people with whom you exchange e-mail messages can be certain that messages actually were sent by you, and are therefore safe to open. In addition, commercial certificates often sign files that are provided for download from various Web sites. If you trust the company who holds the certificate you should feel confident that a signed file is safe to download.

USING WALLETS

Microsoft Wallet is a security feature that enables you to store your personal and credit card information safely on your PC. You can then authorize the sending of that information to Web sites as necessary. The information in the Wallet is password protected and encrypted to prevent unauthorized use of the information.

㉑ *Click the Programs tab.*

㉒ *If you wish to select a different program for one of these tasks, select it from the list boxes.*

㉓ *If you sometimes use a Web browser other than Internet Explorer, select this check box.*

㉔ *Click the Advanced tab.*

㉕ *Select the options that suit your needs.*

㉖ *To restore the defaults, click here.*

㉗ *Click the OK button to complete the task.*

FIND IT ONLINE

See the Internet Explorer Forum at
http://computingcentral.msn.com/topics/ie4/.

Personal Workbook

Q&A

1 How can you make certain that a search engine looks for two words that are together?

_____

_____

_____

2 What is a _URL_?

_____

_____

_____

3 What does underlined text on a Web page usually represent?

_____

_____

_____

4 How can you make it possible to view a Web page without reconnecting to the Internet?

_____

_____

_____

5 How can you make certain that a Web page you visit won't send destructive content to your system?

_____

_____

_____

6 What option can you use to restrict which Web sites can be visited by your PC?

_____

_____

_____

7 How can you create folders to store links to related Web sites?

_____

_____

_____

8 What button can you use to return to the last Web page you visited?

_____

_____

_____

ANSWERS: PAGE 394

Connecting to the Internet and the World Wide Web

Visual Quiz

How can you display this dialog box? What do you need to do to display the expanded folder list that is shown? How can you use this dialog box to find out the last time you visited a Web page?

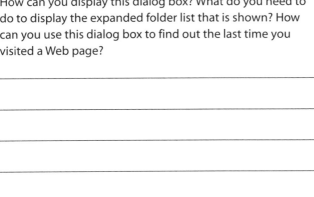

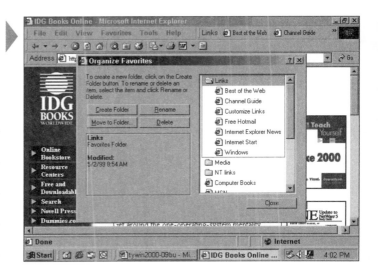

_____

_____

_____

_____

_____

CHAPTER **10**

Using E-mail and News with Outlook Express

Electronic mail, or *e-mail*, is rapidly becoming one of the most popular forms of communication in the world. Using e-mail, you can communicate with people almost anywhere and do so virtually instantly. Someone who receives your message can reply to the message, forward it to someone else, or simply read the message.

Unlike a telephone call, which requires your immediate attention, your e-mail messages are held until you are ready for them. If someone halfway around the world sends you a message, you can read and respond to the message when it is convenient to do so.

When you are ready to receive your e-mail, your system reads all incoming messages from the mail server and moves them into a local inbox in your computer. You can then read, reply to, forward, and file your messages at your convenience.

Newsgroups are gatherings of people on the Internet who discuss topics that interest them. You subscribe to newsgroups and log in to them at your convenience. Newsgroups are organized according to areas of interest, and each group contains so-called *threads,* which are topical sequences of messages. You can initiate a thread on a newsgroup, and you can add your own messages to the threads.

Outlook Express is a program that lets you exchange e-mail with other Internet users and join, read, and post messages to Internet newsgroups. This chapter explains these concepts and describes how to set them up and use them.

When you compose messages or reply to messages that you receive, Outlook Express saves them in your outbox until you are ready to send them. When you connect to the Internet, Outlook Express sends those messages to the mail server, which then forwards them to the intended recipients.

If you want to browse Internet newsgroups, Outlook Express enables you to check out the messages in any of the newsgroups that are available on the news server.

To use Internet mail, you must have an account with a mail server, which your ISP usually provides. To use Internet news, you must have an account with a news server, which your ISP also usually provides. Be sure to set up these accounts before you begin the exercises in this chapter. Your ISP should be able to provide any necessary information.

Creating E-mail Messages

Even if you have another e-mail program, you can use Outlook Express to send and receive e-mail messages that include text, pictures, and other attachments. When you receive messages, you can use Outlook Express to reply to those messages or to forward them to someone else.

The Outlook Express window is customizable, so your view of Outlook Express may not be identical to what is shown on the figures on the facing page. Still, the figures show a fairly typical Outlook Express view. For example, the Folder bar in the upper part of the left pane displays a list of your mail folders. The Inbox folder contains messages that Outlook Express has downloaded into your computer from the mail server. The Outbox folder contains messages that you have composed but that Outlook Express has not yet sent to the mail server. The Sent Items folder contains copies of the e-mail messages that have been sent to the mail server. The Deleted Items folder contains messages that you have deleted from other folders. If you delete messages from the Deleted Items folder, they are gone forever. The Drafts folder is for storing messages that are in progress and that you are not ready to send. The bottom folder is a news server. You will learn what to do with it later in this chapter.

Notice in the figures that folder names sometimes appear in a bold font and are followed by a number in parenthesis. The bold font indicates that the folder contains unread messages, and the number in parentheses specifies how many unread messages are in the folder. Any Outlook Express folder can contain unread messages — if you delete messages without reading them, the Deleted Items folder would show how many unread messages it contained, for example.

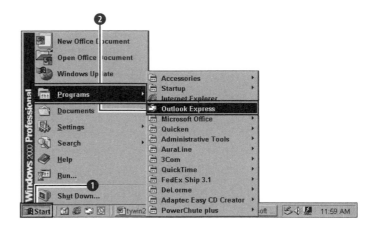

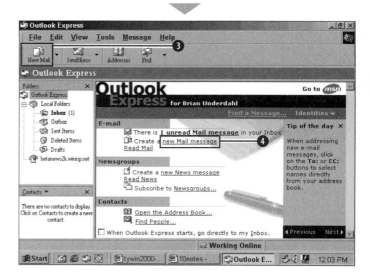

❶ Click the Start button.

❷ Select Programs ➪ Outlook Express.

▶ You may need to confirm whether to make Outlook Express your default e-mail program.

❸ Click the New Mail button to begin composing a new message.

❹ Alternatively, click the new Mail message link.

CROSS-REFERENCE

See "Sending E-mail and Files" later in this chapter.

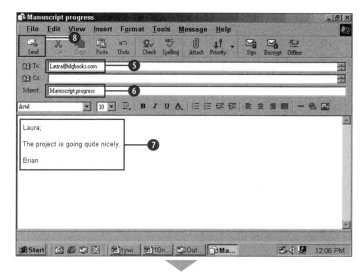

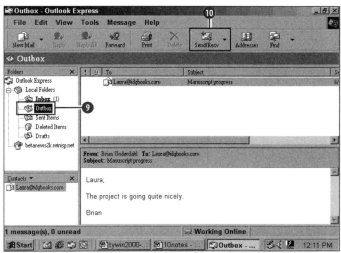

YOU MUST CONNECT TO THE MAIL SERVER

Outlook Express can send and receive e-mail messages only when it is connected to the mail server. You can read existing messages or compose new messages without being connected, but you must connect in order to download new incoming messages or upload new outgoing messages.

BE CAREFUL WITH FORMATTING

Although Outlook Express allows you to format your message just as you would a word processor document, it may not always be safe to assume that the message recipient will see the formatting you've applied. Many people use e-mail software that shows only the text of a message without any formatting. For example, if the message recipient receives their e-mail through AOL, they will not be able to view any formatting that you have applied. If you must include formatting in your message, you may wish to create your message in your favorite word processor and send the message as a file attachment.

⑤ *Enter the recipient's e-mail address in the To box.*

⑥ *Enter a topic in the Subject box.*

⑦ *Enter the text of your message.*

⑧ *Click the Send button to place the new message into your Outbox and close the message editor.*

⑨ *Optionally, click the Outbox folder to view the outbound messages.*

⑩ *Depending on your settings, you may need to click the Send/Recv button to connect to the mail server.*

FIND IT ONLINE

For a free E-mail address see
http://mail.bangkok.com/bangkok/login/login.htm.

Attaching Files to E-mail

Although a simple text note may be all that is needed to put across your message in most cases, you'll probably find that *file attachments* are a handy addition to some e-mail messages. File attachments can be any type of file; word processor document files, spreadsheet files, or graphics images are some typical examples of files that you might send along with an e-mail message.

When you send a file attachment along with an e-mail message, it's always wise to include both a descriptive subject line and a brief message explaining what you have sent. There are several reasons for this. Someone may not be willing to open an unidentified file and risk infecting their system with a computer virus. By adding a personal message, you can offer some reassurance that your file attachment is safe. Also, mail systems sometimes mangle file attachments, so a message telling the recipient what you have sent can make it easier for them to sort out what was received.

When you send file attachments, it's always a good idea to be considerate of the intended recipient. Although you may have a fast Internet connection and may feel that a large graphic image is humorous, if the recipient is connecting via modem or has to pay for connect time, they may not share your sense of humor.

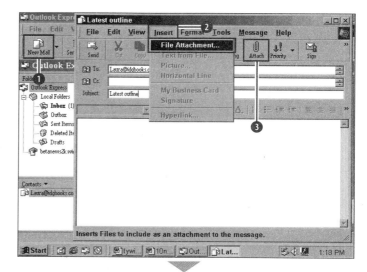

❶ Click the New Mail button.

❷ Select Insert ➪ File Attachment.

❸ Alternatively, click the Attach button.

❹ Select the file location.

CROSS-REFERENCE

See "Creating E-mail Messages" earlier in this chapter.

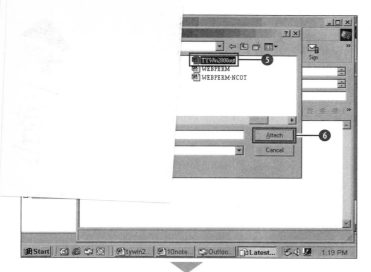

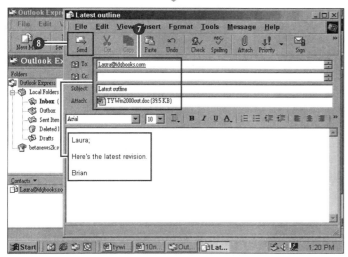

⑤ Select the file you wish to attach.

⑥ Click the Attach button to insert the file into the message.

⑦ Enter the address, subject, and text of your message.

⑧ Click the Send button to complete the task.

▶ Depending on your settings, you may need to confirm that the message will be placed in your Outbox.

FIND IT ONLINE

See **http://www.winzip.com** to download a trial version of WinZip.

Sending E-mail and Files

When you compose an e-mail message, you probably intend for that message to be delivered to the recipient. For the message to be delivered it must be transferred from your Outlook Express Outbox to your mail server so that it can begin its journey across the Internet to the recipient's mailbox.

Depending on how you have configured Outlook Express, you may need to click the Send/Recv button to connect to your mail server. If Outlook Express is configured to check for e-mail automatically, you will not need to initiate the connection yourself unless you would prefer to send and receive any new messages without waiting until the next scheduled connect time.

By default, Outlook Express checks for e-mail every 30 minutes — assuming that Outlook Express is running. You can change this interval or even disable the automatic e-mail checking if you like. Select Tools ⇨ Options to display the Options dialog box. On the General tab, remove the check from the *Check for new messages every xx minute(s)* check box to disable automatic checking. To change the schedule, leave the check box selected and use the spin box to set the new interval. If Outlook Express is not checking for messages automatically, make certain that this option is selected.

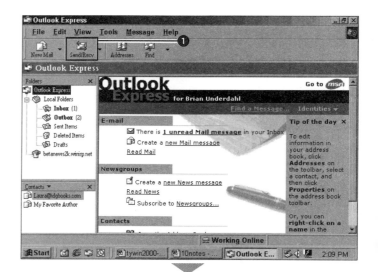

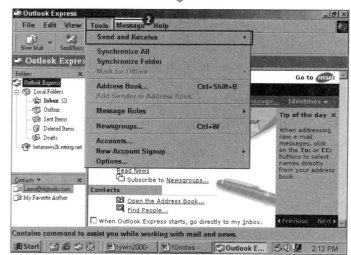

❶ *Click the Send/Recv button.*

❷ *Alternatively, select Tools ⇨ Send and Receive to open the Send and Receive menu.*

CROSS-REFERENCE

See "Reading Your E-mail" later in this chapter.

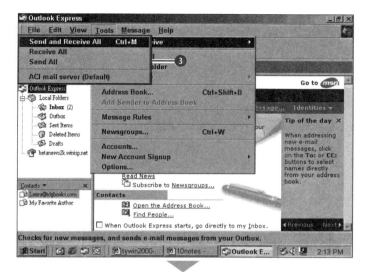

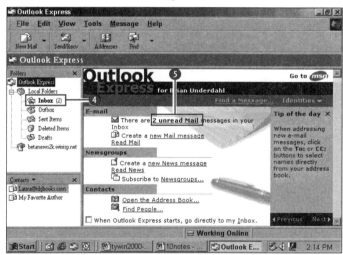

③ *Choose the mail handling option that suits your current needs.*

▶ *You could, for example, choose to receive all new messages without sending your outgoing messages immediately.*

④ *View the number of new messages here — click the Inbox folder icon to open the Inbox.*

⑤ *Alternatively, click this link to open the Inbox.*

TAKE NOTE

▶ CONTROL MESSAGE DELIVERY

By default, Outlook Express automatically attempts to connect to the Internet whenever you place messages in your Outbox. If you'd prefer to hold messages rather than have them sent as soon as you've composed them, select Tools ⇨ Options and click the Send tab. Clear the "Send messages immediately" check box and click OK. You'll need to either send your messages manually or wait until the next scheduled connect time. Holding messages in the Outbox for a few minutes may be a good idea, especially for messages you may wish to reconsider. Once a message has been sent, there's no way to retrieve it — there's no "Unsend" button.

▶ TROUBLESHOOTING PROBLEMS

If Outlook Express seems to be having trouble connecting to your mail server reliably, you may need to do a little troubleshooting. One way to do this is to enable the command logging option. This produces a log file that contains the commands and responses that are sent between your PC and the server. The log file is a text file with the type of server as the filename and log as the extension. For Internet mail this log file is usually pop3.log. To enable logging, select Tools ⇨ Options and click the Maintenance tab. Place a check in the Mail check box in the Troubleshooting section. Your ISP should be able to locate the trouble if you send them a copy of the log file along with a description of the problem you are having.

FIND IT ONLINE

To download a program for mass e-mailings, see **http://www.e-mailworkshop.com/**.

Reading Your E-mail

If you're like most people, you'll probably receive at least as many e-mail messages as you send out. If so, you'll likely want to read and, in some cases, respond to or forward those messages. In addition, you'll need to save any file attachments that you may need for other purposes.

Outlook Express uses a small paper clip icon to show which e-mail messages include attachments. Although you can view the text of a message in the message preview pane that appears in the lower portion of the Outlook Express window, you generally cannot access file attachments without opening the message. Graphics files may appear as part of the message, but most other types of file attachments will appear as icons.

When you open a message that includes a file attachment, the message window includes an Attach box for any file attachments. Each file attachment has its own icon in the Attach box.

After you've opened a message that contains file attachments, you can choose what to do with the attachments. The options vary according to the type of file that is attached, but two options are always available: opening or saving the file. If you choose to open the file, Windows 2000 attempts to determine the file type and use the appropriate method to open the file. If the file is a program, this means that Windows 2000 attempts to run the program. If the file is a data file or a document, Windows 2000 tries to open it in the associated application. If you choose to save the file, Windows 2000 displays the Save Attachment As dialog box. Be sure to note the location where the file is saved so that you can find it later.

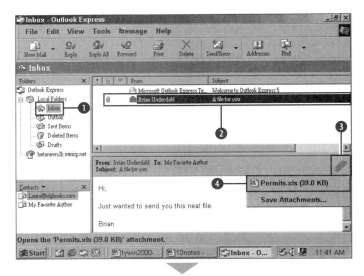

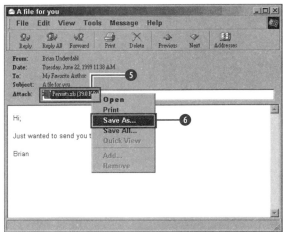

❶ Open the Inbox folder.

❷ Click a message to view in the Preview pane.

❸ If the message contains an attachment, right-click the paperclip icon to display the attachments context menu.

❹ Click here to open the attachment.

▶ Alternatively, double-click the message to open it.

❺ Right-click the attachment to display the context menu.

❻ Select Save As to display the Save Attachment As dialog box.

CROSS-REFERENCE

See "Attaching Files to E-mail" earlier in this chapter.

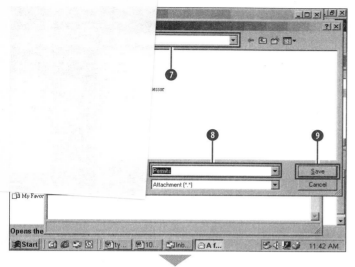

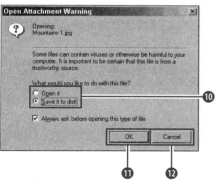

⑦ Select the location to save the file.

⑧ Optionally, specify a name for the file.

⑨ Click the Save button.

⑩ If the Open Attachment Warning dialog box appears, choose to open or save the file.

⑪ Click OK to confirm the action.

⑫ Alternatively, click Cancel to skip opening or saving the file.

FIND IT ONLINE

To learn about viruses see **http://www.icsa.net/ services/consortia/anti-virus/lab.shtml.**

Opening the Newsreader

In the last chapter you learned a little bit about one of the most popular parts of the Internet — the World Wide Web. So far in this chapter you've learned about another of the common uses of the Internet — sending and receiving e-mail messages. Now we'll turn to another useful part of the Internet — Usenet newsgroups. These newsgroups are giant discussion groups in which people from all around the world come together to discuss, argue, and dissect all manner of topics.

The people who frequent newsgroups represent an extremely broad range of personalities. In some newsgroups you'll find experts who can share information that you simply won't be able to find anywhere else. In others you'll find ordinary people who have come together to trade ideas about nearly any esoteric subject you can imagine. In almost any newsgroup you're also likely to run into self-styled "experts" who will do their best to either make you believe their latest conspiracy theory or rake you over the coals if you somehow offend them. To paraphrase an old saying, "let the newsgroup visitor beware" — not all of the information you'll see is quite as reliable as you might hope for.

Before you can use the Outlook Express newsreader, you must set up a news account. Typically your ISP will provide you with the name of their news server and any special information that you might need in order to access the newsgroups.

Continued

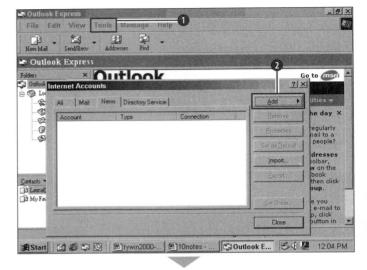

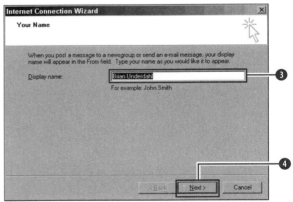

❶ Select Tools ➪ Accounts to open the Internet Accounts dialog box.

❷ Click the Add button and choose News.

❸ Enter the name that you wish to appear on any messages that you post.

❹ Click Next to continue.

CROSS-REFERENCE

See "Finding Newsgroups" later in this chapter.

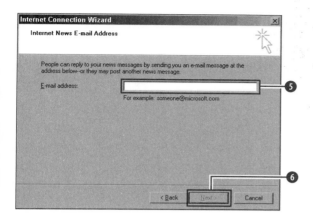

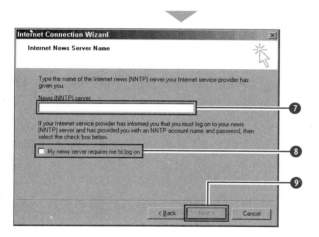

YOU MAY NEED A NEWSGROUP PASSWORD

There are literally thousands of newsgroups on the Internet and many of them cater to very extreme adult tastes. Not all of these newsgroups are suitable for a general audience. Many ISPs limit the range of newsgroups that you can access unless you have specifically requested access to the adult-rated newsgroups. If your ISP has limits on general access to newsgroups, you may need a special logon name and password — which will be provided by your ISP — in order to access the restricted newsgroups.

CONSIDER A SECOND E-MAIL ACCOUNT

One of the biggest problems with posting messages on newsgroups is *spam* — unwanted junk e-mail that can end up clogging your Inbox. Unfortunately, there are all sorts of lowlifes who use special software to scan newsgroups simply to find e-mail addresses. They then flood all of the addresses that they find with bulk e-mail messages advertising everything from get-rich-quick schemes to porno Web sites. In some cases they even sell lists of e-mail addresses to other bulk e-mailers. You may want to open one of the free Web-based e-mail accounts to use only for your newsgroup postings. That way you can close the account and move on to a different one if the spammers get your e-mail address from a newsgroup.

⑤ *Enter the e-mail address that you wish to use for newsgroup purposes.*

⑥ *Click Next to continue.*

⑦ *Enter the name of the newsgroup server as provided by your ISP.*

⑧ *Optionally, click here if you must log on. You will also need to supply a name and password for the news server.*

⑨ *Click Next to continue.*

FIND IT ONLINE

For information on how to conduct research on the Internet, see **http://164.76.4.21/faculty/chew/ internet/research.html.**

Opening the Newsreader
Continued

Once you have set up your newsgroup server account, Outlook Express must download the list of newsgroups that are available on the server. Be prepared to wait several minutes for this process to complete — especially if you have a slow Internet connection. As you will soon discover, there are literally tens of thousands of newsgroups available on the typical newsgroup server. Fortunately you don't have to download the list each time you wish to visit the newsgroups. Outlook Express will keep a record of the existing newsgroups and in the future will only download changes.

Newsgroup messages consist of *message headers* and the actual messages themselves. Message headers are the subject lines, and they are generally descriptive enough to enable you to figure out which messages look interesting enough to read.

When you select a newsgroup so that you can view the messages, Outlook Express doesn't really download all of the messages contained in the newsgroup. Rather it downloads the newest message headers so that you can choose the specific messages that you want to read. By default, Outlook Express downloads up to 300 message headers when you open a newsgroup.

As you browse through the available newsgroups you'll soon notice that most newsgroups contain a large number of messages that are unrelated to the newsgroup topic. Unfortunately, there isn't much you can do to avoid seeing these types of messages. As a rule, the best defense is to simply ignore them. The worst thing you can do is to respond. After the message originator has your e-mail address, you're likely to be buried in unwanted junk e-mail.

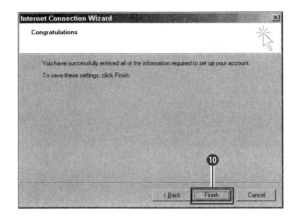

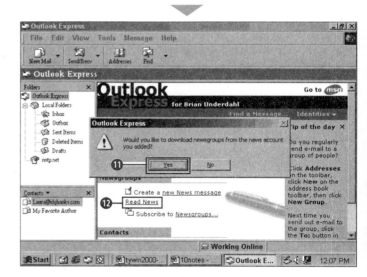

⑩ *Click the Finish button to complete setting up your news account.*

⑪ *Click the Yes button to begin the download of the newsgroup names.*

⑫ *If you did not choose to download the newsgroups earlier, you may need to click the Read News link to begin the download.*

CROSS-REFERENCE

See "Searching for Web Sites" in Chapter 9.

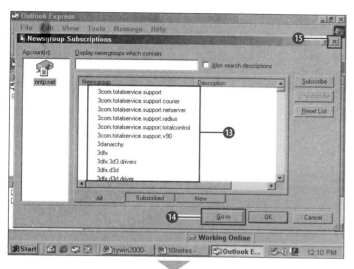

If you like, you have the option to *subscribe* to newsgroups. Subscribing to a newsgroup isn't the same as subscribing to a magazine; you don't pay for a subscription, and you aren't obligated to participate. Subscribing to a newsgroup simply tells Outlook Express that you want the newsgroup to appear in the folder list and that you always want the latest messages from that newsgroup available.

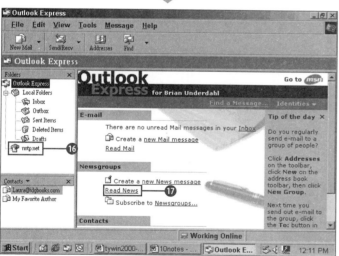

TAKE NOTE

▶ ### CONTROL NEWGROUP OPTIONS

If you would rather download a different quantity of newsgroup headers instead of the default 300 headers, select Tools ➪ Options and click the Read tab. In the News section of this tab you can specify the number of headers you would like downloaded whenever you enter a newsgroup. You can also use the *Mark all messages as read when exiting a newsgroup* check box to avoid having to consider old messages when you return to a newsgroup.

▶ ### AVOID FLAME WARS

Some pretty antisocial types inhabit certain newsgroups. These people will *flame* — insult — anyone who somehow offends them. If someone starts treating you abusively in a newsgroup, the best thing to do is to avoid them and don't start trading insults.

---

⑬ Select a newsgroup that you wish to view.

⑭ Click the Go to button to view the message headers for the selected newsgroup.

▶ When the message headers are displayed, click a header to view the message.

⑮ Click the Close button to close the dialog box.

⑯ To again view the list of newsgroups, click the newsgroup folder.

⑰ Alternatively, click the Read News link to view the list.

▶ You must select a newsgroup and connect to the Internet to view the messages.

FIND IT ONLINE

To find the latest newsgroups fast, see
http://www.newsville.com/fastsearch.html.

Finding Newsgroups

If you find the right newsgroup you may find just the information that you need to solve a problem that you've been working on for months. Unfortunately, finding the message that provides the information that you need can be difficult because a typical news server may contain 60,000 to 100,000 newsgroups. You could spend days just looking through all of the newsgroup names and you still wouldn't know anything about the messages that were contained in more than a small handful of them. By the time you finished your search you'd be so confused you probably wouldn't remember more than a few of the interesting-sounding newsgroups.

Although you'll probably find a lot of intriguing newsgroups just by browsing through the newsgroup list, that's not a very efficient method of locating newsgroups on specific topics. When you're looking for particular topics, it's far better to have Outlook Express narrow the list by only showing those newsgroups with specified words in their names.

You can further refine your newsgroup search by searching the results for a second or even a third word. The figures on the facing page show two methods of refining the search. As shown in the first three figures, you can search for a single term, subscribe to the resulting groups, and then search for the second term within the subscribed groups. The final figure shows another way to reach this goal by including all of the words in a single search phrase. Remember, though, that all of the words must be found in each newsgroup name that qualifies.

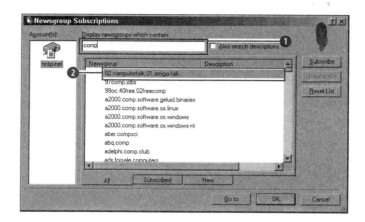

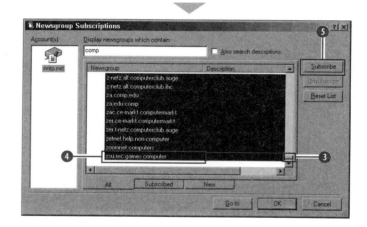

▶ Open the newsgroup list.

❶ Enter the first search phrase in the text box.

❷ Once Outlook Express narrows the list to those containing the phrase, click the first newsgroup in the list.

❸ Drag the scroll box down to the bottom of the scrollbar.

❹ Press and hold Shift as you click the last listed newsgroup.

❺ Click the Subscribe button to move the selected list to the Subscribed tab.

CROSS-REFERENCE

See Chapter 6 for more information on searching for files.

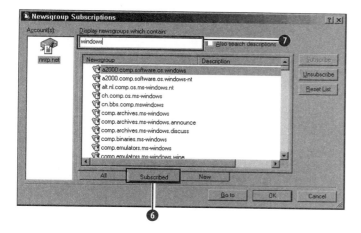

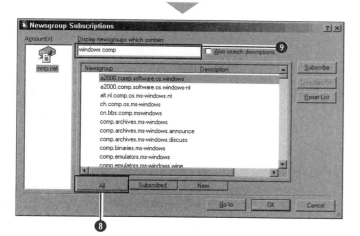

CONSIDER A DIFFERENT METHOD

The Outlook Express newsreader is handy, but it is certainly not the most powerful tool for searching through newsgroup postings. You cannot, for example, look through a series of newsgroups to find every message on specific topics. If someone posts a message in a newsgroup that doesn't happen to be one of those you have selected, you probably won't ever see the message. There are some other tools that can do a far better job of finding newsgroup messages than Outlook Express. One of these is NewsMonger, a program you can download from **http://www.techsmith.com**. NewsMonger looks inside all the messages posted to newsgroups to find what you want.

BROADEN YOUR TOPIC

Locating interesting newsgroups can be a challenge — especially if you are interested in some particularly esoteric topics. If your newsgroup search doesn't seem to produce the desired results, you may need to consider alternative ways of specifying the topic. Try to think of the different names that someone might use for the same topic. You may find that a search produces more results if you use partial rather than complete phrases. For example, use *compu* rather than *computers* and you may have more success.

---

6 *Click the Subscribed tab.*

7 *Enter the second search phrase in the text box to further narrow the list.*

▶ *This narrows the list to only show those newsgroups that include both phrases.*

8 *Alternatively, click the All tab to begin a new search using both phrases at once.*

9 *Enter both search phrases in the text box separated by spaces.*

▶ *Notice that the lists show the same results whether you enter the phrases together or in two steps.*

FIND IT ONLINE

For one of the most comprehensive lists of available newsgroups, see **http://liszt.com/news/**.

Configuring Outlook Express

As you use Outlook Express, you're almost certain to discover certain areas where the program doesn't seem to work just the way you would like it to. Before you decide that Outlook Express isn't for you, though, it's a good idea to play around with some of its customization options. When you do, you'll see that Outlook Express is a very flexible application that you can configure to suit your needs in many different areas.

The figures show you some of the more important Outlook Express configuration options. If you take a few minutes to understand these and the options that are not discussed, you'll be able to fine-tune the way Outlook Express works.

The options on the Send tab can be especially important to your satisfaction with Outlook Express. For example, if you make certain that the *Automatically put people I reply to in my Address Book* option is selected, you'll seldom have to add new e-mail addresses to your messages manually. If you have replied to someone in the past, Outlook Express will already know their e-mail address and you can simply choose it from the Address Book by clicking the To button when you compose a new message.

Although some people like to keep their e-mail messages as short as possible, it is very common to include someone's original text when you reply to a message from them. The *Include message in reply* check box on the Send tab makes certain this happens. If you consider that many people deal with dozens or even hundreds of e-mail messages in an average day, you can understand why including the original message is so important. If you don't include something that places your reply into the proper context, it's entirely possible that the recipient won't understand your reply.

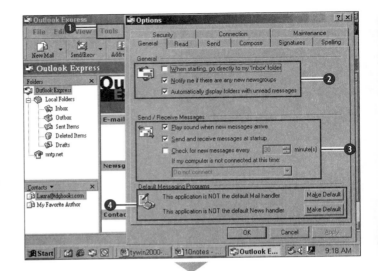

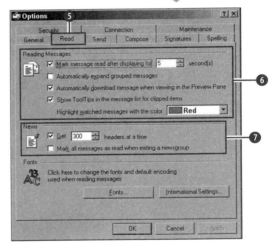

❶ Select Tools ➪ Options to open the Options dialog box.

❷ Select the startup options.

❸ Choose the message sending and receiving options.

❹ Optionally, choose whether to make Outlook Express your default mail and news handler.

❺ Click the Read tab.

❻ Choose options for reading messages.

❼ Select your newsgroup settings.

CROSS-REFERENCE

See "Adding Sounds to Events" in Chapter 13.

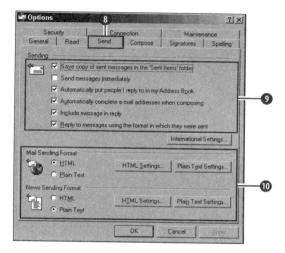

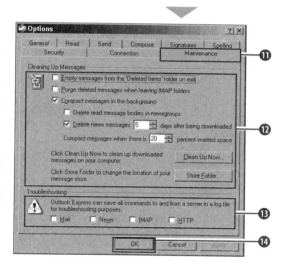

AUTOMATE YOUR E-MAIL

If you sometimes forget to check for new e-mail messages, you can automate the process by using the *Check for new messages every xx minute(s)* option on the General tab of the Options dialog box. If you do select this option, be sure to also select the *Hang up after sending and receiving* check box on the Connection tab. Selecting both of these options will ensure that Outlook Express will regularly check for new messages but will not tie up your telephone line for long intervals.

YOU'VE GOT MAIL

Your PC can play a sound whenever new messages arrive. Be sure the *Play sound when new messages arrive* check box on the General tab is selected. You'll need to use the Sounds and Multimedia applet in Control Panel to assign a sound file to the New Mail Notification event as discussed in Chapter 13. You can even record your own unique sound file to use as the notification that you have new mail.

⑧ *Click the Send tab.*

⑨ *Decide which message sending options you prefer.*

⑩ *Select the formatting options for e-mail and news messages you send.*

⑪ *Click the Maintenance tab.*

⑫ *Select the options for removing old messages.*

⑬ *If necessary, select log files to create for troubleshooting purposes.*

⑭ *Click OK to close the dialog box and confirm your selections.*

FIND IT ONLINE

To find e-mail addresses, try the WhoWhere People Finder at **http://www.whowhere.lycos.com/Email**.

Personal Workbook

Q&A

1 Why do Outlook Express folder names sometimes appear in boldface?

_____

_____

_____

2 What do you need to do before you can save a file that came with an e-mail message?

_____

_____

_____

3 Where do messages you've created wait until they're sent to the mail server?

_____

_____

_____

4 What is the meaning of the number in parentheses following an Outlook Express folder name?

_____

_____

_____

5 How can you find newsgroups that pertain to a specific subject?

_____

_____

_____

6 How can you stop an e-mail message from being delivered once it leaves your Outbox?

_____

_____

_____

7 What message format can you use to make certain that anyone can read your message?

_____

_____

_____

8 How often must you download the entire list of newsgroups?

_____

_____

_____

ANSWERS: PAGE 395

EXTRA PRACTICE

1 Locate newsgroups that discuss Windows 2000.

2 Configure Outlook Express to check for mail every 10 minutes.

3 Create and send an e-mail message to a friend.

4 Attach several files to a message and send it to your e-mail address.

5 When the new message arrives, open one of the attachments.

6 Subscribe to a newsgroup that relates to your favorite vacation activity.

REAL-WORLD APPLICATIONS

✔ You want to find out about relocating to a city halfway across the country. You send an e-mail message to a local real estate office to find out about homes that are available.

✔ You are having trouble finding the proper settings for your printer. You visit a newsgroup relating to that brand and post a message asking if anyone knows which settings you need to use.

✔ You are on a business trip and discover that you forgot an important file for tomorrow's presentation. You send an e-mail to the office and ask a coworker to attach the missing file to their reply.

✔ You are in charge of a class reunion. You search e-mail directories to find some of the "lost" classmates.

Visual Quiz

How can you display this dialog box? If you want to place your outbound messages in the Outbox rather than sending them as soon as you've created them, what setting do you need to adjust?

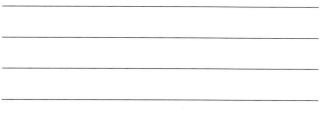

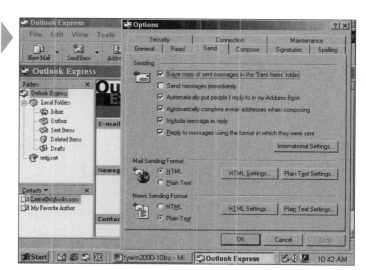

_____

_____

_____

_____

CHAPTER 11

MASTER THESE SKILLS

▶ Opening a New HyperTerminal Connection

▶ Answering a Call with HyperTerminal

▶ Sending Files with HyperTerminal

▶ Receiving Files with HyperTerminal

▶ Capturing a Session Record

▶ Using Telnet

Using HyperTerminal

People sometimes forget that there are other ways for two computers to communicate over a distance other than by connecting them to the Internet. Long before the Internet became widely available, people were exchanging files, sending messages, and even playing games using a telephone line connection to another computer.

Windows 2000 includes HyperTerminal, a program that enables two computers to talk to each other over a phone line or other type of direct connection. Using HyperTerminal you can connect to another computer, exchange files, and even keep a printed log of your online session.

HyperTerminal is a very different type of program than Internet Explorer. Although both programs allow computers to communicate, Internet Explorer is a specialized program that interprets and displays HTML documents such as Web pages. HyperTerminal is a more general communications program that displays the text it receives from another computer without attempting to interpret the text. This makes HyperTerminal a poor choice for displaying Web pages, but it is perfect when you simply want to communicate directly between two PCs — something that Internet Explorer isn't designed to do.

In fact, if you wish to transfer files between two PCs, you'll learn another of HyperTerminal's benefits: Without the overhead on the Internet to deal with, HyperTerminal can transfer files much faster. And if your ISP imposes limits on the size of e-mail messages, you'll be able to avoid bumping up against those limits by using HyperTerminal for file transfers, too.

If you're at all concerned about privacy and security, you may want to consider another of HyperTerminal's advantages. You probably realize that anything you send across the Internet travels through many different computers along the way. Messages and files that travel through so many different computers can be relatively easy prey for snoops. If you use HyperTerminal and connect directly to another computer, you eliminate this potential problem because you aren't using the Internet.

Unlike using Internet Explorer, an online session with HyperTerminal is highly interactive. What you type appears on both computer screens, and you interact with the person or computer at the other end of the connection. Things happen almost immediately without any of the long delays you've become used to when you're browsing the Internet. You may find yourself wishing that browsing the Internet were more like online sessions with HyperTerminal.

Opening a New HyperTerminal Connection

Using HyperTerminal is quite different than using Internet Explorer. When you use Internet Explorer, you connect to the Internet and can then communicate with thousands of different computers. When you use HyperTerminal, you connect directly to one other computer. In HyperTerminal you create a *connection* that contains the specific settings for each computer that you connect to.

When you create and name a HyperTerminal connection, HyperTerminal saves all of the settings for that connection. These settings include items such as the phone number that you dial, which physical connection — such as a modem — that you use for this connection, and any special requirements for communicating with the remote system. When you later click the icon that you selected for the connection, HyperTerminal uses all of the same settings so that you won't have to specify them again.

The figures show the process of setting up a new HyperTerminal connection. HyperTerminal assumes that you want to connect immediately when you have completed the setup. This may be OK if you're dialing in to a computer that is waiting for your call, but if you need to make arrangements with another PC user to set up their computer to answer, you'll probably want do so before you click the Dial button.

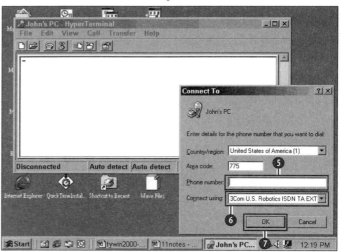

① Click the Start button and select Programs➪ Accessories➪Communications➪HyperTerminal.

② Enter a name for the connection.

③ If you'd like to use a different icon, choose one here.

④ Click the OK button to continue.

⑤ Enter the phone number.

⑥ If necessary, choose the correct connection device.

⑦ Click the OK button to continue.

CROSS-REFERENCE

See "Capturing a Session Record" later in this chapter.

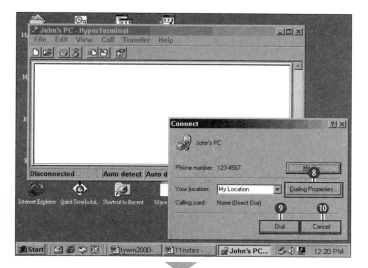

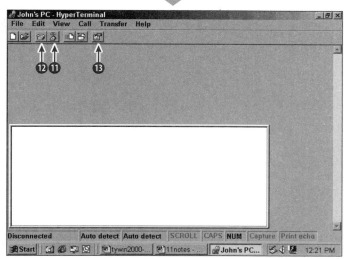

DISABLE CALL WAITING

If you have call waiting or other such services installed on the line that you use for your HyperTerminal connection, be sure to enter the proper code to disable those services before each HyperTerminal call. If you don't disable the service before placing a call, your HyperTerminal connection may be disrupted by the beep or tone that is used to alert you of an incoming call. Call waiting can usually be disabled by dialing *70 at the beginning of a phone number. You may want to check the caller instruction section at the front of your phone book, or ask your telephone company for the correct codes to use in your case. Generally, call waiting is restored once the current call ends.

SEEING WHAT YOU TYPE

The default HyperTerminal settings are designed for connecting to computers that echo the characters you type so that you can see what you have typed. If you connect to another PC you may not see what you are typing — even though the characters appear on the remote PC's screen. To correct this, select File ➪ Properties and then click the Settings tab. Next click the ASCII Setup button. Add a check to the *Echo typed characters locally* check box. You may also need to use the *Send line ends with line feeds* option if everything appears on one line on the remote system, or the *Append line feeds to incoming line ends* option if everything appears on one line on your system.

---

⑧ *To modify the dialing properties, click the Dialing Properties button.*

⑨ *To call now, click the Dial button.*

⑩ *Alternatively, click Cancel to dial later.*

⑪ *Click the Disconnect button to hang up.*

⑫ *Alternatively, click the Call button to dial a call.*

⑬ *Optionally, click the Properties button to change the connection settings.*

FIND IT ONLINE

See **http://www.hilgraeve.com/htpeform.html** to download HyperTerminal Private Edition.

Answering a Call with HyperTerminal

When you use HyperTerminal to communicate between two PCs, you'll soon discover that you have to deal with all of the details of the connection. If all that you've done with your modem in the past is dial in to the Internet, you probably haven't really thought about one of those details — one of the PCs must be set up to answer the call. The other PC, of course, must be set up to call the correct number, as covered in the previous section.

Another important connection detail results from the difference between standalone PCs and computers that are configured as dial-in hosts. When they are communicating over a phone line, PCs typically don't show any of the characters that are being typed on their own keyboard. Rather, they expect that the remote computer will *echo* those characters. But because PCs generally default to not echoing the characters that are received, when two PCs are connected, neither person will be able to see what they are typing unless you make the correct configuration changes. Although this subject was briefly mentioned in the previous section, it is important enough to show in the figures of this task.

You may also need to select the *Send line ends with line feeds* check box or the *Append line feeds to line ends* check box. These two settings are used to force new lines of text to appear on new lines (wrap) instead of overwriting the same line. In most cases, you either make both of these settings on just one of the PCs or make one of the settings — the same one in each case — on, and the other one off, on both PCs. Both PCs, however, should have the *Echo typed characters locally* check box selected.

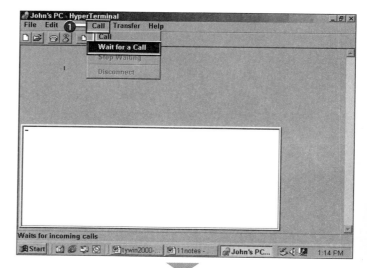

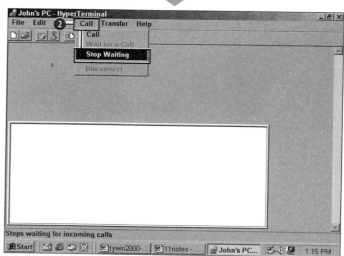

① Select Call ⇨ Wait for a Call to begin waiting for incoming calls.

② Select Call ⇨ Stop Waiting to stop answering calls.

CROSS-REFERENCE

See "Opening a New HyperTerminal Connection" earlier in this chapter.

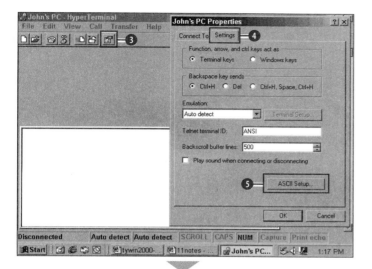

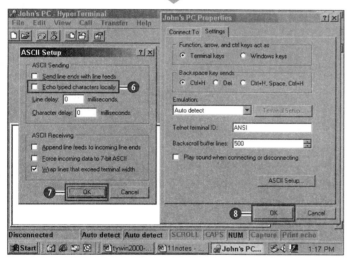

MAKE SURE HYPERTERMINAL ANSWERS

If you set up HyperTerminal to answer incoming calls, you should first disable other software that may attempt to answer calls. For example, if you use fax software to receive incoming faxes, you can create a conflict if both HyperTerminal and the fax software are configured for answering. To avoid this problem, make certain that the fax software is disabled before you tell HyperTerminal to wait for calls.

SWITCHING CALL TYPES

If you use a single phone line for both voice and modem calls, you may be able to switch from a voice call to a modem call by typing the proper commands in the HyperTerminal window. Enter **ATO** on one PC and **ATA** on the other while your voice call is still connected. If the modems connect, hang up the receivers and proceed with your modem call. If the modems don't connect, you'll probably have to hang up and let one of the modems make the call while the other is placed in wait mode.

③ *To change the connection properties, click the Properties button.*

④ *Click the Settings tab.*

⑤ *Click the ASCII Setup button.*

⑥ *Select the Echo typed characters locally check box to see what you type.*

⑦ *Click the OK button to continue.*

⑧ *Click the OK button to complete the task.*

FIND IT ONLINE

To see a list of frequently asked questions about HyperTerminal, see **http://www.hilgraeve.com/ htpefaq.html**

Sending Files with HyperTerminal

One of the best uses of HyperTerminal is for sending files between two PCs. Although you certainly can use the Internet for sending files, a direct connection between two PCs using Hyper-Terminal has certain advantages over using the Internet. Direct file transfers are often quite a bit faster than Internet file transfers. And since direct connections don't send your files through any other computers on the way to their destination, they're more secure than using the Internet for file transfers, too.

One of the major problems with using telephone lines and modems for sending data is that ordinary phone lines were designed only for voice communications. For your computer to send signals across a standard phone connection, the digital signals used inside a computer must first be converted into analog signals — sounds, essentially. This is what a modem does. Your modem also takes the incoming analog signals and converts them back to digital signals that it sends to your PC. Unfortunately, this means that errors in transmitting data are quite common. A little bit of static or other line noise makes the modem "hear" a bit of data incorrectly, and this results in an error in the file you are sending or receiving. A single change in a file could result in a completely unusable file. Or such a change could leave the file *looking* perfect — but with a hidden error in the data that is almost impossible to catch.

To prevent errors from creeping into files that you transfer over phone lines between computers, you use a *file transfer protocol* — a method of checking for and correcting errors in the transmission. Protocols are like languages. Both parties must be speaking the same language or using the same protocol if they're going to

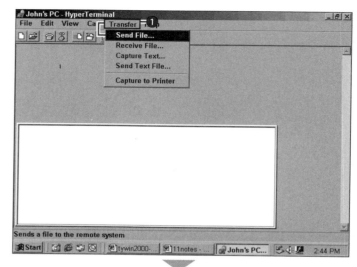

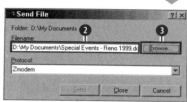

❶ Select Transfer ➪ Send File.

❷ Enter the name of the file to send.

❸ Alternatively, click the Browse button and select the file.

CROSS-REFERENCE

See "Receiving Files with HyperTerminal" later in this chapter.

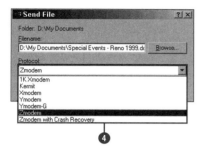

understand each other and accomplish anything. HyperTerminal supports several different protocols, so even if the remote computer isn't using HyperTerminal, you will likely still be able to find at least one protocol supported by both computers.

TAKE NOTE

▶ DIGITAL PHONE LINES

If you have the opportunity to switch to a digital phone line — either ISDN or DSL, you'll find that phone line errors are a thing of the past. Since digital phone lines don't use modems to convert signals between digital and analog, the signal remains completely digital from one computer to the other. The result is a connection that is far faster and more reliable.

▶ CHOOSE ZMODEM PROTOCOL

Zmodem is the best file transfer protocol for use with HyperTerminal. As soon as you begin a Zmodem file transfer to a PC running HyperTerminal, the receiving system automatically starts the transfer without requiring you to do anything on the receiving end. Zmodem also has the ability to restart a file transfer that has been interrupted.

④ Select the file transfer protocol.

⑤ Click the Send button to begin the transfer.

▶ The Send button will not be available unless you are currently connected.

FIND IT ONLINE

See the Computer Shopper BBS listing at **http://www. zdnet.com/computershopper/edit/cshopper/bbs/ index.html.**

Receiving Files with HyperTerminal

O f course, if one computer is going to send a file, it stands to reason that another computer must be ready to receive the file. If you're using HyperTerminal, receiving a file is quite easy. In fact, if both PCs use HyperTerminal and you select the Zmodem file transfer protocol, the file begins transferring when the Send button is clicked on the sending system — you don't even have to tell the receiving system to begin receiving the file. However, if you select a different protocol or if the remote system isn't using HyperTerminal, you may need to initiate the receive file process.

Once you begin a file transfer, HyperTerminal displays a status box that shows you the file transfer progress. It's important that you don't do anything as long as this dialog box is displayed because you may disrupt the file transfer.

Be sure to make note of the location where HyperTerminal saves the files you receive. You may want to create a special download folder so that you can keep track of the files more easily.

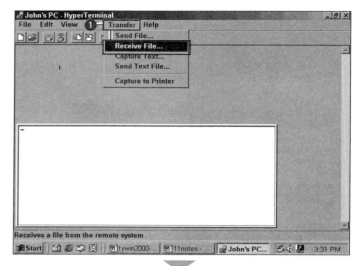

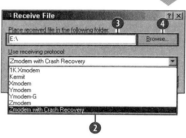

❶ Select Transfer ⏎ Receive File.

❷ Select the file transfer protocol.

▶ Choose Zmodem with Crash Recovery if you are restarting an interrupted Zmodem download.

❸ Enter the name of the folder to use for the received files.

❹ Alternatively, click the Browse button to select the folder.

CROSS-REFERENCE

See "Opening and Saving File Attachments" in Chapter 15.

► CHOOSE YOUR PROTOCOL

When both PCs are using HyperTerminal, Zmodem makes the whole file transfer process quite simple, because only the sender needs to start the file transfer. But if one of the computers is using something other than HyperTerminal, choosing a file transfer protocol becomes a bit more of a challenge. First you must select a protocol that is supported by both systems, and then you must manually initiate the file transfer.

If you are connecting to a mainframe computer, you may need to select Kermit as the file transfer protocol. Generally speaking, mainframe computers do not support most PC-based protocols, so Kermit may be the only option. If you must use Kermit, you will need to issue the correct command to start the transfer on the mainframe. Unfortunately, the command is specific to the particular mainframe system.

► TROUBLESHOOTING FILE TRANSFERS

If you experience problems with file transfers, there can be many possible reasons. The most likely culprit is line noise, and this can be intermittent. If a file transfer fails, try transferring the file again to see if the problem was transitory. If the transfer fails again, wait a moment while you watch the HyperTerminal window. If random characters appear, it's a good indication that you have a poor connection and should try hanging up and calling again. If that is not the problem, try a different file transfer protocol. Even when two programs use the same name for a file transfer protocol, it is possible for incompatibilities to occur.

⑤ *Select the folder.*

⑥ *Click OK to continue.*

⑦ *Click the Receive button to begin the transfer.*

▶ *The Receive button will not be available unless you are currently connected.*

FIND IT ONLINE

Visit Hilgraeve's BBS at **telnet://hbbs.hilgraeve.com/** to find files you can download.

Capturing a Session Record

W hen you're using HyperTerminal, lines of text scroll across and then up your screen. Eventually the earlier text scrolls off the top of the screen and disappears. HyperTerminal maintains a *buffer* so that you can use the scroll bar to go back and look at text that has scrolled off the screen. Typically HyperTerminal's scroll-back buffer can hold up to about 500 lines, but pretty soon earlier text disappears forever as newer lines are added to the bottom of the list.

When you're online with HyperTerminal, you may want to keep a record of information that has appeared on your screen. Because the text scrolls up and eventually out of the buffer, you need methods of saving the text in a file or of printing the text so that it will be available when you need it. Fortunately, HyperTerminal provides you with the tools to capture onscreen text to a file or directly to your printer.

Capturing text in a HyperTerminal window is very different from saving or printing a Web page that you are viewing in Internet Explorer. This difference stems from a very different orientation of the two programs. Internet Explorer deals with complete pages (even if the page appears a little at a time as the page loads). HyperTerminal is solely text-oriented, so when you issue the command to start capturing data, HyperTerminal starts with the next text that is received. This means that HyperTerminal doesn't capture any text that is already on the screen when you issue the command to begin the capture.

Because of this different orientation, it pays to plan ahead. The figures on the facing page show you how to be prepared to capture text as needed without capturing the entire session. Simply begin the capture session as you normally would and then immediately select

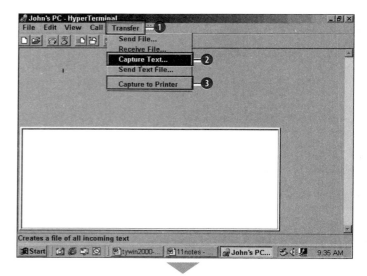

① Select Transfer to display the Transfer menu.

② Select Capture Text to display the Capture Text dialog box.

③ You can also select Capture to Printer to create a printed copy of the session.

④ Enter the name of the text capture file.

⑤ Click the Start button to begin capturing text to the file.

CROSS-REFERENCE

See "Cutting, Copying, and Pasting to the Clipboard" in Chapter 5.

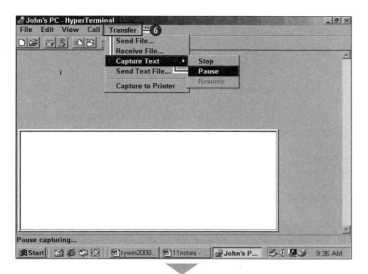

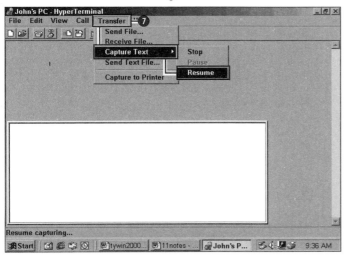

Transfer ⇨ Capture Text ⇨ Pause. Continue with your online session and then, just before you need to begin capturing text, select Transfer ⇨ Capture Text ⇨ Resume. You can pause and resume capturing text as often as necessary.

TAKE NOTE

▶ **PRINTING A SESSION**

If you decide to capture text directly to a printer, remember that many printers — especially laser printers — print one page at a time. The final page may not print until you press a button on the printer. This button is usually labeled "Form Feed" or something similar.

▶ **COPY EARLIER TEXT**

If you didn't begin capturing text soon enough, all is not lost. Highlight the text you need to keep and then select Edit ⇨ Copy to place the text on the Clipboard. Then switch to another program such as WordPad and paste the text. You can scroll up to view text that has scrolled off the screen.

---

⑥ *Select Transfer ⇨ Capture Text ⇨ Pause to pause the text capture while leaving the file open for later captures.*

⑦ *Select Transfer ⇨ Capture Text ⇨ Resume to resume the text capture into the existing capture file.*

▶ *Select Transfer ⇨ Capture Text ⇨ Stop to stop capturing text and close the capture file.*

FIND IT ONLINE

See Spidey's Telnet Gateway list **http://www.geocities.com/Tokyo/3371/telnet.htm**.

Using Telnet

I f the only way you have ever accessed the Internet is
through a Web browser such as Internet Explorer,
you may not realize that there are other areas that
are available to you. The Internet is a giant communications network, and the World Wide Web is just one of
the pieces of that network.

Telnet is one of the standard Internet protocols.
Unlike http as used on the Web, telnet is a text-based
protocol. This makes HyperTerminal a perfect tool for
visiting telnet sites on the Internet. In fact, if you enter a
telnet address in the Windows 2000 Address toolbar or
the Internet Explorer Address bar, Windows 2000 will
automatically start HyperTerminal so that you can view
the specified site.

Because telnet is text-based, you aren't likely to experience the types of delays that you will on the Web.
When you use telnet, you connect to another computer
on the Internet. You can then give the remote computer
instructions which will be carried out as if you were entering them directly from the remote machine. This is
often used for tasks such as remotely administering a
computer (a Web server, for example). Generally you
must supply a user name and sometimes a password to
connect to a computer using telnet.

Many libraries make their catalog available online, as
shown in the figures. You may discover that telnet is an
excellent way to find rare titles that might be available
through a library exchange program.

When you log on to a telnet site, you may be asked to
select a *terminal type*. This simply refers to the set of
commands that your system will respond to. If
VT100 — one of the most common terminal types — is

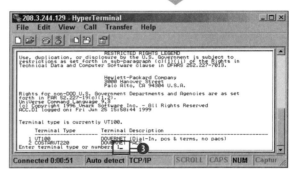

▶ Right-click the Taskbar and
choose Toolbars ⇨ Address
to display the Address
toolbar.

① Enter a telnet address in the
Address bar.

② Once you are connected,
enter your login and press
Enter.

▶ Many public libraries use
"library" as the login.

③ If you are prompted to
choose a terminal type, enter
the VT100 option if available
and press Enter.

CROSS-REFERENCE

See "Using the Address Bar" in Chapter 2.

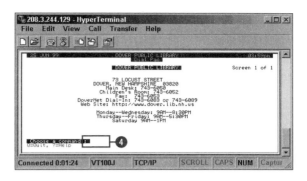

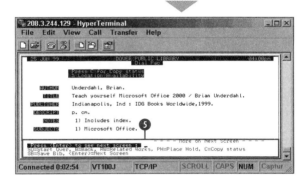

available, choose that option. HyperTerminal automatically *emulates* eight of the most popular terminal types. Click the Properties button and then look in the Emulation list box on the Settings tab for a list of the available types.

TAKE NOTE

▶ FINDING TELNET SITES

If you want to try out telnet, you'll have to search a bit to find active telnet sites. The extreme popularity of the Web has resulted in many of the older Internet protocols, such as telnet, gopher, and ftp, being used far less than they were in the past. Still, telnet retains a certain loyal following if for no better reason than being very fast and simple. You can find thousands of telnet-related sites by doing a search for "telnet" on the Internet.

▶ TELNET AND GAMES

One area where telnet is quite popular is in the world of multiuser games. *Multi User Domains* — MUDs — often use telnet because the games are text-based, and the participants can access the games from almost anywhere in the world via the Internet. To find MUDs, search for both telnet and MUD.

④ *Type your command and press Enter.*

▶ *You can usually display a list of commands by entering a question mark or the word help.*

⑤ *Follow the onscreen prompts in entering your commands.*

▶ *Be sure to log off properly. Many telnet sites can hang temporarily if users do not log off correctly.*

FIND IT ONLINE

Visit the Dover Public Library Online Catalog at **telnet://208.3.244.129/**.

Personal Workbook

Q&A

1 What can you do if you need to keep text that is already on your HyperTerminal screen?

_____

_____

_____

2 What setting must be the same on both the sending and the receiving computer before you can transfer a file?

_____

_____

_____

3 How many computers can you connect at one time using HyperTerminal?

_____

_____

_____

4 What should you do if you can't see anything you type in the HyperTerminal window?

_____

_____

_____

5 What is _telnet_?

_____

_____

_____

6 How can you start printing the text that appears on your screen?

_____

_____

_____

7 How can you prepare HyperTerminal to answer an incoming call?

_____

_____

_____

8 What should you do if someone wants to send you a fax while HyperTerminal is waiting for a call?

_____

_____

_____

ANSWERS: PAGE 395

EXTRA PRACTICE

1. Set up a new connection that you can use to connect to a friend's PC.

2. Transfer several files to another PC.

3. Send a text file to the other PC, and see how that is different than sending other types of files.

4. Capture the text of a session and figure out how you can send the text back to the other computer.

5. Turn on printing and telnet to a library.

6. Use telnet to find out if your library carries books by your favorite author.

REAL-WORLD APPLICATIONS

✓ You're scheduled to participate in an online interview. You use HyperTerminal to keep a complete log of the session for future reference.

✓ You need to transfer some very sensitive files and don't feel you can trust sending them over the Internet. To send them directly, you use HyperTerminal on both PCs.

✓ You have been invited to be a celebrity participant in a multiuser game being hosted in a country halfway around the world. You use HyperTerminal and telnet to connect to the remote host computer across the Internet.

✓ You need to temporarily connect two PCs to transfer files that are too large to fit on diskettes. You use HyperTerminal to transfer the files.

Visual Quiz

How can you display this dialog box? What is the purpose of the Protocol list box?

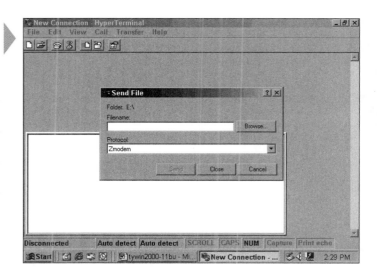

_____

_____

_____

_____

_____

PART

IV

Customizing and Maintaining Windows 2000

Windows 2000 is a very powerful operating system, but that doesn't mean you should simply ignore it. As you'll learn in this part, you can easily change the appearance of Windows 2000 as well as some of the ways that Windows 2000 works.

In addition to customizing Windows 2000, you also need to perform certain routine maintenance tasks if you want your computer to run its best. In some ways these tasks can provide you with valuable insights into how your system operates. When you know what is going on under the surface, you can take a far more active role in making certain that you are getting as much as possible from your PC.

CHAPTER **12**

Changing the Look of Windows 2000

You can easily change the appearance of Windows 2000, and there are a lot of reasons why you might want to do so. Although some of the changes you can make are purely cosmetic, there are other things that can actually make Windows 2000 easier to use. This chapter explains how you can make Windows 2000 appearance changes to suit your personal preferences.

When you set about customizing the appearance of Windows 2000, you'll soon discover that there are a lot of changes that you can make. You can add a pattern or a picture to your desktop so it no longer has the same boring look seen on everyone else's desktop. You can modify the colors used for virtually every element of your screen. You can choose to change the screen resolution to place more things on your screen or to make everything much larger. You can choose the optimal settings to reduce flickering on your monitor. You can add a screen saver to make your screen look like an active art gallery whenever you aren't using your PC. If you don't like the standard taskbar layout, you can modify that, too. Finally, you can make a number of adjustments to your Start menu.

When you start modifying the appearance of Windows 2000, you are really putting the "personal" into personal computing. Other people may not share your tastes, but unless they also share your PC, this should not be a problem. Keep in mind, though, that if each user logs on to Windows 2000 using their own name, they can each have their own personalized Windows 2000 desktop.

In most cases, any appearance changes that you make won't affect how Windows 2000 operates. A few of the changes, though, can affect how a user must interact with Windows 2000. For example, if you activate a screen saver and you specify a password, you must remember the password if you want to get back to Windows 2000 once the screen saver is running. If you move or hide the taskbar, someone might shut down Windows 2000 incorrectly, perhaps causing you to lose any work you haven't saved. When in doubt, use caution with changes that make it difficult for someone to access the standard Windows 2000 screen elements.

Configuring the Desktop

One of the easiest appearance changes you can make to Windows 2000 is also one that can have the most immediate visual impact. Adding a background — or *wallpaper* — image to your Windows 2000 desktop instantly adds a unique touch that can change your desktop from boring to splashy. Working with your PC doesn't have to be boring anymore!

Background images are called wallpaper for a good reason. Wallpaper appears behind the other things on your desktop rather than covering them up. This makes it possible to see all of your desktop icons even though you've added a background image.

You can use several different types of graphics files as background images. The Windows Bitmap (BMP) format is the easiest to use because that format is automatically supported by Windows 2000. If you decide to use a JPEG image, Windows 2000 allows that, too, but you must allow Windows 2000 to activate the Active Desktop in order to use JPEG images as wallpaper.

Even though your desktop wallpaper sits on the desktop behind everything else, some wallpaper images can make it difficult to see the desktop icons, especially if the wallpaper is loaded with a number of dark colors. If you encounter this type of problem with your favorite wallpaper, you may want to try centering the image rather than tiling or stretching it. Another possibility would be to use your favorite graphic editing program to lighten the image somewhat or perhaps to crop the image so that it uses less space on your desktop.

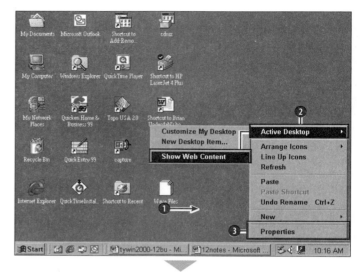

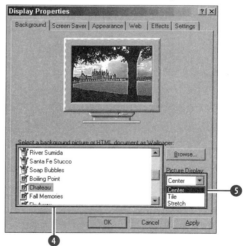

① Right-click a blank space on the desktop to display the desktop context menu.

② Select Active Desktop ➪ Show Web Content to enable JPEG images to be used as wallpaper.

③ Select Properties to open the Display Properties dialog box.

④ Choose an image to use as wallpaper.

⑤ Select the method of displaying the image from the drop-down Display list box.

CROSS-REFERENCE

See "Changing the Resolution" later in this chapter.

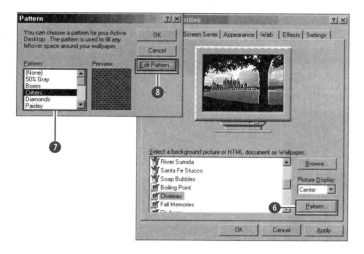

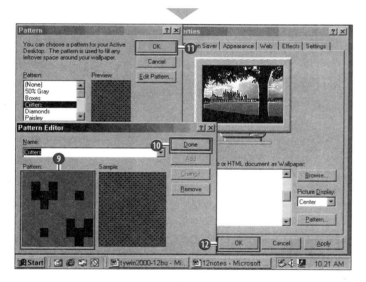

FINDING BACKGROUND IMAGES

You will find that there are many good sources for image files that you can use as desktop wallpaper. JPEG images are easy to find, and use far less disk space than Windows Bitmap images. Most of the images you find on the Internet are JPEG images. Most digital cameras also produce JPEG images. To use an image that you find on a Web page as your Windows 2000 desktop wallpaper, right-click the image and choose Set as Wallpaper from the pop-up context menu. To save multiple images so you can choose one later, right-click each image and choose Save Picture As from the context menu. You may even wish to create a new folder for saving the images you download for use as wallpaper.

RESIZING IMAGES

Digital images that you download or create using your scanner likely won't have the same dimensions as your Windows 2000 desktop. You may end up with blank space around a desktop image, or the image may extend beyond the edges of the screen. Although Windows 2000 offers you the option to stretch the image to fit the desktop, this will produce distorted images unless the original image uses the same 4-wide by 3-high ratio as your screen.

⑥ Alternatively, click the Pattern button to open the Pattern dialog box.

⑦ Choose a pattern from the list box.

⑧ Optionally, click the Edit Pattern button to edit the pattern.

⑨ Click individual squares in the Pattern box to change their color.

⑩ Click Done.

⑪ Click OK.

⑫ Click OK again to complete the task.

FIND IT ONLINE

See **http://www.winfiles.com/apps/98/desktop-misc.html** for a source of desktop management tools.

Changing the Colors

Aside from adding a background image to your desktop, changing the colors used to display the various elements of the Windows 2000 screen can be one of the most visible appearance modifications that you can make. Almost every element on the Windows 2000 screen can be modified to use a different set of colors.

The figures show how you can select your own colors for the various elements of the Windows 2000 screen. Rather than choosing your own color set, you may wish to try out some of the optional color schemes that you can choose from the Scheme list box on the Appearance tab of the Display Properties dialog box. These color schemes provide a complete set of coordinating colors for different purposes. For example, if you have difficulty viewing the screen, you may want to try using one of the high-contrast color schemes. These color schemes are designed to help make the screen much easier to view, especially in poor lighting conditions or for visually impaired users. You may need to experiment with the high-contrast color schemes to see which one works best for you.

Be sure to use the Save As button before you begin making changes so you can return to your saved selections if you find that a new color scheme is not to your liking. Once you've created a new color scheme that you like, save the new scheme, too. Then you'll be able to return quickly to your scheme if someone else uses your PC and changes the color selections.

You may find that the colors and fonts that you select in the Display Properties dialog box don't have much effect on some of your applications. It's just a fact of life that certain programs have their own settings that are not controlled by Windows 2000.

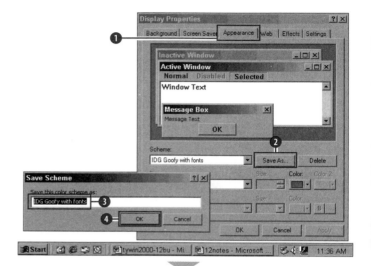

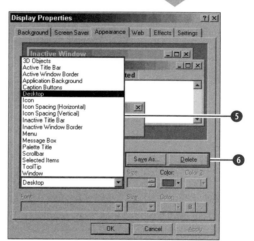

❶ Click the Appearance tab.

❷ Click Save As if you wish to save your current color scheme before you make any changes.

❸ Enter a name for your current scheme.

❹ Click OK to continue.

❺ Choose a screen element from the Item list box to change its current color.

❻ Choose the color and size options for the selected element.

CROSS-REFERENCE

See "Using Dialog Boxes" in Chapter 4.

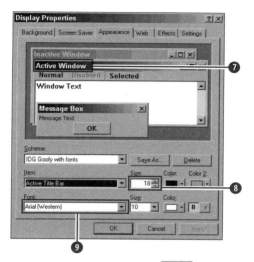

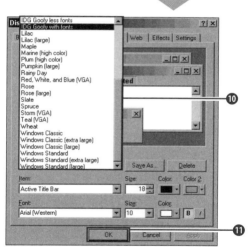

AVOID CHANGING FONTS

Even though you can change the fonts used in dialog boxes, title bars, and the other Windows 2000 text elements at the same time as you are selecting a new color scheme, it's usually best to avoid font changes. When you select alternate fonts you may see a drastic adverse affect on overall system performance. Stick with the default font selections to avoid this potential problem.

USE CARE IN SELECTING COLORS

When you are selecting a color scheme, be careful that you choose contrasting colors for the text and background in any elements that include text. If you pick text colors that are the same as the background colors, you won't be able to see the text, and that circumstance makes it virtually impossible to use Windows 2000. If you accidentally set your text colors this way, choose another one of the Windows 2000 color schemes to reset the colors so that you can see message text.

---

⑦ *Alternatively, click an item in the preview window to select it.*

⑧ *Choose the color and size options for the selected element.*

⑨ *If the selected element includes text, you can choose text options.*

⑩ *Alternatively, select a scheme from the Scheme list box.*

⑪ *Click OK to complete the task.*

FIND IT ONLINE

Visit Moon Valley Software for Windows desktop accessories at **http://www.moonvalley.com/ moonbase/page1.htm**

Changing the Resolution

The *resolution* of your Windows 2000 is the measure of the number of horizontal and vertical picture elements — *pixels* — that can be displayed at one time. There are several factors that control which resolution settings you can use. These include the capabilities of your monitor as well as the amount of memory that is installed on your video display adapter. In this section you will learn how to adjust your display resolution to suit your needs.

In most cases, PC screens use a resolution setting that has a constant ratio of 4 horizontal pixels to 3 vertical pixels. This means that common resolution settings always use the same ratio. Typical settings include 640 by 480, 800 by 600, 1,024 by 768, 1,280 by 1,024, or even 1,600 by 1,200 on very large monitors. In each case, the first number is the number of horizontal pixels and the second is the number of vertical pixels.

Your monitor is an important element in determining which resolution setting will be right for you. If your monitor is small, choosing a higher resolution setting may not be a viable option since everything on your screen could end up too small to see without straining your eyesight. But even if your monitor is a larger model you may discover that some resolution settings simply won't work for you. For example, at some settings you may discover that your screen takes on a strange appearance when you change the resolution settings. The Windows 2000 desktop may not fill the screen, or the desktop may be too wide or too tall. If this happens, you may be able to adjust your monitor's controls to make the screen look normal.

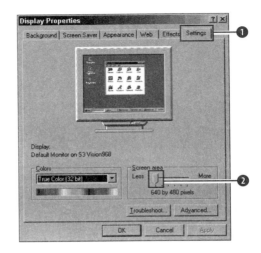

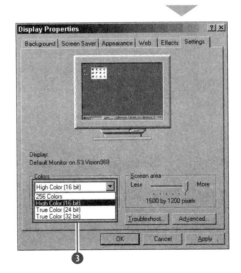

▶ *Right-click a blank space on the desktop and select Properties to open the Display Properties dialog box.*

❶ *Click the Settings tab.*

❷ *Drag the slider to the desired resolution setting.*

❸ *Select the number of colors to display.*

▶ *Choosing more colors may reduce your system's performance.*

CROSS-REFERENCE

See "Setting the Refresh Rate" later in this chapter.

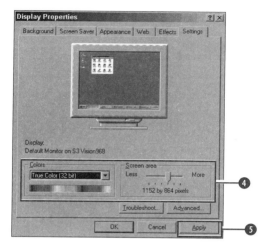

The highest resolution setting commonly recommended for 15-inch monitors is 800 by 600. For 17-inch monitors 1,024 by 768 is the normal recommended setting. If you have a larger or smaller screen, choose a setting that is most comfortable, to reduce the likelihood of eyestrain.

TAKE NOTE

▶ COLOR DEPTH MAY BE AFFECTED

When you change to a higher resolution, you may find that your PC cannot display as many colors as it can at lower resolutions. This is a function of the amount of memory in your display adapter and generally cannot be changed without replacing the adapter. Even so, a 2MB graphics card can display more than 65,000 colors at 1,024 by 768 resolution.

▶ LCD RESOLUTION SETTINGS

If you own a laptop PC or have an LCD display on your desktop, you'll probably discover that although you can change the screen resolution, the screen will be almost unusable at anything other than the highest resolution. The reason for this is that lower-resolution settings require that the image be stretched to fit the screen, and LCD screens typically don't display stretched images very well.

④ Notice that the number of colors and the screen area may interact. You may need to compromise on fewer colors or lower resolution.

⑤ Click Apply to continue.

⑥ Click OK to try out your new settings.

▶ If your screen looks normal after it has been resized, click Yes to keep the new settings.

▶ If you do not confirm the new settings, your desktop will automatically return to the existing settings after 15 seconds.

FIND IT ONLINE

To learn more about recommended resolution settings, see http://www.webopedia.com/Hardware/Monitors/refresh.html.

Setting the Refresh Rate

When you adjust the screen resolution, you may also indirectly change the monitor's *refresh* rate. The refresh rate is the number of times per second that the image on your screen is redrawn. If this rate is too low, your screen will seem to flicker and you may experience fatigue, eyestrain, and headaches. In very extreme cases monitor flicker may possibly trigger seizures in certain individuals.

Even if you don't notice any flicker, you could have problems if the refresh rate is set too low. Flicker can be difficult to spot, but it can be affecting you even if you don't see the flicker.

It is generally recommended that you use a refresh rate setting of at least 70 *Hz* — 70 times per second. Manufacturers often use a lower setting to compensate for inferior equipment or design, so it's important to check this setting whenever you buy a new PC, change monitors, or install a new display adapter card.

Several factors influence the refresh rate settings that you can use. Your monitor generally supports only a limited range of refresh settings for each resolution and color depth setting, and your display adapter has certain refresh rates that it can supply. If Windows 2000 has a listing for your specific monitor manufacturer and model, you can select the *Hide modes that this monitor cannot display* check box to prevent you from selecting a refresh rate that could damage the monitor. You'll find this check box on the Monitor tab of the Monitor and Display Adapter Properties dialog box, but the check box will only be active if Windows 2000 has identified your monitor. If you are able to select this option (and have verified that Windows 2000 has correctly identified your monitor), you'll probably want to select the highest available refresh frequency setting. The highest safe setting will usually produce the best possible display on your screen.

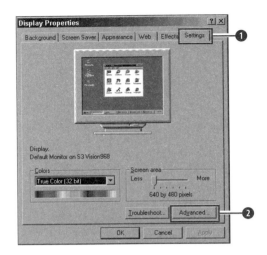

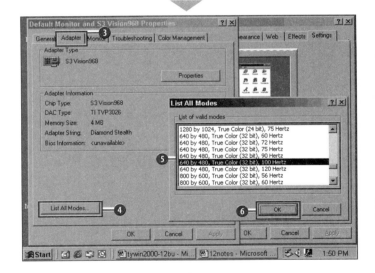

▶ Right-click a blank space on the desktop and select Properties to open the Display Properties dialog box.

❶ Click the Settings tab.

❷ Click the Advanced button.

❸ To see which modes your display adapter supports, click the Adapter tab.

❹ Click the List All Modes button.

❺ View the available modes here.

❻ Click OK to continue.

CROSS-REFERENCE

See "Adding New Hardware" in Chapter 13.

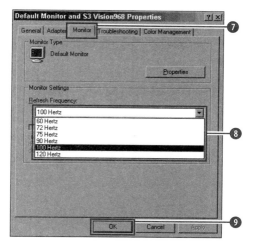

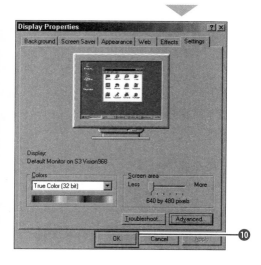

▶ USE CAUTION

If you force the display adapter to choose a refresh rate that is too high for your monitor, you could damage your monitor. All monitors have maximum refresh rate settings that can be used, and these vary according to the screen resolution. If you select a refresh rate that is higher than what is specified in your owner's manual, you could do serious damage and will almost certain void your warranty.

▶ LCD REFRESH SETTINGS

In most cases you cannot set the refresh rate for LCD screens such as those used on laptop PCs. LCD screens use a different method of displaying information than do CRT-based monitors, so refresh-induced flicker is typically not a problem with LCD screens. Some systems with LCD screens do have refresh rate settings, but these are generally only used when an external monitor is connected to the system.

⑦ *Click the Monitor tab.*
⑧ *Select the refresh rate.*
⑨ *Click OK to continue.*

⑩ *Click OK to complete the task.*

FIND IT ONLINE

To learn the acceptable settings for many common monitors, see **http://207.90.189.3/monitors/mdb.htm**.

Using a Screen Saver

S creen savers serve two purposes on a Windows 2000-based PC, and neither of them has anything to do with protecting your monitor from damage. Modern monitors are immune to the type of damage that could burn a permanent image into early computer screens.

The two purposes served by a screen saver are entertainment and security. Having a moving image on your screen when you aren't using your PC may not be high art, but it's probably more entertaining than seeing that budget worksheet staring back at you. Keeping prying eyes from seeing your latest budget figures is likely a valid reason for using a screen saver, too.

There are several different types of screen savers that you can choose. The figures on the facing page show that you have many different options that you can configure, and these options vary according to the type of screen saver that you select. A purely graphical screen saver generally has settings that you can use to change the shapes, textures, and resolution settings. Screen savers that display text allow you to specify the text that is displayed, the format of the text, the speed that the text moves across your screen, and the motion. Some screen savers enable you to do even more customization.

Once a screen saver has been activated, pressing any key on the keyboard or moving your mouse will close the screen saver. If you have selected the Password protected check box, you must enter the correct password to restore your screen. You won't need to enter your password when you are previewing the screen saver.

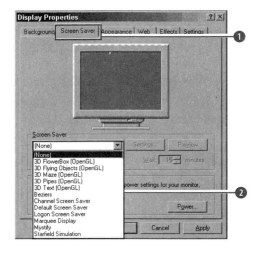

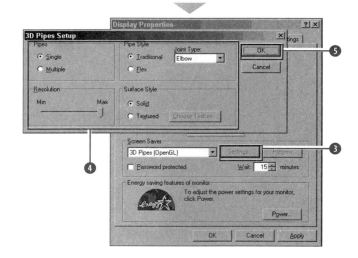

▶ Right-click a blank space on the desktop and select Properties to open the Display Properties dialog box.

❶ Click the Screen Saver tab.

❷ Select a screen saver from the list box.

❸ Optionally, click the Settings button to change how the screen saver operates.

❹ Select the options you prefer.

❺ Click OK to continue.

CROSS-REFERENCE

See "Using Power Management" later in this chapter.

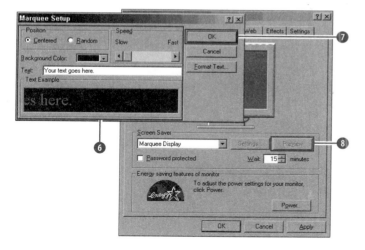

USE A LOGON PASSWORD

If you use a screen saver and a password to prevent other people from accessing your PC, make certain that you have established a password that must be entered to log on to your PC as well. Otherwise, someone would be able to simply turn off the power to your system and then restart to bypass your screen saver password. When you choose to use a password for the screen saver, you use the same password for both logging on and for closing the screen saver.

ACTIVATE A SCREEN SAVER INSTANTLY

You can create a shortcut to your screen saver on your desktop so that you can instantly activate the screen saver by double-clicking the screen saver icon. To do so, open Windows Explorer and navigate to the \Windows\System32 folder. Change to Details view and look in the Type column for screen savers. Use your right mouse button to drag the screen saver to your desktop and choose *Create shortcut(s) here* from the context menu. Then when you plan to be away from your desk for a few moments you can start the screen saver immediately, bypassing the specified waiting period.

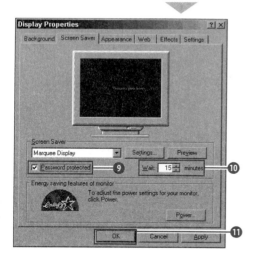

6 If you selected a text-based screen saver, choose your text options.

7 Click OK to continue.

8 Optionally, click Preview to see the screen saver in full screen mode.

9 If you wish to use your logon password to close the screen saver, click here.

10 Specify the length of time before the screen saver activates.

11 Click OK to complete the task.

FIND IT ONLINE

Use your favorite image files to create your own screen savers at **http://www.customsavers.com/index_freewarefiles.html**.

Using Power Management

These days PCs serve many different functions, even when someone is not actively sitting at the keyboard interacting with the system. You may leave your PC turned on so that it can receive incoming faxes or so that it can periodically log on to the mail server and check for new messages. These functions require that your PC be running, but there's no reason why you have to waste a lot of electrical power in the process.

Virtually all PCs come with monitors that can go into a very low power standby mode when they receive the appropriate signal from the computer. The monitor generally uses the most power of all your computer's components. Automatically shutting down the monitor may save more than half the power otherwise consumed by your system.

Leaving the system turned on may also be a little easier on your computer's components. Some experts claim that the power surges that result when you turn the power on can cause far more wear than simply leaving the computer on all the time.

If you do leave your system on all the time you may find an *uninterruptible power supply*— UPS — to be a good investment. These units maintain a steady supply of power to your PC, even if the power from the wall outlet is disrupted. Many UPS models can even communicate with a Windows 2000-based PC and perform an orderly shutdown when the UPS batteries start to run low. Of course, a UPS can also offer excellent protection against loss of data when you are actively working with your system, too. Make certain your UPS is large enough to handle power usage on both your PC and monitor — especially the power surge than can occur when a monitor comes off standby. You should avoid plugging laser printers into the UPS.

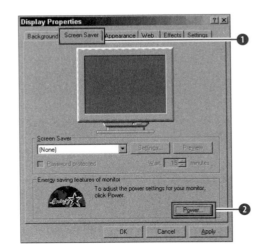

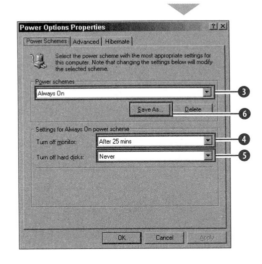

▶ Right-click a blank space on the desktop and select Properties to open the Display Properties dialog box.

❶ Click the Screen Saver tab.

❷ Click the Power button.

❸ Optionally, choose a power scheme that describes how you use your system.

❹ Select the length of time before the monitor goes into standby mode.

❺ Optionally, choose the length of time before your hard disks go into standby mode.

❻ To save your power scheme, click the Save As button and name your settings.

CROSS-REFERENCE

See "Using a Screen Saver" earlier in this chapter.

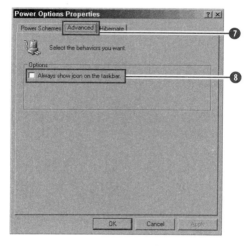

If you use both a screen saver and the energy-saving features of your monitor, you may want to set the screen saver to display more quickly than the energy-saving features. Otherwise, your monitor may turn off before the screen saver is ever displayed.

TAKE NOTE

SCHEDULED TASKS NEED POWER TOO

If you set up your system to perform routine maintenance tasks automatically, your PC must be powered on at the time the tasks are scheduled to activate. This is another good reason why you may want to leave your system running and use the power management options to minimize power consumption.

POWER MANAGEMENT OPTIONS VARY

Your power management options may not be the same as those shown in the Power Options Properties dialog box in the figures on the facing page. Laptop computers generally have more extensive power management options than do desktop systems. Even so, using the power management options that are available on your system is a good way to conserve energy.

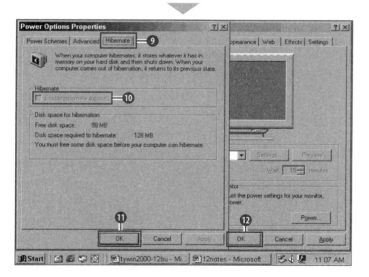

⑦ Click the Advanced tab.

⑧ Optionally, click here to show the Power Options icon in the system tray.

▶ Depending on your system's capabilities, you may see additional options on this tab.

⑨ Click the Hibernate tab.

⑩ If your system is compatible with the hibernate option, click here to activate this option.

⑪ Click OK to continue.

⑫ Click OK to complete the task.

FIND IT ONLINE

See **http://www.apcc.com** for information on Windows 2000-compatible UPS systems.

Moving and Hiding the Taskbar

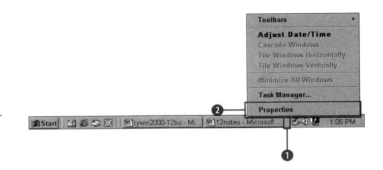

Windows 2000 is designed to allow you to have quite a few different things happening on your PC at the same time. To make it easier for you to see what programs are running and to switch between programs, Windows 2000 normally displays the *Taskbar* at the bottom of the screen. In this section you'll learn how to place the taskbar in the location that is most convenient for you, how to resize the taskbar, and how to hide it when you want to maximize the active screen area.

The Taskbar generally contains several different elements. The Start button displays the Start menu. The Quick Launch toolbar has icons to show the desktop, to start Internet Explorer and Outlook Express, and icons you may have added for quick access to your favorite programs. Next is an area that contains buttons for any programs that you currently have open. Finally, the system tray contains icons for system services such as the clock.

As you open additional programs, the program buttons on the taskbar can become pretty small as they are squeezed into the available space. If the buttons become too small, it can be difficult to read the button titles so that you can make certain you are clicking the correct button. There are several ways to deal with this problem. You can drag the top edge of the taskbar up to accommodate two or more rows of buttons — when you drag the taskbar edge the taskbar always resizes itself in full-row increments. You can also dock the taskbar along one of the sides of the screen — this provides considerably more room for program buttons.

If you only want the taskbar to appear when you really need it, select the Auto hide option in the taskbar Properties dialog box.

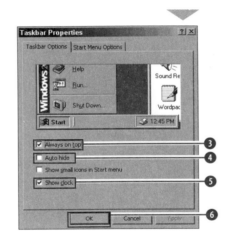

❶ Right-click a blank space on the Taskbar to display the context menu.

❷ Select Properties.

❸ Optionally, select Always on top to reserve space for the Taskbar.

❹ Select Auto hide if you want the Taskbar to disappear when you don't need it.

❺ If you don't want to see the clock in the system tray, deselect this option.

❻ Click OK to apply your changes.

CROSS-REFERENCE

See "Adding Toolbars to the Taskbar" later in this chapter.

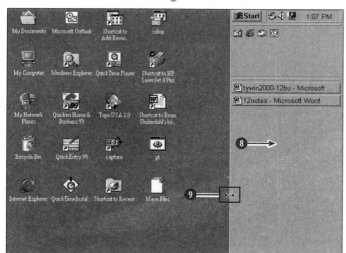

⑦ *To resize the Taskbar, drag the edge.*

⑧ *To move the Taskbar, point to a blank spot on the Taskbar and drag it to one of the edges of the screen to dock it at that edge.*

⑨ *Drag the edge of the Taskbar if you want to adjust the size in the Taskbar's new location.*

TAKE NOTE

► LOCATING A HIDDEN TASKBAR

If you cannot see the taskbar, you can usually display it by moving the mouse pointer just past the bottom edge of the screen. If the Auto hide check box is selected and the taskbar is docked at the bottom of the screen, this will cause the Taskbar to pop up. If the taskbar does not appear, try moving the mouse pointer just past the other edges of the screen until the taskbar appears.

► ACCESSING THE TASKBAR

Programs sometimes hide the taskbar to prevent you from doing anything else while they're running. This is most common with software installation programs. There are times, however, when you need to do something else, such as explore your hard disk to find a place to install a program. When the taskbar is hidden, press the Windows key or Ctrl+Esc to pop up the Start menu and display the taskbar. This method works no matter where the taskbar is hiding.

FIND IT ONLINE

See **http://www.softseek.com/Utilities/ Taskbar_Start_Menu_and_Explorer_Enhancements/ Taskbar_Tools/** for an assortment of Taskbar tools.

Adding Toolbars to the Taskbar

As handy as the Windows 2000 taskbar is, it's possible to make the taskbar far more useful by adding toolbars to the taskbar. In this section you'll learn how to make use of toolbars to enhance your taskbar.

You're probably already familiar with one of the taskbar toolbars. The Quick Launch toolbar contains icons that you can click to quickly view your desktop, browse the Internet, or check your e-mail. You may even have added some of your own shortcuts to the Quick Launch toolbar. But the Quick Launch toolbar is only one of the toolbars that you can add to the taskbar.

The Address toolbar is one of the most useful of the toolbars that you can add to the taskbar. If you know the URL of a Web page you'd like to visit, the quickest way to go directly to the site is to add the Address toolbar to the taskbar and then enter the URL into the Address bar. After you type the address and press Enter, Internet Explorer opens and takes you directly to the Web site, bypassing any start pages that Internet Explorer normally opens first.

The Links toolbar provides you with one-click access to the links on the Internet Explorer Links bar. By clicking one of the links you can quickly visit the associated Web site.

The Desktop toolbar enables you to access anything that appears on your Windows 2000 desktop. You don't have to minimize the open windows to click a desktop icon since all of those icons appear in the Desktop toolbar.

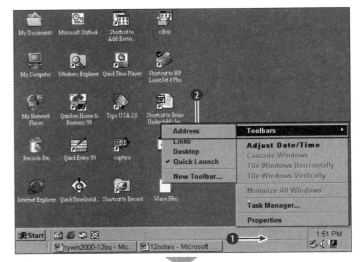

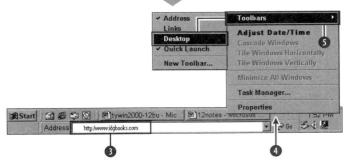

▶ *You may wish to expand the Taskbar to two rows before you add new toolbars.*

① *Right-click a blank space on the Taskbar to display the context menu.*

② *Select Toolbars ⇨ Address to add the Address toolbar to the Taskbar.*

③ *To use the Address toolbar, enter a Web page address and press Enter.*

④ *Right-click a blank space on the Taskbar to display the context menu.*

⑤ *Select Toolbars ⇨ Desktop to display the Desktop toolbar.*

▶ *You may wish to remove the Address toolbar.*

CROSS-REFERENCE

See "Moving and Hiding the Taskbar" earlier in this chapter.

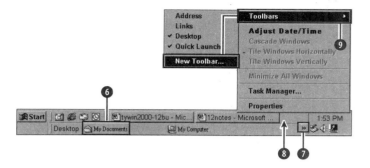

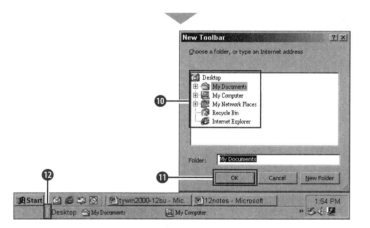

ADD NEW TOOLBARS

Adding a custom toolbar to the taskbar may be the most useful addition of all. When you select Toolbars ➪ New Toolbar from the taskbar context menu, you can specify any folder as the source of the toolbar shortcuts. The folder you specify could be a document folder that you must access often, or you might want to create a new folder and add important shortcuts to that folder. When you select the new folder as the source for the new toolbar, all of the items in that folder will appear as icons on the new toolbar, thus providing you with quick access to the items. You could even create several different folders with shortcuts to programs and documents that relate to specific projects. This would enable you to have several custom toolbars for all of your projects.

RESIZE THE TASKBAR

If you add toolbars to the taskbar, you'll quickly discover that there really isn't room in a single row for program buttons and toolbars. Drag the top edge of the taskbar up to add an additional row so that the new toolbars don't have to share a row with the buttons for your open programs.

---

⑥ Click an item to open it.

⑦ Alternatively, click the arrows to display the remaining items on the toolbar.

⑧ Right-click a blank space on the Taskbar to display the context menu.

⑨ Select Toolbars ➪ New Toolbar.

⑩ Choose a folder to use as the source for the new toolbar.

⑪ Click OK to add the toolbar.

⑫ Optionally, drag a toolbar handle onto the desktop to make the toolbar into a floating toolbar.

FIND IT ONLINE

To download a system tray manager, see
http://www.metaproducts.com/trayicon.html.

Controlling the Start Menu

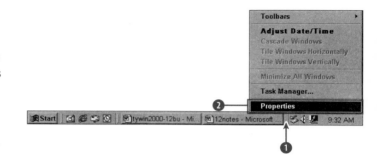

Y ou may not put a lot of thought into the Windows 2000 Start menu, but face it — the Start menu is probably the one part of Windows 2000 that you use most often. That's one reason why this section is so useful — it will show you how to control your Start menu.

The Start menu is an interesting device. Through it you can open programs, access your recently used documents, and modify the way that your PC operates. In Windows 2000 the Start menu is also customizable.

When you add items to the Start menu using the drag-and-drop methods you learned in Chapter 4, Windows 2000 assumes that you are intentionally reorganizing the menus and stops sorting the program and folder shortcuts that appear on the menus. This may be fine for a short time, but eventually you'll probably install some new programs, and those new items will not appear where you might expect in the menus. As the figures on the facing page show, you can easily correct this using the re-sort button.

Although the Advanced option is not shown in use in the figures on the facing page, selecting that option enables you to view the Start Menu folder in Internet Explorer just as if you right-click the Start button and choose Explore. Remember, though, that in Windows 2000 there are actually several Start Menu folders. If you right-click the Start button and choose Explore All Users, you will see a separate Start Menu folder. Your Start menu is actually composed of the contents of your personal Start Menu folder and the All Users Start Menu folder.

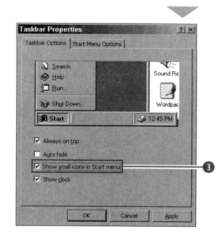

① Right-click a blank space on the Taskbar to display the context menu.

② Select Properties.

③ Optionally, select Show small icons in Start menu to reduce the size of the Start menu.

CROSS-REFERENCE

See "Adding an Entry to the Start Menu" in Chapter 4.

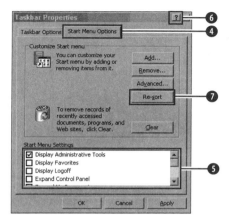

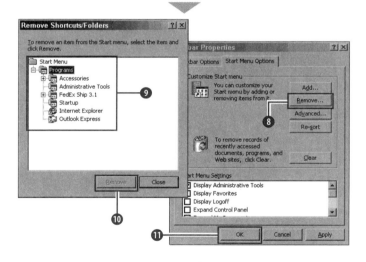

④ Click the Start Menu Options tab.

⑤ Select the options you prefer.

⑥ To learn more about an item, click the question mark and then click the item with the question mark pointer.

⑦ Click Re-sort to place the Start menus back into alphabetical order.

⑧ To remove an item from the Start menu, click the Remove button.

⑨ Select the item to remove.

⑩ Click Remove.

⑪ Click OK to complete the task.

FIND IT ONLINE

For more information on using the Windows Key, see
http://courses.ncsu.edu/classes/aee226/tips.htm.

Personal Workbook

Q&A

1 What will happen if you change the screen resolution setting but don't click the Yes button?

_____

_____

_____

2 How can you make a hidden taskbar pop up without moving the mouse?

_____

_____

_____

3 How can you find a hidden taskbar using the mouse?

_____

_____

_____

4 What do you need to activate before you can use a JPEG image as your desktop wallpaper?

_____

_____

_____

5 What can you do to restore order to the Start menu if items are no longer being sorted?

_____

_____

_____

6 How can you reduce the size of the icons on the Start menu?

_____

_____

_____

7 What is the fastest way to choose a desktop element on the Appearance tab of the Display Properties dialog box so that you can change the element's color?

_____

_____

_____

8 How can you view the items in the Control Panel folder without opening the folder?

_____

_____

ANSWERS: PAGE 396

EXTRA PRACTICE

1 Try out a different screen resolution setting.

2 Move the taskbar to the left side of your screen.

3 Try one of the sample color schemes.

4 Sort your Start menu into alphabetical order.

5 Try several different refresh rates to see which produces the best display.

6 Add a toolbar that shows the contents of the My Documents folder to the taskbar.

REAL-WORLD APPLICATIONS

✔ Your company has several PCs in public areas of your office. You add the company logo as wallpaper.

✔ You need to make certain that people won't be able to view the salary budget worksheet when you are away from your desk. You apply a password-protected screen saver to prevent unauthorized access.

✔ You have added several new programs to your PC, and your Start menu is a mess. You change to small icons and re-sort the menu to make your system easier to use.

✔ You use your PC a lot and have been experiencing headaches. You adjust your monitor refresh rate to correct the problem.

Visual Quiz

How can you display this dialog box? How do the controls on this tab interact?

_____

_____

_____

_____

_____

_____

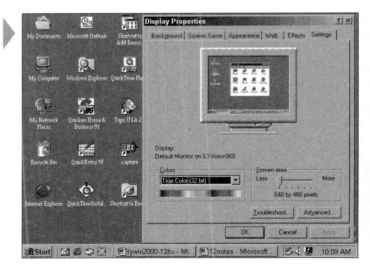

CHAPTER **13**

MASTER THESE SKILLS

- ▶ **Changing to a Single-Click Mouse**
- ▶ **Configuring Mouse Speed**
- ▶ **Configuring Keyboard Speed**
- ▶ **Adding Sounds to Events**
- ▶ **Adding New Hardware**
- ▶ **Using the Registry Editor**

Changing How Windows 2000 Works

In this chapter, you learn how to make some changes to the way Windows 2000 functions. These changes are typically not splashy and visually appealing changes to the appearance of Windows 2000. Rather, they are changes that may help you to be more productive in using Windows 2000. These changes can help make your PC work in ways that are easier for you.

Changes that you make to the way Windows 2000 works don't have to make your PC into a completely different type of machine. Rather, you should think of most of these as simple, subtle tweaks that give your computer a tune-up. If you change something so much that the difference jumps out at you, you've probably gone too far. Think of small adjustments and you'll get the idea of how much change is called for in most cases.

The reasons for customizing the way Windows 2000 works are as varied as the people who use PCs. For example, if you are a very fast typist you might want to configure your keyboard for lightning-fast response. But if you're a hunt-and-peck typist, that setting could make your keyboard repeat characters too quickly. If you set your PC to automatically check for new e-mail messages while you do other things around your office, you might want a sound file to play when a message arrives so you don't have to constantly check the screen. In this chapter, you learn how to deal with all these issues to make your Windows 2000-based PC easier to use.

Most of the settings discussed in this chapter are accessed through the *Control Panel*. The Control Panel is the central location where you'll find the tools you need to configure and control nearly all aspects of how your PC runs under Windows 2000. The Control Panel contents can vary depending on your system's configuration, so your Control Panel may have a slightly different set of icons than are shown in the figures.

We have carefully selected items for this chapter so that none of them pose any danger to your system. Be aware, however, that some tools — especially the Registry Editor — can cause major problems if you make changes just to see what will happen. When in doubt, don't change anything you don't understand.

Changing to a Single-Click Mouse

D o you ever get frustrated when things don't seem to function in a logical manner? If so, you have probably asked yourself why your mouse doesn't always work the same way. Sometimes all you need is a single mouse click and other times you have to double-click. Actually, you can configure your mouse to use single clicks rather than double clicks. When you do, your mouse will work pretty much the same whether you're clicking a link on a Web page or clicking a document icon on your desktop.

Windows 2000 uses the terms *single-click style* and *double-click style* to indicate the two types of mouse behavior. In the single-click style, a single click of the left mouse button selects an object, and a double click opens it. In the double-click style, moving the mouse over an object selects the object, and a single click opens it. When you're browsing the Web, moving your mouse over a link selects the link and a single click opens the link.

Although it may sound like a single-click style mouse is the best choice since your mouse will always work the same way, you may soon discover that there are big differences between browsing the Internet and working with your files and folders. For example, consider how often you are likely to select multiple files on your PC. You probably don't select multiple objects on a Web page, so you may not realize how difficult it can be to get in the habit of correctly selecting more than one object with a single-click mouse. First, you move the mouse pointer over an object, and then you hold down either the Shift key or the Ctrl key, depending on whether you wish to select a contiguous range or several individual items. Next, you move the mouse pointer to the next item you wish to select. If you don't want to select everything between the first and last item, the

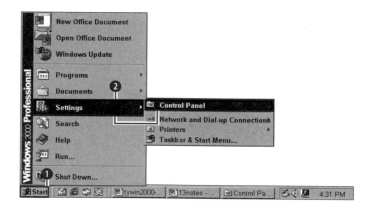

1 Click the Start button.

2 Select Settings ➪ Control Panel.

3 Select Tools ➪ Folder Options to open the Folder Options dialog box.

CROSS-REFERENCE
See "Configuring Mouse Speed" later in this chapter.

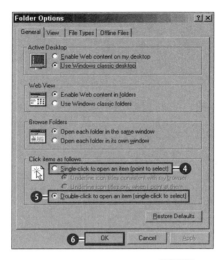

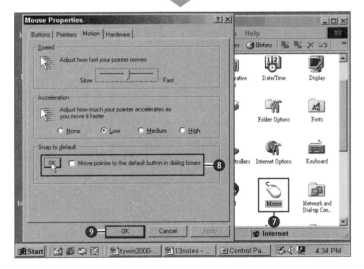

process gets a little tricky. You must move the mouse pointer carefully so that it touches only the items you want to select. If you select an item in error, move the mouse pointer onto the object and then away from it.

TAKE NOTE

▶ TOUCH PADS CAN BE TRICKY

If you configure your mouse to use single clicking rather than double clicking, and you use a laptop PC with a touch pad, you may find that selecting items correctly is extremely tricky. Touch pads move the mouse pointer, but if you tap the touch pad, the tap is generally accepted as a click of the left mouse button.

▶ CHANGE YOUR VIEW

If you select the double-click style, you'll soon discover that it's much easier to use the Windows Explorer details and list views than to use the small or large icons views.

---

④ *Select single-click to use single mouse clicks to open objects.*

⑤ *Alternatively, select double-click to use double mouse clicks to open objects.*

⑥ *Click OK to continue.*

⑦ *Optionally, double-click the Mouse icon.*

⑧ *If you want the mouse pointer to automatically jump to the default button in dialog boxes, select this option.*

⑨ *Click OK to complete the task.*

▶ *You may wish to leave the Control Panel open if you are continuing in this chapter.*

FIND IT ONLINE

For information on a cordless mouse, see
http://www.cordlessmouse.com/.

Configuring Mouse Speed

Your mouse is supposed to make working in the graphical Windows 2000 environment much easier. But if your mouse doesn't seem to work the way it should, using it can seem like pure torture. Your mouse might react too slowly to movements or it might be difficult for you to make it recognize when you have double-clicked something. In this section you'll learn how to correct these types of problems as well as how to choose different mouse pointers.

A PC mouse always has at least two buttons. You normally use the left button for selecting or opening things, and the right button to display those handy context menus. If you're left-handed you may find this button arrangement a little awkward, but there's an easy solution. You can quickly configure Windows 2000 to swap the functions of the two buttons so that using your mouse feels more natural to you.

In addition to changing the way your mouse responds to movements and clicks, there are several other configuration options that you can use, too. You can have a little fun with your mouse by selecting different pointers to replace the standard ones that Windows 2000 uses by default. You can even use *animated cursors* — mouse pointers that use animation to make the mouse pointer a bit more interesting. Animated cursors designed for Windows 95 or for Windows 98 will work fine in Windows 2000.

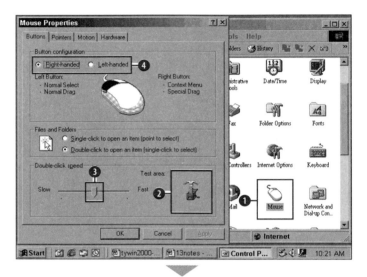

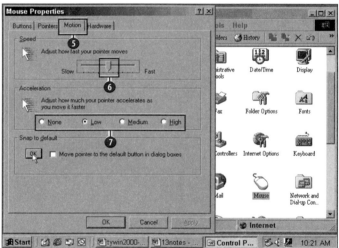

❶ Double-click the Mouse icon in the Control Panel.

❷ Double-click in the test area to test double-click speed.

❸ If necessary, drag the slider right or left to adjust the double-click speed.

❹ Optionally, choose the button configuration to suit your needs.

❺ Click the Motion tab.

❻ Drag the slider right or left to adjust the mouse speed.

❼ Choose the acceleration option you prefer.

CROSS-REFERENCE

See "Configuring Your Keyboard" later in this chapter.

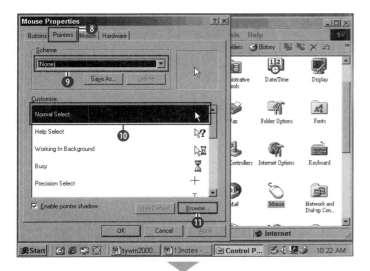

KEEP YOUR MOUSE CLEAN

If your mouse pointer seems to move erratically, the cause may not be that the mouse is configured incorrectly. Erratic mouse movement is most often the result of a dirty mouse or a worn-out mouse pad. If you turn your mouse over you'll probably find that the mouse ball can be easily removed by turning a section of the mouse bottom. Once you have removed the ball you can rinse it off in clean water and then dry it thoroughly. Then check the inside of the mouse for lint or dirt. Don't apply any liquids to the inside of the mouse, but you may want to blow out any dust before you replace the ball. Be sure that the door that holds the ball in place is turned to the proper position before you turn the mouse upright so you don't lose the ball.

USE MOUSE TRAILS

Finding the mouse pointer can sometimes be difficult — especially on some laptop PC screens. If you experience this problem you may want to try the pointer trail option. When you select this option, a series of pointers trail behind the mouse pointer as you move the mouse around on your screen, making it far easier to find the mouse pointer. This can be a good option choice to help a new PC user learn to use a mouse.

---

8 Click the Pointers tab.

9 Optionally, choose one of the available mouse pointer schemes.

10 Select one of the mouse pointers to change.

11 Click the Browse button.

12 Choose one of the available mouse pointers.

13 Preview the pointer here.

14 Click Open to apply the new pointer.

15 Click OK to complete the task.

FIND IT ON THE WEB

You'll find lots of additional Windows mouse pointers at **http://www.dolphinusa.com/cursors/index.htm**.

Configuring Keyboard Speed

You probably use your keyboard more than any other component of your PC. Making certain that your keyboard is both comfortable and working properly is an important part of configuring your system to meet your needs. There are several keyboard adjustments that you can make in Windows 2000, and they are covered in this section.

Keyboard speed can be a major factor in helping to make typing more efficient. The Keyboard Properties dialog box shown on the facing page has two keyboard speed adjustments as well as a related visual adjustment.

The *repeat delay* is the measure of how long you must hold a key down before that character is repeated. Adjust this setting to the shortest delay that is compatible with your typing style.

The *repeat rate* is a measure of how many times per second characters are repeated once you've held the key down long enough to begin repeating characters. Adjust this setting to a rate that feels most comfortable.

The *cursor blink rate* setting controls how quickly the cursor blinks on and off. The rate you select is a matter of personal preference.

You can use the Input Locales settings to choose an alternative keyboard layout, such as one of the Dvorak keyboard layouts. Some people claim that typing on a Dvorak keyboard is faster than typing on a standard QWERTY keyboard layout, but this may depend on how you learned to type.

You can also choose additional language layouts by clicking the Add button on the Input Locales tab of the Keyboard Properties dialog box. When you add a new language, you can also select the layout for the new language keyboard. In most cases you'll probably want to

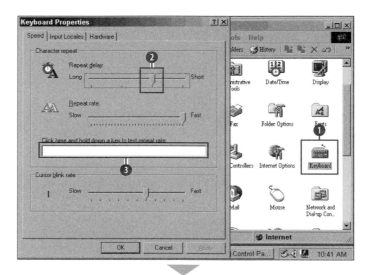

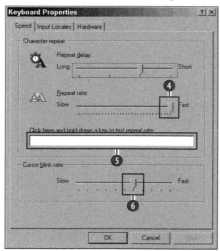

① *Double-click the Keyboard icon in the Control Panel.*

② *Drag the Repeat delay slider left or right to test different settings.*

③ *Click the test box and hold down a key to check the delay setting.*

④ *Drag the Repeat rate slider left or right to test different settings.*

⑤ *Click the test box and hold down a key to check the delay setting.*

⑥ *Drag the slider right or left if you wish to adjust the cursor blink rate.*

CROSS-REFERENCE

See Chapter 8 for information on the accessibility options.

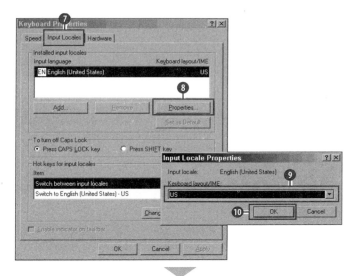

use the same type of layout for all of the languages. Once you have added new languages, you can choose hot keys for switching between languages. The hot keys will have no effect until you install additional languages.

USING FOREIGN LANGUAGES

Foreign languages often include characters that are not shown on a standard keyboard. If you choose to add a new language on the Input Locales tab of the Keyboard Properties dialog box, you'll find that typing those characters will be far easier. Of course, changing keyboard layouts won't actually move the keys on your keyboard. If you choose to use an alternative keyboard layout, remember that what is shown on the keys won't be the same characters that will appear when you type.

TOGGLING CAPS LOCK

If you find that you often press the Caps Lock key in error, you may want to consider the Caps Lock options on the Input Locales tab. You may need to experiment with the two settings to see which method of turning off the Caps Lock feels the most natural to you.

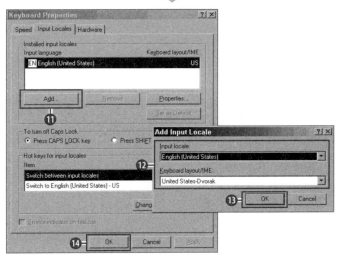

⑦ *Click the Input Locales tab.*

⑧ *Click Properties if you wish to choose a new keyboard layout option.*

⑨ *Select your preferred keyboard layout.*

⑩ *Click the OK button.*

⑪ *Click the Add button if you wish to add additional languages.*

⑫ *Choose the new language and layout.*

⑬ *Click OK*

⑭ *Click OK to complete the task.*

FIND IT ONLINE

For a utility to re-map your keyboard, see
http://www.gdgsystems.com/.

Adding Sounds to Events

Your PC can provide you with audible alerts that signal Windows 2000 *system events*. These system events are common things such as opening Windows 2000, displaying an error message, or emptying the Recycle Bin. In this section you'll learn how to control which sounds are associated with the various system events.

The only sounds that you can associate with events are *wave files*— digital recordings of actual sounds. You can record your own wave files or you can choose from the many thousands of existing wave files that you'll find either on your system or on the Internet.

Wave files tend to be fairly large — especially if they were recorded at a high-quality level or in stereo. In most cases, however, even a low-quality wave sound is more than adequate to signal a system event. There's really no reason why you need a CD-quality recording of Eine Kleine Nachtmusik to let you know that you clicked a button that isn't currently available! It's a far better idea to use short sound clips to signal events.

By default, Windows 2000 does not assign sounds to most events. If it did, your system would be making sounds almost all the time you were working with your system. This could be quite disruptive — especially if you work in a relatively quiet office. There are instances, however, where associating sounds with a majority of system events could be very useful. The audible clues to system events could be very helpful to someone with limited vision or when you need to be aware of events without looking at the screen. You could even record your own messages to help a new PC user learn how to use the system. If you do, remember to keep the sounds as short as possible to minimize file sizes.

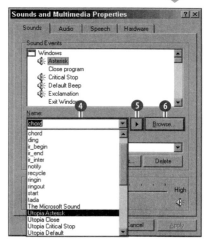

❶ Double-click the Sounds and Multimedia icon in the Control Panel.

❷ Select an event that has a speaker icon indicating that a sound has been assigned to the event.

❸ Click the Play button to play the sound.

❹ Optionally, select a new sound for the event.

❺ Click the Play button to play the new sound.

❻ Alternatively, click the Browse button to search for a different sound.

CROSS-REFERENCE

See "Recording Sounds" in Chapter 17.

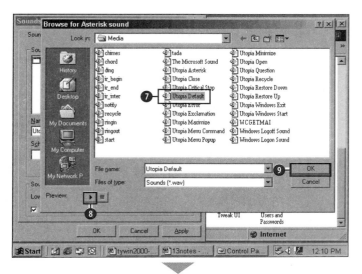

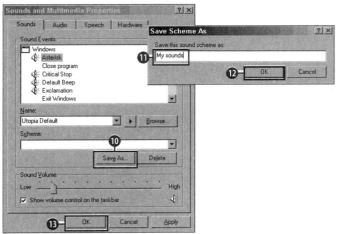

⑦ Select a sound file.

⑧ Click the Play button to hear a preview of the sound.

⑨ Click OK to assign the new sound and close the dialog box.

⑩ Optionally, click Save As to save your sound scheme.

⑪ Type a name for the sound scheme.

⑫ Click the OK button to close the dialog box.

⑬ Click OK to complete the task.

FIND IT ONLINE

See **http://www.dailywav.com/** for new wave sounds daily.

Adding New Hardware

One of the really great features of Windows 2000-based PCs is that they are compatible with nearly all of the new types of hardware or peripherals that you might want to buy to expand your system. In fact, that almost universal compatibility is a huge advantage for PC users because they don't have to put up with a limited range of products when so many manufacturers support the Windows platform.

Windows 2000 makes adding new hardware a fairly easy task. Because Windows 2000 supports *plug and play*, adding new hardware is often as simple as simply installing the new equipment and then starting Windows 2000. In many cases Windows 2000 will recognize that the new piece of hardware has been installed and will automatically load the proper software to support it.

All versions of Windows use software known as *drivers* to support the various pieces of hardware that are installed on the system. This system of using drivers makes it possible for Windows 2000 to support many different types of hardware, because the hardware manufacturer only has to supply a Windows 2000-compatible driver in order for the peripheral to be usable by all of your application programs.

The figures on the facing page and the following pages are a little different from those that accompany most of the tasks in this book. Rather than attempt to detail each step that you might encounter, these figures present an overview of the hardware installation task. The reason for this is simple: there are thousands of different pieces of hardware you could add to your PC, and the process varies somewhat depending on what you're installing. Therefore, we've chosen to show you the screens that best illustrate the important things you need to know about adding new hardware.

Continued

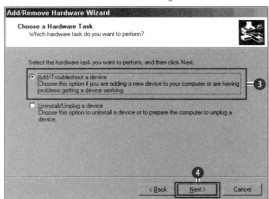

❶ *Double-click the Add/Remove Hardware icon in the Control Panel.*

❷ *Click Next to continue.*

❸ *Make certain the Add/Troubleshoot a device radio button is selected.*

❹ *Click Next to continue.*

CROSS-REFERENCE

See "Using Windows Update" in Chapter 15.

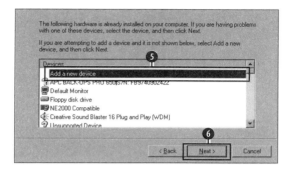

The following hardware is already installed on your computer. If you are having problems with one of these devices, select the device, and then click Next.

If you are attempting to add a device and it is not shown below, select Add a new device, and then click Next.

Devices

Add a new device
APC BACK-UPS PRO 650 S/N: FB9740902422
Default Monitor
Floppy disk drive
NE2000 Compatible
Creative Sound Blaster 16 Plug and Play (WDM)
Unsupported Device

< Back | Next > | Cancel

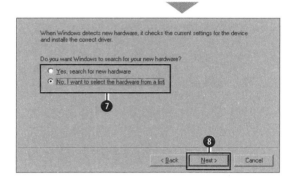

When Windows detects new hardware, it checks the current settings for the device and installs the correct driver.

Do you want Windows to search for your new hardware?

○ Yes, search for new hardware
● No, I want to select the hardware from a list

< Back | Next > | Cancel

⑤ *Select Add a new device.*

⑥ *Click Next to continue.*

⑦ *Choose the option you prefer.*

▶ *In this case, select No, I want to select the hardware from a list to select the new hardware manually.*

⑧ *Click Next to continue.*

FIND IT ONLINE

To find out about new hardware quality before you buy, see **http://www.winreviews.com/**.

Adding New Hardware

Continued

Different types of hardware have varying installation requirements, of course. The figures on the facing page show an example of installing a very common type of peripheral — a printer.

When you install new hardware, Windows 2000 will eventually arrive at a point where you must choose which drivers to install. As the third figure shows, you will often have the option of choosing to use the driver that is supplied with Windows 2000 or to use a driver supplied on disk by the hardware manufacturer. Choosing the correct driver is very important, but your choice may not be an easy one. You can be certain that a driver that is supplied along with Windows 2000 is Windows 2000-compatible, but that driver may not always support the more advanced features of your hardware. The manufacturer-supplied driver will, of course, support every possible feature of the hardware, but may not work too well with Windows 2000. You may want to resolve the dilemma by looking at the file dates on the manufacturer's disk. If the files all seem to be from well before Windows 2000 was released, you may want to try the Windows 2000-supplied drivers first. You can always update the drivers later if you discover that some important features are not supported.

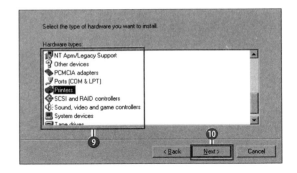

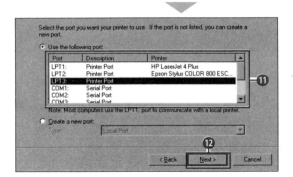

⑨ *Choose the type of device you are adding.*

⑩ *Click Next to continue.*

⑪ *If you are adding a printer, select the port.*

⑫ *Click Next to continue.*

CROSS-REFERENCE

See "Installing Programs" in Chapter 4.

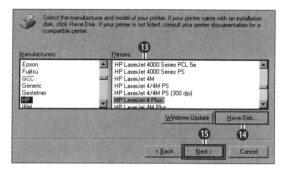

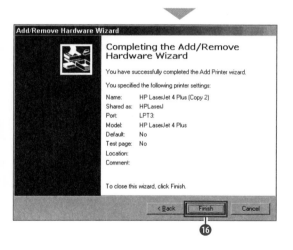

⑬ *Choose the manufacturer and model.*

⑭ *Alternatively, click the Have Disk button and follow the on-screen directions to use a driver disk supplied by the manufacturer.*

⑮ *Click Next to continue.*

▶ *Depending on the device you are installing, you may see several screens where you must make selections before you arrive at the final screen.*

⑯ *Click Finish to complete the task.*

▶ **MAKE SURE IT'S COMPATIBLE**

Although most hardware that works with Windows 98 will also work with Windows 2000, not all equipment is Windows 2000-compatible. The reason for this is usually that the hardware manufacturer has not supplied the proper type of drivers for Windows 2000. You cannot use *virtual device drivers* — VxDs — with Windows 2000 because they can allow peripherals to cause damage to your hardware or data. Although Windows 98 allows VxDs to be used, Windows 2000 protects your system from potential damage by preventing VxDs from operating. When in doubt, contact the manufacturer and ask if Windows 2000 is specifically supported — before you buy.

▶ **CONSIDER USB**

Windows 2000 supports *USB* — Universal Serial Bus peripherals. If you have the option, you may wish to consider buying USB peripherals whenever possible because Windows 2000 automatically recognizes and installs them as soon as they are connected. Since all USB peripherals are external devices, they can be installed without opening your PC. In theory, you could add well over 100 USB devices to your system, but it's unlikely that you'll ever approach that in the real world. Your PC must have USB ports in order to use USB devices, but those ports can be added to most older PCs that lack USB capabilities. Some devices such as the 3Com U.S. Robotics ISDN TA include both serial and USB ports to make it easier for you to use the port that best suits your needs.

Using the Registry Editor

Windows 2000 uses a special database called the *Registry* to maintain system settings and to control how your system functions. The Registry is a complex structure that is absolutely vital to proper operation of your PC. In this section, you'll see how to edit the Registry to make a simple change to Windows 2000.

There are many changes that you can make by editing the Registry. In every case you'll be looking for a specific *key* — which is one of the values held in the Registry. Different Registry keys hold different types of values. Many of the keys hold complex numeric values, but some are like the key used in the example on the facing page — they hold simple text values.

The example used in this case shows you how to modify a Registry key to rename the Recycle Bin. If you right-click the Recycle Bin you'll notice that the context menu does not include a rename command. Editing the Registry is the only way you can rename the Recycle Bin, so it is a good example of how you can use the Registry to accomplish tasks that cannot be done any other way.

Most of the time when you use the Registry editor you'll be making a change that does something more profound than simply renaming the Recycle Bin. Even so, the same procedures apply no matter what type of change you are making. First you must locate the correct key, and then you must change the correct item to show the new value. You must make certain that you enter the correct value type — in this case, text — for the value that you are changing.

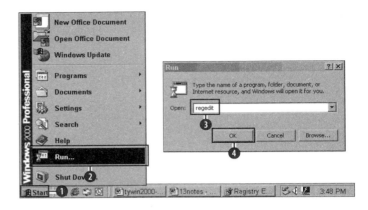

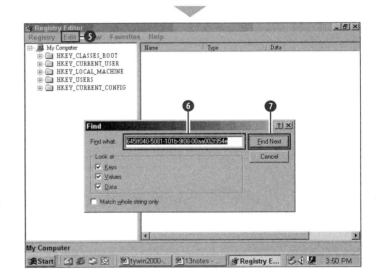

❶ Click the Start button.

❷ Select Run.

❸ Enter **regedit** in the text box.

❹ Click OK to continue.

❺ Select Edit ➪ Find.

❻ Enter the value to find — in this case 645ff040-5081-101b-9f08-00aa002f954e.

▶ This happens to be the Recycle Bin key that you will modify.

❼ Click Find Next.

CROSS-REFERENCE

See "Looking for Problems with Device Manager" in Chapter 15.

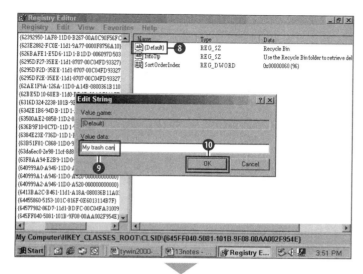

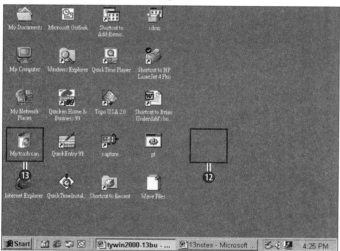

USE EXTREME CAUTION

Making changes to the Windows 2000 Registry without using extreme caution can be very dangerous. You can render your system incapable of starting Windows 2000 if you make changes at random. Whenever you are instructed to edit the Registry, always make certain you are making the change to the correct location within the Registry. Many different Registry keys are quite similar — if you don't find the exact key you are looking for, don't assume that a similar-appearing key is the one you want.

SAVE REGISTRY KEYS

Before you make a change in the Registry, it's a good idea to save the section that you are about to change. That way you'll be able to easily reverse the change if necessary. To save a section of the Registry, select the item you intend to change and then choose Registry ⇨ Export Registry File. Assign a meaningful name to the file so you will recognize it if you need it later. You can double-click a saved Registry file to import it back into the Registry.

---

⑧ *Double-click the value you want to change — {Default} in this case.*

⑨ *Enter the new value.*

⑩ *Click OK.*

⑪ *Click Close to close the Registry editor.*

⑫ *Click a blank space on your desktop.*

⑬ *Press F5 to see your change.*

FIND IT ONLINE

To find out more about the Registry, see
http://www.regedit.com/.

Personal Workbook

Q&A

1 How can you change your keyboard layout without actually moving any keys?

_____

_____

_____

2 Where do you go to assign sounds to Windows 2000 events?

_____

_____

_____

3 What type of peripheral installs automatically when you plug in its cable?

_____

_____

_____

4 What do you call mouse pointers that show a brief animation?

_____

_____

_____

5 What can you do to change the number of times keys repeat when they are held down?

_____

_____

_____

6 What type of sound files can you associate with system events?

_____

_____

_____

7 Where do you find most of the system configuration tools?

_____

_____

_____

8 How can you save a Registry key so it can be easily restored?

_____

_____

_____

ANSWERS: PAGE 397

EXTRA PRACTICE

1. Change the sound that plays when Windows 2000 starts.

2. Change your mouse to operate as a single-click mouse.

3. Set your keyboard repeat rate to the fastest position and see how quickly keys repeat.

4. Change your keyboard layout to one of the Dvorak layouts and try typing a letter.

5. Try one of the dinosaur animated cursors.

6. Add a new printer.

REAL-WORLD APPLICATIONS

✔ You need to create a fancy document that has to be in your customer's office halfway across the country, but your customer does not have the correct software installed to open the document. You install the same brand and model of printer your customer owns and print the document to a file that you e-mail to them for printing.

✔ You are helping someone with limited vision set up their PC. You associate different sounds with all the important system events so that they can tell when something happens on their computer.

✔ You are having problems controlling your mouse. You change the mouse speed and acceleration settings so that the mouse moves more comfortably.

Visual Quiz

How can you display this dialog box? How can you tell which events have associated sounds? How can you hear the sounds?

_____

_____

_____

_____

_____

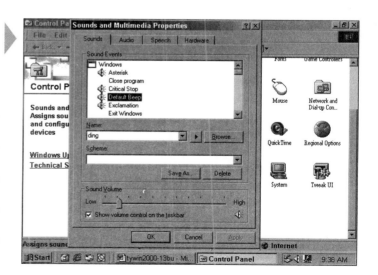

CHAPTER 14

MASTER THESE SKILLS

▶ Checking for Disk Errors

▶ Improving Disk Performance

▶ Using the Disk Cleanup Tool

▶ Backing Up Files

▶ Preparing for Disk Problems

Managing Your Disks

Your disk drives are some of the most important hardware components in your PC. They hold all of the programs that you run, but even more importantly, your disk drives store all of the data files that you save. If something goes seriously wrong with your disk drives, you could lose all of that valuable information in a fraction of a second. In this chapter, you'll learn how to take some steps to protect yourself from disk-related problems.

There are several types of problems that you may encounter with your disk drives, and Windows 2000 includes tools to help you find and correct these problems. These tools include an error checker that you can use to make certain that there are no physical or file system errors on your disks. Another tool improves system performance by making certain your files aren't fragmented and spread all over your disks in several pieces. A disk cleanup tool helps you to remove files that are simply wasting space and serving no useful purpose. Finally, a backup program helps you to protect your valuable data by making archival copies of your important files.

Windows 2000 supports several different *file systems* — different methods of storing data on your disks. Because file systems are so central to the core of an operating system, you must always be certain to use tools that were designed specifically for the file system that you are using. But because at least one of the Windows 2000 file systems — *NTFS 5* — is a new version that has never been used before, it is not compatible with any older disk utilities or tools. To ensure the safety of your files, you must never attempt to use a third-party disk utility on a Windows 2000-based PC unless that utility is specifically designed for Windows 2000. Note, however, that all of the disk tools that are included with Windows 2000 are safe to use no matter which Windows 2000 file system is in use on your PC.

Although Windows 2000 supports several different file systems, there is no easy way in Windows 2000 to change back and forth between file systems. Some third-party partition management software is able to convert between different file systems, but because that is not a Windows 2000 feature, it will not be covered in this book.

Checking for Disk Errors

Disk errors can be hazardous to the health of your data. Fortunately, disk drives tend to be a reliable piece of hardware, so disk errors aren't something you should encounter too often. Unfortunately, disk errors usually occur without giving you much warning. In fact, you can have disk errors and not even be aware that there is a problem until it's too late.

Disk errors generally fall into one of two categories. *File system* errors are the most common type of disk errors. Disk space is allocated using special information tables that are stored on the disk. Errors in these tables can result in space being marked as in use when in fact it should be free. Other, more serious file system errors can cause two or more files to be allocated the same disk space.

Physical errors are places where the disk is physically unable to read or write reliably. All hard disks have some physical errors, but in most cases you won't be aware of them because hard drives automatically compensate for a certain number of physical errors. When the drive is initially prepared for use, any existing physical errors are mapped out, and the drive automatically skips the bad spots. After the drive has been prepared, any new physical errors are called *bad sectors*. When you check for disk errors, you can choose to scan for bad sectors so that they will not be used in the future.

Any type of disk errors can cause serious problems. You can lose important files, or your entire system could lock up and refuse to function. An error-checking program, as shown on the facing page, looks for disk errors of various types and attempts to correct them.

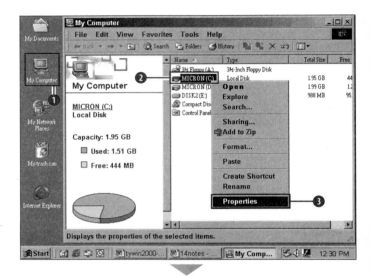

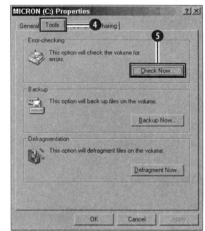

❶ Double-click the My Computer icon on your desktop.

❷ Right-click the drive you wish to check.

❸ Select Properties from the context menu.

❹ Click the Tools tab.

❺ Click the Check Now button.

CROSS-REFERENCE

See "Improving Disk Performance" later in this chapter.

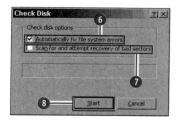

Many disk errors can be traced to a simple cause: PC users who don't bother to properly shut down their systems. Unless you use the Shut Down option on the Start menu, you may still have important files open when you turn off your PC. These open files can be corrupted, and the file system can easily lose track of the space allocated to the files.

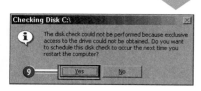

TAKE NOTE

▶ USE NTFS

One method of avoiding many file system errors is to use an NTFS-style partition. When you first install Windows 2000, you are given the option to convert from less secure types of file systems to NTFS. Although NTFS is more secure than other file systems, it is not an option if you must dual boot your PC, because only Windows 2000 can use NTFS 5 partitions.

▶ EXCLUSIVE ACCESS IS REQUIRED

As the final figure shows, a disk can only be checked for errors if the error-checking program can have exclusive access to the drive. Often this means restarting your system so that any errors can be found and corrected.

⑥ Select this option to make certain that file system errors are corrected.

⑦ Select this option to scan for physical errors.

⑧ Click Start to begin the scan.

⑨ If this message appears, click Yes to perform the scan when you restart.

▶ You may wish to restart your system immediately to scan your disks now.

▶ If you have more than one hard drive, you can schedule all of them for a disk check before restarting.

FIND IT ONLINE

For information on removing unneeded files after running ScanDisk see **http://search.zdnet.com/ pcmag/pctech/content/solutions/oe1704a.htm.**

Improving Disk Performance

If you've used your computer for some time, you may have noticed that it seems to be getting a bit slower the more you use it. This reduction in performance isn't due to wear. Rather, the problem is that your files are becoming *fragmented*—spread out in numerous pieces in various areas of the disk.

Disk space fragmentation is easy to visualize if you think about the space in a shopping mall parking lot. If you arrange to meet a group of your friends at the mall early in the morning when the shops are just opening, it will probably be fairly easy for you to find a group of spaces where you can all park right next to each other. If you wait until later in the day, the lot will fill up and you'll all have to look for those random parking spots spread out around the lot.

Disk space allocation generally works pretty much like the parking spaces in the mall parking lot. Files that are created and saved first get the first available spaces. Later files use the spaces further out on the disk. But when a file is deleted from the disk, an open space is available for new files. If the next new file can fit into the opening, it is stored *contiguously*. But if the file is too large to fit into one space, it is fragmented into two or more pieces.

Reading and writing fragmented files takes longer, and this has an adverse effect on system performance. Because your disk drives are much slower than most of the components in your computer, the effects of disk fragmentation are somewhat exaggerated in their overall impact on system performance.

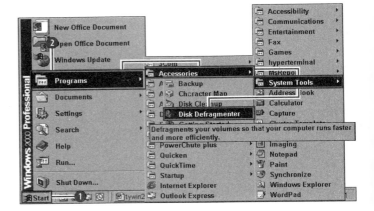

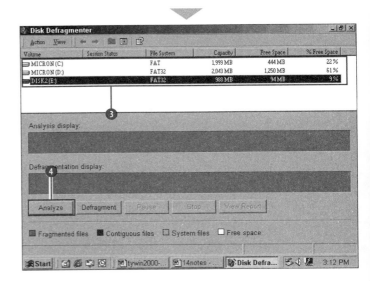

❶ Click the Start button.

❷ Select Programs ⇨ Accessories ⇨ System Tools ⇨ Disk Defragmenter.

❸ Select the drive you wish to defragment.

❹ Click the Analyze button to see if the drive needs defragmentation.

CROSS-REFERENCE

See "Using the Disk Cleanup Tool" later in this chapter.

The disk defragmenter can work efficiently only if nothing attempts to write to your hard disk while it is working. Anything that writes to your hard disk will either delay the disk defragmenter or make it restart the process. Be sure to stop your e-mail program and any other applications before you start the disk defragmentation.

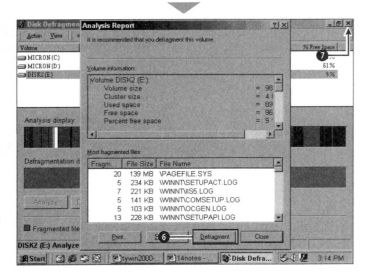

> **TAKE NOTE**
>
> ▶ **EVEN NTFS BECOMES FRAGMENTED**
>
> Although NTFS partitions use more advanced file storage techniques that reduce the amount of file fragmentation that occurs on them, they are not immune to file fragmentation. Executive Software, the manufacturer of the Windows 2000 disk defragmenter software, reports that fragmentation can be a serious problem on NTFS partitions, and that this may be a major performance drain.
>
> ▶ **FREE SOME SPACE**
>
> Disk defragmentation can take considerably longer if your hard disk is almost full. This can also prevent the defragmenter from doing as complete a job as it could if there is plenty of free space. Adequate free space provides room for moving files as the disk is defragmented.

5 When the analysis is complete, click View Report to see the analysis.

6 If you want to defragment the drive, click the Defragment button.

▶ If the drive is very full or highly fragmented, defragmentation may take considerable time.

7 Click the Close button to complete the task.

> **FIND IT ONLINE**
>
> For information on defragmentation, see **http://www.execsoft.com/products/dknt20/ntfragwp.htm**.

Using the Disk Cleanup Tool

Your hard disk probably contains dozens if not hundreds of useless files that are simply wasting space. All of these excess files take away room that could be used more productively, and they reduce your computer's performance, too.

You could take the time to remove those old files manually, but Windows 2000 provides you with a tool to make the process much simpler. The Disk Cleanup tool automates the process of cleaning up unneeded files.

When you open the Disk Cleanup tool, you'll find that there are a number of different types of files that may be wasting your disk space. One of these types — temporary Internet files — is stored on your hard disk so that Internet Explorer can later load those same Web pages more quickly. Generally, though, the amount of time that is saved is rather small unless you are returning to the same page within a few minutes of your last visit. Otherwise it's likely that the page will have changed and the new page would have to be loaded anyway.

There are a number of other types of space-wasting files that the Disk Cleanup tool can remove. You can view a description of each file type by selecting its type in the *Files to delete* list box. Depending on the type of file that you've selected, you may see a View Files button near the bottom of the dialog box. In most cases, viewing the files won't serve much purpose because it is often hard to determine whether a particular file is worth saving.

Of course, you can limit the amount of space wasted by Recycle Bin and temporary Internet files by configuring the Recycle Bin and Internet Explorer options, too. These subjects were covered in Chapters 6 and 9, respectively. If you configure those two items correctly, you probably won't need to use the Disk Cleanup tool as often.

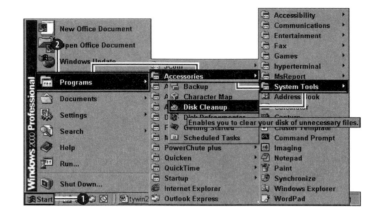

➊ Click the Start button.

➋ Select Programs ➪ Accessories ➪ System Tools ➪ Disk Cleanup.

➌ Select the drive you wish to clean.

➍ Click the OK button to continue.

CROSS-REFERENCE

See "Uninstalling Programs" in Chapter 4.

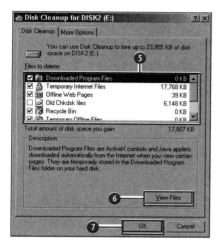

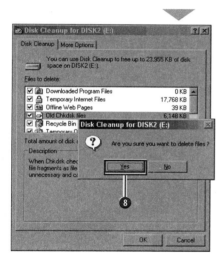

USE MORE OPTIONS

Although the More Options tab of the Disk Cleanup dialog box is not covered in the figures here, it offers two additional ways to free disk space. You can remove Windows 2000 components that you aren't using. You can also uninstall programs that you no longer need. You may find that you can free several hundred megabytes by junking old programs.

DEFRAGMENT AFTER CLEANUP

After you use the Disk Cleanup tool to remove unnecessary files, you may want to run the disk defragmentation tool so that your system makes better use of the available space. The disk defragmenter can do a better job of moving files into contiguous space if it has more free space to work with. In addition, defragmenting immediately after freeing up disk space makes it far less likely that new files you add later will have to be fragmented.

⑤ Select the types of files to remove.

⑥ If you want to look at the files first, click the View Files button.

⑦ Click the OK button to continue.

⑧ Click Yes to confirm that you wish to delete the files.

▶ The files you delete using the Disk Cleanup tool are permanently removed and cannot be recovered.

FIND IT ONLINE

To download a utility that watches all file system activity, see **http://www.sysinternals.com/filemon.htm.**

Backing Up Files

Unfortunately, there are many different types of problems that can cause you to lose important files. Power outages, computer viruses, disk failures, and simple human error can all conspire to wipe out data that you need. Backing up your files is the best way to protect yourself against losing your important data. Backing up your files can also be a fairly quick and easy process — especially if you understand what you are doing.

You can back up your files to tape, to diskettes, to another hard drive, or to a network location. The basic procedure, as shown in the figures, will be similar no matter what type of destination media you choose. Of course, your choice of backup media will affect the process somewhat because different types of media have different capacities. If you fill up the backup media, you'll need to insert additional media to continue the backup.

One of the best ways to ensure that you'll actually back up your files is to keep your backups small so that they take less time to complete. For example, if you store your document files in the My Documents folder, you can concentrate on backing up that folder, and your backups will take only a few minutes. In most cases there's little reason to back up your program files, because you probably have the installation disks and could simply reinstall programs if necessary.

You don't have to use the Backup Wizard to back up your files. If you prefer you can click the Backup tab to skip using the wizards that appear on the welcome tab. Using the Backup Wizard does ensure that you select all of the necessary options before you begin the actual backup, however.

Continued

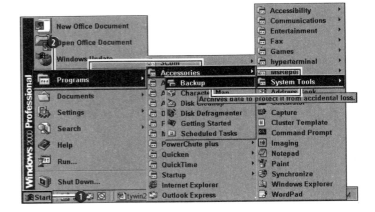

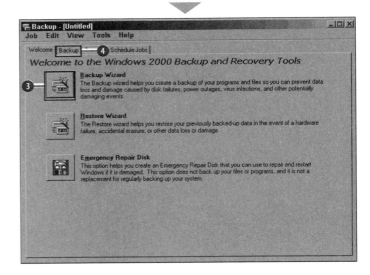

① *Click the Start button.*

② *Select Programs ⇨ Accessories ⇨ System Tools ⇨ Backup.*

③ *Click the Backup Wizard button to begin selecting the backup options.*

④ *Alternatively, click the Backup tab to set the backup options manually.*

CROSS-REFERENCE

See "Opening the My Documents Folder" in Chapter 1.

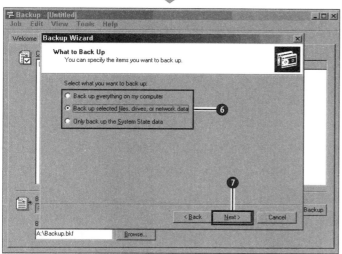

5 Click Next to continue.

6 Choose the type of backup.

7 Click the Next button to continue.

Backing Up Files

Continued

When you select what you wish to back up, you can select entire drives, individual folders, or even individual files. You'll find that the backup selection windows look very similar to Windows Explorer, with one important exception. Each folder and file in the backup selection windows has a check box in front of the folder or file icon. To include an item in the backup, add a check to the item's check box. You can also click a computer or folder icon to open the folders so that you can make individual file or folder selections.

Once you've selected the files to back up, you must select the backup destination. You may have a limited set of options, depending on how your system is configured. Generally, if you have a tape drive, it will be your first choice. Tape drives are made specifically for backing up files and can be the easiest backup media to use. A network drive can be another excellent backup destination — especially if you work in an office that has a file server on the network. Backing up to a network destination is usually quite fast and offers very good protection for your files. If you have a removable media drive such as a ZIP drive, that drive may also be a good choice for a backup destination. Diskettes are generally acceptable only for relatively small backups because using diskettes can involve a lot of disk swapping.

You may be prompted to insert additional backup media during the backup. This is especially likely if you're backing up to diskettes. Be sure you have enough diskettes, tapes, or other backup media ready before you begin the backup. Format the media or erase any old files before you start the backup.

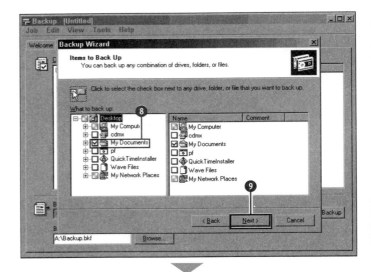

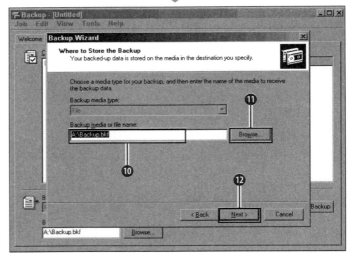

⑧ Choose the files or folders you wish to back up.

⑨ Click Next to continue.

⑩ Choose the backup destination.

⑪ Alternatively, click the Browse button and locate the destination.

⑫ Click Next to continue.

CROSS-REFERENCE

See "Adding New Hardware" in Chapter 13.

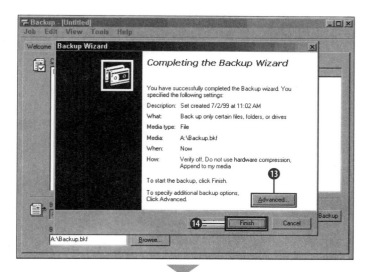

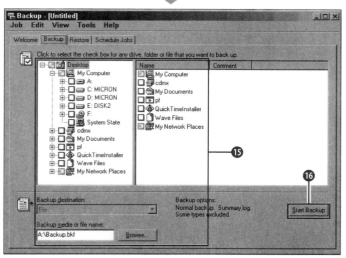

▶ DON'T CHOOSE YOUR HARD DISK

Never choose a folder on your hard disk as the backup destination. Backups are intended to protect you against problems such as hard disk failures, so if you were to place your backups on your hard disk, you would be losing that protection and wasting disk space. It's far better to simply limit the size of your backups by backing up only the files you really need, and using diskettes as the backup media, than to place backups on your hard disk.

▶ STORE BACKUPS OFFSITE

After you've gone to the trouble of backing up your important files, you may want to consider storing the backups someplace away from your computer. Backups are meant to protect you in the event of a disaster, and they can't do it if the same disaster destroys your backup media. If you are backing up files from your office, consider taking the backups home. At the very least, use a fireproof storage location such as the office safe.

⑬ *Optionally, click the Advanced button to choose additional backup options.*

⑭ *Click Finish to begin the backup.*

⑮ *If you chose to bypass the Backup Wizard, choose the backup options.*

⑯ *Click the Start Backup button to begin the backup.*

FIND IT ONLINE

To find technical support for Backup and other consumer products, see **http://support.microsoft.com/ support/search/c.asp.**

Preparing for Disk Problems

No matter how careful you may be, there are some problems that could really ruin your day. A hard disk failure would be one of those problems, especially if you aren't prepared for it.

Having a backup of your important data files is a good first step toward protecting yourself against catastrophic disk failures, but if a really serious error occurs, a backup may not be enough. In extreme cases, a disk error could even prevent you from starting your system. This could be the result of a power failure at just the wrong time or even a computer virus that wipes out the partition information. Most of your hard disk may still be intact, but if you can't access it, your data may as well be toast!

Windows 2000 uses an *Emergency Repair Disk* — ERD — to store all of the information necessary to restore your system's partition information. This disk is used when your system will not boot or when you see a fatal error message on a blue background — the infamous "blue screen of death" or BSOD. If your system will not start Windows 2000, you can insert the ERD in drive A and reboot. You will then need to follow the on-screen directions for recovering from the error.

In some cases you may also be able to correct system problems by starting Windows 2000 in *safe mode*. This is a special operating mode that may allow your computer to start by bypassing all but the most basic Windows 2000 drivers and components. In safe mode you won't be able to use functions and services that were bypassed, but you may be able to solve many problems. For example, if your system won't restart after you add new hardware, you may be able to restart in safe mode and remove the offending item. To start in safe mode, Press F8 when your system begins loading Windows 2000 and choose Safe Mode.

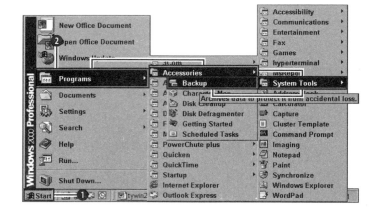

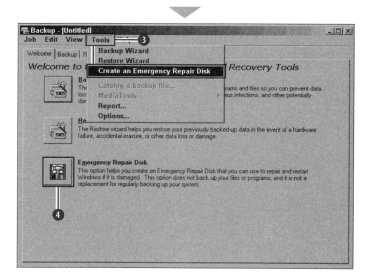

❶ Click the Start button.

❷ Select Programs ➪ Accessories ➪ System Tools ➪ Backup.

❸ Select Tools ➪ Create an Emergency Repair Disk.

❹ Alternatively, click the Emergency Repair Disk button.

CROSS REFERENCE

See "Looking for Problems with Device Manager" in Chapter 15.

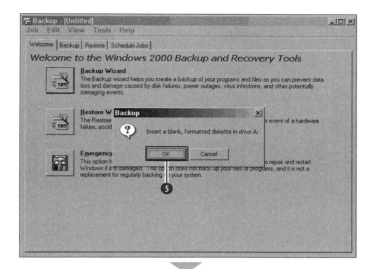

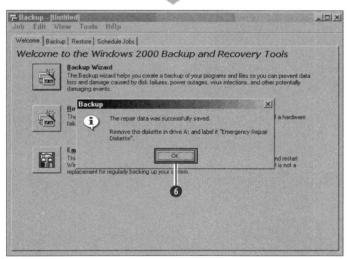

⑤ Insert a blank diskette in drive A and click OK.

▶ You can only create an ERD in drive A because you must be able to boot from the ERD.

⑥ When the files have been copied, click OK.

▶ Carefully label and store the ERD.

FIND IT ONLINE

For help troubleshooting a problem, see
http://support.microsoft.com/support/tshoot/default.asp?FR=0.

Personal Workbook

Q&A

1 What tool can you use to remove old files that are no longer needed on your PC?

_____

_____

_____

2 What type of disk errors can prevent your PC from using specific places on your hard disk?

_____

_____

_____

3 What is the difference between contiguous and fragmented files?

_____

_____

_____

4 How can you reduce the size of backups and the time required to perform them?

_____

_____

_____

5 What will happen if you attempt to scan for errors on a disk that is in use?

_____

_____

_____

6 What do you call a diskette that stores your system's partition information?

_____

_____

_____

7 What operating mode should you attempt to use first if Windows 2000 won't load?

_____

_____

_____

8 How can you free up additional space if the disk cleanup tool doesn't do as much as you'd like?

_____

_____

_____

ANSWERS: PAGE 398

EXTRA PRACTICE

1. Back up your My Documents folder.

2. Use the More Options tab on the Disk Cleanup dialog box to see how much additional disk space you can free by removing Windows 2000 components you don't use.

3. Run Disk Defragmenter and check to see which files are fragmented.

4. Print the list of fragmented files and compare it to the list after you run the disk defragmentation.

5. Check your hard disk for errors.

6. Create an updated copy of your ERD.

REAL-WORLD APPLICATIONS

✔ Your PC has been in use for several months and is starting to run very slowly. You run the disk defragmenter to restore the performance so that you can keep the same system for a while longer.

✔ An earthquake shakes your office. To make certain that your hard drive wasn't damaged, you run the error checker and choose the option that looks for physical errors.

✔ A computer virus strikes your system and prevents it from booting. You use your ERD to restore the partition information so that you can use your PC.

✔ You need to work on some large video files but discover that you are low on disk space. You use the disk cleanup tool to free some space.

Visual Quiz

How can you display this dialog box? How can you tell if your hard disk needs defragmentation? What can you do to make the defragmentation more successful?

_____

_____

_____

_____

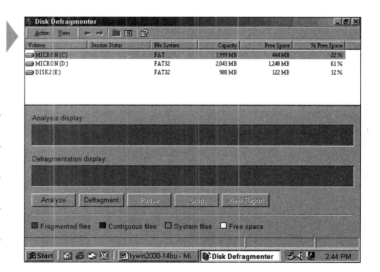

CHAPTER **15**

MASTER
THESE
SKILLS

▶ **Using Windows Update**
▶ **Tuning Up with the Maintenance Wizard**
▶ **Looking for Problems with Device Manager**
▶ **Using Component Services**
▶ **Using Computer Management**
▶ **Viewing the Event Logs**
▶ **Viewing the Performance Monitor**
▶ **Using the Task Manager**

Maintaining Your System

You want your PC to run correctly and efficiently. Just as with any other piece of equipment you might use, this means you must do some periodic maintenance in order to make certain your system is operating as well as it should. In this chapter, you'll learn how to use the Windows 2000 tools to keep your computer in top shape.

Many of the maintenance procedures that you can perform require that you have system administrator-level access to your PC. If you normally log in with more restricted access, you may want to use an administrator login temporarily as you follow along in this chapter. Otherwise you will probably not be able to complete all of the tasks.

Most of the tasks that are covered in this chapter are primarily intended as problem solvers. You won't be using these tools on a daily basis, but knowing about these tools will help you to know where to turn when a problem does arise. The system maintenance tools are the types of tools that you hope you'll never need, but which you'll be glad to have when they're necessary.

One of the tools covered in this chapter is unique. *Windows Update* is a free service that enables you to automatically download and install the latest updates to Windows 2000. Often these updates may include drivers or security updates that can be vital to the health of your system. Even if you don't find yourself using the other tools you learn about in this chapter, you'll want to use Windows Update regularly.

Before you begin the exercises it's important to inject a note of caution. Using any type of tool involves a certain amount of risk. You could, for example, stab yourself with a simple screwdriver or accidentally flatten your thumb when pounding in a nail with a hammer. Computer maintenance tools are no different — if you use them incorrectly you could cause damage. In the case of computer maintenance tools, the damage would likely be to your data rather than to your body, but neither is a desirable outcome. The best way to prevent problems is to use common sense. If you don't know what you are doing, don't just blunder ahead with the "I wonder what will happen if I do this?" attitude. Caution is your best ally!

Using Windows Update

W indows 2000 includes a feature called Windows Update that uses the Internet to make certain your copy of Windows 2000 is up-to-date. If newer drivers are available to make your PC work a little better, Windows Update can download and install them. Similarly, if a security update is available, Windows Update can handle this task, too.

When you visit the Windows Update Web site, you will see a list of the available updates that you can choose to download. After you've selected the updates you wish to download, Windows Update displays your selections so that you can verify that the list is correct.

You are also given the opportunity to view the installation instructions for the software that you've selected. It's a good idea to take the opportunity, because you may not be able to easily find those instructions later. It may also be a good idea to print a copy of the instructions, especially if you're not completely sure you understand the entire download and update process.

In most cases you won't have to do anything special to install the software updates. Most updates install themselves automatically after they are downloaded. It may be necessary to restart your PC after the update has been installed, especially if the update changed critical system files. Most system files cannot be changed while they are in use, so the restart is required before the update will be completed.

After you click the Start Download button, you'll see a dialog box that reports on both the download and the installation progress. You don't need to do anything while this dialog box is being displayed. Depending on the size of the updates you selected, the download could take several minutes to several hours, and it's best not to try to do anything else on your PC during this process.

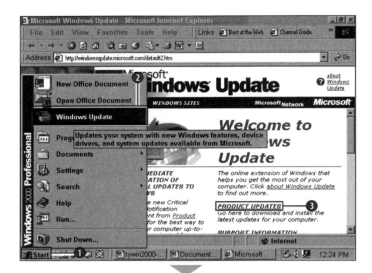

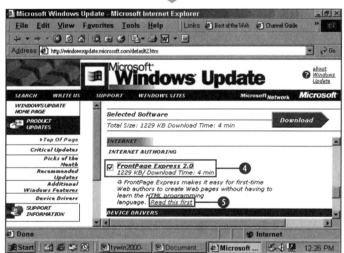

① Click the Start button.

② Choose Windows Update.

③ Once you have connected to the Web site, click the Product Updates link to continue.

④ Choose the updates to download and install.

⑤ Click the "Read this first" link to view the readme file.

CROSS-REFERENCE

See "Installing Programs" in Chapter 4.

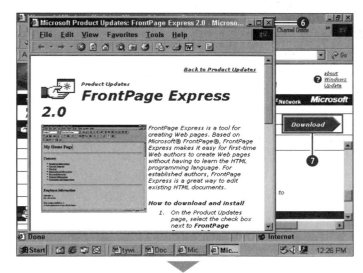

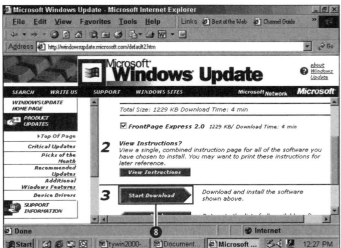

TAKE NOTE

CHOOSING UPDATES

Depending on when you visit, Windows Update may offer several classes of system updates. Critical updates are important fixes that you should download because they may address security issues that could have serious consequences if not corrected. Many of the other types of updates are optional but are often a good choice, especially the items listed as recommended updates. Some of the updates are samples that Microsoft provides to show you a new piece of software, such as a trial version of a new game. It's up to you to decide which of these updates are worth the time it takes to download them.

CHECK OFTEN

Make regular visits to the Windows Update Web site to ensure that your PC always has the latest upgrades to Windows 2000 and possibly solve some issues you weren't even aware existed. Because many system updates are actually bug fixes, you could have a problem and not know about it until it's too late.

⑥ *When you have finished reading the information on the update, click the Close button.*

⑦ *Click the Download button to continue.*

⑧ *When you have verified the list of downloads, click the Start Download button.*

▶ *Follow the on-screen instructions to complete the updates.*

FIND IT ONLINE

For updates to other Microsoft products see
http://www.microsoft.com/downloads/search.asp.

Tuning Up with the Maintenance Wizard

The Maintenance Wizard is a Windows 2000 tool that schedules important system maintenance tasks to run at regular intervals. In most cases these are routine items that you should probably do, but which you probably put off or forget about more often than you should. By using the Maintenance Wizard to schedule these tasks, the jobs will get done and you won't have to feel guilty about avoiding them in the future.

The Maintenance Wizard schedules several different tasks. First, the Maintenance Wizard schedules the cleanup of your Start menu. Then it sets up the Disk Defragmenter tool, using the option to optimize the loading of your program files. You may forget to do this manually after you've added or removed programs from your system, so having this as a scheduled task helps keep your PC's performance at its peak. Next, the Maintenance Wizard schedules checks and repairs for any disk errors. Because you may not always realize when an event has caused disk errors, scheduling this check on a regular basis helps prevent more-serious problems. Finally, the Maintenance Wizard schedules the Disk Cleanup tool to remove unnecessary files that clog your hard disk.

If you haven't performed any routine system maintenance in some time, some of the Maintenance Wizard scheduled tasks may take considerable time to complete the first time they are run. Although choosing the *When I click Finish, perform each scheduled task for the first time* option is a good way to make certain your system won't have problems when the tasks are run, selecting this option may tie up your PC for quite some time. Still, because you will probably see much improved system performance after the maintenance tasks are run, it may be worthwhile to choose the option if you can afford the time.

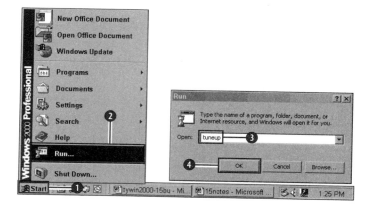

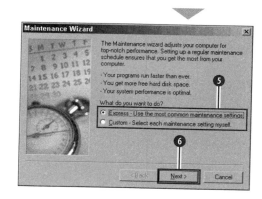

❶ Click the Start button.

❷ Select Run.

❸ Enter **tuneup** in the Open text box.

❹ Click OK to continue.

❺ Choose the Express option to use the default settings.

❻ Click Next to continue.

CROSS-REFERENCE

See Chapter 16 for information on the Task Scheduler.

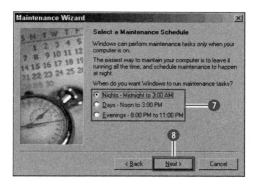

TAKE NOTE

▶ LEAVE YOUR SYSTEM POWERED ON

After the Maintenance Wizard schedules the system maintenance events, be sure that you leave your system running at the scheduled time. If you prefer not to leave your computer on all the time, choose a maintenance schedule that allows the tasks to be performed at a time when you are comfortable leaving the system on, such as during lunch. If you select the custom setup rather than the express setup, you'll also be able to more closely control the task schedule. For even more control over the schedule, you can open the Scheduled Tasks folder after the Maintenance Wizard has created a schedule.

▶ USE THE CUSTOM OPTION

If you select the Custom radio button, you'll see additional options that are not shown in the figures on the facing page. You'll have the option of selecting the settings for each of the routine maintenance items that the Maintenance Wizard schedules, and you can choose to eliminate one or more of them from the schedule.

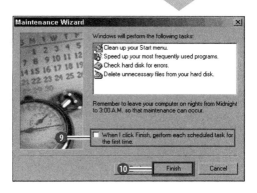

⑦ Choose the time schedule you prefer.

⑧ Click Next to continue.

⑨ Optionally, click here to run the tasks immediately.

⑩ Click Finish to complete the task.

FIND IT ONLINE

For information on rescheduling Maintenance Wizard tasks, see **http://support.microsoft.com/support/windows/serviceware/win98/3azbee60.asp**.

Looking for Problems with Device Manager

The Device Manager is a tool that enables you to examine the devices that are installed in your system. Using the Device Manager you can find out all sorts of very technical information, such as what *system resources* each device is using, which drivers are in use, and whether any devices are having problems.

System resources can be a real problem when you want to install new hardware into your computer. There are a limited number of system resources available, and most hardware that you add requires the use of at least some of them. In this section you'll learn how to discover whether you have a system resource problem that is causing parts of your computer to refuse to work properly.

If some of the devices installed in your PC are experiencing a problem, Device Manager will use either a yellow exclamation point or a red X to indicate the problem. Device Manager primarily looks for conflicts in which two or more devices are trying to use the same resources at the same time. These resources include *interrupt requests* (IRQs), *input/output* (I/O) addresses, *direct memory access* (DMA), and *memory* addresses. Most problems you'll encounter will be with IRQs. In some cases you can choose new, nonconflicting resource settings on the Resources tab of the device's Properties dialog box. Deselect the Use automatic settings check box and choose one of the optional configurations.

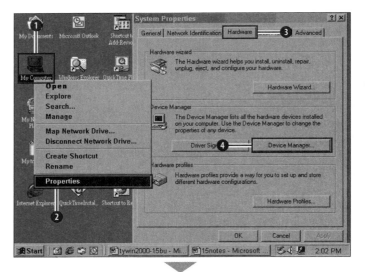

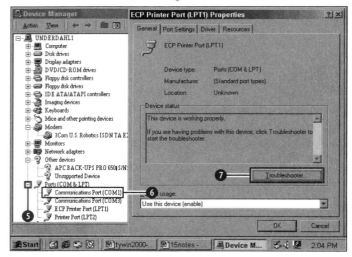

❶ *Right-click the My Computer icon on your desktop.*

❷ *Select Properties.*

❸ *Click the Hardware tab.*

❹ *Click the Device Manager button.*

❺ *Click the box next to a device type to view the individual devices.*

❻ *Double-click a device you wish to examine.*

❼ *If necessary, click the Troubleshooter button to resolve problems.*

CROSS-REFERENCE

See "Adding New Hardware" in Chapter 13.

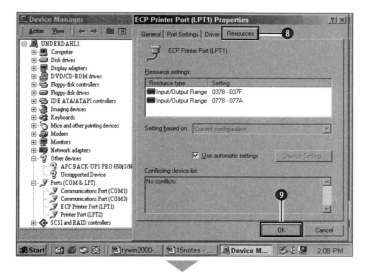

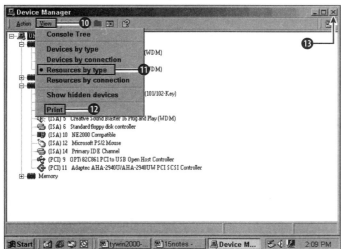

TAKE NOTE

▶ **RESERVE RESOURCES FOR LEGACY HARDWARE**

Modern PCs and peripherals use a method known as *plug and play* to assign system resources. Older peripherals, such as scanner adapter cards, sound boards, or modems, may not support plug and play (in that case they are called *legacy* devices), or they may require specific system resource allocations. If you encounter this problem, you may be able to reserve certain resources using *bios setup options*. To do so, you will need to reboot your system and press the correct key combination to enter your computer's bios setup screens. Because different brands of PCs use different methods of setting bios options, you'll have to refer to your owner's manual to learn how to make these types of settings on your computer.

▶ **UNINSTALL PROBLEM DEVICES**

If you can't resolve a resource conflict by selecting different device settings in Device Manager, you may be able to solve the problem by removing all the conflicting devices using the Uninstall option on each device's right-click context menu. Then shut your computer down, wait a few seconds, and restart the system. Use the option to enter your system's bios setup and look for the setting to reset the plug-and-play resource table. This will be worded differently on different computers. When your system restarts, Windows 2000 should find the devices and try to assign them new, nonconflicting resources.

⑧ *To view or modify the resources used by the selected device, click the Resources tab.*

⑨ *Click OK when you are finished viewing the selected device.*

⑩ *Click View to display the View menu.*

⑪ *To view specific resources, select Resource by type.*

⑫ *To print the list, select Print.*

⑬ *Click Close to complete the task.*

FIND IT ONLINE

If you have problems printing Device Manager information, see **http://support.microsoft.com/support/windows/serviceware/win98/e9r9r64w6.asp**.

Using Component Services

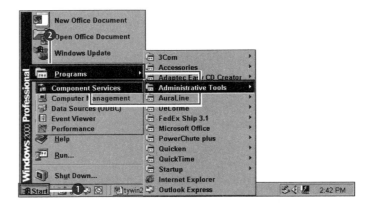

Your Windows 2000-based PC uses a number of *services* to accomplish many of the tasks that your expect it to perform. These services are essentially background applications such as the fax service that you use to send and receive faxes or the print spooler that enables you to continue working while your computer sends a long print job to your printer.

Component Services is the name of the application that enables you to view and control all of those system services. Each service has several options that you can control, but the most important options are the current running status and the startup setting.

Services must be running before they can be used. For example, if the ClipBook service is not running you will be able to use the Windows 2000 Clipboard, but you will not be able to view and save Clipboard objects except by pasting them into documents. If you start the ClipBook service, you will be able to use the ClipBook Viewer.

You can start services manually, or set them to start automatically. The automatic option makes those services available whenever they are needed, but the manual option gives you more control over which items are running on your system.

As the final figure on the facing page shows, services often depend on other services. If you are considering changing the settings for a particular service, it is important to check the Dependencies tab. If you intend to start a service that is currently stopped, all of the services in the Depends On box must also be running. If you are considering stopping a running service, none of the services listed in the Needed By box will be able to function if you do so. This tab can take a moment to be displayed because Windows 2000 needs to search for the dependencies before the items can be shown.

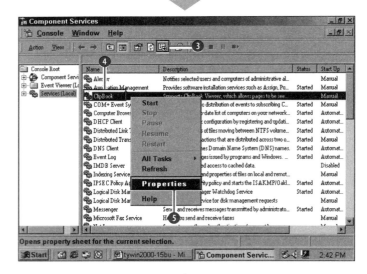

1 Click the Start button.

2 Select Programs ⇨ Administrative Tools ⇨ Component Services.

3 Optionally, click the Export List button to save the list in a text file.

4 Right-click the service you wish to modify.

5 Select Properties.

CROSS-REFERENCE

See "Controlling the Start Menu" in Chapter 12.

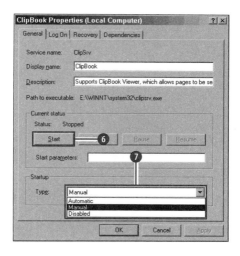

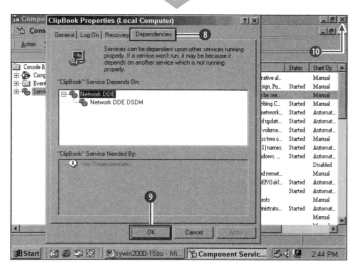

⑥ *Use these buttons to control the service's current status.*

⑦ *Optionally, select the startup option.*

⑧ *To view the service dependencies, click the Dependencies tab.*

⑨ *Click OK when you are finished viewing the selected service.*

⑩ *Click Close to complete the task.*

PRINTING THE SERVICES LIST

You won't find a print command or a print button within the Component Services application, but that won't prevent you from printing the services list if you're willing to go to a little extra trouble to do so. To print the list, make certain that none of the services are selected and then click the Export List button. This will enable you to save the list in a text file that you can later open in Notepad and print from that application.

STOP UNNEEDED SERVICES

If your computer doesn't need some of the services that are started by default, you can stop those services and set their startup option to manual or disabled. For example, if none of your hard disks use NTFS partitions, you could stop the Distributed Link Tracking Client service. Stopping unneeded services may improve your system performance because each running service uses a certain amount of memory and CPU time.

Using Computer Management

Just as the Component Services application enables you to manage system services, Computer Management helps you to view and control many other pieces of your system. In this section you'll have a very brief glimpse of just how many different areas of your computer you can access through this application.

As you explore the various areas of the Computer Management window you'll probably notice that some sections seem familiar. For example, the final figure shows you an alternate method of accessing the disk de-fragmentation tool that you learned about in Chapter 14. The Device Manager, which you saw earlier in this chapter, is another example of a section of the Computer Management window that will be familiar to you. Bringing all of these tools together into one place provides you with a central location where you can perform many different system management tasks.

The Computer Management window uses the same type of tree-structured display you see in Windows Explorer. When an icon is connected to the vertical line by a box, the icon represents an object that contains additional items. A plus sign in the box represents a collapsed item, while a minus sign indicates an expanded item. When you select an item in the *console tree*, the right-hand pane displays the contents of the selected item.

You can right-click most items in the contents pane to display a pop-up context menu. The context menu will vary according to the type of object that is selected, but Properties will always be one of the choices. In some cases the Properties selection will merely show you information about the selected object, but in others you'll be able to change certain properties. For example, if you right-click a disk drive in the Disk Management object and choose Properties, you can change the volume label of the disk.

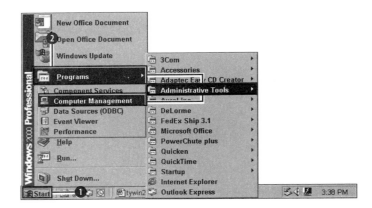

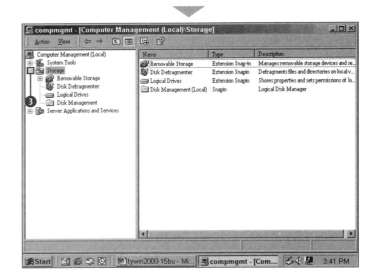

❶ Click the Start button.

❷ Select Programs ➪ Administrative Tools ➪ Computer Management.

❸ Click the boxes to the left of objects to expand or contract the display.

CROSS-REFERENCE

See "Using Component Services" earlier in this chapter.

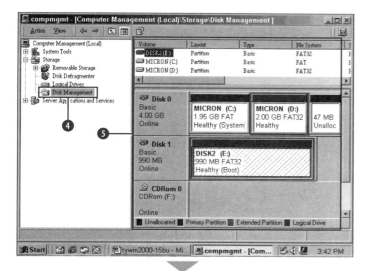

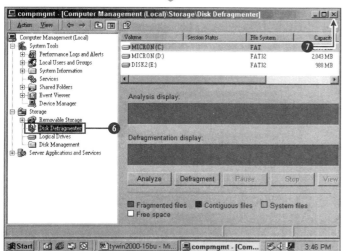

④ Select a branch to view its contents.

⑤ View the contents here.

▶ The options that are available will vary depending on which branch you are viewing.

⑥ Select a different branch to view its contents.

⑦ Click Close to complete the task.

FIND IT ONLINE

To learn how to resolve password-related management problems, see **http://support.microsoft.com/support/kb/articles/q234/3/06.ASP**.

Viewing the Event Logs

A lot goes on behind the scenes in Windows 2000. Most of the time you're probably aware of only a small fraction of all the events that occur as you are using your PC. Of course, many of these events are simply system services that load when they are needed, but a few events either fail to complete, or they produce nonfatal errors that may compromise their success.

Windows 2000 maintains *logs* that list the messages that occur as events happen. These event logs provide a wealth of information about programs that were started, warnings regarding processes that weren't completely successful, and serious errors that may prevent certain functions from being available. You can use the information in these logs to troubleshoot problems.

Messages in the event logs are similar to the error messages that may appear on your screen, but you'll probably find that the event log messages are far more useful. Event log messages are typically considerably more complete than most on-screen error messages, and they may include suggestions about how to correct a problem. By looking at a series of event log messages, you may also be able to determine that an earlier event in a sequence of events was the trigger for a later error. On-screen error messages, of course, lack this type of historical information that can be so important to finding the cause of a problem.

There's another subtle difference between the typical on-screen error message and an event log message. If you wish to keep a record of most on-screen error messages, you'll likely have to manually write down the information that is presented. Drag your mouse across an event log message, right-click, and select Copy to place the text on the Clipboard.

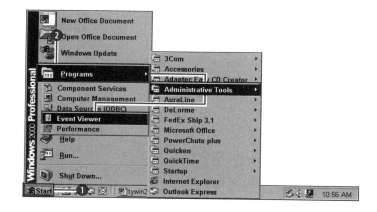

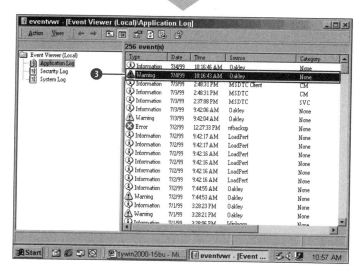

❶ Click the Start button.

❷ Select Programs ⇨ Administrative Tools ⇨ Event Viewer.

❸ Double-click an event message to view the message.

CROSS-REFERENCE

See "Viewing the Performance Monitor" later in this chapter.

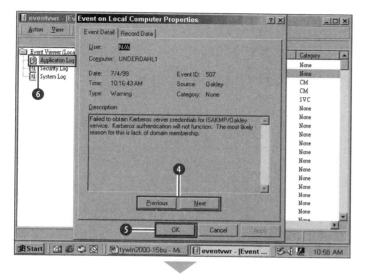

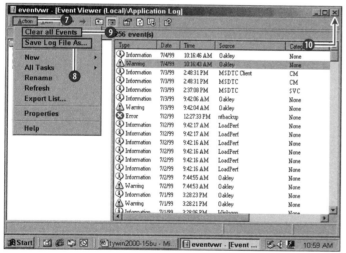

④ Click here to view other messages in the log.

⑤ Click OK to close the message.

⑥ Select a log to view its contents.

⑦ When an event log is selected, click Action to display the Action menu.

⑧ Select Save Log File As if you wish to keep the log for future reference.

⑨ Select Clear all Events if you wish to start a fresh log.

⑩ Click Close to complete the task.

Viewing the Performance Monitor

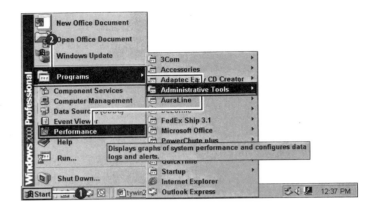

No matter how fast your computer operates, you probably feel at times like it's just not as fast as it should be. By using the Windows 2000 Performance Monitor, you can find out the specific processes that are using your computer's power and determine if it's possible to make some improvements.

When you first start the Performance Monitor, the display will just sit there showing no information. You must add *counters* that display the information you are seeking in order for the Performance Monitor to provide anything useful.

There are several types of counters that you can add to the display. To be most useful, you'll probably want to add counters that display related types of information. For example, counters that display percentages will probably be more meaningful combined with other counters that display percentages rather than with counters that display the number of items per second. Or you may choose to display several different items that relate to the same type of activity — such as several disk-related counters if you are attempting to diagnose disk performance problems.

While you are selecting counters to add to the display, you'll probably find it quite useful to click the Explain button that appears in the Add Counters dialog box. When this button is clicked, a message box appears that describes each counter as you select it. The message box remains open until you choose to close it, and the description changes as you select different counters. This makes it possible for you to view the descriptions of different counters without constantly having to click the Explain button for each new counter you select. These descriptions are especially useful if you aren't certain which counters will provide the details you need.

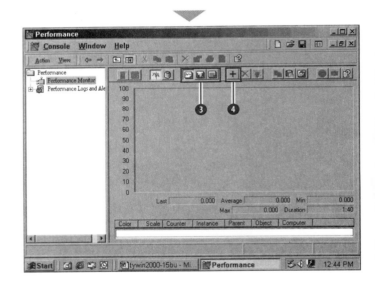

1 Click the Start button.

2 Select Programs ⇨ Administrative Tools ⇨ Performance.

3 Choose the display type by clicking one of these buttons.

4 Click the Add button to add new counters to the display.

CROSS-REFERENCE

See "Viewing the Event Logs" earlier in this chapter.

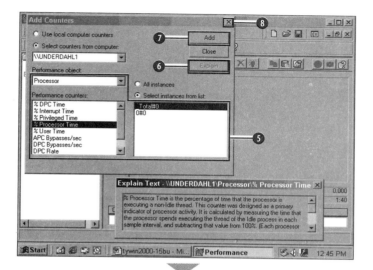

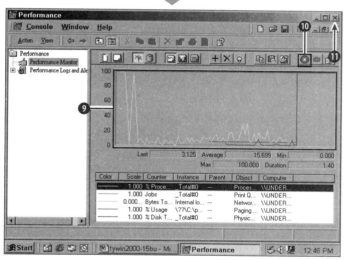

CHOOSE PROCESSES CAREFULLY

Although you could choose to monitor dozens of different system processes, remember that simply monitoring those processes uses a certain amount of CPU time. Rather than taking a shotgun approach, try to narrow your focus and monitor only a few important processes. You may discover that you need to add an additional item or two to the monitor list to get the true picture of what is happening, but you may also discover that certain processes that you are monitoring are adding no useful information.

LOOKING FOR BOTTLENECKS

One of the best ways to use the Performance Monitor is to look for *bottlenecks* — processes that are having a major adverse effect on system performance. For example, if you discover that some of the disk-related processes are using nearly all of their available resources, while processor-related items have plenty of room to spare, it's a good guess that better hard disks will improve system performance more than a faster processor.

⑤ Choose the counters here.

⑥ Click Explain to see the counter description.

⑦ Click Add to add a selected counter.

⑧ Click the Close button when you are finished adding counters.

⑨ View the counters here.

⑩ Click here if you wish to freeze the display.

⑪ Click Close to complete the task.

FIND IT ONLINE

To learn how to add a counter to a Performance Monitor chart, see **http://support.microsoft.com/ support/ntserver/serviceware/nts40/371q76n6.asp**.

Using the Task Manager

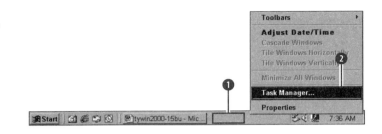

Even though Windows 2000 is one of the most reliable PC operating systems ever, it is still possible for a poorly written program to crash. Generally this does not affect any other programs that are running, but you may occasionally find it necessary to forcibly shut down the program that has stopped responding. The *Task Manager* can generally handle this process quite well.

In addition to shutting down applications, the Task Manager can report on and control all of the background tasks that run on your PC. As the figures show, the Task Manager shows you the percentage of CPU usage each process consumes, how much total CPU time the process has used during the current session, and how much memory each process is using.

In addition to right-clicking the taskbar and selecting Task Manager from the context menu, you can also open the Task Manager by pressing Ctrl+Alt+Del and clicking the Task Manager button. Pressing Ctrl+Alt+Del will also provide additional options such as the ability to lock your system so that a password is needed to access it.

If you use Task Manager to shut down an application or to close a process needed by the application, you could lose any unsaved information in the application. It's always better to attempt to close open applications from within the application itself whenever that option is available.

If you continue to have problems with a program locking up, you may want to dig a little deeper at diagnosing the problem. One technique that is often successful is to uninstall the offending program and then reinstall it. This is especially true if the program had been working correctly before you installed a different application that may have overwritten an important file shared by several programs.

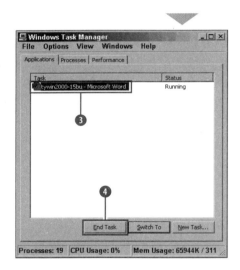

① Right-click a blank space on the taskbar.

② Select Task Manager from the context menu.

③ If you need to shut down a program that is not responding, select it here.

④ Click the End Task button to close the program.

CROSS-REFERENCE

See "Using the Troubleshooters" in Chapter 3.

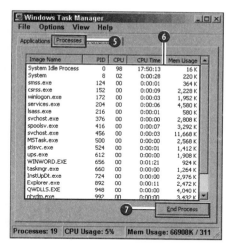

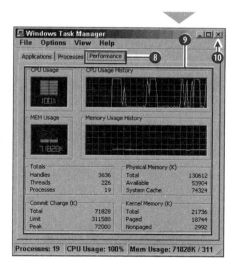

TAKE NOTE

SHUT DOWN PROCESSES CAREFULLY

Even though the Task Manager enables you to select specific processes to be shut down, you should use extreme caution with this option. It is often very difficult to determine the importance of running processes, or even which services they provide. If you shut down a process that is vital, you could cause your programs to malfunction or even make your system unstable. You may be able to determine the purpose of a process by using the Windows 2000 Start menu Search ➪ For Files or Folders command to locate the executable named on the Processes tab. Right-click the program and choose Properties to view information about the program. The program's location may provide additional useful clues to its purpose.

CLOSE TASK MANAGER

It's always a good idea to close Task Manager when it is no longer needed. Even though the display on the Performance tab may be quite interesting, showing that information uses both memory and CPU power.

---

⑤ Click the Processes tab.

⑥ If you need to shut down a process, select it here.

⑦ Click End Process to close the selected process.

⑧ Click the Performance tab.

⑨ View the performance statistics here.

⑩ Click Close to complete the task.

FIND IT ONLINE

To select which process information will be displayed, see **http://support.microsoft.com/support/ntworkstation/serviceware/ntw40/e9jvx18b5.asp**.

Personal Workbook

Q&A

1 What tool can you use to make certain your Windows 2000 system files are up-to-date?

_____

_____

_____

2 Where can you find out if your system has experienced any security problems?

_____

_____

_____

3 Where can you look to see which IRQs are in use on your system?

_____

_____

_____

4 How can you shut down a program that is not responding?

_____

_____

_____

5 What is the purpose of the Maintenance Wizard?

_____

_____

_____

6 Where can you find out if any items depend on a system service that you are considering shutting down?

_____

_____

_____

7 What do you call the items you add to the performance monitor display?

_____

_____

_____

8 What happens if you format a disk using the Computer Management tool?

_____

_____

_____

ANSWERS: PAGE 399

EXTRA PRACTICE

1. Visit the Windows Update Web site.

2. Read the instructions for one of the available updates.

3. Open a program and then use Task Manager to close the program.

4. Use Device Manager to see if any of the devices on your system are reporting problems.

5. Look at the event logs to see if there are any errors.

6. Use the Performance Monitor to see how many disk accesses occur when you open several different documents.

REAL-WORLD APPLICATIONS

✔ You want to improve the performance of your system so that you can wait another six months before you buy a new PC. You use the Maintenance Wizard to make certain your computer gets regular tune-ups.

✔ Your computer is connected to a network, and you suspect that someone has been trying to break in to your files. You use the event logs to see if there have been any security event messages to confirm your suspicions.

✔ You need to maximize the memory that is available for a large graphics project you need to work on. You use Component Services to prevent several unneeded services from being loaded automatically.

Visual Quiz

How can you display this list in the Device Manager? How can you print a reference list showing which system resources are in use?

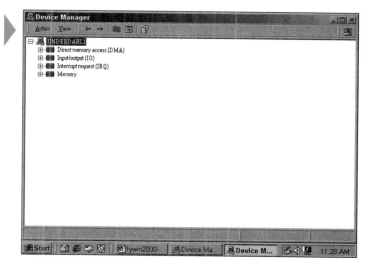

PART

V

Contents of 'Desktop'

Name

My Computer
Network Neigh
Internet Explor
Microsoft Outloo
Recycle Bin
My Briefcase
3252-9
3259-6
3261-8
3262-6
3281-2
3286-3
DE Phone List
Device Manager
In
Iomega Tools

Using Windows 2000 Accessories

Windows 2000 includes a number of extras that add value to your system. In this part you'll learn how to use those accessories to get a bit more done with your computer.

One of the accessory applications can really simplify your life. As you'll soon see, you can schedule routine maintenance tasks so that Windows 2000 does most of the drudge work for you and keeps your PC in top shape.

You'll also see that Windows 2000 has considerable multimedia capabilities. You'll learn how to use multimedia content and even how to create a bit of your own.

Finally, you'll have a quick look at several accessory applications that enable you to do things like add foreign characters to your documents, avoid macro viruses, and even have a fun break.

CHAPTER 16

MASTER
THESE
SKILLS

▶ Setting Up Scheduled Tasks

▶ Modifying a Scheduled Task

▶ Administering Task Scheduler

Using Task Scheduler

Your PC needs regular maintenance in order to keep running at its best. In this chapter, you'll learn how to use the Windows 2000 Task Scheduler to make certain that the items necessary to the goal of keeping your system functioning efficiently are performed on a regular schedule.

The Task Scheduler enables you to schedule different applications to run at specified intervals. If you use the Maintenance Wizard to set up routine maintenance as discussed in Chapter 15, those regular maintenance tasks are added to the Task Scheduler. You can adjust the settings for those tasks using the Task Scheduler, too.

Although the Task Scheduler is primarily intended as a method of running routine maintenance, you can also use Task Scheduler to run other applications on a regular schedule. Adding other types of tasks to the schedule is not very difficult, but you'll need to know how to program the application you wish to use. To be useful as a scheduled task, the task must be one that can be completed without user intervention. For example, if you have an application that you can program to log on to your account at an online brokerage, download vital stock market information, analyze the information, and then page you if you need to buy or sell some shares, you have a good candidate for a scheduled task. Opening your word processor — which just sits there waiting for you to type — would be a poor candidate for a scheduled task.

In this chapter, you'll learn how to use the Task Scheduler to schedule the same type of routine tasks as those you can schedule with the Maintenance Wizard. Although the same general techniques will apply if you wish to schedule a different type of task, the specifics of setting up macros in an application are simply too specific to individual programs to be useful here. Still, once you learn how to use the Task Scheduler, you should find that scheduling other types of tasks is not too difficult. But even if you never use the Task Scheduler for anything except routine system maintenance, you'll still reap the benefit of a PC that runs better than it otherwise would.

Setting Up Scheduled Tasks

etting up scheduled tasks involves a bit more than simply adding a new program shortcut to the Scheduled Tasks folder. When you add a task to the schedule, you probably want to accomplish something a bit more useful than simply opening a program. If the program just sits there waiting for you to do something, it probably won't be very useful as a scheduled task. The program you run must have the capability to do something without your input if it is to accomplish anything useful as a scheduled task.

When you run the Windows 2000 Maintenance Wizard, you have the option to schedule several system maintenance tasks, such as checking your hard drive for errors, at specified intervals. These scheduled tasks are good examples of the types of tasks you should consider when you decide to add new items to the schedule. When the tasks that are set up by the Maintenance Wizard are run, they accomplish a useful purpose whether you're around or not.

If you have used the Maintenance Wizard, you may already have one or more tasks scheduled the first time you open the Scheduled Tasks folder. Even so, you can safely add the task shown in the figures even if you have already enabled the Maintenance Wizard to schedule tasks.

The Task Scheduler is always running in the background. To set up or modify scheduled tasks, you must open the Scheduled Tasks folder. The figures on the facing page show you how to start adding a scheduled task using the Scheduled Task Wizard. The following two pages show you how to complete this exercise.

Continued

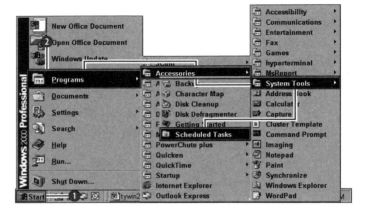

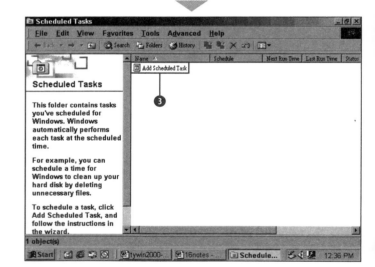

1 Click the Start button.

2 Select Programs ➪ Accessories ➪ System Tools ➪ Scheduled Tasks.

3 Double-click Add Scheduled Task to open the Scheduled Task Wizard.

CROSS-REFERENCE

See "Modifying a Scheduled Task" later in this chapter.

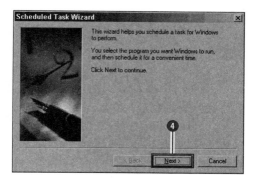

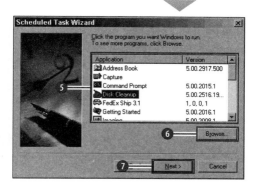

④ *Click Next to continue.*

⑤ *Select the program you wish to schedule.*

⑥ *Alternatively, click the Browse button to locate the program.*

⑦ *Click Next to continue.*

Setting Up Scheduled Tasks

Continued

When you are setting up a scheduled task, you must choose the schedule for the task to run. This involves selecting both the interval between runs and the time of day when you want the task to run.

In choosing the interval, you have a number of options from which to choose. In most cases you'll choose one of the first three options — daily, weekly, or monthly. You can also choose to run a task once, every time you start your system, or every time you log on.

The *One time only* option might be a good choice if you are testing a scheduled task to make certain that you can rely upon it. You could schedule the task to run once and then observe the results to see if the task needs any fine-tuning.

The *When my computer starts* and *When I log on* options may be most useful for tasks you perform every time you use your PC. For example, if you always log on to the Internet and download the latest weather forecast, you might use one of these options. It's generally not a good idea to use these options to schedule a task that takes a long time to complete — such as defragmenting your hard disk.

Once you have selected the interval, you can choose the time to run the task. Certain types of tasks, of course, must run at specific times. In most cases, however, you'll want to select a time that allows the task to run when you aren't using your PC. This is especially true for tasks that need exclusive access to your system or for those that may use so many resources that your computer runs very slowly when they are being processed. Often a very good schedule is to run tasks late at night when you aren't likely to be doing anything else with your computer. You can always reschedule a task if you find the current schedule isn't working out for some reason.

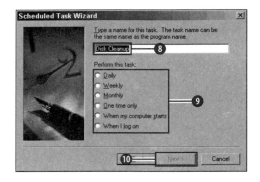

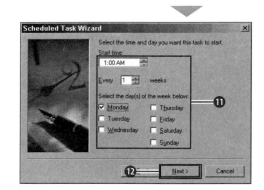

8 Optionally, enter a name for the task.

9 Select the task interval.

10 Click Next to continue.

11 Select the time options you prefer.

12 Click Next to continue.

CROSS-REFERENCE

See "Adding a Task" later in this chapter.

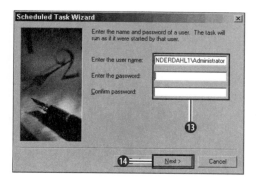

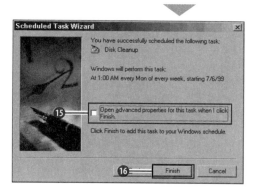

LEAVE THE POWER ON

Your PC can run scheduled tasks only if the system is running at the scheduled time. You can save power by turning off your monitor, your printer, and any other external peripherals that aren't needed to complete the task, but your computer must be running. If your system is off at the scheduled time, Windows 2000 will attempt to run the task as soon as possible after the scheduled time, but this may cause tasks to run while you are using your computer.

MAKE SURE YOU HAVE ACCESS

As you are setting up scheduled tasks you must enter a user name and password. It is important to remember that the specified user must have the proper access rights to complete the task — otherwise the task will not complete.

⑬ *Enter the user name and password of an appropriate user for this level of task.*

⑭ *Click Next to continue.*

⑮ *Optionally, click here to further configure the task.*

⑯ *Click Finish to complete the task.*

FIND IT ONLINE

To download a program that will remind you at a given time, see **http://www.geocities.com/siliconvalley/ network/614**.

Modifying a Scheduled Task

You've probably noticed that your scheduled tasks could use a bit of tweaking here and there. Perhaps you've discovered that certain tasks take longer than you expected and aren't completed by the time you want to use your system. Or perhaps you've discovered that some tasks need to be moved to different days to avoid conflicts with other tasks. No matter the reason, you can easily adjust existing tasks to suit your needs.

The figures show how you can modify a scheduled task. In most cases you will primarily deal with the options on the Schedule and Setting tabs of the dialog box. The options contained on the Task tab are mainly used to set the parameters for the specific program you are running. For example, if you specify the name of the document file to open by including that name following the program name on the command line, you would specify the complete command line in the Run text box.

Most of the settings that you can adjust will seem familiar because they're the same choices you selected when you first set up the task schedule. There are, however, some interesting settings on the Settings tab that you haven't seen before.

The Scheduled Task Completed section includes the option to delete the scheduled task after it completes. This section also lets you limit the amount of time a task can run. The default is 72 hours, but you can set whatever limits you prefer. This option might be useful if you want to run a task fairly often but want it to end before you use your system for something else.

The Idle Time section delays or stops a task if you're using your system at the scheduled time. These options can help make scheduled tasks less obtrusive because they won't interfere with your use of your PC.

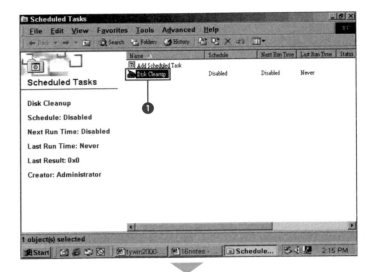

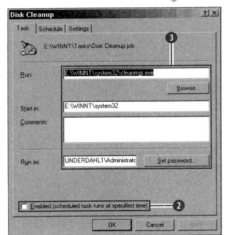

▶ Open the Scheduled Tasks folder if it is not already open.

① Double-click the task you wish to modify.

② Select this check box to enable the task, or deselect it to disable the task.

③ If you need to change any of the program settings, use these options.

CROSS-REFERENCE

See "Tuning Up with the Maintenance Wizard" in Chapter 15.

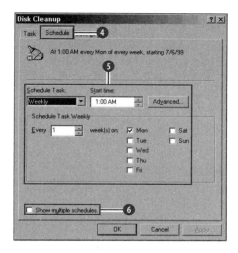

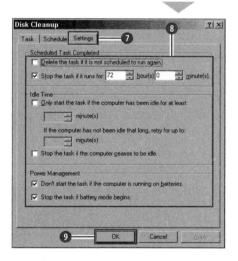

The Power Management settings are useful primarily on laptop systems where they can help save power by not allowing scheduled tasks to run when your computer is running on batteries.

▶ **DISABLE WITHOUT REMOVING**

If you have created a task that you would like to temporarily disable, remove the check from the *Enabled (scheduled task runs at specified time)* check box on the Task tab. This will prevent the task from running, but will not change the schedule. If you later add a check back to this check box, the task will revert to the same schedule, and you will not have to reestablish the schedule.

▶ **USE MULTIPLE SCHEDULES**

If you need to run the same task at times that don't seem to fit the available interval options, select the *Show multiple schedules* check box on the Schedule tab. This will enable you to add several different schedules for the task — each with its own interval and time settings.

④ *Click the Schedule tab.*

⑤ *Select the schedule options you wish to use.*

⑥ *Click here if you wish to use more than one schedule.*

⑦ *Click the Settings tab.*

⑧ *Choose the appropriate settings for this task.*

⑨ *Click OK to complete the task.*

FIND IT ONLINE

If you have problems scheduling disk error checking, see http://support.microsoft.com/support/kb/articles/q179/3/69.asp.

Administering Task Scheduler

If you depend on the Task Scheduler to handle a number of critical processes on your system, you'll almost certainly want to maintain good control of the Task Scheduler. In this section, you learn how to use the options on the Advanced menu to do so.

As you learned earlier in this chapter, you can temporarily suspend a scheduled task if you don't want it to run as scheduled. If you wish to pause all scheduled tasks, you can also stop the Task Scheduler. You may find that you need to do so if you wish to run certain critical functions that require all available processing power to be completed within a reasonable amount of time.

If it is important to know if tasks were completed properly, you have two options. To be advised if a scheduled task did not run, choose Advanced ➪ Notify Me of Missed Tasks. Each time you select this option it changes from off to on or from on to off.

You can also choose to view the log that records the running of all scheduled events. By viewing this log, you can determine whether the events you scheduled were completed successfully. If there were problems, you might need to suspend a task while you figure out how to correct the problem. You can also view the scheduled tasks log by opening SchedLgU.txt in your Windows folder.

If you are notified of tasks that did not complete, be sure to examine the events log to learn more about the problem that prevented the tasks from completing.

When you set up new tasks, the Task Scheduler uses your current user name and password settings as the defaults. If you sometimes log in using a different user name and password, you may not have adequate permissions to complete all of the scheduled tasks. To prevent this from being a problem, you can configure the

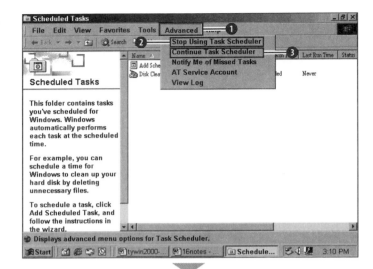

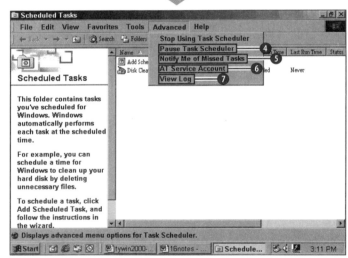

▶ *Open the Scheduled Tasks folder if it is not already open.*

① *Click Advanced to open the menu.*

② *Select this option to stop the Task Scheduler.*

③ *If the Task Scheduler is paused, select this option to continue it.*

④ *If the Task Scheduler is running, select this option to pause it.*

⑤ *Select this option for notification of tasks that did not run.*

⑥ *Select this option to choose a specific user account.*

⑦ *Select this option to view the log.*

CROSS-REFERENCE

See Chapter 15 for more information on administering your computer.

Task Scheduler to always use a specific user name and password. Make certain that the user name you specify has sufficient rights to perform all of the tasks that you schedule.

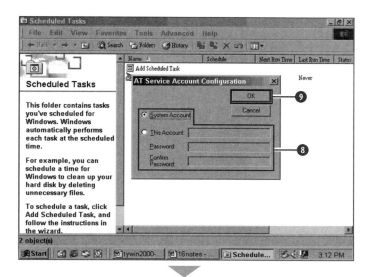

TAKE NOTE

TROUBLESHOOTING SCHEDULED EVENTS

If the scheduled events log shows that certain tasks are consistently unable to complete successfully, you can look for additional clues within the log. You might find, for example, that there is a conflict between two task schedules. If a scheduled task runs successfully but takes too long to complete, it might prevent a later task from completing.

CLEAR THE LOG

The Task Scheduler log is a cumulative file — new entries are added to the existing file, making an ever-larger file. You may wish to stop the Task Scheduler on occasion and use Notepad to remove the oldest entries from the file.

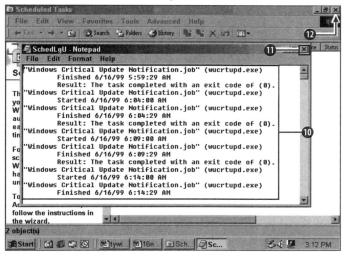

⑧ If you are setting the account options, choose the appropriate account configuration settings.

⑨ Click OK to continue.

⑩ If you have opened the log, view the entries here.

⑪ Click the Close button to continue.

⑫ Click the Close button to complete the task.

FIND IT ONLINE

To learn about the Windows Scripting Host, see
**http://www.vb-web-directory.com/vbscript/
vbs_wsh.shtml.**

Personal Workbook

Q&A

1 How can you get an on-screen notification that advises you when a scheduled task did not run?

_____

_____

_____

2 How can you suspend a task?

_____

_____

_____

3 If you receive a notice that a task did not run, how can you find the problem?

_____

_____

_____

4 Why might you want to enter a descriptive name for a task?

_____

_____

_____

5 How can you specify that you wish to repeat a scheduled task twice daily?

_____

_____

_____

6 What setting can you use to automatically stop a task if you start to use your system?

_____

_____

_____

7 To be a good candidate for a scheduled task, what capability does a program need?

_____

_____

_____

8 How can you set up scheduled tasks that need more permissions than your normal user name allows?

_____

_____

_____

ANSWERS: PAGE 399

EXTRA PRACTICE

1. Add the Disk Defragmenter as a scheduled task.

2. Modify the schedule to run the task once a week.

3. Suspend the task.

4. View the event log to see which events have completed.

5. Resume the task, but change the schedule to every two weeks.

6. Pause the Task Scheduler, and then resume it.

REAL-WORLD APPLICATIONS

✔ You often use an application that creates hundreds of files and deletes other files. You schedule the Disk Defragmenter to run every other night to maintain system performance.

✔ You have a program that can check your stock market portfolio automatically. You schedule the program to run every weekday one hour after the markets open.

✔ You browse the Internet quite often. You schedule the Disk Cleanup program to automatically remove all temporary Internet files every Friday just after you leave for the weekend. You also schedule the disk checking and defragmenting tasks to run over the weekend so that your system is running at top efficiency when you return to the office on Monday.

Visual Quiz

How can you display this dialog box? How can you delay the task startup until 15 minutes after you stop using your system?

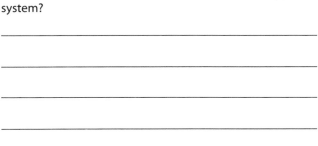

_____

_____

_____

_____

_____

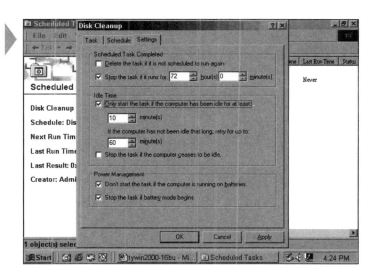

CHAPTER **17**

MASTER
THESE
SKILLS

▶ **Using Media Player for Sound**
▶ **Using Media Player for Video**
▶ **Using CD Player**
▶ **Recording Sounds**
▶ **Using the Volume Controls**
▶ **Configuring Multimedia**

Using Multimedia

Today's PCs provide a lively and interesting computing experience. Much of that excitement is the direct result of the very high level of *multimedia* capability that is common on virtually all of today's computers. In this chapter, you learn how to use the extensive multimedia features that are available in Windows 2000.

The term multimedia encompasses a broad range of audio and video presentations. You won't find every multimedia feature used in every instance, but the field does include many different areas. In this chapter, we use a rather loose definition of multimedia that allows for simple sound files as well as complex productions that include both video and audio tracks in a single file.

These days you'll find multimedia used in many different ways. Web pages, games, and even mainstream business applications often have multimedia features that enhance their impact. Many PC users are finding that they can use multimedia to take their documents out of the boring category and into the area of exciting presentations that simply weren't possible for the average user only a few short years ago.

Windows 2000 supports a number of different types of multimedia content. The standard tools in Windows 2000 can play — and in some cases create — various audio and video formats. For example, you can play back sound files that are digital recordings of actual sounds and you can also play sound files that are closer to a musical score because your PC is actually creating the sounds using the directions in the file. You can play video files that are simply recorded video clips and you can play files that have an audio track synchronized with the video track.

Of course, using multimedia does impose certain requirements on your computer. You need sound, video, and music devices installed and properly configured to support multimedia. Every Windows 2000 system has at least some multimedia capability. For example, even a bare bones Windows 2000 PC can play a video clip. Virtually all PCs also include at least basic sound capabilities, too. You may need to add a set of speakers to realize these capabilities if your system in one of the rare PCs that didn't come with them.

Using Media Player for Sound

Windows 2000 uses an application called Media Player to play back most types of multimedia presentations. Windows 2000 associates Media Player with several different types of multimedia files, so if you double-click the most common types of multimedia files or click a Web link to a multimedia file, Windows 2000 will generally open Media Player to play the media clip.

Playing sound files is certainly one of Media Player's most basic multimedia capabilities. Sound files come in two flavors. *Digital* recordings are actual recordings of sounds and, except for variations in speaker and sound card quality, sound pretty much the same on any system. The most common type of digital recordings are *wave* files — these use the .WAV file extension.

MIDI files are essentially instructions that tell your sound card how to synthesize a piece of music. That is, your sound card actually creates the music in much the same manner as an electronic organ might. MIDI files can sound quite different on different PCs. MIDI files generally use the .MID file extension.

MIDI files are generally quite small compared with WAV sound files. MIDI sequences are limited to music, whereas wave sounds can be a recording of any type of sound, even human speech. In fact, as you'll learn later in this chapter, you can record your own wave sound files easily using the tools that come with Windows 2000. Creating your own MIDI files is far more difficult and requires specialized software that does not come with Windows 2000.

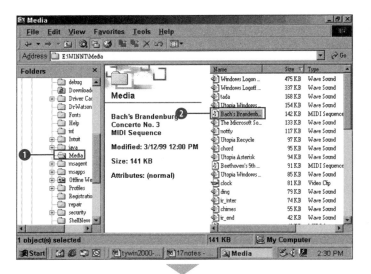

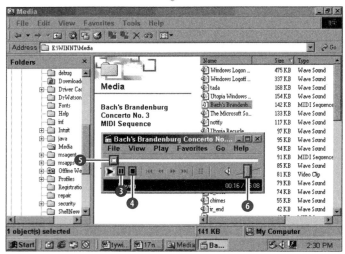

▶ Open Windows Explorer.

❶ Open the Media folder — it will be under your Windows 2000 folder.

❷ Double-click a sound file to open it in Media Player.

❸ Click here to pause the playback.

❹ Click here to stop the playback.

❺ Drag the slider to fast-forward or rewind the playback.

❻ Use this slider to adjust the playback volume.

CROSS-REFERENCE

See "Using Media Player for Video" later in this chapter.

Although you'll find a number of different file formats used for sound files, the Windows 2000 Media Player will likely be able to play the file. There are a few older sound file formats that aren't common enough to have much support these days, but with those exceptions aside, you'll likely find that Media Player can play virtually any sound file.

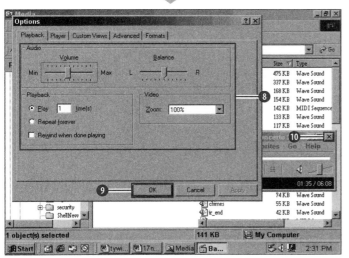

▶ LOCATING SOUND FILES

If you spend any time looking, you'll find there are more sound files than you could ever listen to. Until the novelty wears off, however, you'll easily be able to locate plenty of sound files that you can play. Some sound files are automatically copied to your hard drive when you install Windows 2000. You can usually find more sound files on the installation CD-ROMs for most major office suites as well as on the Internet. To learn which types of sound files the Media Player can play, open the Media Player and select View ⇨ Options. Then click the Formats tab and scroll through the list.

▶ CONTROLLING THE VOLUME

When you play back sound files you may discover that wave files and MIDI files play at different levels. See "Using the Volume Controls" later in this chapter to learn how to correct this inconsistency.

7 *Select View ⇨ Options to change the playback options.*

8 *Select the options you prefer.*

9 *Click OK to continue.*

10 *Click the Close button to complete the task.*

FIND IT ONLINE

Visit the Media Player home page at **http://www.microsoft.com/windows/mediaplayer/default.asp**.

Using Media Player for Video

Because your monitor looks so much like a TV set, it probably comes as no surprise that you can play videos on your computer screen. In fact, there's very little that you can do with a PC that seems more impressive than playing a video clip complete with synchronized sound. The Windows 2000 Media Player can play several different types of video files.

The video files that Media Player supports may appear under several different names, including Microsoft streaming media, video, MPEG movie, Indeo video, QuickTime, and RealMedia. Some of these file formats use a number of different file extensions — depending on the software that was used to create the file. You don't need anything other than Media Player to view any of these types of video files, no matter how they were created.

Video files generally take a lot of disk space. For example, a 90-second color video file with stereo sound may take over 11MB of space. Most video that is destined for viewing on a PC is intended to be viewed in a small window and not full-screen. Full-screen video files would take a prohibitive amount of disk space and a lot of computing power to display properly.

Several methods are used to reduce the size of video files. Reducing the size of the video window is the most common step used. The *frame rate* — the number of images displayed per second — may also be reduced. When the number of frames per second drops, videos tend to become choppy looking.

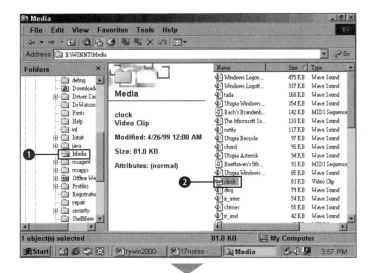

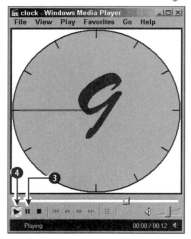

▶ Open Windows Explorer.

❶ Open the Media folder — this will be under your Windows 2000 folder.

❷ Double-click a video file to open it in Media Player.

❸ Click here to pause the playback.

❹ Click here to resume the playback.

CROSS-REFERENCE

See "Using Media Player for Sound" earlier in this chapter.

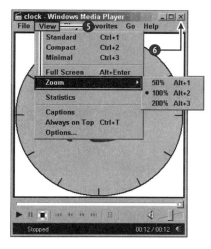

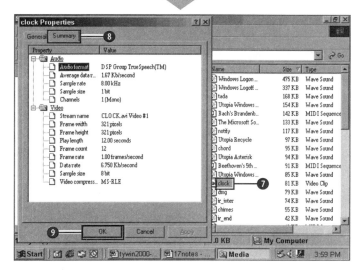

▶ TV VERSUS PC VIDEO

You may wonder why your high-powered PC cannot show most videos full-screen — something that is easy for even the cheapest television set. One reason for this apparent discrepancy is that your computer screen is typically much higher resolution than a standard TV. Higher resolution requires far more data to be processed in the same amount of time. In addition, your computer screen is *refreshed* at a much higher rate than the typical TV screen, and this characteristic greatly increases the rate that data must be supplied, too. Finally, your TV is a single-purpose device that does just one thing, while your PC is generally asked to perform many different tasks at the same time.

▶ ZOOMING THE VIDEO

If you aren't happy with the size of the video window, you can try zooming it to see if the picture is acceptable. You can press Alt+Enter while the video is playing to expand the video to full-screen, or you can select one of the options on the View ⇨ Zoom menu. Remember, though, that the video will have the same resolution regardless of the zoom setting. If you make the video much larger than normal size, the video will appear blocky and out of focus.

⑤ *If you wish to change the playback window size, select View ⇨ Zoom and choose the size.*

▶ *Alternatively, press Alt+Enter to play the video full-screen.*

⑥ *Click the Close button to close Media Player.*

⑦ *To view the video file information, right-click the video file and choose Properties.*

⑧ *Click the Summary tab.*

⑨ *Click OK to complete the task.*

FIND IT ONLINE

To find videos you can download, see **http://windowsmedia.microsoft.com/OnDemand/ondemand.asp?Cat=MU&go.x=14&go.y=13**.

Using CD Player

If you enjoy listening to music while you work with your PC, there's no reason why you can't play audio CDs in your CD-ROM drive. In fact, Windows 2000 includes an excellent program — *CD Player* — specifically designed for this use.

The Windows 2000 CD Player is far better than the standard CD Player that comes with other versions of Windows. In fact, the Windows 2000 CD Player is the same as the Deluxe CD Player that Windows 98 users can get only by buying the Plus! 98 upgrade.

Each audio CD has a unique identification number that identifies what is contained on the CD. When you insert a new audio CD, the CD Player has the ability to download the title, artist, and song titles information from sites on the Internet that maintain huge databases of information about audio CDs. This information is then stored so that it can be displayed the next time you insert the same audio CD. If you like, you can also enter a play list so that the songs are played in the order you prefer, even skipping pieces you don't want to hear.

As the figures on the facing page show, the CD Player was designed to look like the buttons and controls on the front of a CD player that you might find in a typical home stereo system. There are buttons for playing, pausing, and ejecting a CD, as well as buttons that enable you to skip forward and back. You can choose what information you'd like to see on the front panel readout and even choose to play the tracks in random order or to preview each track for a few seconds. If the play list information is available, CD Player also shows the name of the album, artist, and current track.

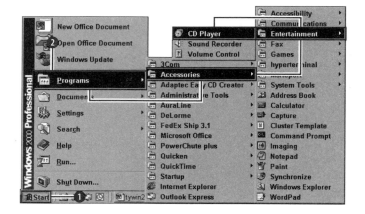

❶ Click the Start button.

❷ Select Programs ➪ Accessories ➪ Entertainment ➪ CD Player.

❸ If CD Player does not have the CD information, click OK to download the information from the Internet.

❹ Use these controls to control the playback.

❺ Use this control to adjust the playback volume.

CROSS-REFERENCE

See "Configuring Multimedia Devices" in this chapter.

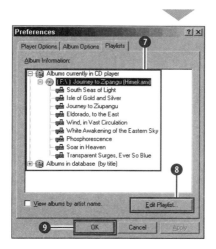

⑥ To view the CD information, select Options ⇨ Playlist.

⑦ Select CDs to view or modify here.

⑧ If you wish to modify the selected CD play list, click here.

⑨ Click OK to complete the task.

Recording Sounds

If you wish to use sounds to attach to system events, to include with an e-mail message, or for any other purpose, you aren't limited to using existing sound files. You can also create your own sounds using the Sound Recorder, an application that lets you record sound files. In this section you'll learn how to use the Sound Recorder to create sound files from a microphone attached to your system. You can also record sounds from any of the other sound card inputs — such as the line input.

The Sound Recorder is a fairly simple application, but it does have some interesting features that you can use to modify sound files. For example, you can add an echo or reverse a sound so that it plays backwards. If the recording's volume isn't correct, you can adjust it up or down. If you want, you can change the speed, too.

When you make a recording you can choose from several different options that affect both the quality of the recording and the amount of disk space that it will require. Lower-quality recordings use less disk space and may be adequate for most purposes.

You can select from the CD, Radio, and Telephone quality settings or select a specific format and attributes. These settings include the *sample rate* — the number of sound samples per second that are recorded. CD quality uses a sample rate of 44,100 Hz. You can use a much lower rate, such as 11,025 Hz, or even 8,000 Hz if you're recording the human voice.

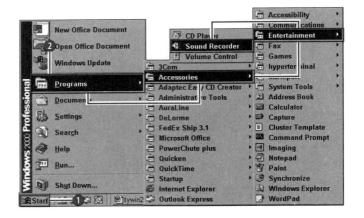

❶ Click the Start button.

❷ Select Programs ⇨ Accessories ⇨ Entertainment ⇨ Sound Recorder.

❸ Select File ⇨ Properties to set the recording properties before you begin recording.

CROSS-REFERENCE

See "Adding Sounds to Events" in Chapter 13.

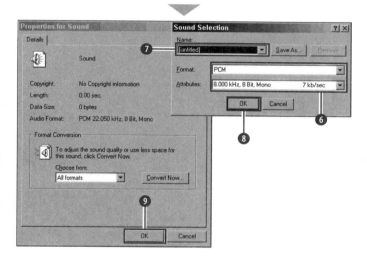

The *bit rate* determines the number of volume levels that can be recorded. Sixteen-bit recordings can store 65,536 levels, whereas 8-bit recordings store only 256 levels. Eight-bit is fine for voice. Some formats even permit 4-bit recordings.

Stereo recordings take twice the space of mono recordings. Always use mono unless you are recording from a stereo source.

Continued

④ *Choose the format type.*

⑤ *Optionally, click the Convert Now button to select the format settings.*

⑥ *Choose a format and attributes.*

⑦ *Alternatively, select one of the defined formats.*

⑧ *Click OK to close the dialog box.*

⑨ *Click OK to return to Sound Recorder.*

Recording Sounds

Continued

After you have selected the recording properties that are appropriate for the way you intend to use the recording, you can make your recording. Then you can have a little fun by applying any of the special effects to modify your recording.

Sound Recorder depicts the recorded sounds by varying the thickness of the line in the viewing window in the middle of the Sound Recorder window. Thicker lines indicate higher volume levels. The shape of the line is not an indicator of the frequencies that were recorded — only of the overall volume level.

If you have used a tape recorder, the Sound Recorder controls should seem quite familiar. If you forget what any of the controls does, hold your mouse pointer over the button for a few seconds to see a description of the control.

You can use the selections on the Effects menu to modify sound files. Keep in mind, however, that it's pretty easy to add distortion as you are applying special effects to a sound file. The quality settings you selected determine the amount of data within the file. Almost any special effect will modify the file in ways that degrade the sound output. If you don't care for the results after you have applied a special effect, select File ⇨ Revert to return to the last saved version of the file.

You can use the Edit menu options to change the length of the recording or to mix two sound files together. For example, if you clicked the record button and waited a few seconds to begin speaking, you could move

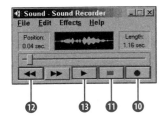

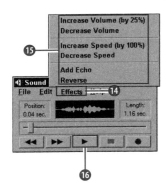

⑩ Click the Record button to begin recording.

⑪ Click the Stop button to end the recording.

⑫ Click the Rewind button to return to the beginning of the recording.

⑬ Click the Play button to hear the recording.

⑭ Select Effects to display the Effects menu.

⑮ Select an effect to apply to your recording.

⑯ Click Play to hear the changes in the recording.

CROSS-REFERENCE

See "Using the Volume Controls" later in this chapter.

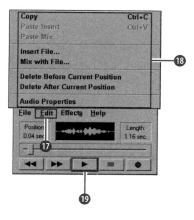

the position slider to the very beginning of your speech and then choose Edit ⇨ Delete Before Current Position to remove the silence at the beginning of the recording. You may need to play the recording several times to locate the correct point to begin your changes. You can also combine several short clips by using the Edit ⇨ Insert File command.

TAKE NOTE

► TROUBLESHOOTING RECORDING PROBLEMS

If you click the Record button but Sound Recorder doesn't record any sound, first make certain that your microphone is plugged in correctly. If the microphone is plugged in correctly, check to make certain that the microphone input is enabled in the volume control, as shown in the next section of this chapter. There should not be a check mark in the Mute check box.

► CREATE A SECRET MESSAGE

You can record a secret message by using Effects ⇨ Reverse to reverse the recording so that it becomes unintelligible. Your intended recipient must use his or her own copy of Sound Recorder to once again reverse the file and hear the message. This won't, of course, provide very much security, but it is an example of how you can have a little fun with the special effects.

---

⑰ Select Edit to display the Edit menu.

⑱ Select the action you wish to perform.

⑲ Click Play again to hear the new changes.

⑳ Select File ⇨ Save As to save the file — you will need to enter a name for the file.

㉑ Click the Close button to complete the task.

FIND IT ONLINE

To download sound files, see **http://www.filefarm.com/ filefarm/windows/subjects/422/.**

Using the Volume Controls

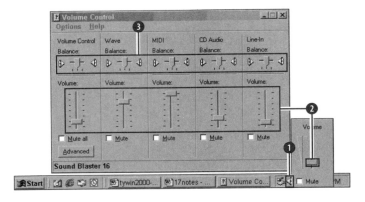

As you play different sounds through your PC, you have probably noticed that it's necessary to adjust the volume to compensate for different loudness levels and background noise conditions. In this section you'll learn how to use the Windows 2000 volume controls so you don't always have to reach for the knob on your speakers.

Windows 2000 has a small volume control slider that pops up when you click the speaker icon in the system tray. In addition to this single control that adjusts all sound sources identically, Windows 2000 has a more sophisticated volume control that you can use to adjust each individual sound source independently. If you've ever been blasted by sound when you switch from one sound source to another, you'll appreciate this capability to balance the different sound sources.

The full volume control also includes sliders that you can use to adjust the left/right balance. Depending on your sound card, you may also be able to adjust the bass, treble, and loudness settings.

Once either volume control is displayed, you can adjust the volume by dragging the slider up or down. To turn the sounds off, click the Mute check box. Drag the horizontal sliders to adjust the left/right balance.

If you are using Sound Recorder or another application to record a sound file, you may discover that the sound file includes unexpected background noise. In many cases, this unwanted noise comes from the other input sources that connect to your sound card. Each of the individual sound sources has a Mute check box that

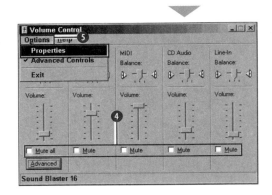

❶ Click the speaker button once for the small volume control, or double-click for the full volume control.

❷ Drag these sliders to adjust volume.

❸ Drag these sliders to adjust balance.

❹ Select these check boxes to mute the sound.

❺ To choose the control, select Options ➪ Properties.

CROSS-REFERENCE

See "Using CD Player" earlier in this chapter.

is intended to silence that sound source, but unfortunately many sound cards don't completely mute the sounds from a source, even if this check box is selected. For the best results, reduce all unused sound sources to the lowest volume level in addition to selecting their Mute check boxes. Then adjust the remaining source to the proper level for recording.

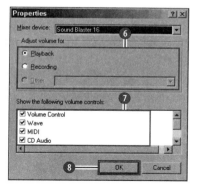

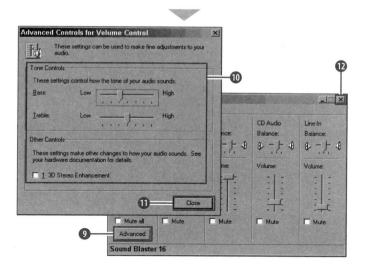

TAKE NOTE

USING POWERED SPEAKERS

If you have a set of powered speakers, you may need to experiment with the volume control settings to discover which settings produce the highest-quality sound. The amplifiers in some powered speakers may produce excess distortion if the volume level from your PC is too high or too low. Too low a volume level from your PC may also result in excess hum from the speakers.

SELECT THE CORRECT CONTROLS

Make certain that you select the correct set of volume controls. Generally, you can select the set of controls either for playback or for recording. Depending on your sound card, choosing the incorrect set may make it more difficult to adjust the individual volume levels correctly. As the figures on the facing page show, you can also choose which of the individual volume controls will appear on the full volume control.

⑥ Choose the set of controls you wish to use.

⑦ Choose the controls to appear on the full volume control.

⑧ Click OK to close the dialog box.

⑨ Click Advanced to adjust the tone and other settings.

⑩ Adjust the settings to suit your preferences.

⑪ Click Close.

⑫ Click the Close button to complete the task.

FIND IT ONLINE

To find audio and video files, see **http://www.realaudio.com/R/HPbc-1/R/realguide.real.com**.

Configuring Multimedia

If you want the most from your PC's multimedia capabilities, you may want to configure the way Windows 2000 uses those capabilities. Windows 2000 tends to be somewhat conservative in its default multimedia settings, so adjusting the configuration may improve the performance of your multimedia devices. The figures on the facing page show you how to open the Multimedia Properties dialog box and configure the audio options. The following pages continue the task by showing you how to configure the speech capabilities in Windows 2000.

There are a number of multimedia settings that may be unfamiliar to you. For example, one of the figures on the facing page shows the Speakers tab of the Advanced Audio Properties dialog box. Select the configuration that most closely represents your speaker setup. This is especially important if you have a very good set of speakers attached to your PC. Otherwise, Windows 2000 may not take advantage of all the advanced features built into your speaker system.

You'll also find performance settings for both playback and recording. The first type of setting is for *hardware acceleration*. This setting determines how much processing power is used to improve audio playback and recording features. Although the default setting uses partial hardware acceleration, you'll probably find that your system has no problem using full acceleration. Using a lower setting may be effective as a method of troubleshooting audio-related problems, but will result in poorer audio performance.

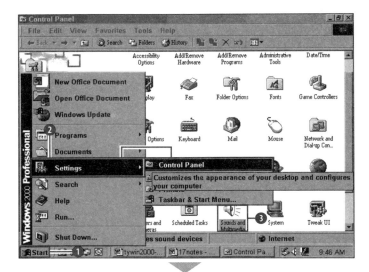

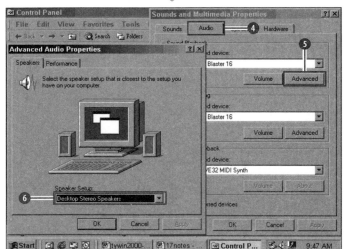

❶ Click the Start button.

❷ Select Settings ➪ Control Panel.

❸ Double-click the Sounds and Multimedia icon.

❹ Click the Audio tab.

❺ Click the playback Advanced Properties button.

❻ Select your speaker setup.

CROSS-REFERENCE

See "Using Computer Management" in Chapter 15.

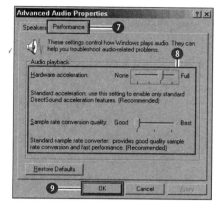

The second audio performance setting is the *sample rate conversion quality*. This setting determines the quality level of audio playback and recording. The default setting produces the lowest quality while imposing the smallest possible drain on system resources. If you prefer that your system sound as good as possible, you'll want to try one of the higher quality settings.

You will need to experiment with these settings to find the best set for your needs. Faster computers are generally better able to handle the higher-quality settings at the right end of the two scales.

Continued

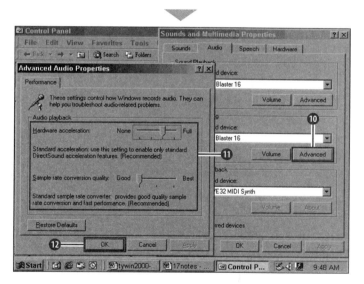

7 *Click the Performance tab.*

8 *Select the playback settings you prefer.*

9 *Click the OK button.*

10 *Click the recording Advanced Properties button.*

11 *Select the recording settings you prefer.*

12 *Click the OK button.*

TAKE NOTE

CHOOSING DEVICES

If your system has more than one device that has audio capabilities installed, you may need to choose the correct device in each of the *Preferred device* list boxes. For example, if you happen to have both a high-quality sound card and a modem with audio capabilities, Windows 2000 may not know which to use for multimedia purposes. You'll want to make certain the correct device is selected.

SET THE VOLUME LEVELS

Since different audio sources may have considerably different sound levels, you may need to adjust each of them to produce output levels that are more even. If you click any of the Volume buttons in the Sounds and Multimedia Properties dialog box, you will open the full volume control, which has individual controls for each sound source.

FIND IT ONLINE

To download the Real player, visit **http://www. realaudio.com/**.

Configuring Multimedia

Continued

Windows 2000 has speech synthesis capabilities built in as a part of its multimedia capabilities. If you use the Windows 2000 Narrator, you are hearing the Windows 2000 speech synthesizer. You've probably noticed, however, that the speech synthesizer sometimes uses rather odd pronunciations. Fortunately, as a part of configuring the Windows 2000 multimedia capabilities, you can adjust the way the speech synthesizer pronounces words.

Synthetic speech is often difficult to understand because it tends to be mechanical sounding. When you compound the odd sound with poor pronunciation, it can be easy to become confused with what the speech synthesizer is trying to say.

You can adjust the way Windows 2000 pronounces specific words. By default, Windows 2000 tries to figure out how words should sound based on their spelling. This can often result in words sounding considerably different than they should. This is especially true in the case of proper names or many foreign words. By taking a few minutes to adjust the pronunciation, you can produce greatly improved results that are far easier to understand.

To change the way Windows 2000 pronounces words, you must first add those words to the speech dictionary as shown in the second figure. After the word is added to the dictionary, you can adjust the pronunciation. If you type in a word that is already in the dictionary, you'll have the opportunity to change the way it is pronounced.

Once you have fine-tuned the pronunciation, you can choose to e-mail the changes to Microsoft. Other

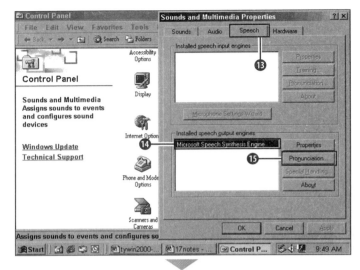

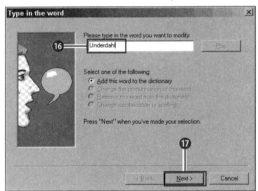

⑬ To adjust pronunciation, click the Speech tab.

⑭ Select the Microsoft Speech Synthesis Engine.

⑮ Click the Pronunciation button.

⑯ Type the word you wish to adjust.

⑰ Click Next to continue.

CROSS-REFERENCE

See "Using the Narrator" in Chapter 8.

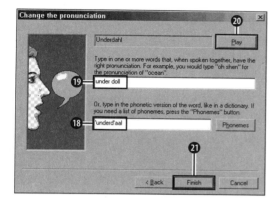

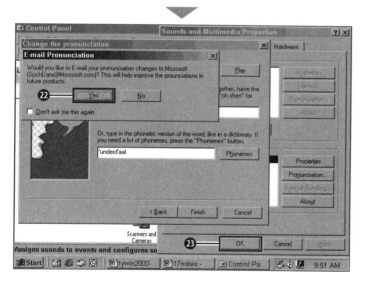

people, of course, may offer alternative pronunciations for certain words. It's likely that Microsoft will choose the most popular variation when alternate pronunciations are submitted. Still, it might be nice to be assured that future speech synthesis products may do a better job of speaking your name!

UNDERSTANDING PHONEMES

Phonemes are essentially building blocks of sounds that you string together to indicate how a word should be pronounced. If you've ever looked up a word in a dictionary you've seen examples of how phonemes are used to describe the pronunciation of words. As the figures show, you can use phonemes to indicate the correct pronunciation of an often mispronounced word so that Windows 2000 will speak the word correctly.

USING SIMILAR-SOUNDING WORDS

If you find that selecting the correct phonemes is somewhat difficult, you may be able to derive the correct pronunciation using similar-sounding words. For example, you can tell Windows 2000 that Underdahl sounds like "under doll" and Windows 2000 will offer 'underd'aal as the correct set of phonemes. You may need to experiment with several different spellings before you discover the one that results in a natural-sounding word.

⑱ Enter the phonetic pronunciation.

⑲ Alternatively, enter similar-sounding words.

⑳ Click the Play button.

㉑ Click the Finish button when the word is correctly pronounced.

㉒ Click Yes if you would like to send Microsoft the corrected pronunciation.

㉓ Click the OK button to complete the task.

FIND IT ONLINE

See http://www.speech.cs.cmu.edu/cgi-bin/cmudict for a machine-readable pronunciation dictionary for North American English.

Personal Workbook

Q&A

1 Which Windows 2000 tool would you use to record a voice message?

_____

_____

_____

2 What is the quickest method of displaying the full volume control?

_____

_____

_____

3 What type of files does the Sound Recorder produce?

_____

_____

_____

4 How can you make CD Player skip the same song on an audio CD every time you play the CD?

_____

_____

_____

5 Why are most video files shown in a small window?

_____

_____

_____

6 What do you call the phonetic building blocks that define how words are pronounced?

_____

_____

_____

7 What type of files are instructions that are used to synthesize music on your PC?

_____

_____

_____

8 What does the thickness of the line that is displayed in the Sound Recorder represent?

_____

_____

_____

ANSWERS: PAGE 400

EXTRA PRACTICE

1. Open the full volume control and adjust each of the individual controls to suit your preferences.

2. Enter a play list for your favorite audio CD.

3. Play a sound file while you adjust the left/right speaker balance using the full volume control.

4. Play a video file and notice the difference as you select different zoom settings.

5. Record a message that tells you when new messages arrive.

6. Add echo to your message so that is sounds like you are in a large room.

REAL-WORLD APPLICATIONS

✔ You have a name that people often mispronounce. You use the speech synthesizer settings to determine the correct phonemes so you can e-mail them as a part of your e-mail signature.

✔ You like to listen to a particular audio CD, but one of the tracks is damaged, so it always skips whenever it is played. You edit the play list for the CD so that track is automatically bypassed.

✔ You have the audio signal from your satellite receiver connected to your sound card so you can listen to a foreign broadcast while you work. You use the full volume control to adjust the line-in input so that the satellite sound is at the correct listening level.

Visual Quiz

How can you display this application? How can you tell how long the file will play? Can you tell what type of file is being played?

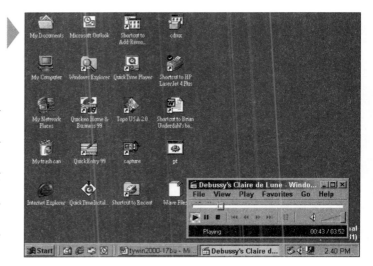

_____

_____

_____

_____

CHAPTER **18**

MASTER
THESE
SKILLS

▶ **Using the Calculator**
▶ **Using Character Map**
▶ **Using Notepad**
▶ **Creating Documents in WordPad**
▶ **Using Imaging for Windows**
▶ **Using Paint**
▶ **Playing Some Games**
▶ **Opening and Closing the Command Prompt Window**
▶ **Using the Command Prompt Window**
▶ **Getting Command Help**

Using the Accessory Applications

Windows 2000 has a number of items that somewhat loosely fit into the category of accessories. These are programs that enable you to do some of the simple tasks that you might expect from your computer, but which don't really require the services of an expensive dedicated application program.

This chapter introduces you to these accessories so that you can learn what you can do in Windows 2000 without buying and installing some fancy new program. As you'll discover, the Windows 2000 accessories are quite capable. They may not be as powerful as you might need for heavy-duty use, but they'll certainly do a very creditable job and suit your needs for occasional use.

Computers are extremely versatile machines, but there's one fact you cannot avoid — they need the proper software to accomplish anything of value. That's one of the main reasons Windows 2000 includes these accessories. The accessories enable you to handle simple tasks without much difficulty. Many of the Windows 2000 accessories are based, at least in their concept, on programs that computer users had to either purchase or create for themselves in earlier operating system versions. Some of the accessory programs that come with the package are actually slightly disguised "lite" versions of popular utility programs that Microsoft has licensed for Windows 2000. For example, the Calculator accessory will not replace your favorite spreadsheet program, nor do the drawing tools in Paint rival those found in sophisticated graphics programs. But if all you need is to make some quick calculations or create a simple sign, you will find the Windows 2000 accessory programs handy.

No discussion of Windows 2000 accessories would be complete without some mention of the *command prompt*. Although it could be argued that the command prompt is a throwback to the early days of computing before graphical user interfaces took over, it is just as valid to say that the command prompt provides you with a powerful tool that can be extremely important. There simply are tasks that are much easier when the computer user has the ability to type in a single command that accomplishes more than dozens of mouse clicks ever could.

Using the Calculator

The first of the accessory applications that we will cover in this chapter is the Calculator. This handy little tool is an on-screen version of a pocket calculator, but it offers unique features that make it far more useful.

The Calculator is actually two different types of calculators in one application. When all you need is a simple calculator that includes basic capabilities such add, subtract, multiply, and divide functions, a square root function, a percent function, a reciprocal function, and memory, the standard calculator will easily meet your needs. If you need more advanced features such as base conversions, statistical functions, and logarithms, you can choose the scientific calculator. It has many additional functions like those you'd find on a sophisticated calculator used by a scientist or engineer.

You can use the calculators either by using your keyboard or by clicking the calculator keys with your mouse. If you want to use the keyboard you'll probably find it easier to use the numeric keypad; make certain the Num Lock indicator is lit.

The calculator keys work just the same as they do on a pocket calculator. The Backspace button removes the last digit you entered. The CE button clears the current entry from the display without modifying the current calculation. The C button zeros out the Calculator.

An M in the gray box above the memory key column indicates that a value has been stored in the calculator's memory. The MC button resets memory to zero, and MR displays the value in memory. MS stores the value currently displayed into memory, and M+ adds the value currently displayed to the value that is in memory.

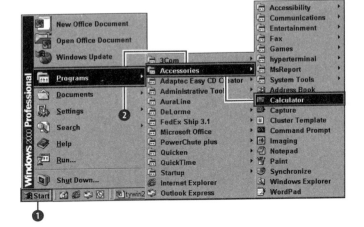

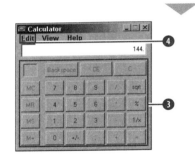

❶ Click the Start button.

❷ Select Programs ➪ Accessories ➪ Calculator.

❸ Enter your calculation using the on-screen keys or your keyboard.

❹ To copy or paste data, use the Edit menu.

CROSS-REFERENCE

See Chapter 5 for more information about using the Clipboard.

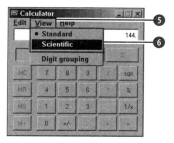

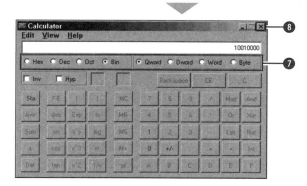

When you are displaying the scientific calculator, a gray box appears above the right parenthesis button. This box indicates the current nesting level when you are entering a formula that use parentheses to control the calculation order.

TAKE NOTE

▶ CONVERTING NUMBER BASES

The scientific calculator includes several radio buttons that you can use to convert numbers to different numbering systems. For example, if the Dec radio button is selected, you can enter a base-10 number. To convert the number to a binary number, you can click the Bin button. When you choose a different numbering system, you may find that some of the keys will be grayed out to indicate that they are unavailable. For example, since binary numbers can only include 1s and 0s, all of the other number keys will be grayed out when you click the Bin button.

▶ USE THE CLIPBOARD

One of the big advantages of the on-screen calculator is that you can copy your results to the Clipboard and then paste them into a document. Use Ctrl+C to copy the result to the Windows 2000 Clipboard and then use Ctrl+V to paste the number into your document.

⑤ To choose a different view, click the View menu.

⑥ Select the type of calculator you wish to use.

⑦ To convert a number to a different base, use these options.

⑧ Click the Close button to complete the task.

FIND IT ONLINE

See **http://www.fdgroup.co.uk/neo/fsi/** for an advanced Windows calculator.

Using Character Map

If you need to enter foreign language characters into your documents, you will find that Windows 2000 provides an essential tool to facilitate this process. The Character Map is a program that provides you with easy access to all of the characters that are contained within a character set.

If you use a standard keyboard, there are probably about 100 keys on the keyboard. Of these, over 20 are dedicated to functions other than entering characters into your documents. This means that even using the Shift key you are limited in the number of different characters that you can enter directly. By using the Character Map, you can easily choose any character you wish to insert into a document — no matter how difficult typing that character directly might be.

Although the Character Map is well suited to enter foreign characters into documents, you'll find that the program has other practical uses, too. For example, if you need to create a document that uses *bullets* you can easily choose any of the special characters that are generally contained in most character sets. You might choose uniquely shaped arrows or even sequentially numbered clock faces for special bullet points for a change of pace from the standard bullets that are used in most presentations.

In addition to bullets, you might find Character Map quite handy if you want to insert standard typographic symbols into a document. Using standard typographic symbols such as the copyright symbol — © — looks far more professional than improvising with normal characters like (c).

You may find that your word processor offers a shortcut to Character Map through a command such as Insert ⇨ Symbol.

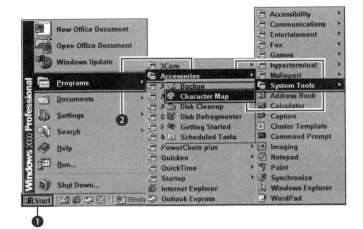

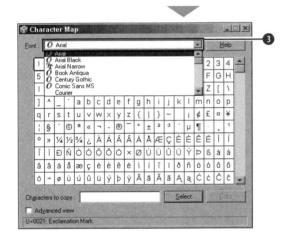

❶ Click the Start button.

❷ Select Programs ⇨ Accessories ⇨ System Tools ⇨ Character Map.

❸ Choose the font you wish to use.

▶ Different fonts may not all contain the same set of extended characters.

CROSS-REFERENCE

See Chapter 5 for more information about working with documents.

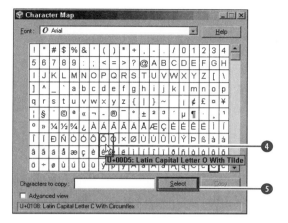

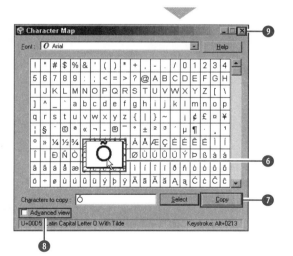

UNDERSTANDING UNICODE

Windows 2000 supports *Unicode* character sets. These are character sets that use 16 bits of data to define the character set rather than the 8 bits that are used for all character sets in Windows 98, Windows 95, and MS-DOS. Eight-bit character sets are limited to fewer than 256 different characters, but Unicode character sets have the potential for 65,536 characters in a single character set. This enables special characters to be created for purposes such as displaying Chinese ideographic symbols. Currently there are approximately 21,000 Chinese ideographic symbols defined and about 39,000 total Unicode characters that are defined.

CREATE YOUR OWN CHARACTERS

Windows 2000 includes a special application — *Private Character Editor* — that you can use to create unique letters and logos for your library. To open the Private Character Editor, click the Start button and choose Run. In the Open text box type **eudcedit** and click OK. After you have created your own characters and saved them in a font file, you can then copy those characters into a document from the Character Map just as you would any standard character.

④ To view the description of a character, hold the mouse pointer over the character.

⑤ Double-click the character or click Select to select the character.

⑥ Alternatively, click the character to view a magnified version.

⑦ Click Copy to copy the selected characters to the Clipboard.

⑧ If you wish to use the advanced Unicode features, click here.

⑨ Click the Close button. Remember to paste the characters into your document.

FIND IT ONLINE

See the Unicode Consortium Web site at
http://www.unicode.org for more information.

Using Notepad

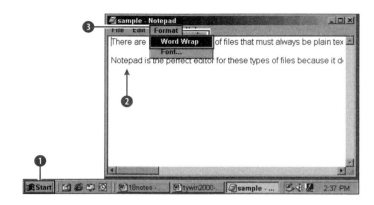

otepad is a simple text editor that you can use for memos, short letters, and various Windows 2000 text file types. Because it supports only plain text files, Notepad is safe to use for files that must not contain anything except plain text.

There are a number of types of files that must always be plain text files. These include setup files that use the .INF extension, and log files that use the .LOG extension. These files cannot contain anything except plain text — otherwise they will be unusable. Notepad is the perfect editor for these types of files because it does not attempt to alter their format and always saves new files as plain text files. If you were to attempt to create one of these files in a word processor program such as WordPad or Microsoft Word, you would have to remember to specifically save the file as a plain text file.

Use the Format ⇨ Word Wrap option for letters, memos, and documents. The paragraphs reform themselves as you change the size of the window. When Word Wrap is on, the horizontal scroll bar goes away and you can see text that would normally extend past the right side of the Notepad window. If it is important to see each line of text on the correct line, be sure to turn word wrap off and use the scroll bar to see the true layout. You may wish to maximize the Notepad window to see more of each line.

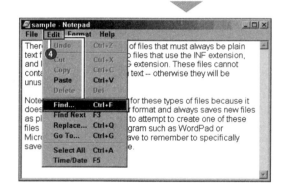

❶ Click the Start button and select Programs ⇨ Accessories ⇨ Notepad.

❷ Type your text in the document window.

❸ Select Format ⇨ Word Wrap to wrap lines to the width of the Notepad window.

❹ To locate specific text, choose Edit ⇨ Find.

CROSS-REFERENCE

See "Creating Documents in WordPad" later in this chapter.

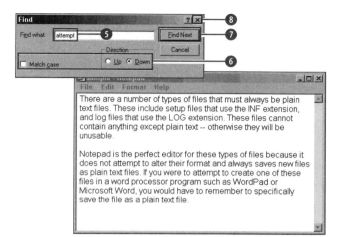

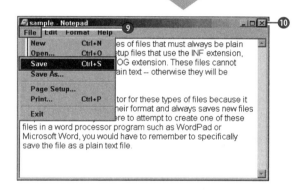

WINDOWS 2000 NOTEPAD

The Windows 2000 version of Notepad has some important differences that may confuse you if you're used to using Notepad in Windows 98. The primary difference is that in the Windows 2000 version of Notepad you can use the Format ⇨ Font command to select a font and attributes to apply to your Notepad document. Note, however, that the same formatting is applied to your entire document — you cannot make just one part of the document bold, for example. Even when you apply a font format change to your Notepad document, Notepad will save the document as a plain text document.

PRINTING NOTEPAD DOCUMENTS

When you try to print text files in Notepad you may discover that short and long lines of text alternate in the printout. This problem is usually caused by the default margin settings Notepad uses. Often, text documents have too many characters per line to fit within the default margins, and this accounts for the odd appearance of the printouts. You can select File ⇨ Page Setup to adjust the margins to enable the printed text to better fit the page. When you're changing margins, consider the capabilities of your printer. Many printers cannot print closer than 0.25 inches from the edge of the paper.

⑤ *Type the search word or phrase.*

⑥ *Select any appropriate search options.*

⑦ *Click Find Next.*

⑧ *Click the Close button to close the Find dialog box.*

⑨ *Select File ⇨ Save to save your work.*

⑩ *Click the Close button to complete the task.*

FIND IT ONLINE

Download a replacement for Notepad at **http://www.alberts.com/AuthorPages/00013878/ Prod_82.htm.**

Creating Documents in WordPad

If you need a bit more power than is available in Notepad, WordPad may be just what you need. You could think of WordPad as "Word Lite" because WordPad is a simple word processor that has some of the features of Microsoft Word. WordPad will read, edit, and write WordPad documents in Word format. WordPad also allows you to do many things you can't do in Notepad, such as apply text formatting as needed.

Even if you use another more powerful word processor than WordPad, you may find that WordPad is a good option on occasion. For example, if you normally use a different word processor such as Word Pro or WordPerfect, WordPad may do a better job of correctly showing the formatting contained in a Word document. Different brands of word processing programs often have some difficulty maintaining document fidelity when opening a foreign document format. See the "Take Note" section for a tip on an important use for WordPad even if you normally use Word.

WordPad works much like any other word processor. As you type, you can tell your current position on the page using the ruler as a guideline. You can easily apply formatting using the toolbar buttons, and, unlike Notepad documents, you can format individual sections of the document as necessary.

Using the View ⇨ Options command, you can select such options as the default measurement unit, the parts of WordPad that appear on your screen, word wrap settings, and the way WordPad selects blocks of text when you manipulate it with your mouse. For example, if you need to create a form that needs to fit a specific layout, choosing the correct unit of measure is a big help.

Continued

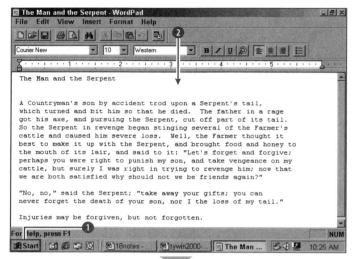

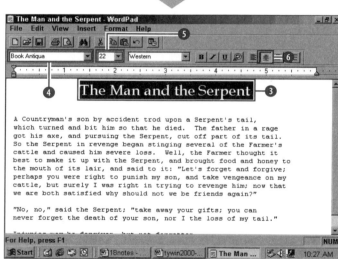

❶ Click the Start button and select Programs ⇨ Accessories ⇨ WordPad.

❷ Type your text in the document window.

❸ To format the title, select the title line.

❹ Choose a font from this list box.

❺ Choose a font size.

❻ Select the appropriate alignment.

CROSS-REFERENCE

See Chapter 8 for information about printing documents.

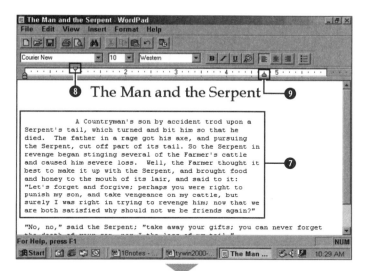

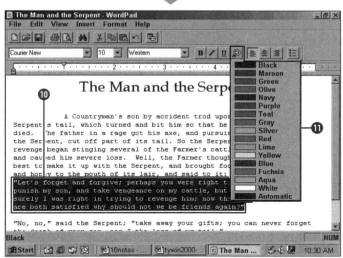

AVOID MACRO VIRUSES

If you suspect that a Word document is infected with a macro virus, you can safely open that document in WordPad. Because WordPad does not execute macros, any macro viruses contained in the document will not be able to run when the document is open in WordPad. To be completely safe, you can copy the text from WordPad to the Clipboard, start a new WordPad document, and paste the text into the new document. When you save your new document, it will be completely virus-free and safe to open in Word.

SET YOUR OPTIONS

WordPad doesn't save many of the document options, such as fonts and styles, that you may wish to use as the defaults for new documents. To make it easier to format new documents according to your preferences, you may want to set those options yourself when you begin a new document. If you press Ctrl+A to select the entire document, any changes you make will then apply to the entire document. You can later apply specific formatting changes to individual portions of your document as necessary.

⑦ To change margin settings, click anywhere inside the section you wish to change.

⑧ Move this marker to select a first-line indent.

⑨ Move this marker to select a right margin.

⑩ To apply a formatting change such as text color, select the text you wish to change.

⑪ Click the color button and choose a text color.

Creating Documents in WordPad

Continued

Although no one would argue that WordPad has all the features of a full-blown word processor such as Microsoft Word, WordPad has many more capabilities than a simple text editor such as Notepad. In a WordPad document, you can use different fonts, font sizes, font styles, and even colors for the text. You can also embed objects such as bitmap images to enhance your WordPad document.

You can save WordPad documents in several different formats. By default, WordPad documents are saved in Word 6 format, but you can also select Rich Text Format (RTF), which preserves the text formatting you've applied. WordPad also offers several plain text formats that differ in the specific character set used in the document. Unless you use accented characters such as those you might find in many European languages, any of the text formats work well.

You can insert objects into your WordPad documents. When you insert an object into a WordPad document, the appearance of WordPad may change while you're working with the object. To return WordPad to the normal appearance, click outside the object. If you choose to insert an object into a document, remember that many objects lose their effectiveness when the document is printed rather than being viewed on a computer screen. There's no way, for example, to effectively use an embedded sound file on a printed page!

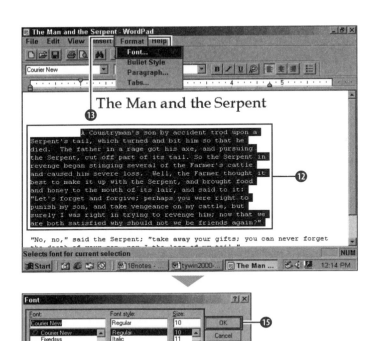

⑫ To format a block of text, select the block.

⑬ Select Format ⇨ Font to select the font formatting options.

⑭ Choose your format options.

⑮ Click OK to continue.

CROSS-REFERENCE

See Chapter 7 for more information about working with documents.

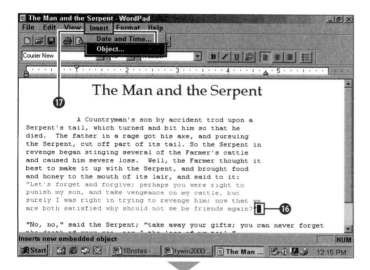

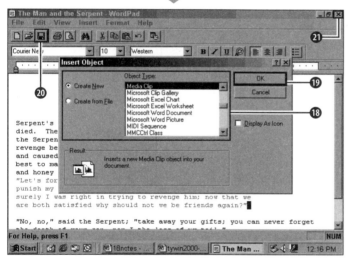

16 To insert an object into your document, click the spot where you wish to place the object.

17 Select Insert ⇨ Object.

18 Select the object.

19 Click OK to continue, and follow the prompts to insert the type of object you selected.

20 Click Save to save your document.

21 Click the Close button to complete the task.

TAKE NOTE

► CREATE A DOCUMENT TEMPLATE

If you often use WordPad to create new documents, you may want to create a document template that you can use as the basis for new documents. Create a blank document that includes your preferred font, alignment, margin, and other settings. Save that blank document as your template. When you wish to create a new document, open your template file and then immediately use File ⇨ Save As to give your new document a different name. This will save you the time required to make these settings with each new document.

► OBJECT TYPES YOU CAN INSERT

When you chose Insert ⇨ Object, you'll probably see a few types of objects that you don't recognize. Although you may wish to experiment with some of them by seeing what appears when you insert them into a document, many of the object types aren't intended for general use. Many object types are specific to one of the programs installed on your PC and won't work correctly in a WordPad document. Generally, though, they won't do any harm and you may enjoy playing around to see what is available. Inserting an object places the object into your document. If you double-click the inserted object you can edit the object. Whether you are able to edit the object directly in the document or in the application that created the object depends on the properties of the two applications.

FIND IT ONLINE

Download CwordPad, with spell checking and a thesaurus, at **http://www.cetussoft.com/cwordpad.htm**.

Using Imaging for Windows

Imaging is a program that is intended to help you work with your scanner as well as to view and annotate faxes. Even if your scanner includes its own simple faxing application, you may find Imaging quite useful.

A simple faxing program may be good enough if all you want to do is send someone an unaltered copy of a single page. But if you need to scan and fax multiple pages or need to add annotations to a page, you may find Imaging to be just what you need. When you scan a document using Imaging, you can add additional pages or even replace scanned pages that didn't come out quite right. Once you've scanned all of the pages you can easily add any annotations electronically before you send off your fax.

When you send or receive faxes, you may want to add a response to something in the text. You can use the annotation tools to add lines, text, highlighting, or even a yellow sticky note to the image.

The annotation toolbar has a number of interesting tools you can use to add your notes to an image. If you're not certain about the function of one of the buttons, move your mouse over the button. You'll see a description of the button in the status line. If you apply an annotation but don't like the results, you can remove the annotation. Imaging also allows you to reverse the last thing you did using the Undo button, and the Redo button will redo the last thing that was undone. The Cut, Copy, and Paste buttons also work in the usual way when you have selected an annotation.

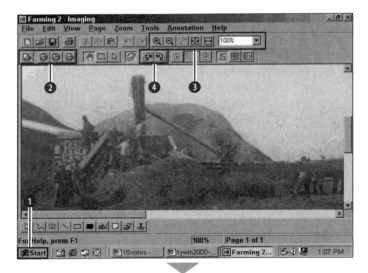

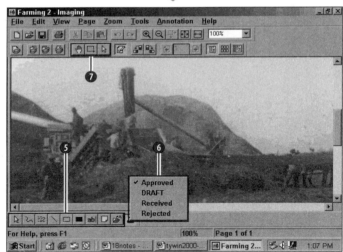

❶ Click the Start button and select Programs ➪ Accessories ➪ Imaging.

❷ Use these tools to scan an image.

❸ Use these tools to control the zoom.

❹ Use these tools to rotate the image.

❺ To add an annotation, select a tool.

❻ To use the rubber stamp annotation, select the stamp after you click the button.

❼ To select a part of the image, use these tools.

CROSS-REFERENCE

See the section "Using Paint" later in this chapter for more information about creating and modifying image files.

After you've scanned and annotated the images you want to send as a fax, you can use the File ➪ Print command to send a fax. Select FAX as your printer before you click the OK button in the Print dialog box. Remember to set the printer selection back to your normal system printer when you're finished sending the fax. You aren't limited to faxing from Imaging — you can print images on your normal printer, too.

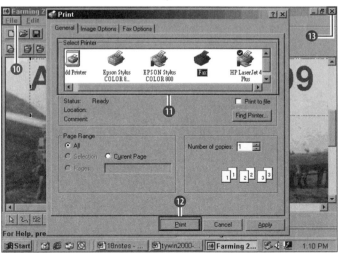

8 *Drag an annotation to place it where you want it.*

9 *Use the annotation's handles to resize the annotation.*

10 *To print or fax the image, select File ➪ Print.*

11 *Choose the destination and options.*

12 *Click Print.*

13 *After you save the image, click the Close button to complete the task.*

FIND IT ONLINE

Find Paint Shop Pro, a complete image creation and manipulation program at **http://www.jasc.com/psp.html**.

375

Using Paint

Paint is a program that you can use to create or modify *bitmap images*—graphic image files such as those produced by scanners or digital cameras. Although both Imaging and Paint work with the same types of images, the two programs have a very different purpose. Paint enables you to create an image completely from scratch and to make changes that simply aren't possible in Imaging—such as spray painting over an area in an image.

While you are working in Paint you make extensive use of two toolbars. The toolbox that appears along the left side of the Paint window includes all of the tools that you use to draw or erase images. The color box at the bottom of the window enables you to choose the colors that you will use with the various drawing tools.

To use the drawing tools, select the tool from the toolbox. The tools in the top row allow you to select a region on the screen. The eraser tool erases parts of the picture with the background color. You erase by dragging the mouse cursor across the picture. The Fill tool fills the portion of the picture that you point to with color. The Pick Color tool sets the foreground and background colors to the color in the picture that you click. The Magnifier tool zooms in on the picture to allow you to work with smaller details. The Pencil tool and the Brush tool draw as you drag the cursor around the screen. The Airbrush tool sprays a pattern as you drag the tool around the picture. The Text tool lets you type text. The Line tool draws straight lines. The remaining Paint tools draw curves, rectangles, many-sided shapes, ellipses, and rounded rectangles.

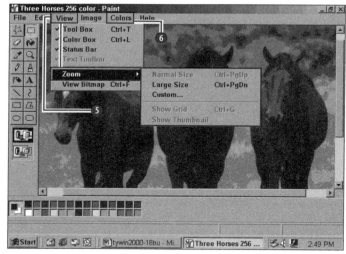

① Click the Start button and select Programs ⇨ Accessories ⇨ Paint.

② Use these tools to draw.

③ Use this box to select tool options as appropriate.

④ Use this box to select colors.

⑤ To change the zoom level, select View ⇨ Zoom and choose the level.

⑥ If you want to use custom colors, select Colors ⇨ Edit Colors.

CROSS-REFERENCE

See "Using Imaging for Windows" earlier in this chapter.

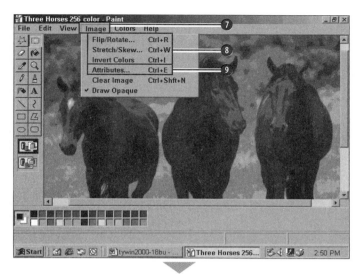

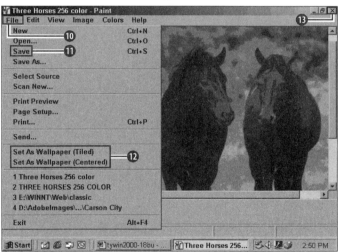

Many of the tools have optional size or shape settings that you select in the area below the toolbox. In addition, the colors that are used alternate between the foreground and background color as you switch between the right and left mouse buttons.

TAKE NOTE

▶ PAINT HAS SEVERAL UNDO LEVELS

If you begin modifying an image and then discover that you have made a major mistake, you can use the Edit ⇨ Undo command to undo the last drawing action you performed. If you select the same command again, Paint will undo the previous action. You can continue selecting this command to undo several different actions, but remember that undo is sequential. You cannot keep your latest action while undoing the previous one.

▶ PICK YOUR COLOR

If you want to match a color exactly, select the Pick Color tool and then click the right or left mouse button on a patch of the desired color. The Paint drawing tools will use the selected color as their right- or left-click color, respectively.

⑦ *Click Image to view the Image menu.*

⑧ *Use these options to apply special effects to the image.*

⑨ *Use this option to resize the image.*

⑩ *Click File to open the File menu.*

⑪ *Click Save to save the image.*

⑫ *Select one of these options if you want to use the image as your desktop wallpaper.*

⑬ *Click the Close button to complete the task.*

FIND IT ONLINE

Download paint and draw gadgets at
http://www.goldendawn.com/gad/gd-gad5.htm.

Playing Some Games

Some people think that computers are no fun at all. If you're one of those people, it may be time to take a short break and have a look at the diversions that are included in Windows 2000. After all, people who never have any fun can get to be pretty boring!

The figures show the four games that are included with Windows 2000. The games are FreeCell, Minesweeper, 3D Pinball, and Solitaire. To make certain we don't spoil your fun, we're not going to tell you too much about them, but provide just a brief description of each of them.

FreeCell is a solitaire card game that starts with eight stacks of cards across the screen. Like any other solitaire game, the objective is to build complete same-suit stacks of cards.

Minesweeper is a game that has a number of mines hidden under the blocks that you click. When you reveal a safe spot, the numbers tell you how many mines are in adjacent blocks. Your goal is to reveal all the safe blocks without hitting a mine.

3D Pinball is an electronic version of the old arcade favorite pinball machines. When you fire your ball into play, your goal is to keep it in play and rack up points. You use the flippers to throw the ball back into the bumpers.

Solitaire is the standard solitaire card game. You can choose from several optional games to keep things interesting.

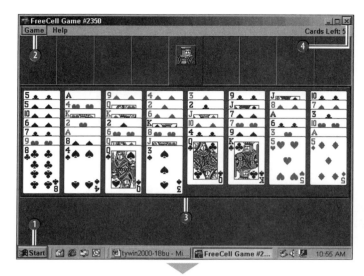

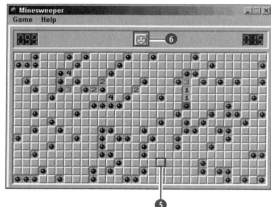

① Click the Start button and select Programs ➪ Accessories ➪ Games and choose your favorite.

② Select Game ➪ New Game to begin.

③ Click the source and destination to move cards.

④ Click Close.

⑤ Click blocks to expose their contents.

⑥ Click here to begin a new game.

CROSS-REFERENCE

See "Configuring Multimedia" in Chapter 17.

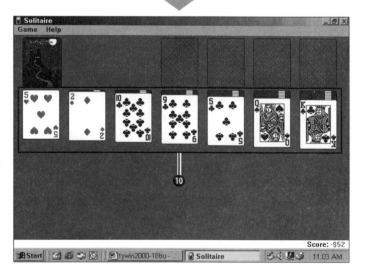

TAKE NOTE

TAKE NOTE

INSTALLING NEW GAMES

If you've decided that you just can't get enough of playing games on your PC, you may be in for a surprise if you attempt to use some popular titles on your Windows 2000 system. Because Windows 2000 is a secure operating system, applications must follow certain rules to run under Windows 2000. In the case of games, manufacturers often ignore some important rules in order to improve the performance of their products. One important rule that games often ignore is that no application should ever attempt to write directly to any of your hardware. Although you have no way to determine this directly, the result of this rule-bending means that a game that writes directly to hardware won't operate under Windows 2000. Look for system requirements that specifically mention Windows 2000. If the package doesn't mention Windows 2000, but does specify Windows NT 4, you may still be safe. If neither Windows 2000 nor Windows NT 4 are mentioned, you should probably avoid the program.

LEARNING THE GAMES

One advantage to playing games on your PC is that the rules of the game are easy to find. Each of these games has a Help menu that can assist in learning how to play the game.

⑦ Press the Spacebar to launch the ball.

⑧ Press Z to move the left flipper.

⑨ Press / to move the right flipper.

⑩ Drag cards to move them.

▶ You may want to limit yourself to a specified amount of play time!

FIND IT ONLINE

See **http://happypuppy.com/compgames/ index.html** for demo and shareware games.

Opening and Closing the Command Prompt Window

The Windows 2000 *graphical user interface* (GUI) will handle the computing needs of most users. As powerful as the Windows 2000 GUI may be, though, it's not possible to do everything by clicking a mouse. Accomplishing some tasks is too difficult or even impossible without access to the *command line*, the old standby from the earliest days of personal computing.

Windows 2000 gives you a complete set of DOS commands. Almost anything that was possible to do from the command prompt on DOS-based PCs is still possible on a Windows 2000 PC. A few obsolete commands are no longer available, but they've been replaced by more-efficient ways of doing things directly from the Windows 2000 GUI.

When you open the *Command Prompt window*, you can enter DOS commands. The Command Prompt window can appear as an actual window, or it can be expanded to full-screen view. Nearly all tasks that require the use of DOS can be done using the Command Prompt window.

To Windows 2000, the Command Prompt window is simply another program that you can run on your PC. When you select Programs ⇨ Accessories ⇨ Command Prompt from the Start menu, you're actually running a program named Cmd.exe that is normally found in the C:\Windows folder. Cmd.exe is a special type of program, called a *command processor*, that executes the commands you enter at the command prompt.

The Command Prompt window is versatile. You can shrink the window down so much that it is virtually impossible to read any of the text in the window, or you can expand it to cover the entire screen. You can control the number of lines displayed in the window. You can also control the colors that are displayed in the window.

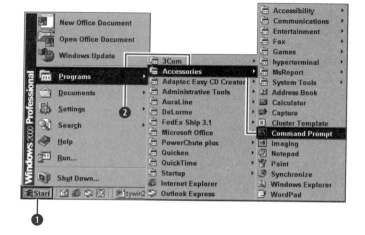

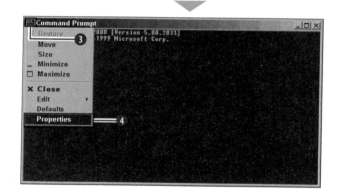

① Click the Start button.

② Select Programs ⇨ Accessories ⇨ Command Prompt.

③ To adjust the window setting, click here to display the menu.

④ Select Properties.

CROSS-REFERENCE

See "Using the Command Prompt Window" next in this chapter.

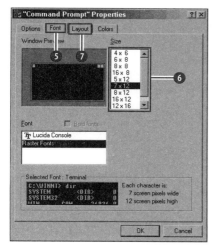

When you're finished working in the Command Prompt window, close the window by typing **EXIT** and pressing Enter, or by clicking the Close button in the upper-right corner of the window.

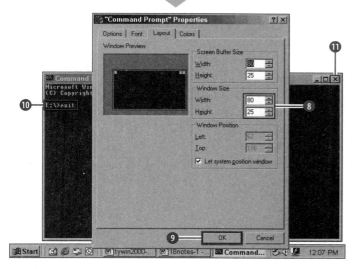

TAKE NOTE

RUNNING MS-DOS PROGRAMS

Although you can run many MS-DOS programs in the Windows 2000 Command Prompt window, not all MS-DOS programs will work properly. The reason for this is usually that a program attempts to perform an action — such as directly accessing video memory — that Windows 2000 prohibits in order to protect your system and your data from damage. Windows 2000 extends the operating system security controls to the Command Prompt window.

PROGRAMS MUST BE SHUT DOWN PROPERLY

To avoid losing data, you must shut down DOS programs properly. If the Command Prompt window shows the program name but does not show the "finished" message, choose the proper command from the program's menus to exit the program before you attempt to close the Command Prompt window. Otherwise, any files the program had open may be corrupted, and you might lose data.

⑤ *Click the Font tab.*

⑥ *Select the font to use in the window.*

⑦ *Click the Layout tab.*

⑧ *Choose the window size settings.*

⑨ *Click OK and confirm how to apply your changes.*

⑩ *Type exit to close the window.*

⑪ *Alternatively, click the Close button.*

FIND IT ONLINE

For a more powerful command line, see
http://www.jpsoft.com/.

Using the Command Prompt Window

S imply opening and closing the Command Prompt window doesn't accomplish very much. To do anything useful at the command prompt, you need to enter DOS commands. In the earlier example, you typed the EXIT command to close the command processor and the Command Prompt window. In this section you'll learn how to use other, more useful DOS commands.

Using DOS commands can sometimes be confusing. You may enter a command that you're certain is correct only to be greeted with the message "*xxx* is not recognized as an internal or external command, operable program or batch file." This message is simply telling you that the command processor cannot find an internal command or a program that matches what you typed on the command line. This doesn't necessarily mean that what you typed was incorrect — only that the command processor cannot find it. You may need to give it a little extra help

One way to give the command processor the help it needs to find a program is to include the complete *path* to the program. For example, if Myprog.exe is in the C:\Allmine folder, you could enter the command as **C:\allmine\myprog** and press Enter. Sometimes this may not work because the program you want to run may not be able to find all its data files. In that case, you'll need to use the CD — Change Directory — command to change to the program's folder before you execute the program. In this example you would first type **CD \allmine** and press Enter, and then type **myprog** and press Enter.

The figures on the facing page show a few examples of using MS-DOS commands.

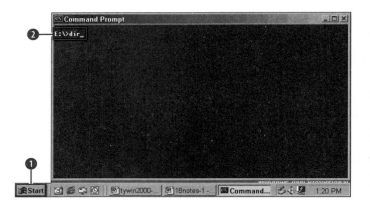

❶ If necessary, click the Start button and select Programs ➪ Accessories ➪ Command Prompt.

❷ Type your command on the command line and press Enter.

❸ To learn command options, enter the command followed by a space and /?.

❹ If necessary, press Enter to complete the display.

▶ You cannot enter a new command until the previous command is completed and the command prompt returns.

CROSS-REFERENCE

See "Getting Command Help" later in this chapter.

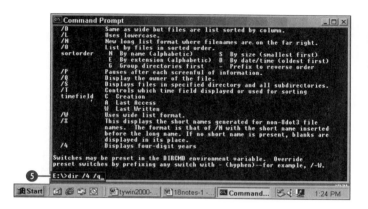

WINDOWS 2000 COMMANDS

If you've used DOS commands in Windows 98, in Windows 95, or in MS-DOS, you'll find that many commands have different options in the Windows 2000 Command Prompt window than what you may be used to. For example, the figures on the facing page show that the DIR command in Windows 2000 includes a number of *parameters* that are not available in the earlier versions of this command. When commands are enhanced in Windows 2000, you will generally find that the older version parameters will continue to function as they did in the past, but you have new options that make the commands even more useful.

EXPAND THE COMMAND PROMPT WINDOW

Although the default size for the command prompt window — 25 rows high by 80 columns wide — is based on the traditional size of PC screens before GUIs became popular, there's no reason why you cannot choose a size that better suits your needs. As the figures on the facing page indicate, increasing the size of the window may make it easier to use certain commands by reducing the amount of scrolling that is required.

⑤ Enter the new command followed by the additional parameters and press Enter.

⑥ Type **exit** and press Enter to close the window.

FIND IT ONLINE

Learn how to change your Command prompt at http://www.vietnam411.com/Computer_Tips/windows/0034.htm.

Getting Command Help

If you aren't a DOS command expert, it can be difficult and confusing to enter commands in the Command Prompt window. Using DOS commands is simply quite different from doing things using your mouse in the Windows 2000 GUI. Not only do you need to type the correct command, but you also may need to include a bunch of esoteric parameters to make the command function as you expect it to.

Windows 2000 includes help information for each of the Windows 2000 DOS commands. To access the help screens you can type the command name followed by /? or by entering **HELP** followed by the command name. Both methods display the same help information.

In addition to information about specific commands, if you simply type **HELP** and press Enter, Windows 2000 will display a list of most of the commands you can enter along with a brief description of the commands. This can be useful when you aren't certain of the exact command that you need to use.

If you need help with a command that is not supported by the HELP command — such as NET or PING — type the command followed by /?. For example, type **NET /?** to learn the syntax of the NET command. HELP supports only the commands that are listed when you type HELP and press Enter.

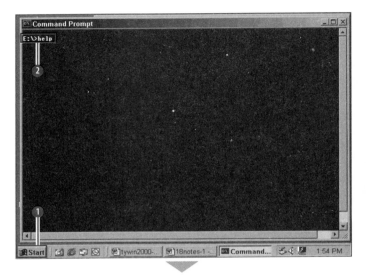

❶ If necessary, click the Start button and select Programs ⟳ Accessories ⟳ Command Prompt.

❷ Type **HELP** on the command line and press Enter to display a list of DOS commands.

❸ To continue, press Enter each time the MORE prompt appears.

❹ Type **HELP** followed by a command name and press Enter to display help for a specific command.

CROSS-REFERENCE

See "Using the Command Prompt Window" earlier in this chapter.

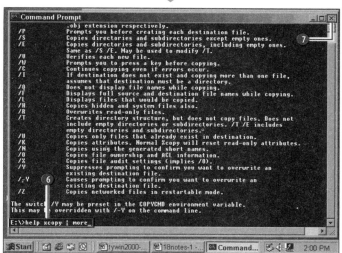

⑤ Add **> PRN** to the end of the command line to make a printed copy of the output.

⑥ Add **| MORE** to the end of the command line to make the output display one page at a time.

⑦ Click the Close button to complete the task.

TAKE NOTE

▶ PRINT THE HELP INFORMATION

DOS commands must be typed correctly without any errors. It can be difficult to remember the exact syntax of DOS commands — especially commands that have a large set of possible parameters you can use. One way to make certain that you enter commands correctly is to make a printed copy of the command's help screens. As the third figure on the facing page shows, you can redirect the output of DOS commands to your printer by adding **> PRN** to the end of the command line. When you press Enter this will cause the output that normally appears on the screen to be sent to your printer. You may need to manually select your printer's form feed after using this option — especially if you have a laser printer. You may also need to press Enter a time or two if the command prompt does not reappear immediately.

▶ PIPING COMMANDS

If you would rather view command help on-screen but find that the help screens scroll off the top of the Command Prompt window before you can read the entire text, you may want to view the text one page at a time. To do so you can *pipe* the output to the MORE command. You can do this by adding **| MORE** at the end of the command line. You may want to examine the MORE command help screens for more information on using this command.

FIND IT ONLINE

Tray Command Line is a free system tray icon that gives you instant access to a small command-line window, http://195.27.241.3/software/windows/tray/sw7.html.

Personal Workbook

Q&A

1 What should you do if the Command Prompt window says "finished" in the title bar?

_____

_____

_____

2 What do you type to close the Command Prompt window?

_____

_____

_____

3 How can you transfer data between the calculator and other applications?

_____

_____

_____

4 What can you do if the lines of text in a Notepad document extend past the right edge of the window?

_____

_____

_____

5 How can you add a picture to a WordPad document?

_____

_____

_____

6 How can you match a color exactly in Paint?

_____

_____

_____

_____

7 What tool can you use to easily enter foreign characters into a document?

_____

_____

_____

8 Which tool can you use to assemble multiple scanned pages for a fax?

_____

_____

ANSWERS: PAGE 401

EXTRA PRACTICE

1. Use the calculator to convert your age into a binary number.

2. Create a text file in Notepad.

3. Create a new Word format document in WordPad.

4. Add several different character formats to your document.

5. Open an image file in Imaging and add a date stamp.

6. Open the Command Prompt window and use the DIR command. Adjust the Command Prompt window to display 35 rows and 90 columns.

REAL-WORLD APPLICATIONS

✔ You receive a Word document that you suspect may be infected with a macro virus. You use WordPad to open the document and copy the text to a new document so that the virus won't infect your system.

✔ You need to send a multiple-page fax to someone overseas. You use Imaging to scan and assemble the pages so that you can transmit the entire fax in one piece to save on long-distance charges.

✔ You are writing a letter to an important potential client in a foreign country. You use Character Map to insert the correct characters into your document so that you can spell the client's name properly and show that you respect their customs and language.

Visual Quiz

How can you display this application? How can you tell the current zoom level? What button would you click to rotate the image 90 degrees clockwise?

_____

_____

_____

_____

Personal Workbook
Answers

Chapter 1

See page 4

1 **What are the three types of things that you will find on the Start menu?**

A: The Start menu includes three different kinds of items — commands, cascading menus, and items that display dialog boxes.

2 **What do three periods following a menu item mean?**

A: Three dots (...) next to the label indicate menu selections that open dialog boxes.

3 **What happens when you click an item on the Start menu that has a small arrow next to the item?**

A: A small arrow next to the label indicates cascading menus. These items display additional menus when you select them.

4 **What does a small diagonal arrow on a desktop icon mean?**

A: A small arrow at the lower-left corner of the icon indicates that the icon is a *shortcut* to the application or document.

5 **How can you make the icons on your desktop align automatically?**

A: If you right-click a blank spot on the desktop and select Arrange Icons ⇨ Auto Arrange, the icons will snap into orderly rows and columns. Any new icons that are added to your desktop will also move into place automatically.

6 **What is the purpose of the Computers Near Me icon?**

A: The Computers Near Me icon provides quick access to the shared resources in your workgroup or your domain.

7 **How can you quickly view your desktop?**

A: The Show Desktop tool button on the Quick Launch toolbar minimizes all open windows to buttons on the taskbar so that you can view the desktop.

8 **How can you quickly switch between two programs without using your mouse?**

A: You can quickly switch between two programs by pressing Alt+Tab.

Personal Workbook Answers

Visual Quiz

Q: How can you display this folder? What must you do to make the folder display the message shown here?

A: Double-click the My computer icon to display the My Computer folder. Select the C drive to display the message.

Chapter 2

See page 24

1 How can you display your personal Start menu items when you open Windows Explorer?

A: To display your personal Start menu, right-click the Start button and choose Explore.

2 How can you run a program that doesn't appear on your Start menu?

A: You can run programs by double-clicking their icon in Windows Explorer.

3 What will happen if you click the History button?

A: If you click the History button, the Folders Explorer Bar will be replaced by the History Explorer Bar.

4 How can you preview the contents of graphics files without opening them?

A: You can preview the contents of graphics files by selecting them in Windows Explorer.

5 How can you make Windows Explorer display file previews in place of file type icons?

A: To display previews of the file contents rather than file type icons, choose thumbnail view.

6 How can you locate all of the folders you opened last week?

A: To locate the folders that you opened last week, click the Last Week folder in the history list and then open the My Computer folder.

7 Which Windows Explorer toolbar can you use to listen to music over the Internet?

A: You can use the Radio toolbar to listen to radio stations on the Internet.

8 Which Windows Explorer toolbar can you use to visit the "Best of the Internet" Web site?

A: You can use the Links toolbar to visit the "Best of the Internet" Web site.

Visual Quiz

Q: How does this view differ from the standard Windows Explorer view, and how can you make Windows Explorer display image previews like this?

A: This Windows Explorer view is different because thumbnail view was selected and the Explorer bars were closed to provide maximum room for the previews. You can choose Thumbnail from the drop-down View list and click the Explorer Bar Close button to make Windows Explorer look like this.

Chapter 3

See page 50

1 How can you print an entire topic and all of its subtopics as one document?

A: To print an entire topic and its subtopics, right-click the topic in the Contents tab and choose Print. Select the option to include all subtopics.

Personal Workbook Answers

2 **How can you copy a help topic?**

A: You can copy a help topic by selecting the topic text, right-clicking the selected text, and choosing Copy.

3 **What is the Favorites tab used for?**

A: The Favorites tab saves your place so that you can return to a help topic easily.

4 **How can you find a topic the quickest when you know the correct keyword?**

A: You can find topics quickly by typing the correct keyword in the Index tab.

5 **How can you find a topic if your keyword is not indexed?**

A: If your keyword does not appear in the index, type the keyword in the Search tab.

6 **How can you toggle the display of the left pane of the help window?**

A: You can toggle the display of the left pane by clicking the Hide or Show buttons.

7 **Which help system component is intended to step you through solutions to problems?**

A: The troubleshooters step you through problem solutions.

8 **How can you get more help if you can't find the answer in the Windows 2000 Help system?**

A: You can get more help if you can't find the answer in the Windows 2000 Help system by using the Web resources link.

Visual Quiz

Q: **How would you display the list shown in the figure? How would you print the entire MS-DOS command list**

A: To display this list you would open the MS-DOS Commands topic in the Reference category on the Contents pane. To print the entire list you would right-click the topic, choose Print, choose *Print selected heading and all subtopics*, and click OK.

Chapter 4

See page 66

1 **If you have items you want to run automatically whenever you start Windows, where should you place them?**

A: Place items in the Startup folder to make them run when you start Windows 2000.

2 **How many options can you select at the same time from a group of radio buttons?**

A: You can select one option at the same time from a group of radio buttons.

3 **Which Control Panel icon do you use when you want to install a new program?**

A: You use the Add/Remove Programs icon in Control Panel when you want to install a new program.

4 **What does the size of the scroll box often indicate?**

A: The size of the scroll box generally indicates the percentage of the document that is visible onscreen.

Personal Workbook Answers

See page 94

5 **What type of action prevents some older programs from running on Windows 2000?**

A: Programs that attempt to directly access hardware cannot run on Windows 2000.

6 **What are *desktop shortcuts*?**

A: Desktop shortcuts are icons on your desktop that open documents, Web sites, or programs.

7 **What window would you use to add the services you would need to use your PC as a Web server?**

A: To use your PC as a Web server you would open the Add/Remove Programs window and choose the Add Windows Components option.

8 **What will happen if you select No when Windows 2000 tells you that you are closing an application and haven't saved your work?**

A: If you close a program without saving your work, you will lose any unsaved changes.

Visual Quiz

Q: **How can you display this window? What can you tell from the status column?**

A: Right-click the taskbar and choose Task Manager. The Status column tells you that all currently loaded programs are running correctly.

Chapter 5

1 **What happens when you drag and drop data between two different documents without holding down any keys?**

A: If you drag and drop data between two different documents, you will copy the data unless you hold down the Alt key to move the data.

2 **How can you save paper while still seeing how your printed output will appear?**

A: To save paper while still seeing how your printed output will appear, use the Print Preview option.

3 **How can you control the format of data you paste from the Clipboard?**

A: You can control the format of data you paste from the Clipboard by using the Edit ➪ Paste Special command.

4 **What shortcut can you use to copy selected text to the Clipboard?**

A: You can use Ctrl+C to copy selected text to the Clipboard.

5 **What happens to data that you've copied to the Clipboard when you copy additional data to the Clipboard?**

A: When you copy additional data to the Clipboard, the new data replaces existing data that you've copied to the Clipboard.

6 **What is the best way to print multiple copies of the same document?**

A: The best way to print multiple copies of the same document is to use the Number of copies spin control.

7 **How can you print using a printer that isn't connected to your PC or your network?**

A: To use a printer that isn't connected to your PC or your network, use the Print to file option.

8 **If you are unable to open a document that appears on the Documents list, what might be the cause?**

A: If you are unable to open a document that appears on the Documents list, the cause might be that the file has been deleted or moved.

Personal Workbook Answers

Visual Quiz

Q: How can you display this dialog box? How can you change the number of copies that are printed?

A: Select File ⇨ Print to display the Print dialog box. Use the Number of copies spin box to set the number of copies that are printed.

Chapter 6

See page 122

1 What will happen if you don't click the New button between searches?

A: If you don't click the New button between searches you will add new conditions to your previous search rather than creating a totally new search.

2 How can you specify that you want to limit your search to files larger than a certain size?

A: To specify that you want to limit your search to files larger than a certain size, click the Size checkbox and choose the size option that suits your needs.

3 How can you temporarily bypass the Recycle Bin and delete a file permanently?

A: You can temporarily bypass the Recycle Bin and delete a file permanently by holding down Shift as you delete a file.

4 Why is it more dangerous to delete files from diskettes than from hard disks?

A: It is more dangerous to delete files from diskettes than from hard disks because Windows 2000 does not provide a Recycle Bin for diskettes.

5 How can you change the Recycle Bin sort order?

A: You can change the Recycle Bin sort order by clicking one of the column headings to sort according to the values in that column.

6 What steps must you take before saving a search for future use?

A: Before saving a search for future use you must first run the search and then click in the Search Results pane.

7 How can you reuse a search you've saved?

A: To reuse a search you've saved, double-click the saved search on your desktop and then click the Search Now button.

8 How can you find a file if all you know are two words that occur together somewhere in the filename?

A: You can find a file if all you know is two words that occur together somewhere in the filename by adding an asterisk before the first word, a question mark between the words, and an asterisk following the second word.

Visual Quiz

Q: How do you display this dialog box? Which part of the dialog box do you use to control how much disk space the Recycle Bin uses? What would you do if you didn't want to confirm that deleted items should go to the Recycle Bin?

A: Right-click the Recycle Bin and select Properties to display the dialog box. Use the slider to control the amount of space that is used. To bypass the prompt when you delete files, remove the check from the Display delete confirmation dialog check box.

Chapter 7

See page 148

1 How can you tell that you're seeing the name of a computer that is on the network?

A: Computer names on the network have two backslashes before the name.

Personal Workbook Answers

2 **When you're trying to find a file, how much of the network can you search at any one time?**

A: When you're trying to find a file, you can search one computer at one time.

3 **What happens to folders that are contained in a folder that you share on the network?**

A: When you share folders, any folders contained in the shared folders are also shared unless you specifically exclude them from sharing.

4 **What happens to your Network Places icons when the computers they refer to are no longer available?**

A: When the computers referred to by Network Places icons are no longer available, the icons remain, but clicking those icons will display a message telling you that the computer is not available.

5 **What network protocol is necessary if you want to share an Internet connection?**

A: The TCP/IP network protocol is necessary if you want to share an Internet connection.

6 **Why does a network printer need drivers installed on PCs that aren't connected to the printer?**

A: A network printer needs drivers installed on PCs that aren't connected to the printer so that they can send the proper commands to use the printer.

7 **How can you allow people access to master documents in a shared folder without allowing them to make changes?**

A: You can allow people access to master documents in a shared folder without allowing them to make changes by granting only read access to the folder.

8 **What do you use to control who has access to shared resources?**

A: You can control who has access to shared resources by using user names and passwords.

Visual Quiz

Q: **How can you display a window like this one? Why does it show three computers but no Entire Network icon?**

A: To display this window, double-click the My Network Places icon, and then double-click the Computers Near Me icon. Because Computers Near Me shows your workgroup or domain, the Entire Network icon does not appear in this view.

Chapter 8

See page 176

1 **Where do you need to go to add the On-Screen Keyboard to the Utility Manager?**

A: To add the On-Screen Keyboard to the Utility Manager you must open the File menu in the On-Screen Keyboard.

2 **What tool do you use to view screen contents at up to nine times normal size?**

A: To view screen contents at up to nine times normal size you use the Magnifier.

3 **What tool do you use to listen to dialog boxes?**

A: To listen to dialog boxes you use the Narrator.

4 **How can you make it possible to press the Shift, Ctrl, or Alt key first and then a second key without holding down the first key?**

A: To make it possible to press the Shift, Ctrl, or Alt key first and then a second key without holding down the first key, enable the StickyKeys option.

5 **How can you make Windows 2000 ignore keys that are held down too long?**

A: To make Windows 2000 ignore keys that are held down too long, enable the FilterKeys option.

6 **What option can you use to flash a window when Windows 2000 plays a sound?**

A: To flash a window when Windows 2000 plays a sound you can use the SoundSentry option.

7 **How can you make it possible to use the keyboard to move the mouse pointer?**

A: You can use the keyboard to move the mouse pointer by enabling the MouseKeys option.

8 **What tool can you use to control when the Magnifier, Narrator, and On-Screen Keyboard start?**

A: You can control when the Magnifier, Narrator, and On-Screen Keyboard start using the Utility Manager.

Visual Quiz

Q: **How can you display a window like this one? Why does it show 4 in the spin box?**

A: To display this window, click the Start button. Then select Programs ⇨ Accessories ⇨ Accessibility ⇨ Magnifier. The spin box sets the magnification level, which is currently set to 4 power.

Chapter 9

See page 196

1 **How can you make certain that a search engine looks for two words that are together?**

A: To make certain that a search engine looks for two words that are together, enclose the search phrase in quotes.

2 **What is a *URL*?**

A: A URL is a Uniform Resource Locator — another name for Web page addresses.

3 **What does underlined text on a Web page usually represent?**

A: Underlined text on a Web page usually represents a link that you can click to view another Web page.

4 **How can you make it possible to view a Web page without reconnecting to the Internet?**

A: To make it possible to view a Web page without reconnecting to the Internet, select Favorites ⇨ Add to Favorites and make certain the Make available offline check box is selected.

5 **How can you make certain that a Web page you visit won't send destructive content to your system?**

A: To make certain that a Web page you visit won't send destructive content to your system, add that Web page to the Restricted security zone.

6 **What option can you use to restrict which Web sites can be visited by your PC?**

A: To restrict which Web sites can be visited by your PC you can use the Content Advisor option on the Content tab of the Internet Options dialog box.

Personal Workbook Answers

7 **How can you create folders to store links to related Web sites?**

A: You can create folders to store links to related Web sites by using the Favorites ⇨ Organize Favorites command and then selecting Create Folder.

8 **What button can you use to return to the last Web page you visited?**

A: You can return to the last Web page you visited by clicking the Back button.

Visual Quiz

Q: How can you display this dialog box? What do you need to do to display the expanded folder list that is shown? How can you use this dialog box to find out the last time you visited a Web page?

A: To display this window, select Favorites ⇨ Organize Favorites. Click a folder in the list to expand the folder so you can see its contents. Click an item to see information about the item, including when you last visited the site.

Chapter 10

See page 214

1 **Why do Outlook Express folder names sometimes appear in boldface?**

A: Outlook Express folder names appear in boldface when they contain unread messages.

2 **What do you need to do before you can save a file that came with an e-mail message?**

A: To save a file that came with an e-mail message, you must either open the message and right-click the attachment or click the Attachment button in the Preview pane.

3 **Where do messages you've created wait until they're sent to the mail server?**

A: Messages you've created wait in the Outbox folder until they're sent to the mail server.

4 **What is the meaning of the number in parentheses following an Outlook Express folder name?**

A: The number in parentheses following an Outlook Express folder name indicates the number of unread messages in the folder.

5 **How can you find newsgroups that pertain to a specific subject?**

A: To find newsgroups that pertain to a specific subject you can enter search phrases in the Newsgroup Subscriptions dialog box.

6 **How can you stop an e-mail message from being delivered once it leaves your Outbox?**

A: In most cases you cannot stop an e-mail message from being delivered once it leaves your Outbox. Be sure you really want to send a message before you click Send.

7 **What message format can you use to make certain that anyone can read your message?**

A: You can use the plain text message format to make certain that anyone can read your message.

8 **How often must you download the entire list of newsgroups?**

A: You only need to download the entire list of newsgroups the first time you access the news server. Later you will only download updates to the list.

Personal Workbook Answers

Visual Quiz

Q: How can you display this dialog box? If you want to place your outbound messages in the Outbox rather than sending them as soon as you've created them, what setting do you need to adjust?

A: To display this window, select Tools ⇨ Options. To delay sending messages until you click the Send/Recv button, click the Send tab and remove the check from the *Send messages immediately* check box.

Chapter 11

See page 234

1 **What can you do if you need to keep text that is already on your HyperTerminal screen?**

A: If you need to keep text that is already on your HyperTerminal screen, use your mouse to select the text and then use Edit ⇨ Copy to place it on the Clipboard.

2 **What setting must be the same on both the sending and the receiving computer?**

A: Before you can transfer a file, the file transfer protocol setting must be the same on both the sending and the receiving computer.

3 **How many computers can you connect at one time using HyperTerminal?**

A: You can connect two computers using HyperTerminal.

4 **What should you do if you can't see anything you type in the HyperTerminal window?**

A: If you can't see anything you type in the HyperTerminal window, you should use the Echo typed characters locally option.

5 **What is *telnet*?**

A: Telnet is a text-based Internet protocol.

6 **How can you start printing the text that appears on your screen?**

A: To begin printing new text, select Transfer ⇨ Capture to Printer.

7 **How can you prepare HyperTerminal to answer an incoming call?**

A: You can prepare HyperTerminal to answer an incoming call by selecting Call ⇨ Wait for a Call.

8 **What should you do if someone wants to send you a fax while HyperTerminal is waiting for a call?**

A: If someone wants to send you a fax while HyperTerminal is waiting for a call you must tell HyperTerminal to not answer the call by selecting Call ⇨ Stop Waiting.

Visual Quiz

Q: How can you display this dialog box? What is the purpose of the Protocol list box?

A: To display this window, select Transfer ⇨ Send File. You use the Protocol list box to choose the file transfer protocol to use for sending files to another computer.

Chapter 12

See page 252

1 **What will happen if you change the screen resolution setting but don't click the Yes button?**

A: If you change the screen resolution setting but don't click the Yes button, Windows 2000 will restore your previous setting.

Personal Workbook Answers

2 **How can you make a hidden taskbar pop up without moving the mouse?**

A: You can make a hidden taskbar pop up without moving the mouse by pressing the Windows key or Ctrl+Esc.

3 **How can you find a hidden taskbar using the mouse?**

A: You can find a hidden taskbar using the mouse by moving the mouse just past the edge of the screen where the taskbar is hiding.

4 **What do you need to activate before you can use a JPEG image as your desktop wallpaper?**

A: Before you can use a JPEG image as your desktop wallpaper you need to activate the option to show Web content on your desktop.

5 **What can you do to restore order to the Start menu if items are no longer being sorted?**

A: To restore order to the Start menu if items are no longer being sorted, click the Re-sort button on the Start Menu Options tab of the Taskbar Properties dialog box.

6 **How can you reduce the size of the icons on the Start menu?**

A: To reduce the size of the icons on the Start menu, select the *Show small icons in Start menu* option on the Taskbar Options tab of the Taskbar Properties dialog box.

7 **What is the fastest way to choose a desktop element on the Appearance tab of the Display Properties dialog box so that you can change the element's color?**

A: The fastest way to choose a desktop element on the Appearance tab of the Display Properties dialog box so that you can change the element's color is to click the item in the preview window.

8 **How can you view the items in the Control Panel folder without opening the folder?**

A: You can view the items in the Control Panel folder without opening the folder by selecting the Expand Control Panel option on the Start Menu Options tab of the Taskbar Properties dialog box.

Visual Quiz

Q: **How can you display this dialog box? How do the controls on this tab interact?**

A: To display this window, right-click a blank space on the desktop and choose Properties. Click the Settings tab to show these controls. The Colors and Screen area controls may interact if you try to choose a color setting and a resolution setting at the maximum end of the range — your display adapter may not support the highest number of colors at the highest resolution.

Chapter 13

See page 274

1 **How can you change your keyboard layout without actually moving any keys?**

A: You can change your keyboard layout without actually moving any keys using the Input locales tab of the Keyboard Properties dialog box.

2 **Where do you go to assign sounds to Windows 2000 events?**

A: You can assign sounds to Windows 2000 events using the Sounds and Multimedia dialog box.

3 **What type of peripheral installs automatically when you plug in its cable?**

A: USB peripherals install automatically when you plug in the cable.

4 **What do you call mouse pointers that show a brief animation?**

A: Mouse pointers that show a brief animation are called animated cursors.

5 **What can you do to change the number of times keys repeat when they are held down?**

A: To change the number of times keys repeat when they are held down, you change the repeat rate in the Keyboard Properties dialog box.

6 **What type of sound files can you associate with system events?**

A: You can associate wave sound files with system events.

7 **Where do you find most of the system configuration tools?**

A: You find most of the system configuration tools in the Control Panel.

8 **How can you save a registry key so it can be easily restored?**

A: You can save a registry key so it can be easily restored by selecting Registry ➪ Export Registry File.

Visual Quiz

Q: **How can you display this dialog box? How can you tell which events have associated sounds? How can you hear the sounds?**

A: To display this window, open the Control Panel and double-click the Sounds and Multimedia icon. Events that have sounds are indicated by a speaker icon. Click the Play button to hear a sound.

Chapter 14

See page 292

1 **What tool can you use to remove old files that are no longer needed on your PC?**

A: You can use the disk cleanup tool to remove old files that are no longer needed on your PC.

2 **What type of disk errors can prevent your PC from using specific places on your hard disk?**

A: Physical disk errors can prevent your PC from using specific places on your hard disk.

3 **What is the difference between contiguous and fragmented files?**

A: Contiguous files are located in one piece on your disk. Fragmented files are spread out in multiple pieces in various locations.

4 **How can you reduce the size of backups and the time required to perform them?**

A: To reduce the size of backups and the time required to perform them, you can limit your backups to include only your important data files.

5 **What will happen if you attempt to scan for errors on a disk that is in use?**

A: If you attempt to scan for errors on a disk that is in use, Windows 2000 will ask if you want to schedule the error check for the next time you restart your system.

6 **What do you call a diskette that stores your system's partition information?**

A: You call a diskette that stores your system's partition information an Emergency Repair Disk or ERD.

Personal Workbook Answers

7 **What operating mode should you attempt to use first if Windows 2000 won't load?**

A: If Windows 2000 won't load, try to start your system in safe mode.

8 **How can you free up additional space if the disk cleanup tool doesn't do as much as you'd like?**

A: You can free up additional space if the disk cleanup tool doesn't do as much as you'd like by using the More Options tab and removing unneeded Windows 2000 components and unused programs.

Visual Quiz

Q: **How can you display this dialog box? How can you tell if your hard disk needs defragmentation? What can you do to make the defragmentation more successful?**

A: To display this window, select Programs ⇨ Accessories ⇨ System Tools ⇨ Disk Defragmenter from the Start menu. To check if a drive needs to be defragmented, click the Analyze button. To make the defragmentation more successful, free up additional disk space.

Chapter 15

See page 308

1 **What tool can you use to make certain your Windows 2000 system files are up to date?**

A: You can use Windows Update to make certain your Windows 2000 system files are up-to-date.

2 **Where can you find out if your system has experienced any security problems?**

A: You can find out if your system has experienced any security problems by opening the event logs and looking at the security log.

3 **Where can you look to see which IRQs are in use on your system?**

A: You can look in the Device Manager to see which IRQs are in use on your system.

4 **How can you shut down a program that is not responding?**

A: To shut down a program that is not responding, open the Task Manager, select the program, and click the End Task button.

5 **What is the purpose of the Maintenance Wizard?**

A: The Maintenance Wizard helps you to schedule important routine system maintenance tasks that can help keep your system running correctly.

6 **Where can you find out if any items depend on a system service that you are considering shutting down?**

A: You can find out if any items depend a system service that you are considering shutting down by looking at the Dependencies tab of the Properties dialog box for the service.

7 **What do you call the items you add to the performance monitor display?**

A: The items you add to the performance monitor display are called counters.

Personal Workbook Answers

8 **What happens if you format a disk using the Computer Management tool?**

A: If you format a disk, you will destroy any data that is on the disk. It doesn't matter if you are using the Computer Management tool or a different method to format the disk.

Visual Quiz

Q: **How can you display this list in the Device Manager? How can you print a reference list showing which system resources are in use?**

A: To display this list, select View ⇨ Resources by type. To print the list, select View ⇨ Print.

Chapter 16

See page 330

1 **How can you get an on-screen notification that advises you when a scheduled task did not run?**

A: You can get an on-screen notification that advises you when a scheduled task did not run by choosing Advanced ⇨ Notify Me of Missed Tasks.

2 **How can you suspend a task?**

A: You can suspend a task by removing the check from the Enable check box.

3 **If you receive a notice that a task did not run, how can you find the problem?**

A: If you receive a notice that a task did not run, you can find the problem by examining the log file.

4 **Why might you want to enter a descriptive name for a task?**

A: You might want to enter a descriptive name for a task if you have more than one variation on the same task so that you can keep track of the different variations.

5 **How can you specify that you wish to repeat a scheduled task twice daily?**

A: You can specify that you wish to repeat a scheduled task twice daily by using the *Show multiple schedules* check box and setting up two different daily schedules.

6 **What setting can you use to automatically stop a task if you start to use your system?**

A: You can use the *Stop the task if the computer ceases to be idle* setting to automatically stop a task if you start to use your system.

7 **To be a good candidate for a scheduled task, what capability does a program need?**

A: To be a good candidate for a scheduled task, a program needs to be able to complete a task without human intervention.

8 **How can you set up scheduled tasks that need more permissions than your normal user name allows?**

A: You can set up scheduled tasks that need more permissions than your normal user name allows by using the Advanced ⇨ AT Service Account command.

Personal Workbook Answers

Visual Quiz

Q: How can you display this dialog box? How can you delay the task startup until 15 minutes after you stop using your system?

A: To display this dialog box, double-click the task that you wish to modify. To delay the task until 15 minutes after you stop using your system, specify 15 in the *Only start the task if the computer has been idle for at least xx minutes* spin box.

Chapter 17

See page 342

1 Which Windows 2000 tool would you use to record a voice message?

A: You can use Sound Recorder to record a voice message.

2 What is the quickest method of displaying the full volume control?

A: You can display the full volume control by double-clicking the speaker icon in the system tray.

3 What type of files does the Sound Recorder produce?

A: The Sound Recorder produces wave files.

4 How can you make CD Player skip the same song on an audio CD every time you play the CD?

A: You can make CD Player skip the same song on an audio CD every time you play the CD by editing the play list.

5 Why are most video files shown in a small window?

A: Most video files are shown in a small window to reduce the size of the file.

6 What do you call the phonetic building blocks that define how words are pronounced?

A: The phonetic building blocks that define how words are pronounced are called *phonemes*.

7 What type of files are instructions that are used to synthesize music on your PC?

A: MIDI files are instructions that are used to synthesize music on your PC.

8 What does the thickness of the line that is displayed in the Sound Recorder represent?

A: The thickness of the line that is displayed in the Sound Recorder represents the volume of the recorded sound at that position in the file.

Visual Quiz

Q: How can you display this application? How can you tell how long the file will play? Can you tell what type of file is being played?

A: To display the Media Player, double-click a multimedia file. The counter in the lower right corner of the Media Player shows the current position and the length of the file. A sound file is being played; if a video file were being played, the video would appear in the Media Player window.

Chapter 18

See page 362

1 What should you do if the Command Prompt window says "finished" in the title bar?

A: If the Command Prompt window says "finished" in the title bar, click the Close button to close the window.

Personal Workbook Answers

2 **What do you type to close the Command Prompt window?**

A: You can close the Command Prompt window by typing EXIT.

3 **How can you transfer data between the calculator and other applications?**

A: You can transfer data between the calculator and other applications by copying and pasting.

4 **What can you do if the lines of text in a Notepad document extend past the right edge of the window?**

A: If the lines of text in a Notepad document extend past the right edge of the window you can select Format ⇨ Word Wrap to wrap the lines so you can see everything.

5 **How can you add a picture to a WordPad document?**

A: You can add a picture to a WordPad document by selecting Insert ⇨ Object and then choosing the type of object.

6 **How can you match a color exactly in Paint?**

A: You can match a color exactly in Paint by clicking the Pick Color tool on the color to make the color the left-click color.

7 **What tool can you use to easily enter foreign characters into a document?**

A: You can use the Character Map to easily enter foreign characters into a document.

8 **Which tool can you use to assemble multiple scanned pages for a fax?**

A: You can use Imaging to assemble multiple scanned pages for a fax.

Visual Quiz

Q: How can you display this application? How can you tell the current zoom level? What button would you click to rotate the image 90 degrees clockwise?

A: To display Imaging, click the Start button and choose Programs ⇨ Accessories ⇨ Imaging. The current zoom level is shown in the status bar and in the Zoom list box. Click the Rotate Right button to rotate the image 90 degrees clockwise.

Index

Symbols & Numbers

... (ellipses), 6
* (asterisk), 128–129
\ (backslashes), 153
- (minus), 29
+ (plus), 29
? (question mark), 128
3D Pinball game, 378

A

accessibility options
about, 177
Accessibility Wizard, 178–179
FilterKeys, 188
Magnifier, 180–181
Narrator, 182–183
online help, 183, 185, 189
On-Screen Keyboard, 184–185
options, 178–179, 186–189
shortcuts, 188–189
starting/stopping tools, 186–187

StickyKeys, 188
ToggleKeys, 189
Utility Manager, 186–187
accessories
about, 363
bitmap images, creating, 376–377
Calculator, 364–365
Character Map, 366–367
Command Prompt window, 380–385
DOS commands, 380–385
faxes, annotating, 374–375
foreign language characters, 366–367
games, 378–379
graphic image files, 376–377
Imaging, 374–375
Notepad, 368–369
Paint, 376–377
scanner tools, 374–377
text editor, 368–369
word processor, 370–371
WordPad, 370–371
account, creating for Outlook Express, 224–226
active control, dialog boxes, 87
active window, defined, 20
Add Network Place Wizard, 152–153
adding
hardware, 284–285
networked resources, 152–153
printers, 161
sounds, 282–283

Index

INDEX

Continued

Continued

Index

Continued

INDEX

Continued

INDEX

Continued

INDEX

Index

W

X

Z

my2cents.idgbooks.com

Register This Book — And Win!

Visit **http://my2cents.idgbooks.com** to register this book and we'll automatically enter you in our fantastic monthly prize giveaway. It's also your opportunity to give us feedback: let us know what you thought of this book and how you would like to see other topics covered.

Discover IDG Books Online!

The IDG Books Online Web site is your online resource for tackling technology — at home and at the office. Frequently updated, the IDG Books Online Web site features exclusive software, insider information, online books, and live events!

10 Productive & Career-Enhancing Things You Can Do at www.idgbooks.com

- Nab source code for your own programming projects.

- Download software.

- Read Web exclusives: special articles and book excerpts by IDG Books Worldwide authors.

- Take advantage of resources to help you advance your career as a Novell or Microsoft professional.

- Buy IDG Books Worldwide titles or find a convenient bookstore that carries them.

- Register your book and win a prize.

- Chat live online with authors.

- Sign up for regular e-mail updates about our latest books.

- Suggest a book you'd like to read or write.

- Give us your 2¢ about our books and about our Web site.

You say you're not on the Web yet? It's easy to get started with IDG Books' *Discover the Internet*, available at local retailers everywhere.